W9-AYO-412

lonely planet

USA

TOP SIGHTS, AUTHENTIC EXPERIENCES

Karla Zimmerman
Ray Bartlett, Andrew Bender, Alison Bing, Stephanie
d'Arc Taylor, Ashley Harrell, Adam Karlin, Ali Lemer,
Vesna Maric, MaSovaida Morgan, Christopher Pitts,
Kevin Raub, Greg Ward

Contents

Left: Yosemite National Park (p325)

Plan Your Trip
USA's Top 12

INGUS KRUKLITIS/SHUTTERSTOCK ©

New York City

The USA's dynamic mega city

Home to striving artists, hedge-fund moguls and immigrants from every corner of the globe, New York City (p35) is constantly reinventing itself. A staggering number of museums, parks and ethnic neighborhoods are scattered through the five boroughs. Do as locals do and hit the streets. Every block reflects the character and history of this dizzying kaleidoscope, and on even a short walk you can cross continents. Above: Times Square (p68). Right: Brooklyn Bridge (p75)

OLIVER FOERSTNER/SHUTTERSTOCK ©

Date: 1/19/21

917.3 USA 2020
Zimmerman, Karla,
USA : top sights, authentic
experiences /

1

LOUIELEA/SHUTTERSTOCK ©

JOSEPH DUBE ARSENAULT/SHUTTERSTOCK ©

Grand Canyon National Park

Jaw-dropping, red-rock chasm

The sheer immensity of the Grand Canyon (p253) is what grabs you at first – a two-billion-year-old rip across the landscape that reveals the earth's geologic secrets with commanding authority. But it's nature's artistic touches, from sun-dappled ridges and crimson buttes to lush oases and a ribbon-like river, that hold your attention and demand your return. To explore the canyon, take your pick of adventures: hiking, biking, rafting or mule riding.

2

ROBERT CICCHETTI/SHUTTERSTOCK ©

Washington, DC

The nation's monument-laden capital

No matter what your politics, it's hard not to fall for the nation's capital (p91). A buzz percolates among the city's grand boulevards, iconic monuments and power-broking buildings. There's no better place for exploring American history, whether tracing your hand along the Vietnam Veterans Memorial, checking out the parchment-scrawled Constitution at the National Archives, or gaping at Abe Lincoln's hat at the Smithsonian Institution. Above: Washington Monument (p94)

3

New Orleans

Southern charmer where the good times roll

Caribbean-colonial architecture, Creole cuisine and a riotous air of celebration beckon in New Orleans (p197). Nights are spent catching Dixieland jazz, blues and rock in bouncing live-music joints, and the city's annual festivals (such as Mardi Gras) are famous the world over. The Big Easy is also a food-loving town that celebrates its many culinary influences. Feast on lip-smacking jambalaya, soft-shelled crab and Louisiana *cochon* (pulled pork) before hitting the good-time bar scene.

San Francisco

Hilly beauty with a beatnik soul

Change is afoot in this boom-and-bust city (p291), currently enjoying a high-profile boom. Amid the fog and clatter of old-fashioned trams, San Francisco's diverse neighborhoods invite long days of wandering, with fabulous restaurants and bohemian nightlife. Highlights include exploring Alcatraz, strolling across the Golden Gate Bridge, and dining inside the Ferry Building. How cool is San Francisco? Trust us – crest that hill to your first stunning waterfront view, and you'll be hooked.

KURLIN POSTCARDS/SHUTTERSTOCK ©

Yosemite National Park

Gorgeous landscape of peaks and waterfalls

Meander through wildflower-strewn meadows in valleys carved by rivers and glaciers, whose hard, endless work makes everything look simply colossal (p325). Thunderous waterfalls tumble over sheer cliffs, ant-sized climbers scale the enormous granite domes of El Capitan and Half Dome, and hikers walk beneath ancient groves of giant trees. Even the subalpine meadows of Tuolumne are magnificently vast.

ARCHITECT: RICHARD MEIER. IMAGE: BONANDBON/SHUTTERSTOCK ©

Los Angeles

Art, beaches and movie stars

A perpetual influx of dreamers, go-getters and hustlers gives this
sprawling coastal city (p267) an energetic buzz. Learn the tricks of
movie-making during a studio tour. Wander gardens and galleries
at the hilltop Getty Center (pictured above; p280). And stargazing?
Take in the big picture at the Griffith Observatory or look for stylish,
earthbound 'stars' at Bar Marmont. Ready for your close-up? You will
be – an hour on the beach guarantees that sun-kissed LA glow.

7

Miami

Beachy Latin—art deco mash-up

Most cities content themselves with one or two highlights, but Miami (p143) seems to have it all. Beyond the stunning beaches and Art Deco Historic District (pictured right; p146), there's culture at every turn. No other US city blends the attitude of North America with the Latin energy of South America and the rhythm of the Caribbean. Throw in pounding nightlife, zippy restaurants and miles of gorgeous sand, and say hello to the Magic City.

FLIPHOTO/SHUTTERSTOCK ©

ROSTY MCFLY/SHUTTERSTOCK ©

ARCHITECT: FRANK GEHRY. IMAGE: NEJDET DUZEN/SHUTTERSTOCK ©

Chicago

Low-key culture amid steely skyscrapers

The Windy City (p117) will blow you away with its architecture, lakefront beaches and world-class museums. But its real lure is its blend of high culture and earthy pleasures. Is there another metropolis that dresses its Picasso sculpture in local sports team gear? Where the demand for hot dogs equals the demand for North America's top restaurants? Winters are brutal, but come summer, Chicago fetes the warm days with festivals and outdoor cafes galore. Far left: North Avenue Beach; Left: Architect Frank Gehry's Jay Pritzker Pavilion (p121)

STORIESFROMANYWHERE/SHUTTERSTOCK ©

ALEX CIMBAL/SHUTTERSTOCK ©

LEONID ANDRONOV/SHUTTERSTOCK ©

Las Vegas

Garish oasis of indulgence

Just when you think you've got a handle on the West – majestic, sublime, soul-nourishing – here comes Vegas (p237) shaking its thing. Beneath the neon lights of the Strip, the city puts on a dazzling show: dancing fountains, a spewing volcano, the Eiffel Tower. But it saves its most dangerous charms for the gambling dens – seductive lairs where the fresh-pumped air and bright colors share one goal: separating you from your money.

10

ROLF_52/SHUTTERSTOCK ©

Austin

Texas' capital keeps it weird

With its alternative vibe and renegade subculture, Austin (p217) rocks great dining, drinking and shopping scenes. It's one of America's music capitals, where a variety of sounds blast on stages nightly. And it's an outdoor playground, where kayakers skim across local lakes, swimmers soak in spring-fed pools, and cyclists hit the urban trails. It's easy to see why this fashionable city is one of America's fastest-growing hot spots.

11

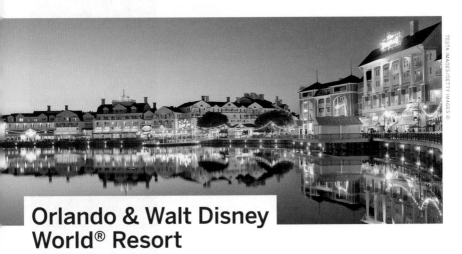

TESTA IMAGES/GETTY IMAGES ©

Orlando & Walt Disney World® Resort

Fantastical theme parks, and their escape

Walt Disney World® Resort (p178) calls itself the 'Happiest Place on Earth' and then delivers the sensation that you are the most important character in the show. Exhilarating rides, eye-popping entertainment and nostalgia are all part of the magical package. Host city Orlando (p190) makes for a lovely, leafy refuge.

12

Plan Your Trip
Need to Know

When to Go

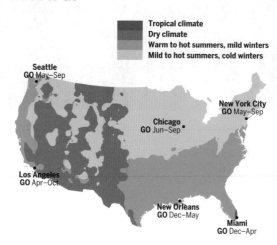

Tropical climate
Dry climate
Warm to hot summers, mild winters
Mild to hot summers, cold winters

Seattle
GO May–Sep

New York City
GO May–Sep

Chicago
GO Jun–Sep

Los Angeles
GO Apr–Oct

New Orleans
GO Dec–May

Miami
GO Dec–Apr

High Season (Jun–Aug)

○ Warm days across the country, with generally high temperatures.

○ Busiest season, with big crowds and higher prices.

○ In ski-resort areas, January to March is high season.

Shoulder (Apr, May, Sep & Oct)

○ Milder temperatures, fewer crowds.

○ Spring flowers (April) and fiery autumn colors (October) in many parts of the country.

Low Season (Nov–Mar)

○ Wintery days, with snowfall in the north, and heavier rains in some regions.

○ Lowest prices for accommodations (aside from ski resorts and warmer getaway destinations).

Currency
US dollar ($)

Language
English, Spanish

Visas
Visitors from the UK, Australia, New Zealand, Japan and many EU countries don't need visas for stays of less than 90 days, though they must get approval from the Electronic System for Travel Authorization (ESTA). Visitors from Canada need neither a visa nor ESTA approval for stays of less than 90 days. Check http://travel.state.gov.

Money
ATMs widely available. Credit cards also widely accepted.

Cell Phones
Phones that operate on tri- or quad-band frequencies will work in the USA. Purchase a pay-as-you-go plan when you arrive.

Time
EST Eastern (GMT/UTC minus five hours); CST Central (GMT/UTC minus six hours); MST Mountain (GMT/UTC minus seven hours); PST Pacific (GMT/UTC minus eight hours).

Daily Costs

Budget: Less than $150

● Campgrounds and hostel dorms: $10–50

● Food from a cafe, farmers market or food truck: $6–15

● Local bus, subway or train tickets: $2–4

Midrange: $150–300

● Double room in midrange hotel: $75–200

● Popular restaurant dinner for two: $30–60

● Car rental per day: from $30

Top End: More than $300

● Double room in a resort or top-end hotel: from $250

● Dinner in a top restaurant: $60–100

● Concert or theater tickets: $60–200

Useful Websites

Lonely Planet (www.lonelyplanet.com/ usa) Destination information, hotel bookings, traveler forum and more.
National Park Service (www.nps.gov) Gateway to America's greatest natural treasures, its national parks.
Eater (www.eater.com) Foodie insight into two dozen American cities.
Punch (www.punchdrink.com) Quirky guides and helpful insights on how to drink well in America's cities.
New York Times Travel (www.nytimes. com/travel) Travel news, practical advice and engaging features.
Roadside America (www.roadsideamerica. com) For all things weird and wacky.

Opening Hours

Typical opening times are as follows:
Banks 8:30am to 4:30pm Monday to Thursday, to 5:30pm Friday (and possibly 9am to noon Saturday)

Bars 5pm to midnight Sunday to Thursday, to 2am Friday and Saturday
Nightclubs 10pm to 4am Thursday to Saturday
Post offices 9am to 5pm Monday to Friday
Shopping malls 9am to 9pm
Stores 9am to 6pm Monday to Saturday, noon to 5pm Sunday
Supermarkets 8am to 8pm, some open 24 hours

Arriving in USA

JFK International Airport (New York)
AirTrain ($5) to subway ($2.75) takes one hour to Manhattan. Express buses to Grand Central or Port Authority cost $19. Taxis $52 plus tolls and tip (45 to 60 minutes).

Los Angeles International Airport LAX Flyaway Bus to Union Station is $9.75 (45 minutes); door-to-door Prime Time and SuperShuttle vans average $17 to $29 (35 minutes to 1½ hours); taxi to Downtown around $50 (25 to 50 minutes).

Miami International Airport Taxis go to Downtown ($22, 25 minutes) and South Beach ($35, 40 minutes), shared Super-Shuttle vans make the trip for $17 to $22, or take Miami Beach Airport Express 150 bus ($2.25) to Miami Beach.

Getting Around

Air Flying is usually more expensive than traveling by train or car, but it's the way to go when you're in a hurry. The domestic air system is extensive and reliable.

Car For maximum flexibility and convenience, and to explore rural America and its wide open spaces, a car is essential. Gas prices are relatively moderate, and you can often score fairly inexpensive rentals, with rates as low as $25 per day.

Train Amtrak has an extensive rail system throughout the USA. Trains are rarely the quickest, cheapest, timeliest or most convenient option, but they're relaxing and scenic.

For more on **getting around**, see p374

Plan Your Trip
Hotspots For...

Fabulous Food

Feasts await, from fresh-shucked oysters and bourbon-soaked bread pudding to smokin' barbecue and duck-fat biscuits. Pack your stretchy pants.

SASI YAISAWANG/SHUTTERSTOCK ©

San Francisco (p291)
The city sets the standard for sustainable, seasonal food and cross-cultural menus.

Ferry Building
Transit hub turned trendy gourmet emporium (p302).

Austin (p217)
The grills are busy around this part of Texas wafting ribs, sausages, pulled pork and other smoked meats.

Franklin Barbecue
The tenderest brisket you'll ever lay lips on (p231).

New Orleans (p197)
A bohemian vibe and cheap restaurants percolate in Faubourg Marigny & Bywater.

Bacchanal
Whatever hits the table will blow your mind. (p212)

Public Art

Ambitious, open-air 'galleries' pop up in town plazas, leafy parks and derelict industrial districts across the country. The groovy eye candy is always free to see.

DENNIZN/SHUTTERSTOCK ©

Miami (p143)
A psychedelic collection of murals brightens warehouses in the gallery-packed Wynwood district.

Wynwood Walls
Top international street artists (p156) change it up.

San Francisco (p291)
The city has long given its public spaces to artists who've left their mark with radical murals.

Clarion Alley
Open-air showcase to watch modern street art. (p315)

Chicago (p117)
Whimsical sculptures by big-name artists dot downtown's streets and green spaces.

Millennium Park
Look for the Bean reflecting the city's skyline. (p120) .

Outdoor Adventures

The landscape's soaring mountains, raging rivers, emerald coves and craggy cliff tops send out their siren song to hikers, paddlers and nature appreciators of all types.

ALBERTO STOCCO/SHUTTERSTOCK ©

Grand Canyon National Park (p253)
The ancient, red-orange chasm is prime for hiking, biking, rafting and sunset gawping.

Mule Riding
Saddle up with Grand Canyon Mule Rides (p259)

Yosemite National Park (p325)
Hikers, climbers and campers will find bliss amid glaciated valleys and earth-shaking waterfalls.

Hiking
Hike the towering cascade on Yosemite Falls Trail (p334).

Los Angeles (p267)
Take in the arcades of Santa Monica Pier, then stroll the oceanside path to the beach.

Bicycling
Take a spin on the South Bay Bicycle Trail (p271).

Eye-Popping Spectacles

If you build it – and razzle-dazzle it with flashing lights and lots of hype – they will come. Some places really pull out all the stops.

TOMS AUZINS/SHUTTERSTOCK ©

Las Vegas (p237)
The Eiffel Tower, a volcano and the Statue of Liberty on the same street? Anything goes in Vegas.

Venetian
Take a gondola ride at the Venetian (p243).

New York City (p35)
Retina-searing neon lights, cabs, skyscrapers and crowds create an urban hustle-bustle like no other.

Broadway
Where there's no business like show business (p54).

Walt Disney World® Resort (p178)
Princesses, pirates, sorcerers, spaceships and a giant talking mouse fill the fairy-tale world.

Magic Kingdom
Cinderella's Castle is an iconic sights (p178).

Plan Your Trip
Essential USA

V. E/SHUTTERSTOCK ©

Activities

The USA has no shortage of spectacular settings for a bit of adventure. No matter your weakness – hiking, biking, kayaking, rafting, surfing, horseback riding, rock climbing – you'll find world-class places to commune with the great outdoors. Take the national parks. They're gigantic outdoor playgrounds designed for everyone to enjoy, from tots toddling down nature trails to grungy rock-climbing champions scaling high-flying domes. Big cities let you get a move on, too, via urban paths such as New York City's High Line and wild, trail-striped green spaces such as Los Angeles' Griffith Park.

Shopping

Streets such as Rodeo Drive in Los Angeles and the Magnificent Mile (aka Michigan Ave) in Chicago are America's retail meccas, with plenty of high-end shops. For something more authentically American, check out the many markets that have work from local potters, jewelry-makers and other artists. The nation's major museums often have terrific gift shops with quality, locally inspired products.

Eating

In a country of such size and regional variation, you could spend a lifetime eating your way across America and barely scratch the surface. Owing to such scope, dining American-style could mean many things: from munching on pulled-pork sandwiches at an old roadhouse to feasting on sustainably sourced seafood in a waterfront dining room. Waves of immigrants have added great variety to American gastronomy by adapting foreign ideas to home soil, from Italian pizza and German hamburgers to Eastern European borscht, Mexican huevos rancheros and Japanese sushi. Classic comfort foods such as mac 'n' cheese, pot roast, grilled cheese sandwiches, biscuits and gravy and fried chicken are also common on local menus.

OLIVER FOERSTNER/SHUTTERSTOCK ©

Drinking & Nightlife

Americans have a staggering range of choices when it comes to beverages. A booming microbrewery industry has brought finely crafted beers to every corner of the country. The US wine industry continues to produce first-rate vintages – and it's not just California vineyards garnering all the awards. Cocktail bars abound, where mixologists blend small-batch liqueurs, whipped egg whites, hand-chipped ice and fresh fruits into snazzy elixirs. Meanwhile, coffee culture continues to prevail, with cafes and roasteries elevating the once-humble cup of coffee to high art.

Entertainment

Live-music venues are thick on the ground, with tunes spilling out of sticky clubs, sunny outdoor amphitheaters, DIY dive bars and everyplace in between. Austin, Chicago and New Orleans host particularly rich gigs, where blues, rock and jazz waft from atmospheric local halls. Many large

★ Best Live Music

Carnegie Hall (p86), New York City

Preservation Hall (p215), New Orleans

Broken Spoke (p235), Austin

Hideout (p138), Chicago

Black Cat (p114), Washington, DC

cities have polished theater scenes that export their musicals and dramas to Broadway in New York City, the theater world's epicenter. Then there's sports, the most popular entertainment of all. Americans are devoted to their favorite team, whether it's baseball, football, basketball or hockey. Watching a game live alongside 40,000 screaming fans at a stadium makes a mighty impression.

From left: Rodeo Drive (p286), Los Angeles; High Line (p50), New York City

Plan Your Trip
Month by Month

ALPHA STOCK/ALAMY ©

January

Snowfall blankets large swaths of the country. Ski resorts kick into high gear, while sun-lovers seek refuge in warmer climes.

❄ Chinese New Year

In late January or early February, you'll find colorful celebrations and feasting anywhere there's a Chinatown. NYC throws a festive parade, though San Francisco's is the best, with floats, firecrackers, bands and plenty of merriment.

February

Aside from mountain getaways, many Americans dread February with its long dark nights and frozen days. For foreign visitors, this can be the cheapest time to travel, with discounted rates for flights and hotels.

❄ Mardi Gras

Held in late February or early March, on the day before Ash Wednesday, Mardi Gras (Fat Tuesday) is the finale of Carnival. New Orleans' celebrations (www.mardigras neworleans.com) are legendary as colorful parades, masquerade balls, feasting and plenty of hedonism rule the day.

March

The first blossoms of spring arrive (at least in the south – the north still shivers in the chill). Meanwhile, drunken spring-breakers descend on Florida.

❄ St Patrick's Day

On the 17th, the patron saint of Ireland is honored with brass bands and ever-flowing pints of Guinness; huge parades occur in New York and Chicago (which goes all-out by dyeing the Chicago River green).

☆ South by Southwest

Each year Austin, TX, becomes ground zero for one of the biggest music festivals in North America. More than 2000 performers play at nearly 100 venues. SXSW is also

Above: Mardi Gras (p200), New Orleans

a major film festival and interactive fest – a platform for groundbreaking ideas.

🎇 National Cherry Blossom Festival

The star of DC's annual calendar celebrates spring's arrival with a kite festival, evening walks by lantern light, cultural fairs and a parade. The three-week event also commemorates Japan's gift of 3000 cherry trees in 1912. It's DC at its prettiest.

April

The weather is warming up, though up north April can still be unpredictable, bringing chilly weather mixed with a few teasingly warm days. Down south it's a fine time to travel.

☆ Jazz Fest

Beginning the last weekend in April, New Orleans hosts the country's best jazz jam (www.nojazzfest.com), with top-notch acts (local resident Harry Connick Jr sometimes plays) and plenty of good cheer. In addition to world-class jazz, there's also great food and crafts.

★ Best Festivals

Mardi Gras, February

South by Southwest, March

National Cherry Blossom Festival, March

Chicago Blues Festival, June

Art Basel, December

May

May is true spring and one of the loveliest times to travel, with blooming wildflowers and generally mild sunny weather.

🎇 Cinco de Mayo

Celebrate Mexico's victory over the French with salsa music and pitchers of margaritas across the country. LA and San Francisco throw some of the biggest bashes.

Above: South by Southwest (p233), Austin

June

Summer is here. School is out; vacationers fill the highways and resorts, bringing higher prices.

✾ Gay Pride

In some cities, gay pride celebrations last a week, but in San Francisco, it's a month-long party (www.sfpride.org), where the last weekend in June sees giant parades. You'll find other great pride events at major cities across the country.

☆ Chicago Blues Festival

It's the globe's biggest free blues fest (www.chicagobluesfestival.us), with three days of the music that made Chicago famous. More than 500,000 people unfurl blankets by the multiple stages that take over Grant Park in early June.

✾ Mermaid Parade

In Brooklyn, NYC, Coney Island (www.coneyisland.com) celebrates summer's steamy arrival with a kitsch-loving parade, complete with skimpily attired mermaids and horn-blowing mermen.

July

Summer is in full swing. The prices are high and the crowds can be fierce, but it's one of the liveliest times to visit.

✾ Independence Day

On July 4, the nation celebrates its birthday with a bang, as nearly every town and city stages a fireworks show. Washington, DC, New York and Chicago are great spots.

August

Expect blasting heat, with temperatures and humidity less bearable the further south you go. You'll find people-packed beaches, high prices and empty cities on weekends, when residents escape to the nearest waterfront.

☆ Lollapalooza

This mondo rock fest (www.lollapalooza.com) sees up to 170 bands spilling off eight stages in Chicago's Grant Park for four days in early August.

October

Temperatures are falling, as autumn brings fiery colors to northern climes.

☆ New York Film Festival

Just one of many big film fests in NYC (Tribeca Film Festival in late April is another goodie); this one features world premieres from across the globe (www.filmlinc.com).

✾ Halloween

In NYC, you can don a costume and join the Halloween parade up Sixth Ave. West Hollywood in Los Angeles and San Francisco's Castro district are also great places to see outrageous outfits.

November

No matter where you go, this is generally low season, with cold winds discouraging visitors despite lower prices (although airfares skyrocket around Thanksgiving).

✾ Thanksgiving

On the fourth Thursday of November, Americans gather with family and friends over day-long feasts – roast turkey, sweet potatoes and loads of other dishes. NYC hosts a huge parade, and there's pro football on TV.

December

Aside from winter sports, December means heading inside and curling up by the fire.

✾ Art Basel

This massive arts fest (www.artbasel miamibeach.com) offers four days of cutting-edge art, film, architecture and design. More than 200 major galleries from across the globe come to the event, with works by some 4000 artists, plus much hobnobbing with a glitterati crowd in Miami Beach.

✾ New Year's Eve

Americans are of two minds when it comes to ringing in the New Year. Some join festive crowds to celebrate, others plot a getaway to escape the mayhem. Whichever you choose, plan well in advance. Expect high prices (especially in NYC).

Plan Your Trip
Get Inspired

MARCOS ANTONIO DE LIMA/SHUTTERSTOCK ©

Read

On the Road (Jack Kerouac; 1957) A journey through post–WWII America.

The Great Gatsby (F Scott Fitzgerald; 1925) A powerful Jazz Age novel.

Beloved (Toni Morrison; 1987) A Pulitzer Prize–winning novel set during the post–Civil War years.

The Adventures of Huckleberry Finn (Mark Twain; 1884) A moving tale of journey and self-discovery.

Blue Highways (William Least Heat-Moon; 1982) A classic of American travel writing.

The Underground Railroad (Colson Whitehead; 2016) Pulitzer Prize–winning novel chronicling a young slave's bid for freedom.

Watch

Singin' in the Rain (1952) Among the best in the era of musicals, with an exuberant Gene Kelly and a timeless score.

Annie Hall (1977) Woody Allen's brilliant romantic comedy, with New York City playing a starring role.

North by Northwest (1959) Alfred Hitchcock thriller with Cary Grant on the run across America.

The Godfather (1972–90) Famed trilogy looking at American society through immigrants and organized crime.

The Last Black Man in San Francisco (2019) Lyrical look at love, family and loss in the rapidly changing city.

Listen

America (Simon & Garfunkel; 1968) Young lovers hitchhiking in search of America.

Smells Like Teen Spirit (Nirvana; 1991) The Gen-X grunge-rock anthem.

Gangsta's Paradise (Coolio; 1995) A hip-hop classic lamenting the cyclical nature of violence.

Born This Way (Lady Gaga; 2011) A gay anthem for a new era in LGBT rights.

Alright (Kendrick Lamar; 2015) The song against injustice chanted at Black Lives Matter protests.

Old Town Road (Lil Nas X; 2019) When country meets rap, this is the super-catchy result.

Above: Brooklyn Bridge (p75), New York City

Plan Your Trip
Five-Day Itineraries

Mighty Metropolises

The bright lights beckon in the nation's largest and third-largest cities. New York is the one that never sleeps, the great dynamo of art, fashion and culture. Big-shouldered Chicago is the Midwest's megacity, a marvel of steely skyscrapers and enormous pizzas.

New York City (p35) Wander in Central Park, get lost in world-class museums, and dive into the city's dizzying nightlife.

Chicago (p117) Wallow in the food scene and gape at eye-popping art and architecture for two days.
✈ 2 hrs to New York City

Southern Roots

For southern hospitality with a dose of cool-cat style, Austin and New Orleans deliver. Two things are certain when you visit these hot spots: you'll stuff your face and you'll hear great live music. Mural-splashed neighborhoods, arty shops and sociable bars add to the fun.

1

Austin (p217)
Soak up the honky-tonks, backyard bars and whimsical restaurants for two days.
✈ 1½ hrs to New Orleans

2

New Orleans (p197)
The antebellum mansions, gumbo, hot jazz and Mardi Gras vibe are hard to resist; three days'll do it.

Plan Your Trip

10-Day Itinerary

Big Apple to Big Easy

Delve into NYC and Washington, DC for world-class museums, iconic buildings and top-notch food and entertainment options. Then head south for sparkling beaches, Disney magic and Cajun cooking on a ramble through Miami, Orlando and New Orleans.

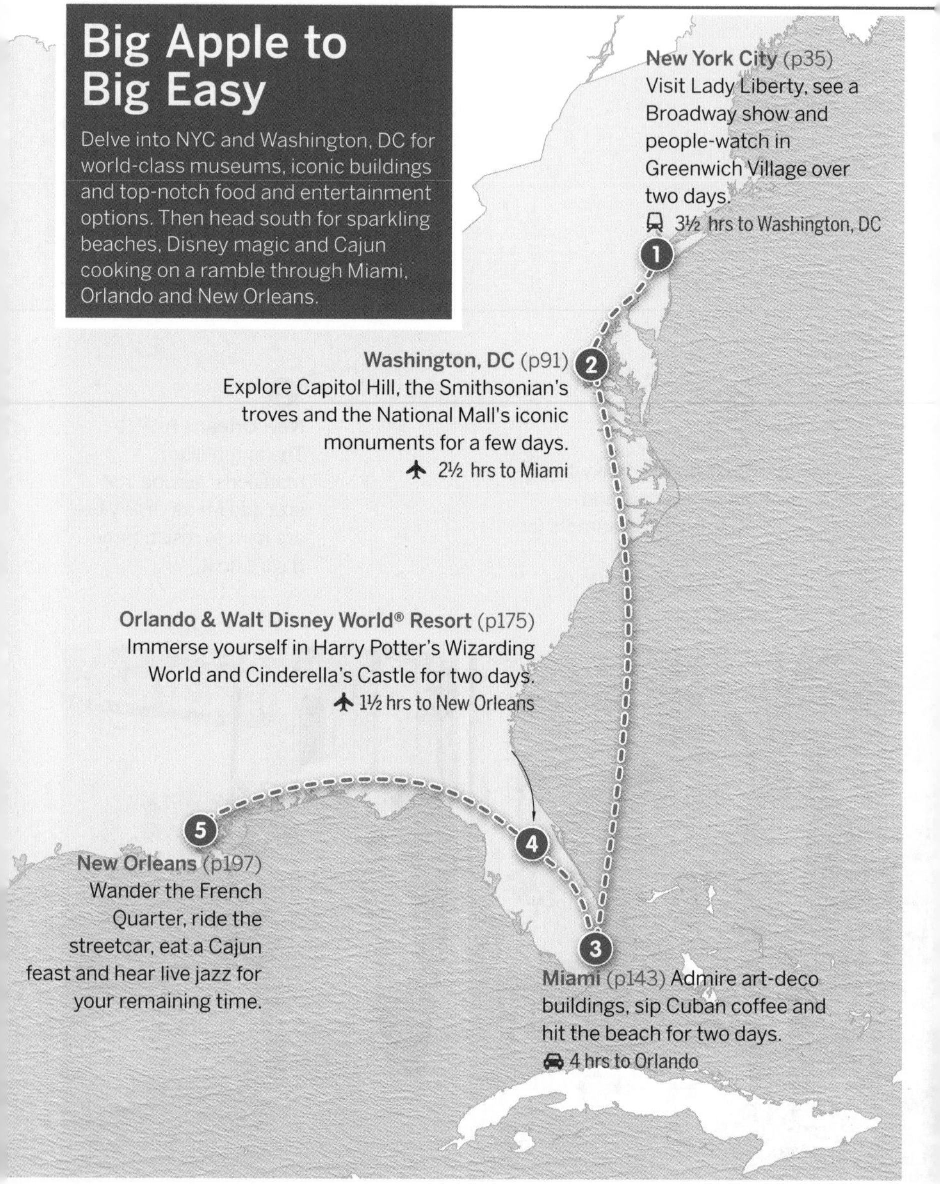

New York City (p35)
Visit Lady Liberty, see a Broadway show and people-watch in Greenwich Village over two days.
🚆 3½ hrs to Washington, DC

Washington, DC (p91)
Explore Capitol Hill, the Smithsonian's troves and the National Mall's iconic monuments for a few days.
✈ 2½ hrs to Miami

Orlando & Walt Disney World® Resort (p175)
Immerse yourself in Harry Potter's Wizarding World and Cinderella's Castle for two days.
✈ 1½ hrs to New Orleans

New Orleans (p197)
Wander the French Quarter, ride the streetcar, eat a Cajun feast and hear live jazz for your remaining time.

Miami (p143) Admire art-deco buildings, sip Cuban coffee and hit the beach for two days.
🚗 4 hrs to Orlando

Plan Your Trip
Two-Week Itinerary

The Wild West

This journey takes in the best of the west, road-tripping through neon-lit Las Vegas, movie-star-rich Los Angeles and freewheeling San Francisco. Yosemite, a national park with mammoth mountains and raging waterfalls, pops up, as does another national park with an awe-inspiring canyon.

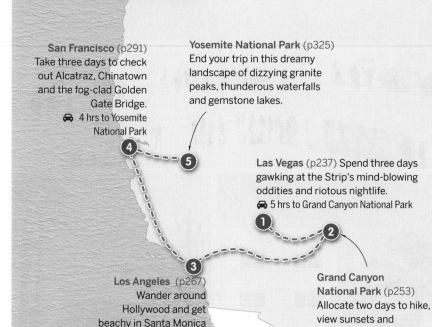

San Francisco (p291) Take three days to check out Alcatraz, Chinatown and the fog-clad Golden Gate Bridge.
🚗 4 hrs to Yosemite National Park

Yosemite National Park (p325) End your trip in this dreamy landscape of dizzying granite peaks, thunderous waterfalls and gemstone lakes.

Las Vegas (p237) Spend three days gawking at the Strip's mind-blowing oddities and riotous nightlife.
🚗 5 hrs to Grand Canyon National Park

Los Angeles (p267) Wander around Hollywood and get beachy in Santa Monica for three days.
🚗 6 hrs to San Francisco

Grand Canyon National Park (p253) Allocate two days to hike, view sunsets and experience one of the planet's great wonders.
🚗 7½ hrs to Los Angeles

Plan Your Trip
Family Travel

MIAZYOU/SHUTTERSTOCK ©

From coast to coast, you'll find superb attractions for all ages: bucket-and-spade fun at the beach, amusement parks, natural history exhibits, hikes in wilderness reserves and plenty of other activities likely to wow young ones. Top spots for family-friendly adventure include Walt Disney World® Resort, FL, with four action-packed theme parks spread across 27,000 acres, and Washington, DC, where the free Smithsonian venues inspire wonder with their dinosaurs, spaceships and zoo animals.

Planning

Weather and crowds are all-important considerations when planning a US family getaway. The peak travel season across the country is from June to August, when schools are out and the weather is warmest. Expect high prices and abundant crowds, meaning long lines at amusement and water parks, fully booked resort areas and heavy traffic on the roads – you'll need to reserve well in advance for popular destinations. The same holds true for winter resorts during their high season of late December to March.

Good to Know

Accommodations Cots and rollaway beds are usually available in hotels and resorts. Children are often not welcome at smaller B&Bs and inns.

Baby items Baby food, formula and disposable diapers (nappies) are widely available in supermarkets and pharmacies (Walgreens, CVS) across the country.

Driving Seat belts or age-appropriate child safety seats are compulsory. Most rental-car companies offer car-seat rentals, but be sure to inquire about availability at the time of booking.

Eating out High chairs or booster seats are usually available, but it pays to inquire ahead of time. At upscale restaurants, children are typically tolerated with more grace early in the evening.

Keeping Costs Down

Accommodations In motels and hotels, children under 17 or 18 years old are usually free when sharing a room with their parents. Homesharing websites are also widely available in the USA and popular with families.

Transport Most public transportation offers reduced fares for children. Children under the age of two can fly for free. Driving is the cheapest way to travel and often the easiest for families.

Eating Many restaurants have children's menus with significantly lower prices – always inquire about options. For moderately healthy, affordable meals on the go, hit up the grocery store for some Uncrustables (frozen peanut butter sandwiches) and fruit.

Activities Most sites and museums offer free admission for children five and under, and reduced admission for children under 12.

Useful Websites

Lonely Planet Kids (www.lonelyplanetkids.com) Loads of activities and great family travel blog content.

★ Best Theme Parks & Zoos

Walt Disney World® Resort (p178)

Universal Orlando Resort (p184)

Legoland (p191)

National Zoo (p103)

Zoo Miami (p153)

My Family Travel Map: North America (shop. lonelyplanet.com) Unfolds into a colorful and detailed poster for kids to personalize with stickers to mark their family's travels. Ages five to eight.

Family Travel Files (www.thefamilytravelfiles. com) Ready-made vacation ideas, destination profiles and travel tips.

Parents Magazine (www.parents.com) Monthly magazine that includes travel tips and advice.

From left: Smithsonian's National Air & Space Museum (p96), Washington, DC; Islands of Adventure (p184), Universal Orlando Resort

Central Park
(p38)

NEW YORK CITY

Broadway (p54)

N
0 — 4 km
0 — 2 miles

North Hudson Park

Riverside Park

Hudson River

Upper West Side & Central Park
Walking past brown-stones on quiet side streets still makes you feel like you've stepped out of a New York movie.

Upper East Side
Home to the so-called 'Museum Mile' – one of the most cultured strips in New York (and possibly the world).

BROADWAY

MUS MOD

West Village, Chelsea & the Meatpacking District
Mellow and raucous, quaint and sleekly contemporary, it's a 'hood to call your own.

Pennsylvania (Penn) Station

Grand Central Terminal

EMP B

East River

SoHo & Chinatown
Offering a delicious, contradictory jumble of cast-iron architecture, strutting fashionistas, temples and hook-hung salami.

HIGH LINE

Financial District & Lower Manhattan
Bold, architectural icons, eateries and a booming residential population; it's no longer strictly business here.

NATIONAL SEPTEMBER 11 MEMORIAL & MUSEUM

Upper New York Bay

ELLIS ISLAND

Governors Island

STATUE OF LIBERTY

Times Square
JASON SPONSELLER/SHUTTERSTOCK ©

Arriving in New York City

JFK International Airport AirTrain ($5) to subway ($2.75) takes one hour to Manhattan. Taxis $52 plus tolls and tip (45 to 60 minutes).

LaGuardia Airport Express bus to Midtown costs $16. Taxis $34 to $53 plus tolls and tip (30 minutes).

Newark Liberty International Airport AirTrain ($5.50) to Newark Airport train station to any train bound for NYC's Penn Station ($13, 25 minutes).

Where to Stay

NYC room prices are high. Weekdays are often cheaper than weekends. No Manhattan neighborhood has a monopoly on a single style and you'll find better-value hotels in Brooklyn and Queens. A few B&Bs and hostels are scattered throughout. See Where to Stay (p89) for details on lodgings by neighborhood.

Central Park

Lush lawns, cool forests, flowering gardens, glassy bodies of water and meandering, wooded paths provide a dose of serene nature amid the urban rush of New York City. Today, this 'people's park' is still one of the city's most popular attractions, beckoning throngs of New Yorkers with concerts, events and wildlife.

Great For...

❶ Need to Know

Map p76; www.centralparknyc.org; 59th to 110th Sts, btwn Central Park West & Fifth Ave; ⊘6am-1am; 🛗; 🚇A/C, B/D to any stop btwn 59th St-Columbus Circle & Cathedral Pkwy (110th St)

★ **Top Tip**

Bring a picnic to the Sheep Meadow, where thousands of people lounge and play on warm days.

JORDI DE RUEDA ROIGÉ/ALAMY ©

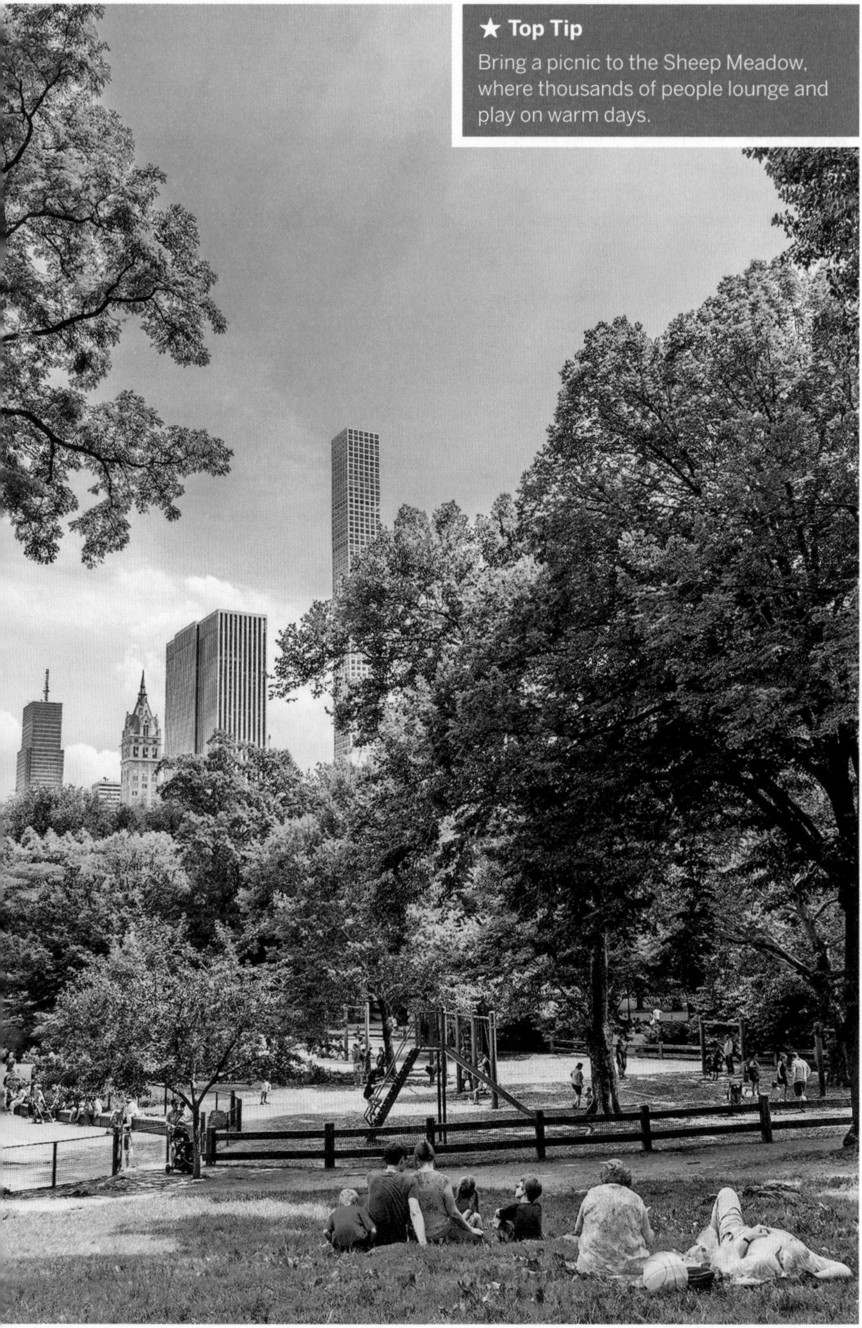

Like the city's subway system, the vast and majestic Central Park, an 843-acre rectangle of open space in the middle of Manhattan, is a great class leveler – which is exactly what it was envisioned to be. Created in the 1860s and '70s by Frederick Law Olmsted and Calvert Vaux on the marshy northern fringe of the city, the immense park was designed as a leisure space for all New Yorkers, regardless of color, class or creed.

While parts of the park swarm with joggers, in-line skaters, musicians and tourists on warm weekends, it's quieter on weekday afternoons, especially in less-well-trodden spots above 72nd St such as the Harlem Meer and the North Meadow (north of 97th St). Or head to the 6-acre Conservatory Garden (access from Fifth Ave at 105th St), which serves as one of the park's official quiet zones. It's beautiful, bursting with crabapple trees, meandering boxwood and, in the spring, lots of flowers.

Folks flock to the park even in winter, when snowstorms inspire cross-country skiing and sledding or just a simple stroll through the white wonderland, and crowds turn out every New Year's Eve for a midnight run. The **Central Park Conservancy** (☎212-310-6600; www.centralparknyc.org/tours) offers ever-changing guided tours of the park, including ones that focus on public art, wildlife and places of interest to kids.

Strawberry Fields

Standing inside the park across from the famous Dakota apartment building, where John Lennon was fatally shot in 1980, is this poignant, tear-shaped garden – a memorial to the slain star. It contains a grove of

Strawberry Fields

stately elms and a tiled mosaic that says, simply, 'Imagine.' Find it at 72nd St on the park's west side.

Bethesda Terrace & Mall

The arched walkways of Bethesda Terrace, crowned by the magnificent Bethesda Fountain (at 72nd St), have long been a gathering area for New Yorkers. To the south is the Mall (featured in countless movies), a promenade shrouded in mature North American elms. The southern stretch, known as Literary Walk, is flanked by statues of famous authors.

> **☑ Don't Miss**
> Tours with the Central Park Conservancy; many are free, others cost $15.

VERGIE AZEVEDO/SHUTTERSTOCK ©

Conservatory Water & Around

North of the zoo (at 74th St) is Conservatory Water, where model sailboats drift lazily and kids scramble about on a toadstool-studded statue of Alice in Wonderland. There are Saturday story hours (www.hcastorycenter.org) at 11am from June to September at the Hans Christian Andersen statue, to the west of the water.

Great Lawn & Around

The Great Lawn is a massive emerald carpet at the center of the park – between 79th and 85th Sts – surrounded by ball fields and London plane trees. Immediately to the southeast is Delacorte Theater, home to an annual Shakespeare in the Park festival, as well as Belvedere Castle, a bird-watching lookout. Further south, between 73rd and 78th Sts, is the leafy Ramble, a popular birding destination. On the southeastern end is the Loeb Boathouse, home to a waterside restaurant that offers rowboat rentals and gondola rides.

Jackie O Reservoir

The Jacqueline Kennedy Onassis Reservoir (at 90th St) takes up almost the entire width of the park and serves as a gorgeous reflecting pool for the city skyline. It is surrounded by a 1.58-mile track that draws legions of joggers in the warmer months. Nearby, at Fifth Ave and 90th St, is a statue of New York City Marathon founder Fred Lebow, peering at his watch.

> **✕ Take a Break**
> Class things up with an afternoon martini at the **Loeb Boathouse** (Map p76; ☎212-517-2233; www.thecentralparkboathouse.com; Lake, near E 74th St; mains lunch $26-38, dinner $30-46; ⊙restaurant noon-3:45pm Mon-Fri, from 9:30am Sat & Sun year-round, 5:30-9:30pm Mon-Fri, from 6pm Sat & Sun Apr-Nov; ⑤B, C to 72nd St, 6 to 77th St).

Central Park

THE LUNGS OF NEW YORK

The rectangular patch of green that occupies Manhattan's heart began life in the mid-19th century as a swampy piece of land that was carefully bulldozed into the idyllic nature-scape you see today. Since officially becoming Central Park, it has brought New Yorkers of all stripes together in interesting and unexpected ways. The park has served as a place for the rich to show off their fancy carriages (1860s), for the poor to enjoy free Sunday concerts (1880s) and for activists to hold be-ins against the Vietnam War (1960s).

Since then, legions of locals – not to mention travelers from all kinds of faraway places – have poured in to stroll, picnic, sunbathe, play ball and catch free concerts and performances of works by Shakespeare.

Loeb Boathouse
Perched on the shores of the lake, the historic Loeb Boathouse is one of the city's best settings for an idyllic meal. You can also rent rowboats and bicycles and ride on a Venetian gondola.

Duke Ellington Circle

Harlem Meer

The Blockhouse   North Woods

Fifth Ave

97th St Transverse

86th St Transverse

The Great Lawn

Central Park West

Conservatory Garden
The only formal garden in Central Park is perhaps the most tranquil part of the park. On the northern end, chrysanthemums bloom in late October. To the south, the park's largest crab apple tree grows by the Burnett Fountain.

Jacqueline Kennedy Onassis Reservoir
This 106-acre body of water covers roughly an eighth of the park's territory. Its original purpose was to provide clean water for the city. Now it's a good spot to catch a glimpse of water birds.

Belvedere Castle
A so-called 'Victorian folly,' this Gothic-Romanesque castle serves no other purpose than to be a very dramatic lookout point. It was built by Central Park co-designer Calvert Vaux in 1869.

The park's varied terrain offers a wonderland of experiences. There are quiet, woodsy knolls in the north. To the south is the reservoir, crowded with joggers. There are European gardens, a zoo and various bodies of water. For maximum flamboyance, hit the Sheep Meadow on a sunny day, when all of New York shows up to lounge.

Central Park is more than just a green space. It is New York City's backyard.

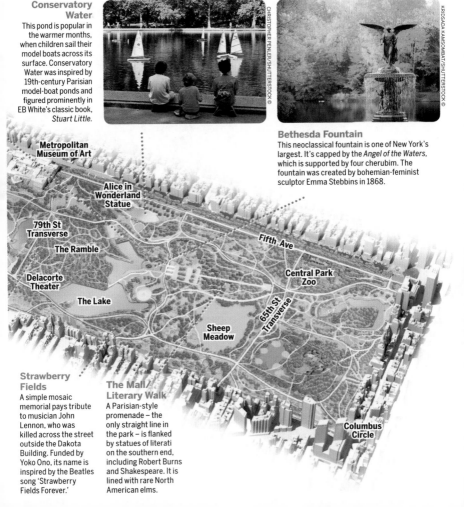

Conservatory Water

This pond is popular in the warmer months, when children sail their model boats across its surface. Conservatory Water was inspired by 19th-century Parisian model-boat ponds and figured prominently in EB White's classic book, *Stuart Little*.

CHRISTOPHER PENLER/SHUTTERSTOCK ©

KRIDSADA KAMSOMBAT/SHUTTERSTOCK ©

Bethesda Fountain

This neoclassical fountain is one of New York's largest. It's capped by the *Angel of the Waters*, which is supported by four cherubim. The fountain was created by bohemian-feminist sculptor Emma Stebbins in 1868.

Metropolitan Museum of Art

Alice in Wonderland Statue

79th St Transverse

The Ramble

Delacorte Theater

The Lake

Fifth Ave

Central Park Zoo

65th St Transverse

Sheep Meadow

Columbus Circle

Strawberry Fields

A simple mosaic memorial pays tribute to musician John Lennon, who was killed across the street outside the Dakota Building. Funded by Yoko Ono, its name is inspired by the Beatles song 'Strawberry Fields Forever.'

The Mall / Literary Walk

A Parisian-style promenade – the only straight line in the park – is flanked by statues of literati on the southern end, including Robert Burns and Shakespeare. It is lined with rare North American elms.

Statue of Liberty & Ellis Island

Stellar skyline views, a scenic ferry ride, a lookout from Lady Liberty's crown, and a moving tribute to America's immigrants at Ellis Island – unmissable is an understatement.

Great For...

☑ Don't Miss

The breathtaking views from Lady Liberty's crown (remember to reserve tickets well in advance).

Statue of Liberty

A Powerful Symbol

Lady Liberty has been gazing sternly toward 'unenlightened Europe' since 1886. Dubbed the 'Mother of Exiles,' she's often interpreted as a symbolic admonishment to an unjust old world. Emma Lazarus' 1883 poem 'The New Colossus' articulates this challenge: 'Give me your tired, your poor, your huddled masses yearning to breathe free, the wretched refuse of your teeming shore.'

History of the Statue

Conceived as early as 1865 by French intellectual Édouard Laboulaye as a monument to the republican principles shared by France and the USA, the Statue of Liberty is still a symbol of the ideals of opportunity and freedom. French sculptor Frédéric-

ℹ Need to Know

Statue of Liberty (☎212-363-3200, tickets 877-523-9849; www.nps.gov/stli; Liberty Island; adult/child incl Ellis Island $18.50/9, incl crown $21.50/12; ⊙8:30am-6pm, hours vary by season; 🚢to Liberty Island, ⑤1 to South Ferry, 4/5 to Bowling Green, then ferry)

✕ Take a Break

Stop by French food hall Le District (p78) for crepes, pastries and frites.

★ Top Tip

If you want to see both the Statue of Liberty and Ellis Island, you must get a ferry before 2pm.

Auguste Bartholdi traveled to New York in 1871 to select the site, then spent more than 10 years in Paris designing and making the 151ft-tall figure known in full as *Liberty Enlightening the World*. It was then shipped to New York, erected on a small island in the harbor and unveiled in 1886. Structurally, it consists of an iron skeleton (designed by Gustave Eiffel) with a copper skin attached to it by stiff but flexible metal bars.

Visiting the Statue

Reserve your tickets online well in advance (up to six months ahead) to access Lady Liberty's crown for breathtaking city and harbor views. If you miss out on crown tickets, you may have better luck with tickets for the pedestal, which also offers commanding views. If you don't score either, don't fret: all ferry tickets to Liberty Island offer basic access to the grounds, including guided ranger tours or self-guided audio tours. Book tickets at www.statuecruises.com to avoid long queues.

Note the 146-stair slog up to the statue's crown is arduous and should not be undertaken by anyone with significant health conditions that might impair their ability to complete the climb.

Liberty Island is usually visited in conjunction with nearby Ellis Island. Ferries leave from Battery Park; South Ferry and Bowling Green are the closest subway stations. (Ferry tickets include admission to both sights.)

Ellis Island

The most famous port of entry in the world, and a physical symbol of the American immigrant story, **Ellis Island** (☎212-363-3200, tickets ⊙877-523-9849; www.nps.gov/elis; ferry incl Liberty Island adult/child $18.50/9;

⏱8:30am-6pm, hours vary by season) is now a National Monument. Operating only from 1892 to 1924, it nonetheless processed some 12 million new arrivals. An estimated 40% of Americans today descend from those millions, making this island central to the story of modern America.

Main Building Architecture

With the Main Building, architects Edward Lippincott Tilton and William A Boring created a suitably impressive and imposing 'prologue' to America. The duo won the contract after the original wooden building burnt down in 1897. Having attended the École des Beaux-Arts in Paris, it's not surprising that they opted for a beaux-arts aesthetic for the project. The building evokes a grand train station, with majestic triple-arched entrances, decorative Flemish bond brickwork, and granite quoins (cornerstones) and belvederes.

Inside, it's the 338ft-long Registry Room (also known as the Great Hall) on the 2nd floor that takes the breath away. Under its beautiful vaulted ceiling, the newly arrived lined up to have their documents checked (people such as polygamists, paupers, criminals and anarchists were turned back). The original plaster ceiling was severely damaged by an explosion of munition barges at nearby Black Tom Wharf. It was a blessing in disguise – the rebuilt version was adorned with striking herringbone-patterned tiles by Rafael Guastavino. The Catalan-born engineer is also responsible for the beautiful tiled ceiling at the Grand Central Oyster Bar & Restaurant at Grand Central Terminal.

Ellis Island

Main Building Restoration

In 1990, following a long and expensive restoration, Ellis Island's dignified beaux-arts-style main building was reopened to the public as the Ellis Island Immigration Museum. Now anybody who rides the ferry to the island can experience a cleaned-up, modern version of the historic new-arrival experience, with the museum's interactive exhibits paying homage to the hope, jubilation and sometimes bitter disappointment of the millions who came here in search of a new beginning. Among them were Hungarian Erik Weisz (Harry Houdini), Italian Rodolfo Guglielmi (Rudolph Valentino) and Brit Archibald Alexander Leach (Cary Grant).

Quick Facts

The Statue of Liberty weighs 225 tons, and stretches 305ft and 1in from ground to torch tip.

MEIQIANBAO/SHUTTERSTOCK ©

Immigration Museum Exhibits

The museum's exhibits are spread over three levels. To get the most out of your visit, opt for the 50-minute self-guided audio tour (free with ferry ticket, available from the museum lobby). Featuring narratives from a number of sources, including historians, architects and the immigrants themselves, the tour brings to life the museum's hefty collection of personal objects, official documents, photographs and film footage. It's an evocative experience to witness personal memories – both good and bad – in the very halls and corridors in which they occurred.

The collection is divided into a number of permanent and temporary exhibitions. 'Journeys: The Peopling of America 1550–1890' on the 1st floor is interesting, but the real focus begins on the 2nd floor, where you'll find the two most fascinating exhibitions. 'Through America's Gate' examines the step-by-step process faced by the newly arrived (including the chalk-marking of those suspected of illness, a wince-inducing eye examination, and 29 questions) in the beautiful, vaulted Great Hall, while 'Peak Immigration Years' explores the motives behind the immigrants' journeys and the challenges they faced once free to begin their new American lives. Particularly interesting is the collection of old photographs, which offers intimate glimpses into the daily lives of these courageous new Americans.

★ Did You Know?

The book of law in the statue's left hand is inscribed with July IV MDCCLXXVI (July, 4, 1776), the date of American independence. The rays on her crown represent the seven seas and continents.

Museum of Modern Art

With a vast collection, scenic sculptural garden, and some of the best temporary shows in New York City, the Museum of Modern Art (MoMA) is a thrilling crash course in all that is beautiful and addictive about art.

Great For...

☑ Don't Miss

The outdoor sculpture garden makes a fine retreat when you have gallery fatigue.

Since its founding in 1929, the museum has amassed almost 200,000 artworks, documenting the creativity of the late 19th century through to today. For art buffs, it's Valhalla.

Visiting MoMA

It's easy to get lost in MoMA's vast collection. To maximize your time and create a plan of attack, download the museum's free smartphone app from the website beforehand. MoMA's permanent collection spans multiple levels. Works are on rotation so it's hard to say exactly what you'll find on display, but Van Gogh's phenomenally popular *The Starry Night* is usually a sure bet. Other highlights of the collection include Picasso's *Les Demoiselles d'Avignon* and Henri Rousseau's *The Sleeping Gypsy*, not to mention iconic American works like

STEFANO POLITI MARKOVINA/ALAMY ©

❶ Need to Know

MoMA; Map p70; 📞212-708-9400; www.
moma.org; 11 W 53rd St, btwn Fifth & Sixth
Aves; adult/child $25/free, 5:30-9pm Fri free;
🕙10am-5:30pm Sat-Thu, to 9pm Fri & 1st Thu;
♿; ⓢE, M to 5th Ave-53rd St; F to 57th St

✕ Take a Break

For a casual vibe, nosh on Italian-
inspired fare at MoMA's **Cafe 2** (Map p70;
📞212-333-1299; www.momacafes.com; 2nd
fl; dishes $12-14; 🕙11am-5:30pm Sat-Thu, to
7:30pm Fri; 🛜).

★ Top Tip

Keep your museum ticket handy, as it
also provides free entry to film screenings and MoMA PS1 (p69) in Queens.

Warhol's *Campbell's Soup Cans* and *Gold
Marilyn Monroe*, Lichtenstein's equally
poptastic *Girl with Ball*, and Hopper's
haunting *House by the Railroad*. Audio
guides are free, available on a device from
the museum or via the app.

A massive redesign in 2019 added more
than 40,000 sq ft of gallery space, as
well as new performance and multimedia
spaces and free galleries at street level.

Abstract Expressionism

One of the greatest strengths of MoMA's
collections is abstract expressionism, a
radical movement that emerged in New
York in the 1940s and boomed a decade
later. Defined by its penchant for irrev-
erent individualism and monumentally
scaled works, this so-called New York

School helped turn the metropolis into *the*
epicenter of Western contemporary art.
Among the stars are Rothko's *Magenta,
Black, Green on Orange,* Pollock's *One
(Number 31, 1950)* and de Kooning's
Painting.

Film Screenings

Not only a palace of visual art, MoMA
screens an incredibly well-rounded selection of celluloid gems from its collection
of over 22,000 films, including the works
of the Maysles Brothers and every Pixar
animation film ever produced. Expect
anything from Academy Award–nominated
documentary shorts and Hollywood classics to experimental works and international retrospectives. Best of all, your museum
ticket will get you in for free (you'll still need
to get a ticket for the film you want to see).

High Line

A resounding triumph of urban renewal, the High Line is a remarkable linear public park built along a disused elevated rail line. Each year, this aerial greenway attracts millions of visitors who come for stunning vistas of the Hudson River, public art installations, willowy stretches of native-inspired landscaping and a thoroughly unique perspective on the neighborhood streets below.

Great For...

ℹ Need to Know

Map p66; ☎212-500-6035; www.thehighline.org; Gansevoort St, Meatpacking District; ⏰7am-11pm Jun-Sep, to 10pm Apr, May, Oct & Nov, to 7pm Dec-Mar; 🚍M14 crosstown along 14th St, M23 along 23rd St, ⑤A/C/E, L to 8th Ave-14th St, 1, C/E to 23rd St, 7 to 34th St-Hudson Yards

✕ Take a Break

A cache of eateries is stashed within Chelsea Market (p80) at the 14th St exit.

★ **Top Tip**

The High Line is an especially romantic place to stroll on a balmy night, when you can see the lit-up city sparkling all around.

History

Long before the High Line was a beacon for eager tourists, happy-snapping families and New Yorkers seeking respite from the street-level grind, it was an unglamorous freight line running through neighborhoods of industry and slaughterhouses. Commissioned in the 1930s as the 'West Side Elevated Line', the idea was to eliminate the rail accidents that claimed more than 500 lives along 'Death Ave' (Tenth Ave).

By the 1980s the rails became obsolete (thanks to a rise in truck transportation). Locals signed petitions to remove the eyesore the tracks had become, but in 1999 a committee called Friends of the High Line was formed to save the rusting iron and transform the tracks into a unique elevated green space. Community support grew and, on June 9, 2009, phase one of the project opened with much ado.

Along the Way

The main things to do on the 1.5-mile-long High Line are stroll, sit and picnic 30ft above the city – while enjoying fabulous views of Manhattan's ever-changing urban landscape. Along the park's length you'll pass by lush native plants, lounge chairs for soaking up some sun and some surprising vantage points over the bustling streets – especially at various overlooks, where bleacher-like seating faces huge panes of glass that frame the traffic, buildings and pedestrians below as living works of art. There's also André Balazs' luxury hotel, the Standard, which straddles the park.

Information, Tours, Events & Eats

As you walk its length you'll find staffers wearing the signature double-H logo who can point you in the right direction or offer you additional information about the converted rails. There are also many staffers behind the scenes organizing public art exhibitions and activity sessions, especially in summer. Special tours and events explore a variety of topics: history, horticulture, design, art and food. Check the schedule at www.thehighline.org for the latest.

The High Line also invites various gastronomic establishments from around the city to set up vending carts and stalls so that strollers can enjoy to-go items on the green. Expect a showing of the finest coffee and ice cream during the warmer months.

What's Nearby?

Whitney Museum of American Art (Map p66; ☑212-570-3600; www.whitney.org; 99 Gansevoort St, at Washington St, Meatpacking District; adult/child $25/free, 7-10pm Fri pay-what-you-wish; ⊙10:30am-6pm Mon, Wed, Thu & Sun, to 10pm Fri & Sat; ⑤A/C/E, L to 8th Ave-14th St) After years of construction, the Whitney's new downtown location opened to much fanfare in 2015. Anchoring the southern reaches of the High Line, this stunning building – designed by Renzo Piano – provides 63,000 sq ft of space for the museum's unparalleled collection of American art. Inside the light-filled galleries you'll find works by all the greats, including Edward Hopper, Jasper Johns, Georgia O'Keeffe and Mark Rothko. Unlike at many museums, special emphasis is placed on the work of living artists.

Hudson River Park (Map p66; ☑212-627-2020; www.hudsonriverpark.org; West Village; ⊙6am-1am; ⊛; ⊟M23 crosstown bus, ⑤1 to Christopher St, C/E to 23rd St) The High Line may be all the rage these days, but one block away stretches a 5-mile-long recreational space that has transformed the city over the past decade. Covering 550 acres (400 of which are on the water) and running from Battery Park at Manhattan's southern tip to 59th St in Midtown, Hudson River Park is Manhattan's wondrous backyard. The long riverside path is a great spot for cycling, running and strolling. Several boathouses (including one in Chelsea near W 26th St and another in the West Village near Houston St) offer kayak hire and longer excursions for the more experienced.

> ☑ **Don't Miss**
>
> The amphitheater-style viewing platforms at 17th and 26th Sts.

MASSIMO SALESI/SHUTTERSTOCK ©

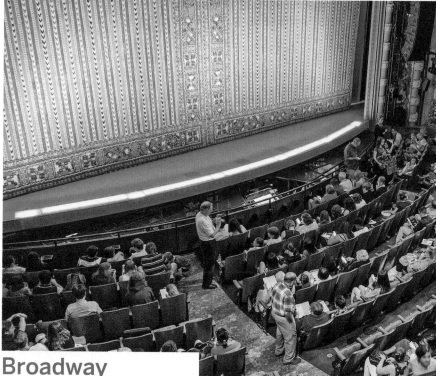

Broadway

Broadway is NYC's dream factory – a place where romance, betrayal, murder and triumph come with dazzling costumes, toe-tapping tunes and stirring scores. Reserve well ahead for top shows, which sell out months in advance.

Great For...

☑ Don't Miss

The **Brill Building** (Map p70; 1619 Broadway, at W 49th St; SN/R/W to 49th St; 1, C/E to 50th St); Carole King and Burt Bacharach both started out here.

Broadway Beginnings

The neighborhood's first playhouse was the long-gone Empire, opened in 1893 and located on Broadway between 40th and 41st Sts. Two years later, cigar manufacturer and part-time comedy scribe Oscar Hammerstein opened the Olympia, also on Broadway, before opening the Republic, now children's theater **New Victory** (Map p70; ✆646-223-3010; www.newvictory.org; 209 W 42nd St, btwn Seventh & Eighth Aves; ♿; SN/Q/R/W, S, 1/2/3, 7 to Times Sq-42nd St; A/C/E to 42nd St-Port Authority Bus Terminal), in 1900. This led to a string of new venues, among them the still-beating **New Amsterdam Theatre** (Aladdin; Map p70; ✆866-870-2717; www.newamsterdamtheatre.com; 214 W 42nd St, btwn Seventh & Eighth Aves; ⊙box office 9am-8pm Mon-Fri, from 10am Sat, 10am-6:30pm Sun; ♿; SN/Q/R/W, S, 1/2/3, 7 to Times Sq-42nd St;

New Amsterdam Theatre

PIT STOCK/SHUTTERSTOCK ©

❶ Need to Know

Theatermania (www.theatermania.com) provides listings, reviews and ticketing for any form of theater.

✕ Take a Break

Seek out beefy brilliance at Burger Joint (p81), hiding in the Parker New York hotel.

★ Top Tip

Check show websites for cheap-ticket digital lotteries, entered the day of or day prior to a performance.

A/C/E to 42nd St-Port Authority Bus Terminal) and **Lyceum Theatre** (Map p70; www.shubert. nyc/theatres/lyceum; 149 W 45th St, btwn Sixth & Seventh Aves; ⓢN/R/W to 49th St).

The Broadway of the 1920s was well known for its lighthearted musicals, commonly fusing vaudeville and music-hall traditions, and producing classic tunes like Cole Porter's 'Let's Misbehave.' At the same time, Midtown's theater district was evolving as a platform for new American dramatists. One of the greatest was Eugene O'Neill. Born in Times Square at the long-gone Barrett Hotel (1500 Broadway) in 1888, the playwright debuted many of his works here, including Pulitzer Prize–winners Beyond the Horizon and Anna Christie. O'Neill's success on Broadway paved the way for other American greats like Tennessee Williams, Arthur Miller and Edward

Albee – a surge of serious talent that led to the establishment of the annual Tony Awards in 1947.

These days, New York's Theater District covers an area stretching roughly from 40th St to 54th St between Sixth and Eighth Aves, with dozens of Broadway and off-Broadway theaters ranging from block-buster musicals to new and classic drama.

Getting a Ticket

Unless there's a specific show you're after, the best – and cheapest – way to score tickets in the area is at the **TKTS Booth** (www.tdf.org/tkts; Broadway, at W 47th St, Midtown; ⏲3-8pm Mon & Fri, 2-8pm Tue, 10am-2pm & 3-8pm Wed, Thu & Sat, 11am-7pm Sun; ⓢN/Q/R/W, S, 1/2/3, 7 to Times Sq-42nd St), where you can line up and get same-day discounted tickets for top Broadway and off-Broadway shows. Smartphone users can download the free TKTS app, which offers rundowns of both Broadway and off-Broadway shows, as well as real-time updates of what's available on that day. Always have a back-up choice in case your first preference sells out, and never buy from scalpers on the street.

The TKTS Booth is an attraction in its own right, with its illuminated roof of 27 ruby-red steps rising a panoramic 16ft 1in above the 47th St sidewalk.

What's On?

Musicals rule the marquees on Broadway, with the hottest shows of the day blending song and dance in lavish, star-studded productions.

Hamilton

Broadway's hottest ticket, Lin-Manuel Miranda's acclaimed musical *Hamilton,* uses contemporary hip-hop beats to recount the story of America's first Secre-

tary of the Treasury, Alexander Hamilton. Inspired by Ron Chernow's biography *Alexander Hamilton,* the show has won a flock of awards, with 11 Tony Awards (including Best Musical), a Grammy for its triple-platinum cast album and the Pulitzer Prize for Drama.

Book of Mormon

Subversive, obscene and ridiculously hilarious, this cutting musical satire is the work of *South Park* creators Trey Parker and Matt Stone and *Avenue Q* composer Robert Lopez. Winner of nine Tony Awards, it tells the story of two naive Mormons on a mission to 'save' a Ugandan village.

Kinky Boots

Adapted from a 2005 British indie film, Harvey Fierstein and Cyndi Lauper's smash

Ambassador Theatre

hit tells the story of a doomed English shoe factory unexpectedly saved by Lola, a business-savvy drag queen. Its solid characters and electrifying energy have not been lost on critics, and the musical has won six Tony Awards, including Best Musical in 2013.

Lion King

A top choice for families with kids, Disney's blockbuster musical tells the tale of a lion cub's journey to adulthood and the throne of the animal kingdom. The spectacular sets, costumes and African chants are worth the ticket alone.

★ Did You Know?

The term 'off Broadway' is not a geographical one – it simply refers to theaters that are smaller in size (200 to 500 seats).

Chicago

It's a little easier to score tickets to *Chicago* than some of the newer musicals, and you'll often find last-minute discounts at TKTS booths around the city. This Bob Fosse/Kander & Ebb classic tells the story of showgirl Velma Kelly, wannabe Roxie Hart, lawyer Billy Flynn and the fabulously sordid goings-on of the Chicago underworld. Revived by director Walter Bobbie, its sassy, infectious energy more than makes up for the tight-squeeze seating.

Harry Potter & the Cursed Child

This popular two-part play is beloved of Potterheads of all ages and winner of six Tony Awards.

Mean Girls

Tiny Fey's musical adaptation of her classic film about the perils of navigating social cliques in high school.

EGROYV/SHUTTERSTOCK ©

❶ Quick Facts

The annual Tony Awards are the Oscars of the theater world, bestowing awards across a host of categories. Check out the latest winners on www. tonyawards.com.

National September 11 Memorial & Museum

Rising from the ashes of Ground Zero, the memorial and museum are a beautiful, dignified response to the city's darkest chapter, as much a symbol of hope and renewal as they are a tribute to the victims of terrorism.

Great For...

☑ Don't Miss

In the museum, look for the 'Angel of 9/11,' the eerie outline of a woman's anguished face on a twisted girder.

Reflecting Pools

Surrounded by a plaza planted with more than 400 swamp white oak trees, the 9/11 Memorial's reflecting pools occupy the original footprints of the ill-fated Twin Towers. From their rim, a steady cascade of water pours 30ft down toward a central void. The flow of the water is richly symbolic, beginning as thousands of smaller streams, merging into a massive torrent of collective confusion, and ending with a slow journey toward an abyss. Bronze panels frame the pools, inscribed with the names of the nearly 3000 people who died in the terrorist attacks of September 11, 2001, and in the World Trade Center car bombing on February 26, 1993. Designed by Michael Arad and Peter Walker, the pools are both striking and deeply poignant.

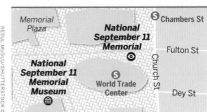

❶ Need to Know

National September 11 Memorial (Map p66; www.911memorial.org; 180 Greenwich St, Lower Manhattan; ⏰7:30am-9pm; ⑤E to World Trade Center, 2/3 to Park Pl, R/W to Cortlandt St) FREE

✕ Take a Break

Head up to Tribeca for great dining options such as Locanda Verde (p78).

★ Top Tip

To minimize queuing, purchase tickets online or at one of the vending machines outside the museum building.

Memorial Museum

The contemplative energy of the monument is further enhanced by the **National September 11 Memorial Museum** (📞212-312-8800; adult/child $26/15, 5-8pm Tue free; ⏰9am-8pm Sun-Thu, to 9pm Fri & Sat, last entry 2hr before close). Standing between the reflective pools, the museum's glass entrance pavilion eerily evokes a toppled tower. Inside the entrance, an escalator leads down to the museum's subterranean main lobby. On the descent, visitors stand in the shadow of two steel tridents, originally embedded in the bedrock at the base of the North Tower. Each over 80ft tall and weighing 50 tons, they once provided the structural support that allowed the towers to soar over 1360ft into the sky. They remained standing in the subsequent sea of rubble, becoming immediate symbols of resilience.

Among he collection are the Vesey Street Stairs. Dubbed the 'Survivors Stairs,' they allowed hundreds of workers to flee the WTC site on the morning of 9/11. At the bottom of these stairs is the moving In Memoriam gallery, its walls lined with the photographs and names of those who perished. Interactive touch screens and a central reflection room shed light on the victims' lives.

Around the corner from the In Memoriam gallery is the NYC Fire Department's Engine Company 21. One of the largest artifacts on display, its burnt-out cab is testament to the inferno faced by those at the scene. The fire engine stands at the entrance to the museum's main Historical Exhibition. Divided into three sections – *Events of the Day, Before 9/11* and *After 9/11* – its collection of videos, real-time audio recordings, images, objects and testimonies provide a rich, meditative exploration of the tragedy, the events that preceded it (including the WTC bombing of 1993), and the stories of grief, resilience and hope that followed.

Empire State Building

The striking art-deco skyscraper has appeared in dozens of films and still provides one of the best views in town – particularly around sunset when the twinkling lights of the city switch on. Although the crowds are substantial, no one regrets making the journey to the top.

The Chrysler Building may be prettier, and One World Trade Center may be taller, but the queen bee of the New York skyline remains the Empire State Building. NYC's biggest star has enjoyed close-ups in around 100 films, from *King Kong* to *Independence Day*. Heading up to the top is a quintessential NYC experience.

Observation Decks

There are two observation decks. The open-air 86th-floor deck offers an alfresco experience, with telescopes (previously coin operated; now free) for close-up glimpses of the metropolis in action. Further up, the enclosed 102nd-floor deck is New York's second-highest observation deck, trumped only by the observation deck at One World Trade Center. Needless to say, the views over the city's five boroughs (and five

---

Great For...

☑ **Don't Miss**

Live jazz held on Thursday to Saturday nights from 9pm to 1am on the 86th floor.

ANDREA IZZOTTI/SHUTTERSTOCK ©

34th St-
Herald Sq   **Empire State**
S W 34th St   **Building**   E 34th St
Park Ave S

W 33rd St   E 33rd St   S
Fifth Ave   33rd St

❶ Need to Know

Map p70; www.empirestatebuilding.com; 20 W
34th St, btwn Fifth & Sixth Aves; 86th-fl observation deck adult/child $38/32, incl 102nd-fl
observation deck $58/52; ⊙8am-2am, last
elevators up 1:15am; ⑤6 to 33rd St, B/D/F/M,
N/Q/R/W to 34th St-Herald Sq

✘ Take a Break

Feast on dumplings, barbecue and
kimchi in nearby Koreatown (32nd St,
between Fifth and Sixth Aves).

★ Top Tip

To beat the crowds, buy tickets online
(worth the $2 convenience fee).

neighboring states, weather permitting) are
quite simply exquisite. The views from both
decks are especially spectacular at sunset,
when the city dons its nighttime cloak in
dusk's afterglow. Alas, the passage to heav-
en will involve a trip through purgatory: the
queues to the top are notorious.

By the Numbers

The statistics are astounding: 10 million
bricks, 60,000 tons of steel, 6400 windows
and 328,000 sq ft of marble. Built on
the original site of the Waldorf-Astoria,
construction took a record-setting 410
days, using seven million hours of labor and
costing a mere $41 million. It might sound
like a lot, but it fell well below its $50 million

budget (just as well, given it went up during
the Great Depression). Coming in at 102
stories and 1454ft from top to bottom, the
limestone phallus opened for business on
May 1, 1931.

Language of Light

Since 1976, the building's top 30 floors
have been floodlit in a spectrum of colors
each night, reflecting seasonal and holiday
hues. Famous combos include orange,
white and green for St Patrick's Day; blue
and white for Chanukah; white, red and
green for Christmas; and the rainbow
colors for Gay Pride weekend in June. For
a full rundown of the color schemes, check
the website.

Iconic Architecture

Head for Midtown for New York City's most iconic architecture, spanning the 20th and 21st centuries.

Start Grand Central Terminal
Distance 1.8 miles
Duration 3.5 hours

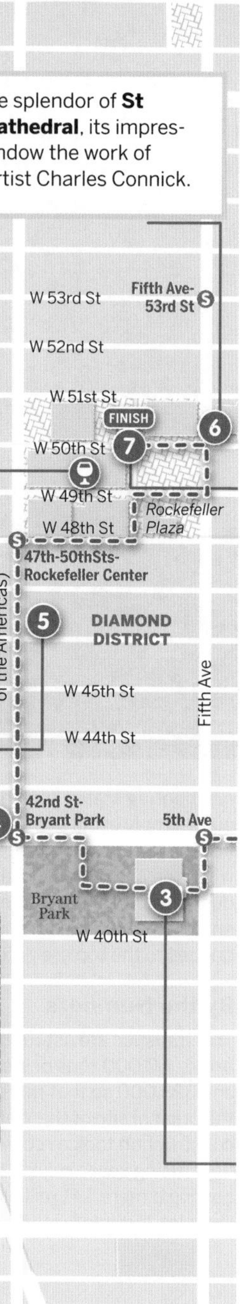

6 Admire the splendor of **St Patrick's Cathedral**, its impressive rose window the work of American artist Charles Connick.

W 53rd St
Fifth Ave-53rd St Ⓢ
W 52nd St
W 51st St
FINISH **7**
6
W 50th St Ⓨ
W 49th St
Rockefeller
W 48th St Plaza
Ⓢ
47th-50thSts-Rockefeller Center

Take a Break Cocktails at **Bar SixtyFive** (p85)

Sixth Ave (Avenue of the Americas)

5
DIAMOND DISTRICT
W 45th St
Fifth Ave
W 44th St

5 The unique **Diamond District** has more than 2600 businesses selling diamonds, gold, pearls, gemstones and watches.

4 Ⓢ
42nd St-Bryant Park 5th Ave
Ⓢ
Bryant Park **3**
W 40th St

4 The soaring **Bank of America Tower**, NYC's fourth-tallest building, is one of its most ecofriendly.

Classic Photo The vista from the **Top of the Rock** (p73) observation deck

7 The **Rockefeller Center** (p76) is a magnificent complex of art-deco skyscrapers and sculptures.

0 — 400 m
0 — 0.2 miles

E 49th St
E 48th St
E 47th St
E 46th St
E 45th St
E 44th St
E 43rd St
E 42nd St
E 40th St

Madison Ave
Park Ave
Lexington Ave
Vanderbilt Ave

Grand Central Terminal

START

42nd St-Grand Central

1 At beaux-arts marvel **Grand Central Terminal** (p72), you can stargaze at the Main Concourse ceiling

3 Step inside the stately **New York Public Library** to peek at its spectacular Rose Reading Room.

2 Slip into the sumptuous art-deco lobby of the **Chrysler Building** (p72), with its inlaid wood and marble

◎ SIGHTS

◎ Financial District & Lower Manhattan

One World Observatory　　Viewpoint

(Map p66; 📞212-602-4000; www.oneworld observatory.com; 285 Fulton St, cnr West & Vesey Sts, Lower Manhattan; adult/child/under-5s $35/29/free; ⏰9am-9pm Sep-Apr, from 8am May-Aug; ⓢE to World Trade Center, 2/3 to Park Pl, A/C, J/Z, 4/5 to Fulton St, R/W to Cortlandt St) Spanning levels 100 to 102 of the tallest building in the Western Hemisphere, One World Observatory offers dazzling panoramic views from its sky-high perch. On a clear day you'll be able to see all five boroughs and some surrounding states, revealed after an introductory video abruptly disappears to allow the dazzling view in through immense picture windows. Not surprisingly, it's a hugely popular attraction. Purchase tickets online in advance, choosing the date and time of your visit.

Museum of Jewish Heritage　　Museum

(Map p66; 📞646-437-4202; www.mjhnyc.org; 36 Battery Pl, Financial District; adult/child $8/free, 4-9pm Wed & Thu free; ⏰10am-9pm Sun-Thu, to 5pm Fri mid-Mar–mid-Nov, to 3pm Fri rest of year; ♿; ⓢ4/5 to Bowling Green, R/W to Whitehall St) This evocative waterfront museum explores all aspects of modern Jewish identity and culture, from religious traditions to artistic accomplishments. The museum's core exhibition covers three themed floors: *Jewish Life a Century Ago, Jewish Renewal* and *The War Against the Jews* – a detailed exploration of the Holocaust through thousands of personal artifacts, photographs, documentary films and survivor testimony. Also commemorating Holocaust victims is the external installation Garden of Stones, a narrow pathway of 18 boulders supporting living trees.

One World Observatory

◉ SoHo & Chinatown

Chinatown Area

(Map p66; www.explorechinatown.com; south of Broome St & east of Broadway; ⑤N/Q/R/W, J/Z, 6 to Canal St; B/D to Grand St; F to East Broadway) A walk through Manhattan's most colorful, cramped neighborhood is never the same, no matter how many times you hit the pavement. Peek inside temples and exotic storefronts. Catch the whiff of ripe persimmons, hear the clacking of mahjongg tiles on makeshift tables, eye dangling duck roasts swinging in store windows and shop for anything from rice-paper lanterns and 'faux-lex' watches to tire irons and a pound of pressed nutmeg. America's largest congregation of Chinese immigrants is your oyster.

◉ East Village & Lower East Side

New Museum of Contemporary Art Museum

(Map p66; ☑212-219-1222; www.newmuseum. org; 235 Bowery, btwn Stanton & Rivington Sts, Lower East Side; adult/child $18/free, 7-9pm Thu by donation; ◷11am-6pm Tue, Wed & Fri-Sun, to 9pm Thu; ⚕; ⑤F to 2nd Ave, R/W to Prince St, J/Z to Bowery, 6 to Spring St) The New Museum of Contemporary Art is a sight to behold: a seven-story stack of ethereal, off-kilter white boxes (designed by Tokyo-based architects Kazuyo Sejima and Ryue Nishizawa of SANAA and New York firm Gensler) rearing above its medium-rise neighborhood. It was a long-awaited breath of fresh air along what was a completely gritty Bowery strip when it arrived back in 2007 – since the museum's opening, many glossy new constructions have joined it, quickly transforming this once down-and-out avenue.

◉ West Village, Chelsea & Meatpacking District

Washington Square Park Park

(Map p66; www.nycgovparks.org; Fifth Ave, at Washington Sq N, West Village; ◷closes midnight; ⚕; ⑤A/C/E, B/D/F/M to W 4th

 New York for Children

While the American Museum of Natural History (p74) and **Central Park** (p38) reign as favorites, other good options include the following:

Bronx Zoo (☑718-220-5100; www.bronx-zoo.com; 2300 Southern Blvd; full-experience adult/child Apr-Oct $37/27, Nov-Mar $29/21, pay-as-you-wish general admission Wed; ◷10am-5pm Mon-Fri, to 5:30pm Sat & Sun Apr-Oct, 10:30am-4:30pm Nov-Mar; ⑤2, 5 to West Farms Sq-E Tremont Ave) This 265-acre zoo is the country's biggest and oldest, with more than 6000 animals and re-created habitats from around the world, from African plains to Asian rainforests. It's deservedly popular, with especially large crowds on discounted Wednesdays and weekends in good weather, and any day in July or August.

Intrepid Sea, Air & Space Museum
(Map p70; ☑877-957-7447; www.intrepidmuseum.org; Pier 86, Twelfth Ave at W 46th St; adult/child $33/24; ◷10am-5pm Mon-Fri, to 6pm Sat & Sun Apr-Oct, 10am-5pm Nov-Mar; ⚕; ⎚westbound M42, M50 to 12th Ave, ⑤A/C/E to 42nd St-Port Authority Bus Terminal) In WWII, the USS *Intrepid* survived both a bomb and kamikaze attacks. This hulking aircraft carrier now plays host to a multimillion-dollar interactive military museum that tells its tale through videos, historical artifacts and frozen-in-time living quarters. The flight deck features fighter planes, military helicopters and high-tech flight simulators.

Bronx Zoo

West & East Villages, Chinatown & Lower Manhattan

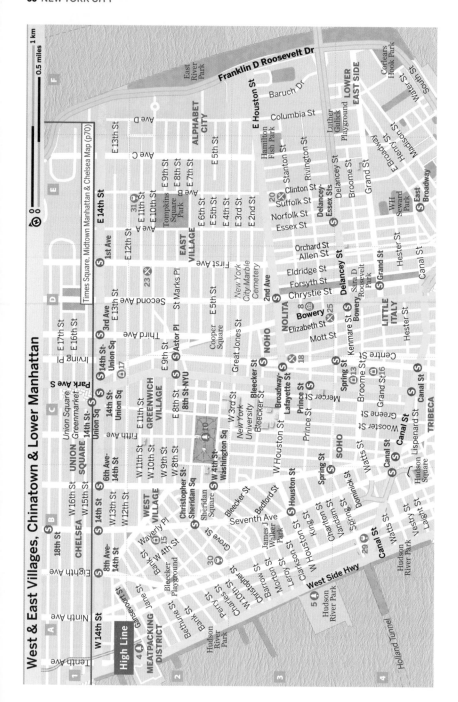

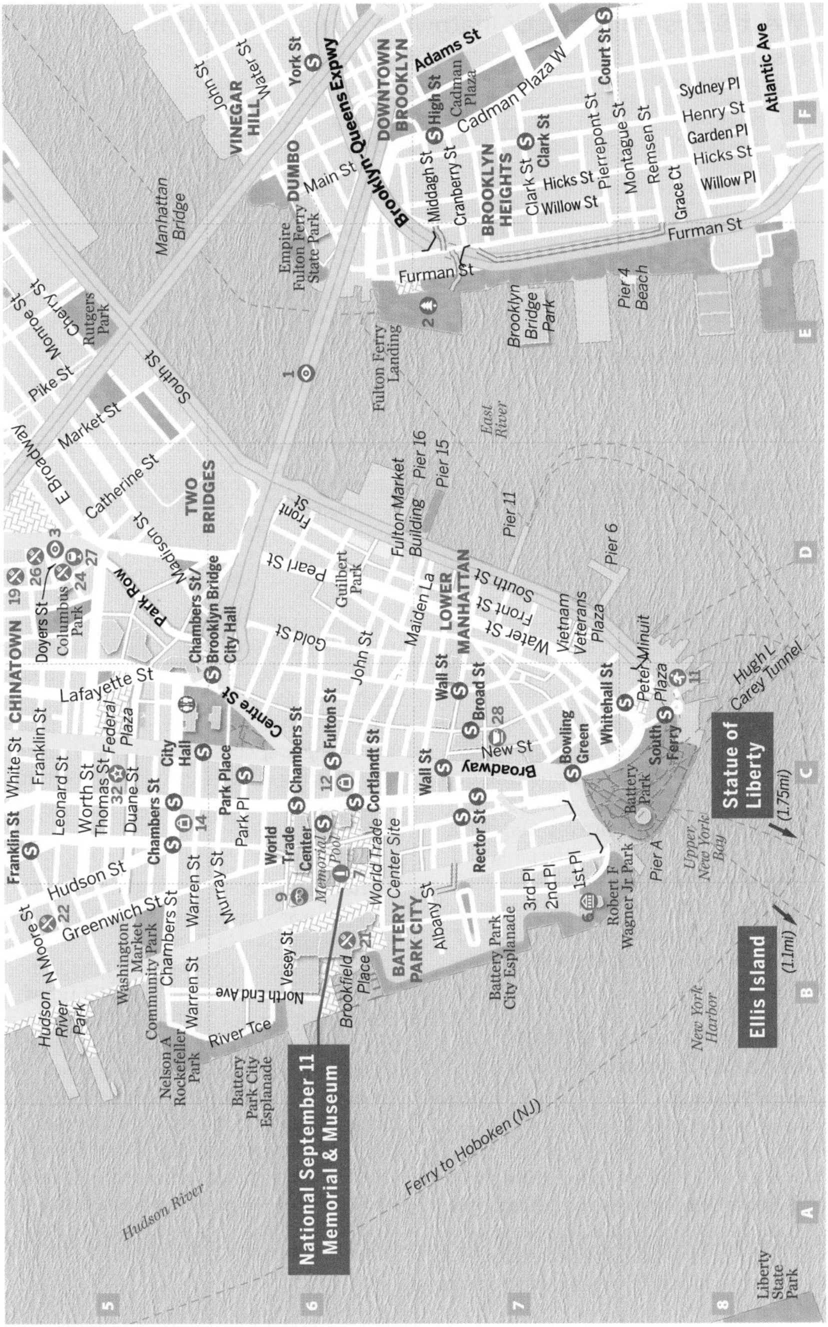

National September 11
Memorial & Museum

Statue of
Liberty

Ellis Island

John St
VINEGAR
HILL
Water St
York St
Main St
DUMBO
Empire
Fulton Ferry
State Park
Fulton Ferry
Landing
Brooklyn-Queens Expwy
DOWNTOWN
BROOKLYN
Adams St
High St
Middagh St
Cranberry St
Cadman
Plaza
Cadman Plaza W
BROOKLYN
HEIGHTS
Clark St
Clark St
Hicks St
Willow St
Pierrepont St
Court St
Montague St
Remsen St
Sydney Pl
Henry St
Garden Pl
Hicks St
Willow Pl
Grace Ct
Atlantic Ave
Furman St
Furman St
Brooklyn
Bridge
Park
Pier 4
Beach

Manhattan
Bridge
Rutgers
Park
Cherry St
S Monroe St
Pike St
Market St
E Broadway
South St
Catherine St
Madison St
TWO
BRIDGES
Front St
St
Pearl St
Guilbert
Park
Fulton Market
Building
Pier 16
Pier 15
East
River
Pier 11
Fulton St
South St
Maiden La
Water St
Front St
LOWER
MANHATTAN
Vietnam
Veterans
Plaza
Pier 6

CHINATOWN
19
White St
Franklin St
Doyers St
26
Columbus
Park
3
24
27
Park Row
Lafayette St
Leonard St
Worth St
Thomas St
32
Duane St
Chambers St
Brooklyn Bridge
City Hall
Centre St
Chambers St
City
Hall
Gold St
John St
Wall St
Broad St
New St
28
Whitehall St
Peter Minuit
Plaza
Hugh L
Carey Tunnel

Franklin St
Hudson St
N Moore St
22
Greenwich St
Washington
Market
Community Park
Warren St
Chambers St
Murray St
Thomas St
Federal
Plaza
14
Park Place
Park Pl
World
Trade
Center
9
Memorial
Pool
1
12
Cortlandt St
World Trade Center Site
Rector St
Broadway
Wall St
Bowling
Green
South
Ferry
Pier A
Battery
Park
S Plaza
11

Hudson
River
Park
Nelson A
Rockefeller
Park
Battery
Park City
Esplanade
Warren St
River Tce
Vesey St
North End Ave
Brookfield
Place
21
BATTERY
PARK
CITY
Albany St
3rd Pl
2nd Pl
1st Pl
Robert F
Wagner Jr Park
6
Battery Park
City Esplanade
Upper
New York
Bay

Hudson River

Ferry to Hoboken (NJ)

New York
Harbor

Liberty
State
Park

(1.75m)

(1.1mi)

5
6
7
8

A B C D E F

West & East Villages, Chinatown & Lower Manhattan

St-Washington Sq, R/W to 8th St-NYU) This former potter's field and square for public executions is now the unofficial town square of Greenwich Village, hosting lounging NYU students, tuba-playing street performers, socialising canines, fearless squirrels, speed-chess pros, and barefoot children who splash about in the fountain on warm days. Locals have resisted changes to the shape and uses of the park, and its layout has remained largely the same since the 1800s. Check out the Washington Square Park Conservancy (www.washingtonsquareparkconservancy.org) for news and events.

◉ Union Square, Flatiron District & Gramercy

Union Square   Square
(Map p70; www.unionsquarenyc.org; 17th St, btwn Broadway & Park Ave S; ⑤4/5/6, N/Q/R, L to 14th St-Union Sq) Union Square is like the Noah's Ark of New York, rescuing at least two of every kind from the curling seas of concrete. In fact, one would be hard pressed to find a more eclectic cross-section of locals

gathered in one public place: suited businessfolk gulping fresh air during their lunch breaks, dreadlocked loiterers tapping beats on their tablas, skateboarders flipping tricks on the southeastern stairs, old-timers poring over chess boards, and throngs of protesting masses chanting fervently for various causes.

◉ Midtown

Times Square   Area
(Map p70; www.timessquarenyc.org; Broadway, at Seventh Ave; ⑤N/Q/R/W, S, 1/2/3, 7 to Times Sq-42nd St) Love it or hate it, the intersection of Broadway and Seventh Ave (aka Times Square) pumps out the NYC of the global imagination – yellow cabs, golden arches, soaring skyscrapers and razzle-dazzle Broadway marquees. It's right here that Al Jolson 'made it' in the 1927 film *The Jazz Singer,* that photojournalist Alfred Eisenstaedt famously captured a lip-locked sailor and nurse on V-J Day in 1945, and that Alicia Keys and Jay-Z waxed lyrically about the concrete jungle.

Radio City Music Hall
Historic Building

(Map p70; www.radiocity.com; 1260 Sixth Ave, at W 50th St; tours adult/child $31/27; ⊙tours 9:30am-5pm; 🚹; 🅂B/D/F/M to 47th-50th Sts-Rockefeller Center) This spectacular moderne movie palace was the brainchild of vaudeville producer Samuel Lionel 'Roxy' Rothafel. Never one for understatement, Roxy launched his venue on December 23, 1932, with an over-the-top extravaganza that included camp dance troupe the Roxy-ettes (mercifully renamed the Rockettes). Guided tours (75 minutes) of the sumptuous interiors include the glorious auditorium, Witold Gordon's classically inspired mural *History of Cosmetics* in the Women's Downstairs Lounge, and the VIP Roxy Suite, where luminaries such as Elton John and Alfred Hitchcock have been entertained.

Rockefeller Center
Historic Building

(Map p70; ☎212-588-8601; www.rockefeller-center.com; Fifth to Sixth Aves, btwn W 48th & 51st Sts; 🅂B/D/F/M to 47th-50th Sts-Rockefeller Center) This 22-acre 'city within a city' debuted at the height of the Great Depression, with developer John D Rockefeller Jr footing the $100-million price tag. Taking nine years to build, it was America's first multiuse retail, entertainment and office space – a sprawl of 19 buildings (14 of which are the original moderne structures). The center was declared a National Landmark in 1987. Highlights include the Top of the Rock (p73) observation deck and **NBC Studio Tours** (Map p70; ☎212-664-3700; www.thetouratnbcstudios.com; 30 Rockefeller Plaza, entrance at 1250 Sixth Ave; 1hr tours adult/child $33/29, children under 6yr not admitted; ⊙8:20am-2:20pm Mon-Thu, to 5pm Fri, to 6pm Sat & Sun, longer hours in summer;).

The Rockefeller Center is also graced with the creations of 30 great artists, commissioned around the punchy theme 'Man at the Crossroads Looks Uncertainly but Hopefully at the Future.' Paul Manship contributed the 18ft *Prometheus*, overlooking the sunken plaza, while Lee Lawrie made the 24ft-tall bronze *Atlas*, in front of

 ### Detour: Queens

The largest of NYC's boroughs, Queens is truly a world apart. Twelve subway lines serve the area, and the NYC Ferry runs from East 34th St across to Long Island City, up to Roosevelt Island on to Astoria.

MoMA PS1 (☎718-784-2084; www.momaps1.org; 22-25 Jackson Ave, Long Island City; suggested donation adult/child $10/free, NYC residents or with MoMA ticket free, Warm Up party online/at venue $18/22; ⊙noon-6pm Thu-Mon, Warm Up parties noon-9pm Sat Jul-early Sep; 🅂G, 7 to Court Sq, E/M to Court Sq-23rd St) At MoMA's hip contemporary outpost, you'll be peering at videos through floorboards, schmoozing at DJ parties and debating the meaning of nonstatic structures.

Museum of the Moving Image (www.movingimage.us; 36-01 35th Ave, btwn 36th & 37th Sts, Astoria; adult/child $15/9, 4-8pm Fri free; ⊙10:30am-5pm Wed & Thu, to 8pm Fri, to 6pm Sat & Sun; 🚹; 🅂M/R to Steinway St) This super-cool complex is one of the world's top film, TV and video museums. Galleries show the best of a collection of 130,000-plus artifacts, including Elizabeth Taylor's wig from Cleopatra.

Rockaway Beach (⊙beach 6am-9pm, boardwalk to 10pm; 🚌Q52-SBS to Rockaway Beach Blvd-Beach 92 St, 🚢NYC Ferry from Wall St-Pier 11, 🅂A to Beach-90 St) It's only a 75-minute ride on the A train from Midtown, or a 57-minute ferry ride from Wall St, to the pier at 108th St to the break for the beach off 90th St in the Rockaways.

MoMA PS1

Times Square, Midtown Manhattan & Chelsea

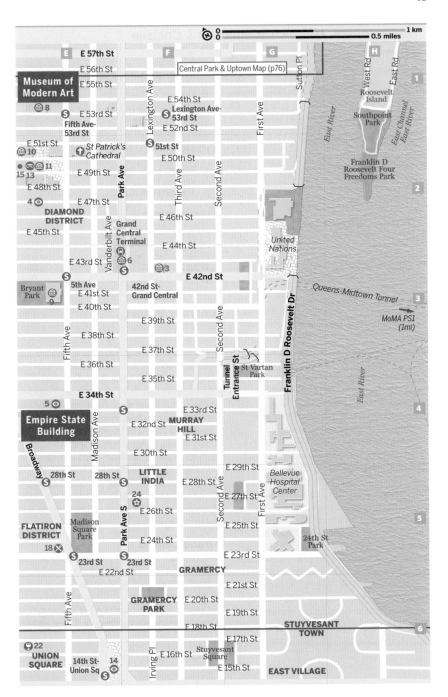

0 — 1 km
0 — 0.5 miles

E | E 57th St
E 56th St
F
Central Park & Uptown Map (p76)
G
H
West Rd | East Rd
Roosevelt Island
1

Museum of Modern Art
E 55th St
E 54th St
Lexington Ave-53rd St
Southpoint Park
East River
East Channel East River

🏛8
🟢 E 53rd St
Lexington Ave
E 52nd St
First Ave

Fifth Ave-53rd St
🟢 51st St
E 50th St

Franklin D Roosevelt Four Freedoms Park

E 51st St
🏛10
St Patrick's Cathedral
Park Ave
Third Ave
Second Ave

●🟢🏛11
15 13
E 49th St

E 48th St
2

4🟢
E 47th St
DIAMOND DISTRICT
E 45th St
Vanderbilt Ave
Grand Central Terminal
E 46th St

🏛6
🟢
E 44th St

United Nations

E 43rd St
🏛3
E 42nd St

🟢
Bryant Park
🏛9
5th Ave
E 41st St
42nd St-Grand Central

Queens-Midtown Tunnel
3

E 40th St
MoMA PS1 (1mi)

Fifth Ave
E 38th St
E 39th St
Second Ave
Franklin D Roosevelt Dr

E 37th St

E 36th St
Tunnel Entrance St
St Vartan Park
East River

E 35th St

E 34th St
5🟢
E 33rd St
4

Empire State Building
Madison Ave
🟢 E 32nd St
MURRAY HILL
E 31st St

Broadway
E 30th St

28th St
🟢
28th St
🟢
LITTLE INDIA
E 29th St
E 28th St
Second Ave
First Ave
Bellevue Hospital Center

24
🟢
E 27th St

E 26th St

FLATIRON DISTRICT
Madison Square Park
E 25th St
Park Ave S

18🟢
E 24th St
24th St Park
5

🟢
23rd St
🟢
23rd St
E 23rd St

E 22nd St
GRAMERCY

E 21st St

GRAMERCY PARK
E 20th St

E 19th St

Fifth Ave
E 18th St
STUYVESANT TOWN
6

E 17th St

🟢22
UNION SQUARE
14th St-Union Sq
🟢
14
Irving Pl
E 16th St
Stuyvesant Square
E 15th St
EAST VILLAGE

Times Square, Midtown Manhattan & Chelsea

Sights
1 Bank of America Tower.......D3
2 Brill Building.......D2
3 Chrysler Building.......F3
4 Diamond District.......E2
5 Empire State Building.......E4
6 Grand Central Terminal.......F3
7 Intrepid Sea, Air & Space Museum.......A2
8 Museum of Modern Art.......E1
9 New York Public Library.......E3
10 Radio City Music Hall.......E2
11 Rockefeller Center.......E2
12 Times Square.......D3
13 Top of the Rock.......E2
14 Union Square.......E6

Activities, Courses & Tours
15 NBC Studio Tours.......E2

Shopping
MoMA Museum & Design Stores.......(see 8)

Eating
16 Burger Joint.......D1
Cafe 2.......(see 8)
17 Chelsea Market.......C6
18 Eataly.......E5
19 Foragers Table.......C6
20 Le Bernardin.......D2
21 Totto Ramen.......C1

Drinking & Nightlife
Bar SixtyFive.......(see 13)
22 Raines Law Room.......E6
Serra.......(see 18)
The Campbell.......(see 6)

Entertainment
23 Carnegie Hall.......D1
24 Jazz Standard.......F5
25 Lyceum Theatre.......D2
26 New Amsterdam Theatre.......D3
27 New Victory Theater.......D3
28 Sleep No More.......B5

the International Building (630 Fifth Ave). Isamu Noguchi's *News* sits above the entrance to the Associated Press Building (50 Rockefeller Plaza), while José Maria Sert's oil *American Progress* awaits in the lobby of central 30 Rockefeller Plaza (formerly known as the GE Building). The latter work replaced Mexican artist Diego Rivera's original painting, rejected by the Rockefellers for containing 'communist imagery.'

Come the festive season, Rockefeller Plaza is where you'll find New York's most famous **Christmas tree** (www.rockefellercenter.com; Rockefeller Plaza; ⌚Dec) Ceremoniously lit just after Thanksgiving, it's a tradition that dates back to the 1930s, when construction workers set up a small tree on the site. In its shadow, **Rink at Rockefeller Center** (☎212-332-7654; www.therinkatrockcenter.com; Fifth Ave, btwn W 49th & 50th Sts; adult $25-33, child $15, skate rental $13; ⌚8:30am-midnight mid-Oct–Apr) is the city's best-known – and smallest – ice-skating rink (which becomes a cafe in summer).

Chrysler Building Historic Building
(Map p70; 405 Lexington Ave, at E 42nd St; ⌚lobby 7am-6:30pm Mon-Fri; SS, 4/5/6, 7 to Grand Central-42nd St) Designed by William Van Alen and completed in 1930, the 77-floor Chrysler Building is the pinup for New York's purest art deco architecture, guarded by stylized eagles of chromium nickel and topped by a beautiful seven-tiered spire reminiscent of the rising sun. The building was constructed as the headquarters for Walter P Chrysler and his automobile empire; unable to compete on the production line with bigger rivals Ford and General Motors, Chrysler trumped them on the skyline, and with one of Gotham's most beautiful lobbies.

Grand Central Terminal Historic Building
(Map p70; www.grandcentralterminal.com; 89 E 42nd St, at Park Ave; ⌚5:30am-2am; SS, 4/5/6, 7 to Grand Central-42nd St, Metro North to Grand Central) Completed in 1913, Grand Central Terminal – commonly, if incorrectly,

called Grand Central Station – is one of New York's most venerated beaux-arts beauties. Adorned with Tennessee-marble floors and Italian-marble ticket counters, its glorious main concourse is capped by a vaulted ceiling depicting the constellations, designed by French painter Paul César Helleu. When commuters complained that the sky is backwards – painted as if looking down from above, not up – it was asserted as intentional (possibly to avoid having to admit an error).

Top of the Rock   Viewpoint

(Map p70; ☑212-698-2000, toll free 877-692-7625; www.topoftherocknyc.com; 30 Rockefeller Plaza, entrance on W 50th St, btwn Fifth & Sixth Aves; adult/child $38/32, sunrise/sunset combo $56/45; ☺8am-midnight, last elevator at 11pm; ⑤B/D/F/M to 47th-50th Sts-Rockefeller Center) Designed in homage to ocean liners and opened in 1933, this 70th-floor open-air observation deck sits atop 30 Rockefeller Plaza, the tallest skyscraper at the Rockefeller Center (p69). Top of the Rock beats

the Empire State Building (p60) on several levels: it's less crowded, has wider observation decks (both outdoor and indoor) and offers a view of the Empire State Building itself. Before ascending, a fascinating 2nd-floor exhibition gives an insight into the legendary philanthropist behind the art deco complex.

◉ Upper East Side

Metropolitan Museum of Art   Museum

(Map p76; ☑212-535-7710; www.metmuseum.org; 1000 Fifth Ave, at E 82nd St; 3-day pass adult/senior/child $25/$17/free, pay-as-you-wish for NY State residents; ☺10am-5:30pm Sun-Thu, to 9pm Fri & Sat; ⛟; ⑤4/5/6, Q to 86th St, 6 to 77th St) The vast collection of art and antiquities contained within this palatial museum (founded in 1870) is one of the world's largest and most important, with more than two million individual objects in its permanent collection: paintings, sculptures, textiles and artifacts from around the

Grand Central Station

ANDERM/SHUTTERSTOCK ©

globe – even an ancient Egyptian temple straight from the banks of the Nile. 'The Met' has 17 acres of exhibition space to explore, so plan to spend several hours here. (Wear comfy shoes.)

Guggenheim Museum   Museum

(Map p76; ☑212-423-3500; www.guggenheim. org; 1071 Fifth Ave, at E 89th St; adult/child $25/ free, cash-only pay-what-you-wish 5-8pm Sat; ☺10am-5:30pm Wed-Fri, Sun & Mon, to 8pm Sat, to 9pm Tue; ♿; ⑤4/5/6, Q to 86th St) A New York icon, architect Frank Lloyd Wright's conical white spiral is probably more famous than the artworks inside, which include works by Kandinsky, Picasso, Pollock, Monet, Van Gogh and Degas; photographs by Mapplethorpe; and important surrealist works. But temporary exhibitions climbing the much-photographed central rotunda are the real draw. Other key works are often exhibited in the more recent adjoining tower (1992).

Pick up the free audioguide or download the Guggenheim app for information about the exhibits and architecture.

◎ Upper West Side & Central Park

American Museum of Natural History   Museum

(Map p76; ☑212-769-5100; www.amnh.org; Central Park West, at W 79th St; suggested admission adult/child $23/13; ☺10am-5:45pm; ♿; ⑤C to 81st St-Museum of Natural History; 1 to 79th St) Founded in 1869, this classic museum contains a veritable wonderland of more than 34 million artifacts – including lots of menacing dinosaur skeletons – as well as the Rose Center for Earth & Space, which has a cutting-edge planetarium. From October through May, the museum is home to the Butterfly Conservatory, a vivarium featuring 500-plus butterflies from all over the world that will flutter about and land on your outstretched arm.

Lincoln Center   Arts Center

(Map p76; ☑212-875-5456, tours 212-875-5350; www.lincolncenter.org; Columbus Ave, btwn W 62nd & 66th Sts; tours adult/student $25/20;

Guggenheim Museum

⊗tours 11:30am & 1:30pm Mon-Sat, 3pm Sun; ; ⑤1, 2, 3 to 66th St-Lincoln Center, A/C or B/D to 59th St-Columbus Circle) **FREE** This stark arrangement of gleaming modernist temples houses some of Manhattan's most important performance companies: the **New York Philharmonic** (Map p76; 🖉212-875-5656; www.nyphil.org; Columbus Ave at W 65th St; tickets $29-125; ⊡), the **New York City Ballet** (Map p76; 🖉212-496-0600; www.nycballet.com; Columbus Ave at W 63rd St; tickets $39 to $204; ⊗box office 10am-7:30pm Mon, to 8:30pm Tue-Sat, 4:30am-7:30pm Sun; ⊡) and the Metropolitan Opera (p87). The lobby of the iconic Opera House is dressed with brightly saturated murals by painter Marc Chagall. Various other venues are tucked in and around the 16-acre campus, including a theater, two film-screening centers and the renowned Juilliard School for performing arts.

🟢 ACTIVITIES

Staten Island Ferry   Cruise

(Map p66; www.siferry.com; Whitehall Terminal, 4 Whitehall St, at South St, Lower Manhattan; ⊗24hr; ⑤1 to South Ferry, R/W to Whitehall St, 4/5 to Bowling Green) **FREE** Staten Islanders know these hulking orange ferries as commuter vehicles, while Manhattanites think of them as their secret, romantic vessels for a spring-day escape. Yet many tourists are also wise to the charms of the Staten Island Ferry, whose 25-minute, 5.2-mile journey between Lower Manhattan and the Staten Island neighborhood of St George is one of NYC's finest free adventures.

🔵 SHOPPING

🔵 Financial District & Lower Manhattan

Philip Williams Posters   Vintage

(Map p66; 🖉212-513-0313; www.postermuseum.com; 122 Chambers St, btwn Church St & W Broadway, Lower Manhattan; ⊗10am-7pm Mon-Sat; ⑤A/C, 1/2/3 to Chambers St) You'll find more than 100,000 posters dating back to 1870 in this cavernous treasure trove, from oversized French advertisements for per-

🔖 Detour: Brooklyn

Brooklyn is an eating-drinking-artsy hot spot, with top sights that are easy to reach by public transportation.

Brooklyn Bridge (Map p66 ⑤4/5/6 to Brooklyn Bridge-City Hall, J/Z to Chambers St, R/W to City Hall, ⑤2/3 to Clark St, A/F to High St-Brooklyn Bridge Station) A New York icon, the Brooklyn Bridge was the world's first steel suspension bridge, and, at 1596ft, the longest when it opened in 1883. Its suspended bicycle-pedestrian walkway delivers soul-stirring views of Manhattan, the East River and the Brooklyn waterfront. The crossing can be challenging – if walking, stay in the pedestrian portion of the lane as cyclists move quickly.

Brooklyn Bridge Park (Map p66 🖉718-222-9939; www.brooklynbridgepark.org; East River Waterfront; ⊗6am-1am, some sections to 11pm, playgrounds to dusk; ⊡⊡; 🚌B63 to Pier 6/Brooklyn Bridge Park, B25 to Old Fulton St/Elizabeth Pl, ⛴East River or South Brooklyn routes to Dumbo/Pier 1, ⑤A/C to High St, 2/3 to Clark St, F to York St) This 85-acre park is one of Brooklyn's best-loved attractions. Wrapping itself around a 1.3-mile bend on the East River, it runs from just beyond the far side of the Manhattan Bridge in Dumbo to the west end of Atlantic Ave in Brooklyn Heights. It's revitalized a once-barren stretch of shoreline, turning a series of abandoned piers into beautifully landscaped parkland with jaw-dropping views of Manhattan.

Brooklyn Bridge

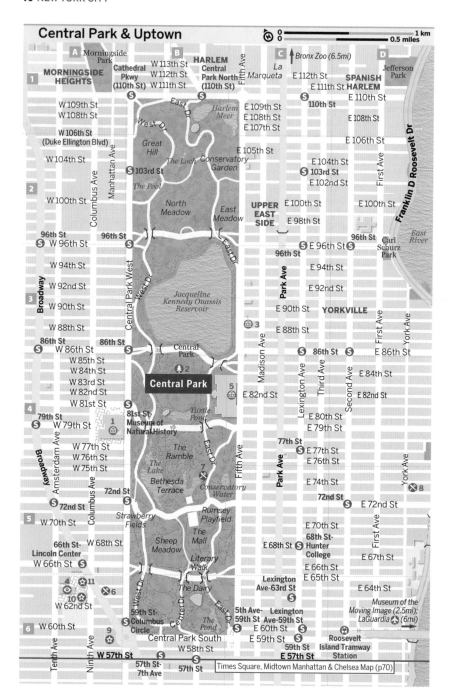

Central Park & Uptown

0 1 km
0 0.5 miles

MORNINGSIDE HEIGHTS

Morningside Park

Cathedral Pkwy (110th St)

W 113th St
W 112th St
W 111th St

HARLEM

Central Park North (110th St)

La Marqueta

Bronx Zoo (6.5mi)

SPANISH HARLEM

Jefferson Park

E 112th St
E 111th St
E 110th St

110th St

E 109th St
E 108th St
E 107th St

Harlem Meer

W 109th St
W 108th St

W 106th St (Duke Ellington Blvd)

East Dr

West Dr

Great Hill

E 108th St
E 106th St

E 105th St

The Loch

Conservatory Garden

W 104th St

103rd St

The Pool

E 104th St
103rd St
E 102nd St

W 100th St

North Meadow

East Meadow

UPPER EAST SIDE

E 100th St
E 98th St

E 100th St

96th St
W 96th St
W 94th St

96th St

East Dr

96th St

E 96th St
96th St

E 94th St
E 92nd St

Carl Schurz Park

East River

W 92nd St

Park Ave

Central Park West

West Dr

Jacqueline Kennedy Onassis Reservoir

W 90th St
W 88th St

E 90th St
E 88th St

YORKVILLE

Broadway

3

86th St
W 86th St

86th St

Central Park

86th St

E 86th St

E 86th St

W 85th St
W 84th St
W 83rd St
W 82nd St
W 81st St

2

Central Park

5

Madison Ave

Lexington Ave

Third Ave

Second Ave

First Ave

York Ave

E 84th St
E 82nd St

E 82nd St

81st St
W 79th St

Museum of Natural History

Turtle Pond

E 80th St
E 79th St

79th St

W 77th St
W 76th St
W 75th St

The Ramble

The Lake

77th St

E 77th St
E 76th St

Amsterdam Ave

Columbus Ave

72nd St

Bethesda Terrace

Conservatory Water

7

Park Ave

First Ave

York Ave

E 74th St

72nd St

8

72nd St

Strawberry Fields

Rumsey Playfield

E 72nd St

Broadway

5

W 70th St

Sheep Meadow

The Mall

E 70th St

W 68th St

68th St-Hunter College

E 68th St

E 67th St

66th St-Lincoln Center
W 66th St

Literary Walk

E 66th St
E 65th St

Lexington Ave-63rd St

The Dairy

4
11

6

E 64th St

10

W 62nd St

West Dr

Center Dr

East Dr

5th Ave-59th St
E 60th St

Lexington Ave-59th St

Museum of the Moving Image (2.5mi); LaGuardia (6mi)

9

59th St-Columbus Circle

The Pond

59th St

Roosevelt Island Tramway Station

W 60th St

Central Park South

E 59th St

Tenth Ave

Ninth Ave

W 58th St

57th St-7th Ave

W 57th St

57th St

E 57th St

Franklin D Roosevelt Dr

Times Square, Midtown Manhattan & Chelsea Map (p70)

Central Park & Uptown

fume and cognac to Eastern European film posters and decorative Chinese *Nianhua* posters. Prices range from $15 for small reproductions to thousands of dollars for rare, showpiece originals like a Cassandre. There's a second entrance at 52 Warren St.

Century 21   Fashion & Accessories

(Map p66; ☑212-227-9092; www.c21stores.com; 22 Cortlandt St, btwn Church St & Broadway, Financial District; ⊘7:45am-9pm Mon-Wed, to 9:30pm Thu & Fri, 10am-9pm Sat, 11am-8pm Sun; ⓢA/C, J/Z, 2/3, 4/5 to Fulton St, R/W to Cortlandt St) For penny-pinching fashionistas, this giant cut-price department store is dangerously addictive. It's physically dangerous as well, considering the elbows you might have to throw to ward off the competition beelining for the same rack. Not everything is a knockout or a bargain, but persistence pays off. You'll also find bespoke tailoring, accessories, shoes, cosmetics, homewares and toys.

⊙ SoHo & Chinatown

Galeria Melissa   Shoes

(Map p66; ☑212-775-1950; www.melissa.com. br/us/galerias/ny; 500 Broadway, btwn Broome & Spring Sts, SoHo; ⊘10am-7pm Mon-Fri, to 8pm Sat, 11am-7pm Sun; 🖮; ⓢ6 to Spring St, R/W to Prince St) This Brazilian designer specializes in downpour-friendly plastic footwear. Recyclable, sustainable, stylish – women's and kids' shoes run the gamut from mod sandals to brogues, runners and, of course, boots.

Saturdays   Fashion & Accessories

(Map p66; ☑212-966-7875; www.saturdays nyc.com; 31 Crosby St, btwn Broome & Grand Sts, SoHo; ⊘store 10am-7pm, coffee bar 8am-7pm Mon-Fri, from 10am Sat & Sun; ☎; ⓢN/Q/R/W, J/Z to Canal St; 6 to Spring St) SoHo's version of a surf shop sees boards and wax paired up with designer grooming products, graphic art and surf tomes, and Saturdays' own line of high-quality, fashion-literate threads for dudes. There's a second branch in the **West Village** (Map p66; ☑347-246-5830; 17 Perry St, at Waverly St, West Village; ⊘10am-7pm; ⓢA/C/E, L to 8th Ave-14th St; 1/2/3 to 14th St).

⊙ West Village, Chelsea & Meatpacking District

Strand Book Store   Books

(Map p66; ☑212-473-1452; www.strandbooks. com; 828 Broadway, at E 12th St, West Village; ⊘9:30am-10:30pm; ⓢL, N/Q/R/W, 4/5/6 to 14th St-Union Sq) Beloved and legendary, the iconic Strand embodies downtown NYC's intellectual bona fides – a bibliophile's Oz, where generations of book lovers carrying the store's trademark tote bags happily lose themselves for hours. In operation since 1927, the Strand sells new, used and rare titles, spreading an incredible 18 miles of books (over 2.5 million of them) among three labyrinthine floors.

🍽 Best Cheap Eats in Chinatown

Nom Wah Tea Parlor (Map p66; ☎212-962-6047; www.nomwah.com; 13 Doyers St; dim sum from $4; ⊙10:30am-10pm Sun-Wed, to 11pm Fri & Sat; ⑤J/Z to Chambers St; 4/5/6 to Brooklyn Bridge-City Hall) Hidden down a narrow lane, 1920s Nom Wah Tea Parlor might look like an American diner, but it's actually the oldest dim-sum place in town. Grab a seat at one of the red banquettes or counter stools and simply tick off what you want on the menu provided.

Xi'an Famous Foods (Map p66; ☎212-786-2068; www.xianfoods.com; 45 Bayard St, btwn Elizabeth St & Bowery; dishes $4.70-12; ⊙11:30am-9pm Sun-Thu, to 9:30pm Fri & Sat; ⑤N/Q/R/W, J/Z, 6 to Canal St, B/D to Grand St) Food bloggers hyperventilate at the mere mention of this small chain's hand-pulled noodles. The burgers are also menu stars: tender lamb sautéed with ground cumin and toasted chili seeds, or melt-in-the-mouth stewed pork. There are 13 other locations throughout the city.

Deluxe Green Bo (Map p66; ☎212-625-2359; www.deluxegreenbo.com; 66 Bayard St, btwn Elizabeth & Mott Sts; mains $5.95-19.95; ⊙11am-11pm Mon-Thu, to midnight Fri & Sat, to 10:30pm Sun; ⑤N/Q/R, J/Z, 6 to Canal St; B/D to Grand St) It's all about the food at this no-frills Chinese spot: gorgeous *xiao long bao* served in steaming drums, heaping portions of greasy noodles and gleaming plates of salubrious, sautéed spinach. Cash only.

Nom Wah Tea Parlour
ROBERT K. CHIN - STOREFRONTS/ALAMY ©

🏛 Midtown

MoMA Design Stores
Gifts & Souvenirs

(Map p70; ☎212-708-9700; www.momastore.org; 11 W 53rd St, btwn Fifth & Sixth Aves; ⊙9:30am-6:30pm Sat-Thu, to 9pm Fri; ⑤E, M to 5th Ave-53rd St) The redesigned flagship store at the Museum of Modern Art (p49) is a fab spot for souvenir shopping. Besides gorgeous books (from art and architecture to culture critiques and kids' picture books), you'll find art posters and one-of-a-kind knickknacks. For furniture, homewares, jewelry, bags and artsy gifts, head to the **MoMA Design Store** (⊙10am to 6:30pm daily) across the street.

❌ EATING

❌ Financial District & Lower Manhattan

Locanda Verde
Italian $$$

(Map p66; ☎212-925-3797; www.locandaverdenyc.com; 377 Greenwich St, at N Moore St, Tribeca; mains lunch $24-36, dinner $27-58; ⊙7am-11pm Mon-Thu, to 11:30pm Fri, 8am-11:30pm Sat, to 11pm Sun; ⑤1 to Franklin St, A/C/E to Canal St) Curbside at the **Greenwich Hotel** (Map p66; ☎212-941-8900; www.thegreenwichhotel.com; r from $650; ❈🛎⊕) is this Italian fine diner by Andrew Carmellini, where velvet curtains part onto a scene of loosened button-downs, black dresses and slick bar staff. It's a place to see and be seen, but the food – perhaps grilled swordfish with farro salad, *orecchiette* with duck sausage, or rigatoni with white-veal Bolognese – is still the main event.

Le District
Food Hall $$$

(Map p66; ☎212-981-8588; www.ledistrict.com; Brookfield Place, 225 Liberty St, at West St, Lower Manhattan; market mains $12-30, Beaubourg dinner mains $19-36; ⊙Beaubourg 8am-10pm Mon, to 11pm Tue & Wed, to midnight Thu & Fri, 10am-midnight Sat, to 10pm Sun, other hours vary; 🛎; ⑤E to World Trade Center, 2/3 to Park

Pl, R/W to Cortlandt St, 4/5 to Fulton St, A/C to Chambers St) Paris on the Hudson reigns at this sprawling French food emporium selling everything from high-gloss pastries and pretty *tartines* to stinky cheese and savory steak-*frites*. Main restaurant Beaubourg does bistro classics such as *coq au vin*, but for a quick sit-down feed, head to the Market District counter for *frites* or the Cafe District for a savory crepe.

🏵 SoHo & Chinatown

Uncle Boons   Thai $$
(Map p66; ☎646-370-6650; www.uncleboons. com; 7 Spring St, btwn Elizabeth St & Bowery, Nolita; small plates $15-18, large plates $25-31; ☺5:30-11pm Sun-Thu, to midnight Fri & Sat; 📶; ⑤J/Z to Bowery; 6 to Spring St) Michelin-star Thai is served up in a fun, tongue-in-cheek combo of retro wood-paneled dining room with Thai film posters and old family snaps. Spanning the old and the new, dishes are tangy, rich and creative. Standouts include the *kob woonsen* (garlic and soy marinated frogs legs), *koong* (grilled head-on prawns) and *kaduuk* (roasted bone marrow satay).

Chefs Club   Fusion $$$
(Map p66; ☎212-941-1100; www.chefsclub.com; 275 Mulberry St, Nolita; prix-fixe $85-125; ☺5:30-10:30pm Mon-Sat; ⑤R/W to Prince St, B/D/F/M to Broadway-Lafayette St) In a building used in part for the show *Will & Grace*, Chefs Club sounds more like a discount warehouse than the spectacular dining spot it really is: visiting chefs prepare a menu for anywhere from three weeks to three months, offering their finest selections in menus that span the flavors of the globe.

🏵 East Village & Lower East Side

Ivan Ramen   Ramen $$
(Map p66; ☎646-678-3859; www.ivanramen. com; 25 Clinton St, btwn Stanton & E Houston Sts, East Village; mains $15-21; ☺12:30-10pm Sun-Thu, to 11pm Fri & Sat; ⑤F, J/M/Z to Delancey-Essex Sts, F to 2nd Ave) After creating two thriving ramen spots in Tokyo, Long Islander Ivan Orkin brought his talents back home. Few can agree about NYC's best ramen, but this intimate shop, where solo

MoMA Design Stores

MATE KAROLY/SHUTTERSTOCK ©

ramen heads sit at the bar watching their bowls take shape, is on every short list. The *tsukumen* (dipping-style) ramen with pickled collard greens and shoyu-glazed pork belly is unbeatable.

Momofuku Noodle Bar   Noodles $$
(Map p66; ✆212-777-7773; https://momofuku-noodlebar.com; 171 First Ave, btwn E 10th & E 11th Sts, East Village; mains $17-27; ⊙lunch noon-4:30pm Mon-Fri, to 4pm Sat & Sun, dinner 5:30-11pm Sun-Thu, to midnight Fri & Sat; ⋒; ⑤L to 1st Ave, 6 to Astor Pl) With just a handful of tables and a no-reservations policy, this bustling phenomenon may require you to wait. But you won't regret it: spicy short-rib ramen; ginger noodles with pickled shiitake; cold noodles with Sichuan sausage and Thai basil – it's all amazing. The ever-changing menu includes buns (perhaps brisket and horseradish), snacks (smoked chicken wings) and desserts.

The open kitchen creates quite a bit of steam, but the devoted crowd remains unfazed.

Momofuku is part of David Chang's crazy-popular, now global, restaurant empire (www.momofuku.com). NYC outposts include two-Michelin-starred **Momofuku Ko** (8 Extra Pl, East Village), which serves up pricey tasting menus ($225) and has a prohibitive, we-dare-you-to-try reservations scheme; **Momofuku Ssäm Bar** (207 Second Ave, East Village), which features large and small meat-heavy dishes; chicken joint **Fuku** (four branches in Manhattan); and another Noodle Bar in the shopping center at Columbus Circle.

🗽 West Village, Chelsea & Meatpacking District

Chelsea Market   Market $
(Map p70; www.chelseamarket.com; 75 Ninth Ave, btwn W 15th & W 16 Sts, Chelsea; mains $10-15; ⊙7am-2am Mon-Sat, 8am-10pm Sun; ⑤A/C/E, L to 8th Ave-14th St) In a shining example of redevelopment and renaissance, Chelsea Market has taken a 19th-century Nabisco cookie factory and turned it into an 800ft-

★ **Top Five for Foodies**

Uncle Boons (p79)

Chelsea Market

Totto Ramen (p81)

Foragers Table (p81)

Chefs Club (p79)

From left: Radio City Music Hall (p69); Chelsea Market; Momofuku Noodle Bar

long food court of mouthwatering diversity. On the site where the beloved Oreo was first conceived, now more than 35 vendors sell everything from tongue-tingling hand-pulled dan dan noodles to Jamaican jerk, fine cheese and whole lobsters.

Foragers Table American $$$

(Map p70; ✆212-243-8888; www.foragers-market.com/restaurant; 300 W 22nd St, at Eighth Ave, Chelsea; mains $20-39; ⊙dinner 5:30-10pm Mon-Sat, to 9pm Sun, brunch 9am-3pm Sat & Sun; ✍; ⑤1, C/E to 23rd St) The owners of this outstanding restaurant run a 28-acre Hudson Valley farm, from which much of the seasonal menu is sourced. It changes frequently, but recent temptations included pan-roasted duck breast with poached pears, mushroom pappardelle with sherry and toasted almonds, and cauliflower steak with sweet potato tahini and sumac onions.

⊗ Midtown

Burger Joint Burgers $

(Map p70; ✆212-708-7414; www.burgerjointny. com; Parker New York, 119 W 56th St, btwn Sixth & Seventh Aves; burgers $9-17; ⊙11am-11:30pm Sun-Thu, to midnight Fri & Sat; ✍; ⑤F to 57th St) With only a small neon burger as your clue, this speakeasy-style burger hut lurks behind the lobby curtain in the Parker New York hotel. Though it might not be as secret as it once was (you'll see the queues), it still delivers the same winning formula of graffiti-strewn walls, retro booths and attitude-loaded staff slapping up beef 'n' patty brilliance.

Totto Ramen Ramen $

(Map p70; ✆212-582-0052; www.tottoramen. com; 366 W 52nd St, btwn Eighth & Ninth Aves; ramen $14-18; ⊙noon-4:30pm & 5:30pm-midnight; ✍; ⑤C/E to 50th St) There might be two other Midtown branches but purists know that neither beats the tiny 20-seat original. Write your name and party size on the clipboard and wait your turn. Your reward: extraordinary ramen. Get the butter-soft *char siu* (pork), which sings in dishes like miso ramen (with fermented soybean paste, egg, scallion, bean sprouts, onion and homemade chili paste).

Le Bernardin   Seafood $$$

(Map p70; ✆212-554-1515; www.le-bernardin. com; 155 W 51st St, btwn Sixth & Seventh Aves; prix-fixe lunch/dinner $93/165, tasting menus $170-198; ☉11:45am-2:30pm & 4:45-10:30pm Mon-Thu, to 11pm Fri, 4:45-11pm Sat; ⑤1 to 50th St; B/D, E to 7th Ave) The interiors may have been subtly sexed-up for a 'younger clientele' (the stunning storm-themed triptych is by Brooklyn artist Ran Ortner), but triple-Michelin-starred Le Bernardin remains a luxe, fine-dining holy grail. At the helm is French-born celebrity chef Eric Ripert, whose deceptively simple-looking seafood often borders on the transcendental. Life is short, and you only live (er, eat!) once.

🍴 Upper East Side

Tanoshi   Sushi $$$

(Map p76; www.tanoshisushinyc.com; 1372 York Ave, btwn E 73rd & 74th Sts; chef's sushi selection $95-100; ☉seatings 6pm, 7:30pm & 9pm Tue-Sat; ⑤Q to 72nd St) It's not easy to snag one of the 22 stools at Tanoshi, a wildly popular, pocket-sized sushi spot. The setting may be humble, but the flavors are simply magnificent. Only sushi is on offer and only *omakase* (chef's selection) – which might include Hokkaido scallops, kelp-cured flake or mouthwatering *uni* (sea urchin). BYO beer, sake or whatnot.

🍴 Upper West Side & Central Park

Épicerie Boulud   Deli $

(Map p76; ✆212-595-9606; www.epicerie boulud.com; 1900 Broadway, at W 64th St; sandwiches $8-14.50; ☉7am-10pm Mon, to 11pm Tue-Sat, 8am-10pm Sun; 🛜🍴; ⑤1 to 66th St-Lincoln Center) A deli from star chef Daniel

Restaurant at Chelsea Market (p80)

Boulud is no ordinary deli. Forget ham on rye – here you can order suckling pig confit, *jambon de Paris* and Gruyère on pressed ciabatta, or paprika-spiced flank steak with caramelized onions and three-grain mustard.

DRINKING & NIGHTLIFE

Financial District & Lower Manhattan

Bluestone Lane   Coffee
(Map p66; 718-374-6858; www.bluestone laneny.com; 30 Broad St, Financial District; 7am-5pm Mon-Fri, 8am-4pm Sat & Sun; J/Z to Broad St, 2/3, 4/5 to Wall St) The second installment in Bluestone Lane's booming US empire of Aussie-style coffee shops, this tiny outpost in the corner of an art deco office block is littered with Melbourne memorabilia. Alongside Wall St suits you'll find homesick antipodeans craving a decent, velvety flat white and a small selection of edibles, including the Australian cafe standard, smashed avocado on toast ($8).

SoHo & Chinatown

Apothéke   Cocktail Bar
(Map p66; 212-406-0400; www.apotheke nyc.com; 9 Doyers St, Chinatown; 6:30pm-2am Mon-Sat, from 8pm Sun; J/Z to Chambers St; 4/5/6 to Brooklyn Bridge-City Hall) It takes a little effort to track down this former opium-den-turned-apothecary bar on Doyers St (look for the 'chemist' sign with a beaker illustration hanging above the doorway). Inside, skilled barkeeps work like careful chemists, using local, seasonal produce from Greenmarkets to produce intense, flavorful 'prescriptions.' The pineapple-cilantro spiced Sitting Buddha is one of the best drinks on the menu.

Ear Inn   Pub
(Map p66; 212-226-9060; www.earinn.com; 326 Spring St, btwn Washington & Greenwich Sts, SoHo; bar 11:30am-4am, kitchen to 2am; ; C/E to Spring St) Want to see what

Jazz Hot Spots

Jazz at Lincoln Center (Map p76; Dizzy's Club Coca-Cola reservations 212-258-9595, Rose Theater & Appel Room tickets 212-721-6500; www.jazz.org; Time Warner Center, 10 Columbus Circle, Broadway at W 59th St; A/C, B/D, 1 to 59th St-Columbus Circle) Perched atop the Time Warner Center, Jazz at Lincoln Center comprises three state-of-the-art venues: midsized Rose Theater; panoramic, glass-backed Appel Room; and intimate, atmospheric Dizzy's Club Coca-Cola. It's the last of these that you're most likely to visit, given its nightly shows (cover charge $5 to $45). The talent here is often exceptional, as are the dazzling Central Park views.

Jazz Standard (Map p70; 212-576-2232; www.jazzstandard.com; 116 E 27th St, btwn Lexington & Park Aves; cover $25-40; shows 7:30pm & 9:30pm; 6 to 28th St) Jazz luminaries like Ravi Coltrane, Roy Haynes and Ron Carter have played at this sophisticated club. The service is impeccable and the Southern food (from Danny Meyer's upstairs **Blue Smoke** restaurant) is great. The club's artistic director is Seth Abramson, a guy who really knows his jazz.

Lincoln Center

SoHo was like before the trendsetters and fashionistas? Come to the creaking old Ear Inn, proudly billed as one of the oldest drinking establishments in NYC. The

NYC's Best Festivals

Tribeca Film Festival (☎212-941-2400; www.tribecafilm.com; ☺Apr) Founded in 2003 by Robert De Niro and Jane Rosenthal, the Tribeca Film Festival is now a major star of the indie movie circuit. Gaggles of celebs come to walk the red carpets each spring.

July Fourth Fireworks (www.macys. com; ☺Jul 4) America's Independence Day is celebrated with fireworks over the East River, starting at 9pm. Good viewing spots include the waterfronts of the Lower East Side and Williamsburg, Brooklyn, or any high rooftop or east-facing Manhattan apartment.

Village Halloween Parade (www. halloween-nyc.com; Sixth Ave, from Spring St to 16th St; ☺7-11pm Oct 31) This is not your average suburban Halloween parade. The largest in the country, with 60,000 participants and millions more spectators, this is an all-out bacchanal, a mix of Mardi Gras and art project, with marchers decked out in spectacular costumes. It begins at 7pm at Sixth Ave and Spring St and continues up Sixth until 16th St

ALEX LLOBET/SHUTTERSTOCK ©

house it occupies was built in the late 18th century for James Brown, an African aide to George Washington. Drinks are cheap and the crowd's eclectic.

🍸 East Village & Lower East Side

Rue B   Bar
(Map p66; ☎212-358-1700; www.rueb-nyc.com; 188 Ave B, btwn E 11th & E 12th Sts, East Village; ☺6pm-4am; ⑤L to 1st Ave) There's live jazz (and the odd rockabilly group) nightly from 9pm to midnight ($10 cover) at this tiny, amber-lit drinking den on a bar-dappled stretch of Ave B. A celebratory crowd packs the small space – so mind the tight corners, lest the trombonist end up in your lap. Photos and posters of jazz greats and NYC icons enhance the ambience.

🍸 West Village, Chelsea & Meatpacking District

Employees Only   Bar
(Map p66; ☎212-242-3021; www.employeesonlynyc.com; 510 Hudson St, btwn W 10th & Christopher Sts, West Village; ☺6pm-4am; ⑤1 to Christopher St-Sheridan Sq) This divine cocktail bar, tucked behind a discreet green awning on Hudson St, is a world-beater. Ace mixologists shake up crazy libations like the Ginger Smash, and the wood-rich art deco space makes everyone feel glamorous. Open until 3:30am, the kitchen plays its part, too, producing delights such as bone-marrow poppers and spicy shrimp on polenta (mains $27 to $31).

🍸 Union Square, Flatiron District & Gramercy

Serra   Rooftop Bar
(Map p70; ☎212-937-8910; www.eataly.com; 200 Fifth Ave, at W 23rd St, Flatiron District; ☺11:30am-10pm Sun-Thu, to 11pm Fri & Sat; ⑤F/M, R/W, 6 to 23rd St) The crown jewel of Italian food emporium **Eataly** (Map p70; ☎212-229-2560; www.eataly.com; ☺7am-11pm) is this covered rooftop garden tucked betwixt the Flatiron's corporate towers. The theme is refreshed each season, meaning

Serra

you might find a Mediterranean beach escape one month and an alpine country retreat the next, but the setting is unfailingly impressive and food and drink always matches up to the gourmet goodies below.

Raines Law Room
Cocktail Bar

(Map p70; www.raineslawroom.com; 48 W 17th St, btwn Fifth & Sixth Aves, Flatiron District; ⏰5pm-2am Mon-Thu, to 3am Fri & Sat, to 1am Sun; ⓢF/M to 14th St, L to 6th Ave, 1 to 18th St) A sea of velvet drapes and overstuffed leather lounge chairs, the perfect amount of exposed brick, expertly crafted cocktails using hard-to-find spirits – these folks are as serious as a mortgage payment when it comes to amplified atmosphere. There's no sign from the street; look for the '48' above the door and ring the bell to gain entry.

🌀 Midtown

The Campbell
Cocktail Bar

(Map p70; 📞212-297-1781; www.thecampbellnyc. com; Grand Central Terminal, D Hall, 89 E 42nd St; ⏰noon-2am; ⓢS, 4/5/6, 7 to Grand Central-42nd St) In 1923 this hidden-away hall was the office of American financier John W Campbell. It later became a signalman's office, a jail and a gun storage before falling into obscurity. In 2017 it was restored to its original grandeur, complete with the stunning hand-painted ceiling and Campbell's original safe in the fireplace. Come for cocktails and you'll feel like you're waiting for Rockefeller or Carnegie to join you.

Bar SixtyFive
Cocktail Bar

(Map p70; 📞212-632-5000; www.rainbowroom. com/bar-sixty-five; 30 Rockefeller Plaza, entrance on W 49th St; ⏰4:30pm-midnight Mon-Fri, 4-9pm Sun, closed Sat; ⓢB/D/F/M to 47th-50th Sts-Rockefeller Center) Sophisticated SixtyFive

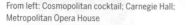
From left: Cosmopolitan cocktail; Carnegie Hall; Metropolitan Opera House

sits on level 65 of the central building of Rockefeller Center (p69), making it the highest vantage point in Midtown that doesn't require a ticket. Views are undeniably breathtaking, but at peak times it can feel like a cattle market: walk-ins are herded into a central standing area. If you want to sit down by a window, you'll need to reserve a table.

There's also balcony seating (weather permitting), which can be reserved with an $85 minimum spend. Dress well (no sportswear or guests under 21) and if you arrive without a reservation, aim for 5pm so you don't have to queue.

At the other end of the corridor is the revamped Rainbow Room, a legendary, elite nightclub turned swanky nosh spot serving Sunday brunch as well as dinner on select evenings (see the website).

⊛ ENTERTAINMENT

For current listings, check out *New York Magazine* and *Time Out*.

Carnegie Hall   Live Music
(Map p70; ☑212-247-7800; www.carnegiehall. org; 881 Seventh Ave, at W 57th St; tours adult/child $17/12; ⊘1hr tours 11:30am, 12:30pm, 2pm & 3pm Mon-Fri, 11:30am & 12:30pm Sat Sep-Jun; ⑤N/R/W to 57th St-7th Ave) The legendary Carnegie Hall may not be the world's biggest concert hall, nor its grandest, but it's definitely one of the most acoustically blessed. Opera, jazz and folk greats feature in the Isaac Stern Auditorium, with edgier jazz, pop, classical and world music in the popular Zankel Hall. Intimate Weill Recital Hall hosts chamber music, debut performances and panel discussions.

ARCHITECT: WALLACE HARRISON; IMAGE: 4KCLIPS/SHUTTERSTOCK ©

Sleep No More — Theater

(Map p70; ☑box office 212-904-1880; www.
sleepnomorenyc.com; 530 W 27th St, btwn Tenth
& Eleventh Aves, Chelsea; tickets from $100;
☺sessions begin 4-7pm; Ⓢ1, C/E to 23rd St) One
of the most immersive theater experiences ever conceived, *Sleep No More* is a
loose, noir retelling of *Macbeth* set inside
a series of Chelsea warehouses that have
been redesigned to look like the 1930s-era
'McKittrick Hotel' (a nod to Hitchcock's
Vertigo); the jazz bar, Manderley, is another
Hitchcock reference, this time to his adaptation of Daphne du Maurier's *Rebecca*.

Metropolitan Opera House — Opera

(Map p76; ☑tickets 212-362-6000, tours 212-
769-7028; www.metopera.org; Lincoln Center,
Columbus Ave at W 64th St; tickets $25-480;
☺box office 10am-10pm Mon-Sat, noon-6pm
Sun; Ⓢ1 to 66th St-Lincoln Center) New York's
premier opera company is the place to see
classics such as *La Boheme, Madame But-*
terfly and *Macbeth*. It also hosts premieres
and revivals of more contemporary works,
such as John Adams' *The Death of Kling-*
hoffer. The season runs from September to
May. Tickets start at $25 and can get close
to $500.

Flea Theater — Theater

(Map p66; ☑tickets 212-226-0051; www.theflea.
org; 20 Thomas St, btwn Timble Pl & Broadway,
Tribeca; tickets from $10; ❸; Ⓢ A/C, 1/2/3 to
Chambers St, R/W to City Hall) One of NYC's
top off-off-Broadway venues, Flea is famous for staging innovative and timely new
works. It houses three performance spaces,
including the 'Siggy,' named for co-founder
Sigourney Weaver. The year-round program
includes music and dance productions, as
well as Sunday shows for young audiences
(aged two and up) and SERIALS, a rollicking
late-night competition series of 10-minute
plays.

ℹ️ INFORMATION

NYC Information Center (Map p70; 📞212-484-1222; www.timessquarenyc.org; Broadway Plaza, at W 45th St; ⊗8am-5pm; 🚇N/Q/R/W, S, 1/2/3, 7, A/C/E to Times Sq-42nd St) There are official NYC Visitor Information Centers throughout the city. The main office is in Midtown.

ℹ️ GETTING THERE & AROUND

TO/FROM THE AIRPORT

JFK International Airport (📞718-244-4444; www.jfkairport.com) It's located 15 miles from Midtown in southeastern Queens. The AirTrain ($5) links to the subway ($2.75), which makes the one-hour journey into Manhattan. Express buses to Grand Central or Port Authority cost $19. Shared vans to Manhattan hotels run from $20 to $26 per person. Taxis cost a flat $52 excluding tolls, tip and rush-hour surcharge.

LaGuardia Airport (LGA; 📞718-533-3400; www.laguardiaairport.com; 🚌M60, Q70) Used mainly for domestic flights, this is the closest airport to Manhattan but the least accessible by public transit: take the Q70 express bus from the airport to the 74th St–Broadway subway station (7 line, or the E, F, M and R lines at the connecting Jackson Heights-Roosevelt Ave station). Express buses to Midtown cost $16. Taxis range from $34 to $53, excluding tolls and tip.

Newark Liberty International Airport (📞973-961-6000; www.newarkairport.com) It is about the same distance from Midtown as JFK (16 miles). Take the AirTrain ($5.50) to Newark Airport train station, and board any train bound for New York's Penn Station ($13). Express buses to Port Authority or Grand Central cost $17. Taxis range from $60 to $80 (plus $15 toll and tip). Allow 45 minutes to one hour of travel time.

BICYCLE

The city's popular bike-share program Citi Bike (www.citibikenyc.com) provides excellent access to most parts of Manhattan, with growing service elsewhere. To use a Citi Bike, either pay for a single ride ($3), or buy a pass (24-hour/three-day passes $12/24 including tax) at any Citi Bike station.

PUBLIC TRANSPORTATION

Check the Metropolitan Transportation Authority website (www.mta.info) for public transportation information (buses and subway). Delays have increased as ridership has expanded.

Subway Inexpensive, somewhat efficient and operates around the clock, though navigating lines can be confusing. Color-coded subway lines are named by a letter or number. Each line is shared by local trains and express trains; the latter make only select stops in Manhattan (indicated by a white circle on subway maps). A single ride is $2.75 with a MetroCard.

Buses Convenient during off hours – especially when transferring between the city's eastern and western sides (most subway lines run north to south). Uses the MetroCard; same price as the subway.

Inter-borough ferries The New York City Ferry (www.ferry.nyc) provides handy transport between waterside stops in Manhattan, Brooklyn and Queens. It costs $2.75 a ride ($1 more to bring a bicycle on board). The free, commuter-oriented Staten Island Ferry (p75) makes constant journeys across New York Harbor.

TAXI & RIDE SHARE

Taxi meters start at $2.50 and increase roughly $5 for every 20 blocks. See www.nyc.gov/taxi for more information.

App-based car-hailing services have taken over the streets of the five boroughs. Now, with nearly five times as many cars as yellow cabs and growing, they're both convenient, indispensable for some, and of course adding to the already terrible traffic problem.

Where to Stay

In general, expect high prices and small spaces. Rates waver by availability, not by high-season or low-season rules. Accommodations fill quickly, especially in summer, and range from cookie-cutter chains to stylish boutiques.

Neighborhood	Atmosphere
Financial District & Lower Manhattan	Convenient to Tribeca's nightlife and ferries. Cheap weekend rates at business hotels.
SoHo & Chinatown	Shop to your heart's content right on your doorstep, but crowds (mostly tourists) swarm the streets.
East Village & Lower East Side	Fashionable and fun, the area feels the most quintessentially 'New York' to visitors and Manhattanites alike.
West Village, Chelsea & Meatpacking District	Thriving, picturesque part of town. Prices soar for traditional hotels, but remain reasonable for B&Bs.
Union Square, Flatiron District & Gramercy	Convenient subway access to anywhere in the city. Steps away from the Village and Midtown; good dining options.
Midtown	In the heart of the postcard version of NYC. One of the most expensive areas in the city; expect small rooms..
Upper East Side	Close to top-notch museums and Central Park. Designer shops on Park Ave. Wallet-busting prices..
Upper West Side & Central Park	Convenient access to Central Park and the Museum of Natural History. More family style than lively scene.
Brooklyn	Better prices; great for exploring some of NYC's most creative neighborhoods..
Queens	Cheaper, tourist-free and NYC's best ethnic restaurants.

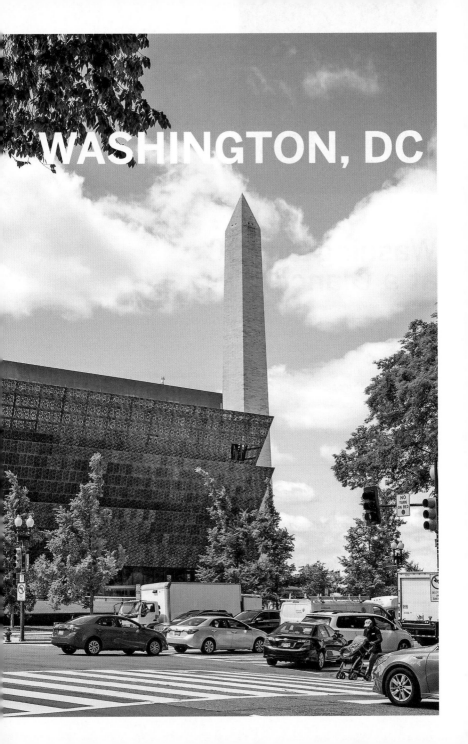

WASHINGTON, DC

Washington, DC at a Glance...

The USA's capital teems with iconic monuments, vast museums and the corridors of power where politicos roam. Seeing the White House and soaring Capitol will thrill, but it's the cobblestoned neighborhoods, global cafes and buzzy quarters popping with live music and beer gardens that really make you fall for DC, no matter what your politics. The city can be a bargain, thanks to the slew of free Smithsonian museums and other gratis institutions. Plan on jam-packed days sightseeing and nights spent with locals sipping DC-made brews and chowing in cozy restaurants.

Two Days in Washington, DC

Start at the National Mall. Check out the **Air & Space Museum** (p96) and the **National Museum of African American History & Culture** (p96). Continue to the **Washington Monument** (p94), **Vietnam Veterans Memorial** (p95) and **Lincoln Memorial** (p94). Have dinner Downtown. Next day, tour Capitol Hill, visit the **National Archives** (p103) and saunter by the **White House** (p102). At night go to U Street or Shaw for eats and drinks.

Four Days in Washington, DC

On day three, explore Georgetown and have lunch there. In the evening, catch a show at the **Kennedy Center** (p113). Start day four at Dupont Circle and gape at mansions along **Embassy Row** (p106). Visit the **National Gallery of Art** (p97), **United States Holocaust Memorial Museum** (p102) and other sights you might have missed. For dinner, browse in Adams Morgan.

Previous page: National Museum of African American History & Culture (p96)
ARCHITECT: DAVID ADJAYE; IMAGE:NIGEL JARVIS/SHUTTERSTOCK ©

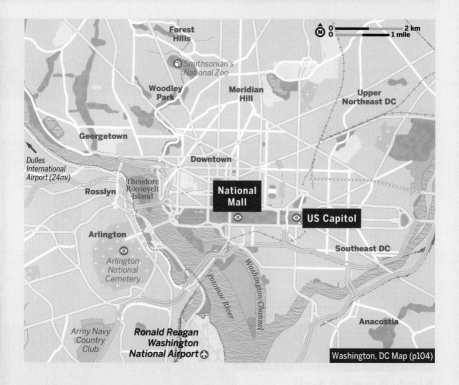

Washington, DC Map (p104)

Arriving in Washington, DC

Ronald Reagan Washington National Airport Metro trains (around $2.65) depart every 10 minutes between 5am and 11:30pm (to 1am Friday and Saturday); 20 minutes to center. Taxis $19 to $26.

Dulles International Airport Silver Line Express bus runs every 15 to 20 minutes to Wiehle-Reston East Metro between 6am and 10:40pm (from 7:45am weekends); 60 to 75 minutes to center, around $11 total. Taxis $62 to $73.

Where to Stay

Washington has loads of posh properties for all the dignitaries who come to town. Design-driven hotels, straightforward chain hotels, B&Bs and apartments blanket the cityscape, too. But nothing comes cheap, especially in popular areas around the White House, Downtown and Dupont Circle.

National Mall

A monument-studded park edged by the magnificent Smithsonian museums, this 2-mile-long expanse is anchored at one end by the Lincoln Memorial, at the other by Capitol Hill, and centered by the Washington Monument.

Great For...

☑ Don't Miss

The Lincoln Memorial step where Martin Luther King Jr gave his 'I Have a Dream' speech.

Memorials & Monuments

Lincoln Memorial (☏202-426-6841; www.nps.gov/linc; 2 Lincoln Memorial Circle NW; ⊗24hr; 🚌Circulator National Mall, MOrange, Silver, Blue Line to Foggy Bottom-GWU) Anchoring the Mall's west end is the hallowed shrine to Abraham Lincoln, who gazes across the Reflecting Pool beneath his neoclassical, Doric-columned abode. The words of his Gettysburg Address and Second Inaugural speech flank the huge marble statue on the north and south walls. On the steps, Martin Luther King Jr delivered his famed 'I Have a Dream' speech; look for the engraving that marks the spot (on the landing 18 stairs from the top).

Washington Monument (www.nps.gov/wamo; 2 15th St NW; 🚌Circulator National Mall, MOrange, Silver, Blue Line to Smithsonian) **FREE** Peaking at 555ft (and 5in) and composed of 36,000 blocks of stone, the Washington Monument is the district's tallest structure. It reopened in fall 2019

Lincoln Memorial

ANDREI MEDVEDEV/SHUTTERSTOCK ©

❶ Need to Know

The DC Circulator National Mall bus route stops by many of the museum and monument hot spots.

✖ Take a Break

Mitsitam Native Foods Cafe (www.mits itamcafe.com; cnr 4th St & Independence Ave SW, National Museum of the American Indian; mains $12-22; ⊙11am-5pm, reduced hours winter; 🚌Circulator National Mall, Ⓜ Orange, Silver, Blue, Green, Yellow Line to L'Enfant Plaza) serves unique, indigenous dishes.

★ Top Tip

Dining options are thin on the Mall, so bring snacks. Museums typically allow you to bring in food.

after being closed for three years for repairs. You need a ticket to access the observation deck. Same-day passes for a timed entrance are available at the kiosk by the monument. During peak season it's a good idea to reserve tickets in advance by phone (877-444-6777) or online (www.recreation.gov) for a small fee.

Martin Luther King Jr Memorial (www.nps.gov/ mlkm; 1964 Independence Ave SW; ⊙24hr; 🚌Cir culator National Mall, Ⓜ Orange, Silver, Blue Line to Smithsonian) Opened in 2011, this was the first Mall memorial to honor an African American. Sculptor Lei Yixin carved the piece, which is rem iniscent in concept and style to the Mt Rushmore memorial. Besides Dr King's striking, 30ft-tall image, known as the Stone of Hope, there are two blocks of granite behind him that represent the Mountain of Despair. A wall inscribed with King's powerful quotes about democracy, justice and peace flanks the piece.

Vietnam Veterans Memorial (www.nps.gov/ vive; 5 Henry Bacon Dr NW; ⊙24hr; 🚌Circulator National Mall, Ⓜ Orange, Silver, Blue Line to Foggy Bottom-GWU) Maya Lin's design for this hugely evocative memorial takes the form of a black, low-lying 'V' – an expression of the psychic scar wrought by the Vietnam War. The monument descends into the earth, with the names of the war's 58,000-plus American casualties – listed in the order they died – chiseled into the dark, reflective wall. It's a subtle but profound mon ument – and all the more surprising as Lin was only 21 when she designed it.

Smithsonian Museums

You could spend your entire trip here. Of the Smithsonian Institution's 19 vast museums, 10 are on the Mall, offering everything from dinosaur skeletons to lunar modules to exquisite artworks. All of the sights are free.

National Air & Space Museum (☎202-633- 2214; www.airandspace.si.edu; cnr 6th St &

Independence Ave SW; ⏱10am-5:30pm; 🚻; 🚌Circulator National Mall, Ⓜ Orange, Silver, Blue, Green, Yellow Line to L'Enfant Plaza) **FREE** The legendary exhibits at this hugely popular museum include the Wright brothers' flyer, Chuck Yeager's Bell X-1, Charles Lindbergh's Spirit of St Louis, Amelia Earhart's natty Vega 5B and the Skylab Orbital Workshop. An IMAX theater, planetarium and flight simulators are all here ($9 to $12 each).

National Museum of African American History & Culture (📞844-750-3012; www. nmaahc.si.edu; 1400 Constitution Ave NW; ⏱10am-5:30pm; 🚻; 🚌Circulator National Mall, Ⓜ Orange, Silver, Blue Line to Smithsonian or Federal Triangle) **FREE** This sensational museum covers the diverse African American experience and how it helped shape the nation. Start downstairs in the sobering 'Slavery and Freedom' exhibition

and work your way up to the community and culture galleries on the 3rd and 4th floors, where African American achievements in sport, music, theater and visual arts are joyfully celebrated. Since opening in late 2016, the museum has been so wildly popular that visitors need a timed entry pass for certain peak times and seasons. The best way to obtain one is via the same-day online release, when tickets are made available at 6:30am on the museum's website.

National Museum of Natural History (📞20 2-663-1000; www.naturalhistory.si.edu; cnr 10th St & Constitution Ave NW; ⏱10am-5:30pm, to 7:30pm some days; 🚻; 🚌Circulator National Mall, Ⓜ Orange, Silver, Blue Line to Smithsonian or Federal Triangle) **FREE** Zip to the 2nd floor's Hope Diamond, a 45.52-karat bauble that's said to have cursed its owners, which included Marie Antoinette. The giant squid (1st floor, Ocean

National Gallery of Art

Hall), live butterfly pavilion and tarantula feedings provide additional thrills at this kid-packed venue. The beloved dinosaur hall, centered on the Nation's T-Rex, has reopened after being revamped.

National Museum of American History

(202-633-1000; www.americanhistory.si.edu; 1300 Constitution Ave NW, btwn 12th and 14th Sts NW; 10am-5:30pm, to 7:30pm some days; ; Circulator National Mall, Orange, Silver, Blue Line to Smithsonian or Federal Triangle) **FREE** This museum has as its centerpiece the flag that flew over Baltimore's Fort McHenry during the War of 1812 – the same flag that inspired Francis Scott Key to pen 'The

---

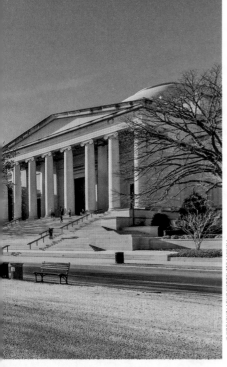

FRANK FELL MEDIA/SHUTTERSTOCK ©

Star-Spangled Banner' (it's on the entry level). Other highlights include Julia Child's kitchen (1st floor) and The First Ladies costume exhibit on the 3rd floor. New exhibits include 'American Enterprise' (1st floor) and 'On with the Show' (3rd floor).

National Gallery of Art

The staggering collection at the **National Gallery of Art** (202-737-4215; www.nga.gov; Constitution Ave NW, btwn 3rd & 7th Sts; 10am-5pm Mon-Sat, 11am-6pm Sun; ; Circulator National Mall, Green, Yellow Line to Archives-Navy Memorial-Penn Quarter) **FREE** spans art from the Middle Ages to the present. The neoclassical West Building showcases European art through to the early 1900s; highlights include works by da Vinci, Manet, Monet and Van Gogh. The IM Pei–designed East Building displays modern and contemporary art – don't miss Pollock's *Number 1, 1950 (Lavender Mist)*, Picasso's *Family of Saltimbanques* and the massive Calder mobile specially commissioned for the entrance lobby. An underground walkway connects the buildings and is made extraordinary by Leo Villareal's light sculpture, *Multiverse*.

You could spend a full day here easily. Consider joining one of the regular volunteer-led tours or taking advantage of the free, multilanguage 'Director's Tour' audioguide, which introduces the gallery's highlights.

★ **Did You Know?**

The Smithsonian Institution holds approximately 155 million artworks, scientific specimens and artifacts, of which less than 2% are on display at any given time.

National Mall

A DAY TOUR

Folks often call the Mall 'America's Front Yard,' and that's a pretty good analogy. It is indeed a lawn, unfurling scrubby green grass from the Capitol west to the Lincoln Memorial. It's also America's great public space, where citizens come to protest their government, go for scenic runs and connect with the nation's most cherished ideals writ large in stone, landscaping, monuments and memorials.

You can sample quite a bit in a day, but it'll be a full one that requires roughly 4 miles of walking.

Start at the ❶ **Vietnam Veterans Memorial**, then head counterclockwise around the Mall, swooping in on the ❷ **Lincoln Memorial**, ❸ **Martin Luther King Jr Memorial** and ❹ **Washington Monument**. You can also pause for the cause of the Korean War and WWII, among other monuments that dot the Mall's western portion.

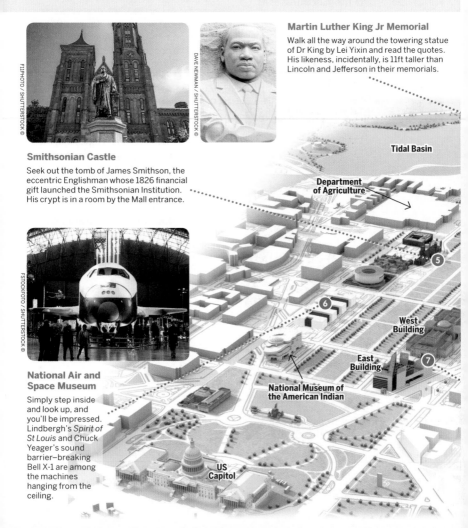

Martin Luther King Jr Memorial

Walk all the way around the towering statue of Dr King by Lei Yixin and read the quotes. His likeness, incidentally, is 11ft taller than Lincoln and Jefferson in their memorials.

DAVE NEWMAN / SHUTTERSTOCK ©

FLIPHOTO / SHUTTERSTOCK ©

Smithsonian Castle

Seek out the tomb of James Smithson, the eccentric Englishman whose 1826 financial gift launched the Smithsonian Institution. His crypt is in a room by the Mall entrance.

FSTOCKFOTO / SHUTTERSTOCK ©

National Air and Space Museum

Simply step inside and look up, and you'll be impressed. Lindbergh's *Spirit of St Louis* and Chuck Yeager's sound barrier–breaking Bell X-1 are among the machines hanging from the ceiling.

Tidal Basin

Department of Agriculture

West Building

East Building

National Museum of the American Indian

US Capitol

Then it's onward to the museums, all fabulous and all free. Begin at the ⑤ Smithsonian Castle to get your bearings – and to say thanks to the guy making all this awesomeness possible – and commence browsing through the ⑥ National Air & Space Museum, ⑦ National Gallery of Art & National Sculpture Garden and ⑧ National Museum of African American History and Culture.

TOP TIPS

Start early, especially in summer. You'll avoid the crowds, but more importantly you'll avoid the blazing heat. Try to finish with the monuments and be in the air-conditioned museums by 10:30am. Also, consider bringing snacks, since the only food available is from scattered cart vendors and museum cafes.

Lincoln Memorial

Commune with Abe in his chair, then head down the steps to the marker where Martin Luther King Jr gave his 'Dream' speech. The view of the Reflecting Pool and Washington Monument is one of DC's best.

ADAM PARENT / SHUTTERSTOCK ©

Korean War Veterans Memorial

National WWII Memorial

Vietnam Veterans Memorial

Check the symbol that's beside each name. A diamond indicates 'killed, body recovered.' A plus sign indicates 'missing and unaccounted for.' There are approximately 1200 of the latter.

Washington Monument

As you approach the obelisk, look a third of the way up. See how it's slightly lighter in color at the bottom? Builders had to use different marble after the first source dried up.

National Museum of American History

National Museum of Natural History

National Museum of African American History and Culture

Feel the power at newest Smithsonian museum, where artifacts include Harriet Tubman's hymnal, Emmett Till's casket, a segregated lunch counter and Michael Jordan's sneakers. The building's design is based on a three-tiered Yoruban crown.

National Sculpture Garden

RARRARORRO / SHUTTERSTOCK ©

National Gallery of Art & National Sculpture Garden

Beeline to Gallery 6 (West Building) and ogle the Western Hemisphere's only Leonardo da Vinci painting. Outdoors, amble amid whimsical sculptures by Miró, Calder and Lichtenstein. Also check out IM Pei's design of the East Building.

Capitol Hill

First-time visitors will be forgiven for assuming Capitol Hill, the city's geographic and legislative heart, is all about power-broking and politics. Truth is, it's mostly a row-house-lined residential neighborhood, but there's no denying that the big-domed building grabs all the attention.

Great For

☑ Don't Miss

The 1507 Waldseemuller World Map (the first to show America) at the Library of Congress.

The Capitol

Since 1800, the **Capitol** (☏202-226-8000; www.visitthecapitol.gov; 1st St SE & E Capitol St; ⊙8:30am-4:30pm Mon-Sat; ⓂOrange, Silver, Blue Line to Capitol South) **FREE** is where Congress, the legislative branch of American government, has met to write the country's laws. The lower House of Representatives (435 members) and upper Senate (100) meet respectively in the south and north wings of the building. Enter via the underground visitor center below the East Front Plaza. Guided tours of the building are free, but tickets are limited and there's often a long wait. It's best to reserve online in advance (there's no fee).

To watch Congress in session, you need a separate gallery pass. US citizens must get one in advance or in person from their representative or senator; foreign visitors

Capitol building

ORHAN CAM/SHUTTERSTOCK ©

Constitution Ave NW
Supreme
Court
1st St NE
Capitol ◎
E Capitol St
◎ *Library of*
Congress
Independence Ave SW
Ⓜ Capitol South

❶ Need to Know

Underground tunnels connect the Capitol, Supreme Court and Library of Congress, making for easy, weather-proof access.

✕ Take a Break

Eastern Market (✆202-698-5253; www.easternmarket-dc.org; 225 7th St SE; ⊗7am-7pm Tue-Fri, to 6pm Sat, 9am-5pm Sun; ⓂOrange, Silver, Blue Line to Eastern Market) is a short stroll away for local foods.

★ Top Tip

Military bands perform on the Capitol steps weekdays (except Thursday) at 8pm June through August.

should take their passports to the House and Senate Appointment Desks on the upper level. Congressional committee hearings are more interesting if you care about what's being debated; check for a schedule, locations and to see if they're open to the public (they often are) at www.house.gov and www.senate.gov.

Supreme Court

The highest court in the USA, the **Supreme Court** (✆202-479-3000; www.supremecourt.gov; 1 1st St NE; ⊗9am-4:30pm Mon-Fri; ⓂOrange, Silver, Blue Line to Capitol South) FREE occupies a pseudo-Greek temple protected by 13,000lb bronze doors. Arrive early to watch arguments (periodic Monday through Wednesday October to April). You can visit the permanent exhibits and the building's two five-story, marble-and-

bronze, spiral staircase year-round. On days when court is not in session you also can hear lectures (every hour on the half-hour) in the courtroom.

Library of Congress

The world's largest **library** (✆202-707-8000; www.loc.gov; 10 1st St SE; ⊗8:30am-4:30pm Mon-Sat; ⓂOrange, Silver, Blue Line to Capitol South) FREE – with 164 million books, manuscripts, maps, photos, films and other items – awes in both scope and design. The centerpiece is the 1897 Jefferson Building. Gawk at the Great Hall, done up in stained glass, marble and mosaics of mythical characters, then seek out the Gutenberg Bible (c 1455), Thomas Jefferson's round library and the reading-room viewing area. Free tours take place between 10:30am and 3:30pm on the half-hour.

◉ SIGHTS

◎ White House Area

White House   Landmark

(☏202-208-1631, 24hr info 202-456-7041; www.
whitehouse.gov; 1600 Pennsylvania Ave NW;
⊗tours 7:30-11:30am Tue-Thu, to 1:30pm Fri &
Sat; Ⓜ Orange, Silver, Blue Line to Federal Triangle
or McPherson Sq) **FREE** The 'President's
House,' built between 1792 and 1800, is an
iconic, imposing building that's thrilling
to see but difficult to access. Tours must
be pre-arranged: Americans must apply
via one of their members of Congress;
non-Americans must ask their country's
embassy in DC for assistance – in reality,
there's only a slim chance that the embassy will be able to help source tickets.
If you're lucky enough to visit, you'll see
several public rooms in the main residence
via self-guided tour.

◎ Georgetown

Dumbarton Oaks   Gardens, Museum

(☏202-339-6400; www.doaks.org; 1703 32nd
St NW; museum free, gardens adult/child $10/5;
⊗museum 11:30am-5:30pm Tue-Sun, gardens
2-6pm; ☐Circulator Georgetown-Union Station)
The mansion's 27 acres of enchanting formal gardens are straight out of a storybook.
The springtime blooms – including heaps
of cherry blossoms – are stunning. The
mansion itself is worth a walk-through to
see exquisite Byzantine and pre-Columbian
art (including El Greco's *The Visitation*) and
the fascinating library of rare books that
date as far back as 1491. From November to
mid-March the gardens are free (and they
close at 5pm). Enter them at R and 31st
Sts NW.

◎ Capitol Hill & South DC

United States Holocaust
Memorial Museum   Museum

(☏202-488-0400; www.ushmm.org; 100 Raoul
Wallenberg PI SW, South DC; ⊗10am-5:20pm,
extended hours Apr–mid-Jun; ☐Circulator, Ⓜ
Orange, Silver, Blue Line to Smithsonian) **FREE**
For a deep understanding of the Holocaust
– its victims, perpetrators and bystanders
– this harrowing museum is a must-see.
The main exhibit gives visitors the identity

United States Holocaust Memorial Museum

card of a single Holocaust victim, whose story is revealed as you take a winding route into a hellish past marked by ghettos, rail cars and death camps. It also shows the flip side of human nature, documenting the risks many citizens took to help the persecuted.

◎ Downtown & Penn Quarter

National Archives   Landmark

(📞866-272-6272; www.archives.gov/museum; 701 Constitution Ave NW, Penn Quarter; ⊙10am-5:30pm; Ⓜ Green, Yellow Line to Archives-Navy Memorial-Penn Quarter) **FREE** It's hard not to feel a little in awe of the big three documents in the Archives: the Declaration of Independence, the Constitution and the Bill of Rights. Taken together, it becomes clear just how radical the American experiment was. The archival bric-a-brac of the Public Vaults makes a flashy rejoinder to the main exhibit. You can reserve tickets (www.recreation.gov) for $1.50 and use the fast-track entrance on Constitution Ave (recommended in spring and summer).

Reynolds Center for American Art & Portraiture   Museum

(📞202-633-1000; www.americanart.si.edu; cnr 8th & F Sts NW, Penn Quarter; ⊙11:30am-7pm; Ⓜ Red, Yellow, Green Line to Gallery Pl-Chinatown) **FREE** The Reynolds Center is one of DC's finest museums. This Smithsonian venue combines the National Portrait Gallery and the American Art Museum into one whopping collection of American art that's unmatched anywhere in the world. Keep an eye out for famed works by Edward Hopper, Georgia O'Keeffe, Andy Warhol, Winslow Homer and loads more celebrated artists.

Ford's Theatre   Historic Site

(📞202-347-4833; www.fords.org; 511 10th St NW, Penn Quarter; ⊙9am-4:30pm; Ⓜ Red, Orange, Silver, Blue Line to Metro Center) **FREE** On April 14, 1865, John Wilkes Booth assassinated Abraham Lincoln here. Free timed-entry tickets provide access to the site, which has four parts: the theater itself (where you see the box seat Lincoln was sitting in when Booth shot him), the basement museum

🏛 DC for Children

Check www.washington.org/family-friendly for the lowdown on sights, activities and restaurants for kids. Top draws beyond the National Museum of Natural History (p96) and National Air & Space Museum (p96) include:

Smithsonian's National Zoo (📞20 2-633-4888; www.nationalzoo.si.edu; 3001 Connecticut Ave NW, Woodley Park; ⊙9am-6pm mid-Mar–Sep, to 4pm Oct–mid-Mar, grounds 8am-7pm mid-Mar–Sep, to 5pm Oct–mid-Mar; Ⓜ Red Line to Cleveland Park or Woodley Park) **FREE** Home to more than 2700 animals and more than 390 species in natural habitats, the National Zoo is famed for its giant pandas, Mei Xiang, Tian Tian and Bei Bei. Other highlights include the African lion pride, Asian elephants, and orangutans swinging 50ft overhead from steel cables and interconnected towers (aka the 'O Line').

International Spy Museum (📞202-393-7798; www.spymuseum.org; 700 L'Enfant Plaza SW, South DC; adult/child $25/15; ⊙10am-6pm Mon-Fri, 9am-7pm Sat & Sun; 👶; Ⓜ Orange, Silver, Blue, Yellow, Green Line to L'Enfant Plaza) One of DC's most popular museums delivers fun, interactive exhibits portraying the flashy world of intelligence-gathering. Highlights include an immersive exhibit exploring communist Berlin, a Situation Room experience of the capture of Osama bin Laden, and an exploration of potential future cyber threats against international security.

National Air & Space Museum (p96)

Washington, DC

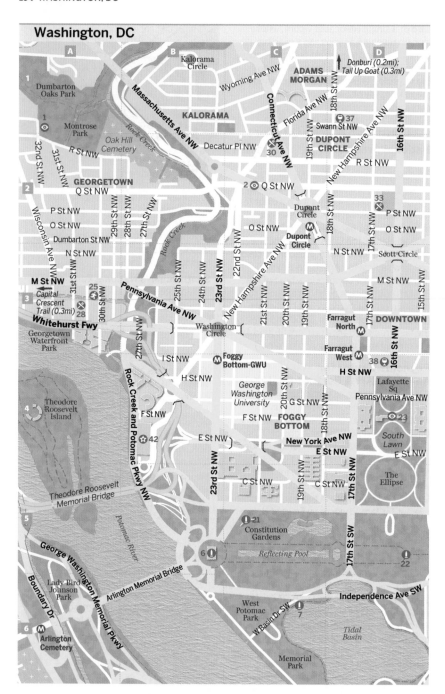

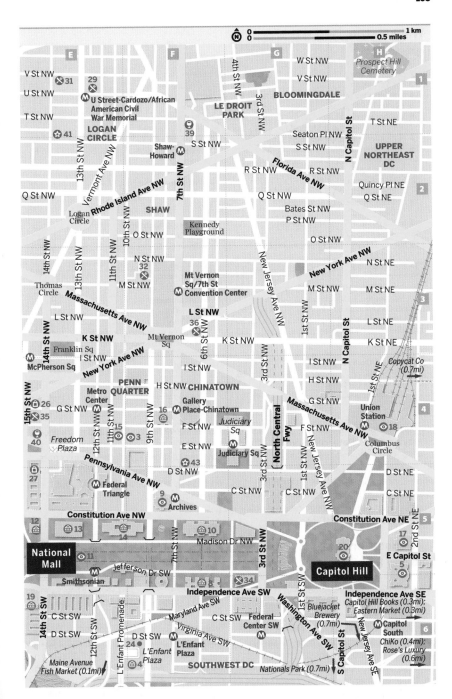

Washington, DC

(displaying Booth's .44-caliber pistol, his muddy boot etc), **Petersen House** (🖉20 2-347-4833; www.fords.org; 516 10th St NW; ☺9am-4:30pm) **FREE** (across the street, where Lincoln died) and the aftermath exhibits. Arrive early (by 8:30am) because tickets do run out. Better yet, reserve online ($3 fee) to ensure admittance.

◎ Dupont Circle

Embassy Row   Architecture
(www.embassy.org; Massachusetts Ave NW, btwn Observatory & Dupont Circles NW; M Red Line to Dupont Circle) Want to take a trip around the world? Stroll northwest along Massachusetts Ave from Dupont Circle (the actual traffic circle) and you pass more than 40 embassies housed in mansions that range from elegant to imposing to discreet. Tunisia, Chile, Turkmenistan, Togo, Haiti – flags

flutter above heavy doors and mark the nations inside, while dark-windowed sedans ease out of driveways ferrying diplomats to and fro. The district has another 130 embassies sprinkled throughout, but this is the main vein.

TOURS

Bike & Roll   Cycling
(🖉202-842-2453; www.bikeandrolldc.com; 955 L'Enfant Plaza SW, South DC; tours adult/child from $44/34; ☺9am-8pm, reduced hours spring & fall, closed early Jan–mid-Mar; M Orange, Silver, Blue, Yellow, Green Line to L'Enfant Plaza) This branch of the bike-rental company (from $16 per two hours) is the one closest to the Mall. In addition to bike rental, it also provides tours. Three-hour jaunts wheel by the main sights of Capitol Hill and the National

Mall. The evening rides to the monuments are particularly good.

DC Brew Tours — Bus

(☎202-759-8687; www.citybrewtours.com/dc; 801 F St NW, Penn Quarter; tours $70-99; ⓂRed, Yellow, Green Line to Gallery Pl-Chinatown) Visit three to four breweries by van. Routes vary but could include DC Brau, Atlas, Hellbender and Port City, among others. Three- to five-hour jaunts feature tastings of 15-plus beers and a light meal. The 3½-hour tour forgoes the meal and pares down the brewery tally. Departure is from outside the Reynolds Center. Tours go daily, at various times.

🛍 SHOPPING

Capitol Hill Books — Books

(☎202-544-1621; www.capitolhillbooks-dc.com; 657 C St SE, Capitol Hill; ⊗10am-8pm Mon-Fri, from 9am Sat & Sun, to 7pm Sun; ⓂOrange, Silver, Blue Line to Eastern Market) A trove of secondhand awesomeness, this shop has so many books that staff have to double-stack them on the shelves. Categories are, er, unconventional, including 'Hinduism and Bobby Knight' and 'Sideshows and Carnivals.' The section on US presidents is huge (Chester Arthur books! An entire shelf of Truman books!).

White House Gifts — Gifts & Souvenirs

(☎202-737-9500; www.whitehousegifts.com; 701 15th St NW, White House Area; ⊗8am-9pm Mon-Sat, 9am-8pm Sun May-Dec, 9am-8pm Mon-Sat, to 6pm Sun Jan-Apr; ⓂRed, Orange, Silver, Blue Line to Metro Center) Not to be confused with the official White House **gift shop** (http://shop.whitehousehistory.org; 1450 Pennsylvania Ave NW; ⊗7:30am-4pm; ⓂOrange, Silver, Blue Line to Federal Triangle) in the White House Visitor Center, this store sells official souvenirs alongside less-orthodox offerings. So while you can still find the certified White House Christmas ornament among the stock, you'll also see caricature Trump bottle openers and the Political Inaction Figures paper-doll set.

🥾 Hit the Trail in Georgetown

Leafy Georgetown offers some great opportunities for active types:

C&O Canal Towpath (www.nps.gov/choh; 1057 Thomas Jefferson St NW, visitor center; 🚌Circulator Georgetown-Union Station) The shaded hiking-cycling path runs alongside a waterway built in the mid-1800s to transport goods to West Virginia. Step on at Jefferson St for a lovely escape from the crowds. Note the canal and environs are being restored and enhanced over the next several years, so you might run into construction along the way; check the latest before setting off.

Capital Crescent Trail (www.cctrail.org; Water St; 🚌Circulator Georgetown-Union Station) Stretching between Georgetown and Bethesda, MD, the constantly evolving Capital Crescent Trail is a fabulous (and very popular) jogging and biking route. Built on an abandoned railroad bed, the 7-mile trail is paved and is a great leisurely day trip. It has beautiful lookouts over the Potomac River, and winds through woodsy areas and upscale neighborhoods.

Hiker on the C&O Canal Towpath

🍴 EATING

🍴 White House Area

Old Ebbitt Grill — American $$

(☎202-347-4800; www.ebbitt.com; 675 15th St NW; mains $18-32; ⊗7:30am-1am Mon-Fri, from 8:30am Sat & Sun, happy hour 3-6pm &

★ **Top Five for Foodies**

Dabney

Tail Up Goat (p110)

Rose's Luxury

ChiKo

Little Serow (p110)

From left: Old Ebbitt Grill (p107); Eastern Market (p101); Busboys & Poets (p111)

POPOVA VALERIYA/SHUTTERSTOCK ©

CORIN/SHUTTERSTOCK ©

11pm-1am; ⓜRed, Orange, Silver, Blue Line to Metro Center) Established in DC in 1856, this legendary tavern has occupied prime real estate near the White House since 1983. Political players and tourists pack into the wood-paneled interior, where thick burgers, succulent steaks and jumbo lump crab cakes are rotated out almost as quickly as the clientele. Pop in for a cocktail and oysters during happy hour.

🚫 Georgetown

Baked & Wired   Bakery $

(☎703-663-8727; www.bakedandwired.com; 1052 Thomas Jefferson St NW; baked goods $3-8; ⊙7am-8pm Mon-Thu, to 9pm Fri, 8am-9pm Sat, 8am-8pm Sun; 🚌Circulator Georgetown-Union Station) This cheery cafe whips up beautifully made coffees, bacon cheddar buttermilk biscuits and enormous cupcakes (like the banana and peanut-butter-frosted Elvis impersonator). It's a fine spot to join university students and cyclists coming off the nearby trails for a sugar buzz. When the weather permits, patrons take their treats outside to the adjacent grassy area by the C&O Canal.

🚫 Capitol Hill & South DC

ChiKo   Asian $$

(☎202-558-9934; www.chikodc.com; 423 8th St SE, Capitol Hill; mains $14-18; ⊙5-11pm Mon-Thu, to midnight Fri & Sat, to 10pm Sun; ⓜOrange, Silver, Blue Line to Eastern Market) ChiKo stands for Chinese and Korean, and it fuses the cuisines with low-key style. Dishes such as pork and kimchi potstickers and chilled acorn noodles wow the foodie masses: it's high-brow fare at a budget price. The restaurant is fast-casual in set-up: order at the counter, then try to score one of the handful of picnic tables in the fluorescent-lit room.

Rose's Luxury   American $$$

(☎202-580-8889; www.rosesluxury.com; 717 8th St SE, Capitol Hill; small plates $14-16, family plates $33-36; ⊙5-10pm Mon-Sat; ⓜOrange, Silver, Blue Line to Eastern Market) Michelin-starred Rose's is one of DC's most buzzed-about eateries. Crowds fork into worldly Southern comfort food as twinkling lights glow overhead and candles flicker around the industrial-chic, half-finished room. Rose's doesn't take reservations, but

MICHAEL VENTURA/ALAMY ©

ordering your meal at the upstairs bar can save time (and the cocktails are delicious).

🍴 Downtown & Penn Quarter

Shouk Israeli **$**

(📞202-652-1464; www.shouk.com; 655 K St NW, Downtown; mains $10; ⊙11am-10pm; 🍴; Ⓜ Green, Yellow Line to Mt Vernon Sq/7th St-Convention Center) Fast and casual, Shouk creates big flavor in its vegan menu of Israeli street food, served with craft beer and tap wines. A crazy-good burger made of chickpeas, black beans, lentils and mushrooms gets stuffed into a toasty pita with pickled turnips, arugula and charred onions. The mushroom-and-cauliflower pita and sweet-potato fries with cashew *labneh* (creamy 'cheese') are lip smacking.

Dabney American **$$$**

(📞202-450-1015; www.thedabney.com; 122 Blagden Alley NW, Downtown; small plates $14-25; ⊙5:30-10pm Tue-Thu, 5-11pm Fri & Sat, 5-10pm Sun; Ⓜ Green, Yellow Line to Mt Vernon Sq/7th St-Convention Center) Chef Jeremiah Langhorne studied historic cookbooks, dis-

covering recipes that used local ingredients and lesser-explored flavors in his quest to resuscitate mid-Atlantic cuisine lost to the ages. Most of the dishes are even cooked over a wood-burning hearth, as in George Washington's time. Langhorne gives it all a modern twist – enough to earn him a Michelin star.

🍴 Dupont Circle

Bistrot du Coin French **$$**

(📞202-234-6969; www.bistrotducoin.com; 1738 Connecticut Ave NW; mains $20-30; ⊙11:30am-midnight Mon-Wed, to 1am Thu & Fri, noon-1am Sat, noon-midnight Sun; Ⓜ Red Line to Dupont Circle) The lively and much-loved Bistrot du Coin is a neighborhood favorite for roll-up-your sleeves, working-class French fare. The kitchen sends out consistently good onion soup, classic *steak-frites* (grilled steak and French fries), cassoulet, open-face sandwiches and 11 varieties of its famous *moules* (mussels). Regional wines from around the motherland accompany the food by the glass, carafe and bottle.

Little Serow   Thai $$$

(www.littleserow.com; 1511 17th St NW; prix-fixe menu $54; ⊙5:30-10pm Tue-Thu, to 10:30pm Fri & Sat; Ⓜ️Red Line to Dupont Circle) Set in a cavern-like green basement, Little Serow has no phone, no reservations and no sign on the door, and it only seats groups of four or fewer (larger parties will be separated). Despite all this, people line up around the block. What for? Superlative northern Thai cuisine. The single-option menu, consisting of six or so hot-spiced courses, changes weekly.

Adams Morgan

Donburi   Japanese $

(📞202-629-1047; www.donburidc.com; 2438 18th St NW; mains $11-13; ⊙11am-10pm; Ⓜ️Red Line to Woodley Park-Zoo/Adams Morgan) Hole-in-the-wall Donburi has 14 seats at a wooden counter where you get a front-row view of the slicing, dicing chefs. *Donburi* means 'bowl' in Japanese, and that's what arrives steaming hot and filled with, say, panko-coated shrimp atop rice, blended with the house's sweet-and-savory sauce.

It's a simple, authentic meal. There's often a line, but it moves quickly. No reservations.

Tail Up Goat   Mediterranean $$

(📞202-986-9600; www.tailupgoat.com; 1827 Adams Mill Rd NW; mains $18-27; ⊙5:30-10pm Mon-Thu, 5-10pm Fri & Sat, 11am-1pm & 5-10pm Sun; Ⓜ️Red Line to Woodley Park-Zoo/Adams Morgan) With its pale-blue walls, light wood decor and lantern-like lights dangling overhead, Tail Up Goat exudes a warm, island-y vibe. The lamb ribs are the specialty – crispy and lusciously fatty, served with date-molasses juice. The housemade breads and spreads star on the menu too – say, flaxseed sourdough with beets. No wonder Michelin gave it a star.

🍽 Logan Circle, U Street & Shaw

Ben's Chili Bowl   American $

(📞202-667-0058; www.benschilibowl.com; 1213 U St NW, U Street; mains $6-10; ⊙6am-2am Mon-Thu, to 4am Fri, 7am-4am Sat, 11am-midnight Sun; Ⓜ️Green, Yellow Line to U Street/African-American Civil War Memorial/Cardozo) Ben's is a DC institution. The main stock in trade is

Ben's Chili Bowl

half-smokes, DC's meatier, smokier version of the hot dog, usually slathered with mustard, onions and the namesake chili. For 60-plus years presidents, rock stars and Supreme Court justices have come to indulge in the humble diner, but despite the hype, Ben's remains a true neighborhood establishment. Cash only.

Busboys & Poets   Cafe $$

(202-387-7638; www.busboysandpoets. com; 2021 14th St NW, U Street; mains $16-22; 7am-midnight Mon-Thu, to 1am Fri, 8am-1am Sat, to midnight Sun; ; Green, Yellow Line to U Street/African-American Civil War Memorial/Cardozo) Busboys & Poets is one of U Street's linchpins. Locals pack the place for coffee, boozy brunches, books and a progressive vibe that makes San Francisco feel conservative. The lengthy, vegetarian-friendly menu spans sandwiches, pizzas and Southern fare such as shrimp and grits. Tuesday night's open-mike poetry reading ($5 admission, from 9pm to 11pm) draws big crowds.

DRINKING & NIGHTLIFE

White House Area

Round Robin   Bar

(202-628-9100; http://washington.intercontin ental.com/food-drink/round-robin-bar; 1401 Pennsylvania Ave NW, Willard InterContinental Hotel; noon-1am Mon-Sat, to midnight Sun; Red, Orange, Silver, Blue Line to Metro Center) Dispensing drinks since 1847, the bar at the Willard hotel is one of DC's most famous watering holes. The small, circular space is done up in classic accents, all dark wood trim, marble bar and leather seats. While it's touristy, you'll likely still see officials here determining your latest tax hike over a mint julep or single malt scotch.

Off the Record   Bar

(202-638-6600; www.hayadams.com/dining/ off-the-record; 800 16th St NW, Hay-Adams Hotel; 11:30am-midnight Sun-Thu, to 12:30am Fri &

Arlington National Cemetery

Arlington National Cemetery (877-907-8585; www.arlingtoncemetery.mil; Memorial Ave; 8am-7pm Apr-Sep, to 5pm Oct-Mar; Blue Line to Arlington Cemetery) **FREE** is the somber final resting place for more than 400,000 military personnel and their dependents. The 624-acre grounds contain the dead of every war the USA has fought since the Revolution. Highlights include the Tomb of the Unknown Soldier, with its elaborate changing-of-the-guard ceremony (every hour on the hour October through March, every half-hour April through September), and the grave of John F Kennedy and his family, marked by an eternal flame. Departing from the visitor center, hop-on, hop-off bus tours are an easy way to visit the cemetery's main sights. Though Arlington is in Virginia, it's only a few Metro stops southwest of the National Mall.

Sat; Orange, Silver, Blue Line to McPherson Sq) Table seating, an open fire in winter and a discreet basement location in one of the city's most prestigious **hotels** (d from $400;), right across from the White House – it's no wonder DC's important people submerge to be seen and not heard (as the tagline goes) here. Experienced bartenders swirl martinis and manhattans for the suit-wearing crowd. Enter through the hotel lobby.

🍴 What's on at The Wharf

The Southwest Waterfront has long been home to the **Maine Avenue Fish Market** (www.wharfdc.com; 1100 Maine Ave SW, South DC; mains $7-13; ⏰8am-9pm; Ⓜ Orange, Silver, Blue, Yellow, Green Line to L'Enfant Plaza), but the area was otherwise unremarkable – until the Wharf shot up. The huge complex of restaurants, hotels, entertainment venues, parks and piers officially opened in late 2017, and now it buzzes.

The public piers are the niftiest bits. The Transit Pier has a winter ice rink, summer mini-golf course and small outdoor stage for free concerts. The Wharf water taxi departs from here, hence the name. The District Pier is the longest dock, jutting well out into the Washington Channel and hosting a big stage for festivals. The Recreation Pier makes for a fine stroll with its benches, swinging seats and boathouse for kayak and paddleboard rentals.

Loads of eateries sit waterside, and more are on the way, as you'll see from the ongoing construction that will add to the Wharf for the next several years.

IO1100J0101101/SHUTTERSTOCK ©

🍸 Capitol Hill & South DC

Copycat Co   Cocktail Bar

(☎202-241-1952; www.copycatcompany.com; 1110 H St NE, Capitol Hill; ⏰5pm-2am Sun-Thu, to 3am Fri & Sat; Ⓜ Red Line to Union Station then streetcar) When you walk into Copycat it feels like a Chinese fast-food restaurant.

That's because it is (sort of) on the 1st floor, where Chinese street-food nibbles are available. The fizzy drinks and egg-white-topped cocktails fill glasses upstairs, in the dimly lit, speakeasy-meets-opium-den-vibed bar. Staff are unassuming and gracious in helping newbies figure out what they want from the lengthy menu.

Bluejacket Brewery   Brewery

(☎202-524-4862; www.bluejacketdc.com; 300 Tingey St SE, South DC; ⏰11am-1am Sun-Thu, to 2am Fri & Sat; 🍴🍽; Ⓜ Green Line to Navy Yard-Ballpark) Beer-lovers' heads will explode in Bluejacket. Pull up a stool at the mod-industrial bar, gaze at the silvery tanks bubbling up the ambitious brews, then make the hard decision about which of the 20 tap beers you want to try. A dry-hopped kolsch? Sweet-spiced stout? A cask-aged farmhouse ale? Four-ounce tasting pours help with decision-making.

🍸 Downtown & Penn Quarter

Columbia Room   Cocktail Bar

(☎202-316-9396; www.columbiaroomdc.com; 124 Blagden Alley NW, Downtown; ⏰5pm-12:30am Tue-Thu, to 1:30am Fri & Sat; Ⓜ Green, Yellow Line to Mt Vernon Sq/7th St-Convention Center) Serious mixology goes on at Columbia Room, the kind of place that sources spring water from Scotland, and uses pickled cherry blossom and barley tea among its ingredients. But it's done in a refreshingly nonsnooty environment. Choose from three areas: the festive Punch Garden on the outdoor roof deck, the comfy, leather-chair-dotted Spirits Library, or the 14-seat, prix-fixe Tasting Room.

🍸 Dupont Circle

Bar Charley   Bar

(☎202-627-2183; www.barcharley.com; 1825 18th St NW; ⏰5pm-12:30am Mon-Thu, 4pm-1:30am Fri, 10am-1:30am Sat, to midnight Sun; Ⓜ Red Line to Dupont Circle) Bar Charley draws a mixed crowd from the neighborhood – young, old, gay and straight. They come for groovy cocktails sloshing in vintage glassware and ceramic tiki mugs, served

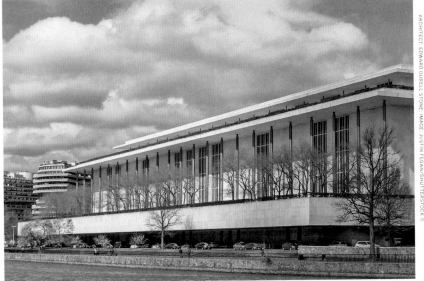

Kennedy Center

at very reasonable prices by DC standards. Try the gin and gingery Suffering Bastard. The beer list isn't huge, but it's thoughtfully chosen with some wild ales. Around 60 wines available too.

🍺 Logan Circle, U Street & Shaw

Right Proper Brewing Co Brewery

(📞202-607-2337; www.rightproperbrewery. com; 624 T St NW, Logan Circle; ⏰5-11pm Mon-Thu, 11:30am-midnight Fri & Sat, to 10pm Sun; Ⓜ Green, Yellow Line to Shaw-Howard U) Right Proper Brewing makes sublime ales in a building that shares a wall with the joint where Duke Ellington used to play pool. It's the Shaw district's neighborhood club-house, a big, sunny space filled with folks gabbing at reclaimed wood tables. The tap lineup changes regularly as the brewers work their magic, but crisp farmhouse ales are an oft-flowing specialty.

⭐ ENTERTAINMENT

Kennedy Center Performing Arts

(📞202-467-4600; www.kennedy-center.org; 2700 F St NW, Foggy Bottom; ⏰box office 10am-9pm Mon-Sat, noon-9pm Sun; 📶♿; Ⓜ Orange,

Silver, Blue Line to Foggy Bottom-GWU) Over-looking the Potomac River, the magnificent Kennedy Center hosts a staggering array of performances – more than 2000 each year in venues including the Concert Hall, home to the **National Symphony** (www.kenne-dy-center.org/nso), and Opera House, home to the **National Opera** (www.kennedy-center. org/wno). Free performances are staged on the Millennium Stage daily at 6pm as part of the center's 'Performing Arts for Everyone' initiative.

Nationals Park Stadium

(📞202-675-6287; www.mlb.com/nationals; 1500 S Capitol St SE, South DC; 📶; Ⓜ Green Line to Navy Yard-Ballpark) The major-league Washington Nationals play baseball at this spiffy stadium beside the Anacostia River. Don't miss the mid-fourth-inning 'Presi-dents' Race' – an odd foot race between giant-headed caricatures of George Wash-ington, Abraham Lincoln, Thomas Jefferson and Teddy Roosevelt. Hip bars and eateries and playful green spaces surround the ballpark, and more keep coming as the area gentrifies.

Black Cat
Live Music

(☎202-667-4490; www.blackcatdc.com; 1811 14th St NW, U Street; tickets $10-25; Ⓜ Green, Yellow Line to U Street/African-American Civil War Memorial/Cardozo) The Black Cat is the go-to venue for music that's loud and grungy with a punk edge. The White Stripes, Arcade Fire and Foo Fighters have all thrashed here. The big action takes place on the Mainstage. The legendary Backstage and Red Room bar are being reimagined on the club's 2nd story; check the website for updates.

Woolly Mammoth Theatre Company
Theater

(☎202-393-3939; www.woollymammoth. net; 641 D St NW, Penn Quarter; average ticket $67; Ⓜ Green, Yellow Line to Archives-Navy Memorial-Penn Quarter) Woolly Mammoth is the edgiest of DC's experimental groups. For most shows, $20 'stampede' seats are available at the box office two hours before performances. They're limited in number, and sold first-come, first-served, so get there early.

ⓘ INFORMATION

Destination DC (☎202-789-7000; www.wash ington.org) is DC's official tourism site, with the mother lode of online information.

ⓘ GETTING THERE & AROUND

TO/FROM THE AIRPORT

Ronald Reagan Washington National Airport (DCA; www.flyreagan.com) is 4.5 miles south of downtown in Arlington, VA.

○ **Metro** The airport has its own Metro station on the Blue and Yellow Lines. Trains (around $2.65) depart every 10 minutes or so between 5am and 11:30pm (to 1am Friday and Saturday); they reach the city center in 20 minutes.

○ **Shuttle van** The Supershuttle (www.super-shuttle.com) door-to-door shared van service goes downtown for $19. It takes 10 to 30 minutes and runs from 5:30am to 12:30am.

○ **Taxi** Rides to the city center take 10 to 30 minutes (depending on traffic) and cost $19 to $26.

Nationals Park (p113)

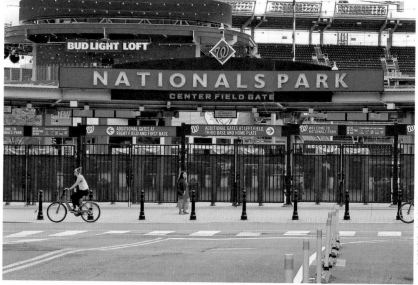

Dulles International Airport (IAD; ✆703-572-2700, 703-572-8296; www.flydulles.com) is in the Virginia suburbs 26 miles west of DC.

○ **Bus & Metro** Washington Flyer's (www.washfly.com) Silver Line Express bus runs every 15 to 20 minutes from Dulles (main terminal, arrivals level door 4) to the Wiehle-Reston East Metro station between 6am and 10:40pm (from 7:45am weekends). Total time to DC's center is 60 to 75 minutes, total bus-Metro cost around $11.

○ **Shuttle van** The Supershuttle (www.supershuttle.com) door-to-door shared van service goes downtown for $33. It takes 30 to 60 minutes and runs from 5:30am to 12:30am.

○ **Taxi** Rides to the city center take 30 to 60 minutes (depending on traffic) and cost $62 to $73.

BICYCLE

Capital Bikeshare (www.capitalbikeshare.com) has stations all over the city. Kiosks issue passes (one day for $8 or three days for $17) on the spot. There's also an option for a 'single trip' ($2), ie a one-off ride of under 30 minutes.

PUBLIC TRANSPORTATION

METRO

○ DC's modern subway network is the Metrorail (www.wmata.com), commonly called Metro.

There are six color-coded lines: Red, Orange, Blue, Green, Yellow and Silver.

○ Trains start running at 5am Monday through Friday (from 7am Saturday, 8am Sunday); the last service is around 11:30pm Sunday through Thursday and 1am on Friday and Saturday.

○ Fare cards are called SmarTrip cards. Machines inside all stations sell them. The plastic, rechargeable card costs $10, with $8 of that stored for fares. You then add value as needed.

○ Fares cost $2.25 to $6, depending on distance traveled and time of day. Fares increase slightly during morning and evening rush hour.

Use the card to enter *and* exit station turnstiles.

DC CIRCULATOR BUS

DC Circulator (www.dccirculator.com) buses run along handy local routes, including Union Station to/from the Mall (looping by all major museums and memorials), Union Station to/from Georgetown (via K St), Dupont Circle to/from Georgetown (via M St), and the White House area to/from Adams Morgan (via 14th St).

Circulator buses operate from roughly 6am to 9pm weekdays (midnight or so on weekends).

Fare is $1. Pay with exact change, or use a SmarTrip card.

TRAIN

Magnificent, beaux-arts **Union Station** (✆202-289-1908; www.unionstationdc.com; 50 Massachusetts Ave NE, Capitol Hill; ⊙24hr, ticketed passengers only midnight-5am; Ⓜ Red Line to Union Station) is the city's rail hub. There's a handy Metro station (Red Line) here for transport onward in the city. Amtrak (www.amtrak.com) arrives at least once per hour from major east-coast cities. Many bus lines (Megabus, Greyhound etc) also use the station.

TAXI & RIDESHARE

○ Fares are meter-based. The meter starts at $3.50, then it's $2.16 per mile thereafter.

○ There's a $2 surcharge for telephone dispatches. Try DC Yellow Cab (✆202-544-1212) if you need a pick-up.

○ Ride-hailing companies Uber, Lyft and Via are popular in the District.

CHICAGO

Chicago at a Glance...

Take cloud-scraping architecture, lakefront beaches and world-class museums, stir in wild comedy, fret-bending guitars and very hefty pizza, and you've got a town that won't let you down.

The city center is a steely wonder, but it's Chicago's mural-splashed neighborhoods – with their inventive storefront restaurants, corner rock clubs and sociable dive bars – that really blow you away. Michelin-starred eateries pop up throughout, serving masterful food in come-as-you-are environs. You can also fork into a superb range of global cuisine.

Two Days in Chicago

Explore the art and greenery of **Millennium Park** (p120), then stop for a deep-dish pizza at **Giordano's** (p136). Take a tour with the **Chicago Architecture Center** (p133) to get the lowdown on the city's skyscrapers. On day two explore the **Art Institute of Chicago** (p122). Grab a stylish dinner in the West Loop, then listen to blues at **Buddy Guy's Legends** (p139).

Four Days in Chicago

On your third day, stroll **Navy Pier** (p129), rent a bicycle and cruise through **Lincoln Park** (p132). If it's baseball season, go watch the Cubs at **Wrigley Field** (p124) In the evening yuck it up at **Second City** (p138). Pick a neighborhood for day four: culture aplenty in **Pilsen & Near South Side** (p132) or brainy museums in **Hyde Park** (p140).

Previous page: Chicago street scene
NEJDET DUZEN/SHUTTERSTOCK ©

Arriving in Chicago

O'Hare International Airport The Blue Line L train ($5) runs 24/7 and departs every 10 minutes and reaches downtown in 40 minutes. Shuttle vans cost $35, taxis around $50.

Midway International Airport The Orange Line L train ($3) runs between 4am and 1am every 10 minutes and reaches downtown in 30 minutes. Shuttle vans cost $28, taxis $35 to $40.

Where to Stay

The Loop and Near North are the most lodging-filled neighborhoods, offering a mix of cool design hotels and chain properties. Ace Hotel, Hoxton and other trendy brands cluster in the West Loop. Posh hostels and apartment rentals are popular in Near North, Wicker Park, Lincoln Park and Wrigleyville.

Millennium Park

This stunning art-filled green space sits in the heart of the Loop. Lovely views, daring works of sculpture, high-tech fountains, hidden gardens, free summer concerts and a winter skating rink are all part of the allure.

Great For...

☑ Don't Miss

The Lurie Garden, filled with prairie flowers and a little river to dip your toes.

The Bean

The park's biggest draw is 'the Bean' – officially titled *Cloud Gate* – Anish Kapoor's 110-ton, silver-drop sculpture. It reflects both the sky and the skyline, and everyone clamors around to take a picture and to touch its silvery smoothness. Good vantage points for photos are at the sculpture's northern and southern ends. For great people-watching, go up the stairs on Washington St, on the Park Grill's northern side, where there are shaded benches.

Crown Fountain

Jaume Plensa's *Crown Fountain* is another crowd-pleaser. Its two 50ft-high glass-block towers contain video displays that flash a thousand different faces. The people shown are all native Chicagoans and they all agreed to strap into Plensa's special dental

Millenium Park and architect Frank Gehry's Pritzker Pavilion

EYESTRAVELLING/SHUTTERSTOCK ©

ⓘ Need to Know

☎312-742-1168; www.millenniumpark.
org; 201 E Randolph St; ⊗6am-11pm; ♿;
Ⓜ Brown, Orange, Green, Purple, Pink Line to
Washington/Wabash

✕ Take a Break

Grab a sandwich and bottle of wine at
Pastoral (p134) for a picnic in the park.

★ Top Tip

Free walking tours take place at
11:30am and 1pm daily from late May to
mid-October.

chair, where he immobilized their heads for
filming. Each mug puckers up and spurts
water, just like the gargoyles atop Notre
Dame Cathedral. A fresh set of nonpuck-
ering faces appears in winter, when the
fountain is dry. On hot days the fountain
crowds with locals splashing in the streams
to cool off. Kids especially love it.

Pritzker Pavilion

Millennium Park's acoustically awesome
band shell, Pritzker Pavilion was designed
by architect Frank Gehry, who gave it his
trademark swooping silver exterior. The
pavilion hosts free concerts at 6:30pm
several nights weekly from June to August,
ranging from indie rock and world music to
jazz and classical. On Tuesday there's usu-

ally a movie beamed onto the huge screen
on stage. Seats are available up close in the
pavilion, or you can sit on the grassy Great
Lawn that unfurls behind.

For all shows – but especially the classical ones, which the top-notch Grant Park
Orchestra performs – folks bring blankets,
picnics, wine and beer. There is nothing
quite like sitting on the lawn, looking up
through Gehry's wild grid and seeing the
grandeur of the skyscrapers forming the
backdrop to the soaring music. If you want
a seat up close, arrive early.

The pavilion also hosts daytime action.
Concert rehearsals take place Tuesday to
Friday, usually from 11am to 1pm, offering
a taste of music if you can't catch the
evening show.

WHITEBLUSH/SHUTTERSTOCK ©

Art Institute of Chicago

The second-largest art museum in the country, the Art Institute has the kind of celebrity-heavy collection that routinely draws gasps from patrons.

Great For...

☑ Don't Miss

Grant Wood's *American Gothic* (Gallery 263), one of America's most famous paintings.

Must-See Works: Floor 2

First up is *A Sunday Afternoon on the Island of La Grande Jatte* by Georges Seurat (Gallery 240). Get close enough for the painting to break down into its component dots and you'll understand why it took Seurat two long years to complete his pointillist masterpiece. Next seek out *Nighthawks* by Edward Hopper (Gallery 262). His lonely, poignant snapshot of four solitary souls at a neon-lit diner was inspired by a Greenwich Ave restaurant in Manhattan. In the next room you'll find *American Gothic* by Grant Wood (Gallery 263). The artist, a lifelong resident of Iowa, used his sister and his dentist as models for the two stern-faced farmers.

WHITEBLUSH/SHUTTERSTOCK ©

E Monroe St

S Michigan Ave

Art Institute of Chicago

Adams/Wabash

E Jackson Blvd

❶ Need to Know

📱312-443-3600; www.artic.edu; 111 S Michigan Ave; adult/child $25/free; ⏱10:30am-5pm Fri-Wed, to 8pm Thu; 🚹; Ⓜ Brown, Orange, Green, Purple, Pink Line to Adams)

✕ Take a Break

The nearby Berghoff (p137), dating from 1898, is tops for a beer and a dose of Chicago history.

★ Top Tip

Ask at the information desk about free talks and tours once you're inside.

Must-See Works: Floors 1 & 3

Stop by Marc Chagall's *America Windows* (Gallery 144). He created the huge, blue stained-glass pieces to celebrate the USA's bicentennial. Another favorite is *The Old Guitarist* by Pablo Picasso (Gallery 391). The elongated figure is from the artist's Blue Period. Not far away is Salvador Dalí's *Inventions of the Monsters* (Gallery 396). He painted it in Austria before the Nazi annexation. The title refers to a Nostradamus prediction that the apparition of monsters presages the outbreak of war.

Other Intriguing Sights

The Thorne Miniature Rooms (Lower Level, Gallery 11) and Paperweight Collection (Lower Level, Gallery 15) are awesome, overlooked galleries. In the light-drenched Modern Wing, the ongoing exhibition 'The New Contemporary' (Galleries 288 and 290–99) bursts with iconic works by Andy Warhol, Roy Lichtenstein and Jasper Johns.

Visiting the Museum

Download the museum's free app, either at home or using the on-site wi-fi. It offers several audio tours through the collection. Highlights, architecture and pop art are among the themes.

Allow two hours to browse the museum's highlights; art buffs should allocate much longer. The museum's main entrance is on Michigan Ave, but you can also enter via the Modern Wing on Monroe St. Advance tickets are available (surcharge $2), but unless there's a blockbuster exhibit going on they're usually not necessary. The entrance queue moves fast.

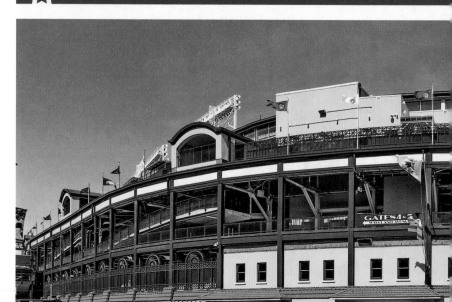

Wrigley Field

Built in 1914, Wrigley Field is the second-oldest baseball park in the major leagues. It's filled with legendary traditions and curses, including a team that didn't win a championship for 108 years.

Environs

The ballpark provides an old-school slice of Americana, with a hand-turned scoreboard, ivy-covered outfield walls and an iconic neon sign over the front entrance. The field is uniquely situated smack in the middle of a neighborhood, surrounded on all sides by houses, bars and restaurants. The grassy plaza just north of the main entrance – aka Gallagher Way – has tables, chairs, a coffee shop and a huge video screen. On nongame days it's open to the public and hosts free movie nights, concerts and alfresco fitness classes; on game days it's a beer garden for ticket holders. Kids love the grassy expanse, where they can run around, play catch or cool off in the splash pad. A slew of new cocktail bars, beer bars

Great For...

☑ **Don't Miss**

Taking a photo under the neon entrance sign.

CARLOS YUDICA/SHUTTERSTOCK ©

❶ Need to Know

☎800-843-2827; www.cubs.com; 1060 W Addison St, Wrigleyville; Ⓜ Red Line to Addison)

✕ Take a Break

It's a pre-game ritual to beer up at **Murphy's Bleachers** (☎773-281-5356; www.murphysbleachers.com; 3655 N Sheffield Ave, Wrigleyville; ⊘11am-2am; Ⓜ Red Line to Addison), steps away from the ballpark.

★ Top Tip

Buy tickets at the Cubs' website or Wrigley box office. Online ticket broker StubHub (www.stubhub.com) is also reliable.

and hip taco, barbecue and fried-chicken eateries beckon across the way on Clark and Addison Sts.

The Curse & Its Reverse

It started with Billy Sianis, owner of the Billy Goat Tavern. The year was 1945 and the Cubs were in the World Series against the Detroit Tigers. When Sianis tried to enter Wrigley Field with his pet goat to see the game, ballpark staff refused, saying the goat stank. Sianis threw up his arms and called down a mighty hex, saying that the Cubs would never win another World Series. Years rolled by, and they didn't. Then in 2016 it happened: the Cubs won the Series in a wild, come-from-behind set of games. The young team scrapped, slugged and pitched its way to victory, exorcising the

curse. The city went insane. At the victory parade a few days later, an estimated five million fans partied with the team.

The Traditions

When the middle of the seventh inning arrives, it's time for the seventh inning stretch. You then stand up for the group sing-along of 'Take Me Out to the Ballgame,' typically led by a guest celebrity along the lines of Mr T, Ozzy Osbourne or the local weather reporter. Here's another tradition: if you catch a home run slugged by the competition, you're honor-bound to throw it back onto the field. After every game the ballpark hoists a flag atop the scoreboard. A white flag with a blue 'W' indicates a victory; a blue flag with a white 'L' means a loss.

Art of the City

This tour swoops through the Loop, highlighting Chicago's revered art and architecture, with a visit to Al Capone's dentist thrown in for good measure.

Start Chicago Board of Trade
Distance 2.5 miles
Duration Two hours

Chicago River

6 Picasso's abstract *Untitled* sculpture is ensconced in **Daley Plaza**. Baboon, dog, woman? You decide.

W Randolph St

Daley Plaza
6
Washington **5**

5 Al Capone's dentist drilled teeth in what's now Room 809 of the **Staypineapple** hotel.

W Madison St

THE LOOP

S LaSalle St
S Clark St
N State St

Monroe

W Adams St

2 Step into the nearby **Rookery** (p128) to see Frank Lloyd Wright's handiwork in the atrium.

Quincy

2

Jackson

W Jackson Blvd

START **1**

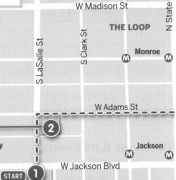

1 Start at the **Chicago Board of Trade** with its art-deco building and rooftop statue of Ceres.

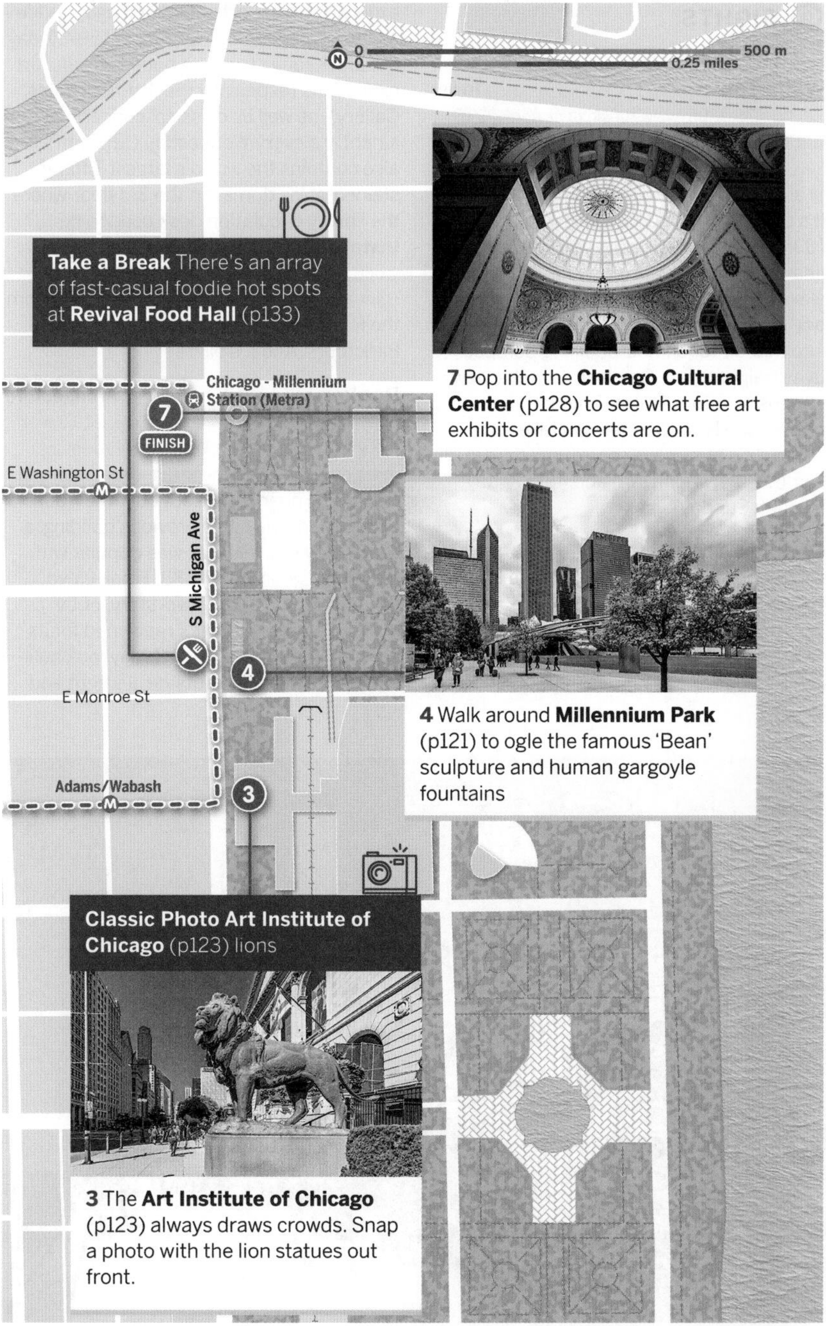

Take a Break There's an array of fast-casual foodie hot spots at **Revival Food Hall** (p133)

Chicago - Millennium Station (Metra)

7 Pop into the **Chicago Cultural Center** (p128) to see what free art exhibits or concerts are on.

(7) FINISH

E Washington St

S Michigan Ave

(4)

E Monroe St

4 Walk around **Millennium Park** (p121) to ogle the famous 'Bean' sculpture and human gargoyle fountains

Adams/Wabash

(3)

Classic Photo Art Institute of Chicago (p123) lions

3 The **Art Institute of Chicago** (p123) always draws crowds. Snap a photo with the lion statues out front.

◉ SIGHTS
◉ The Loop

Willis Tower   Tower
(☎312-875-9696; www.theskydeck.com; 233 S
Wacker Dr; adult/child $24/16; ☺9am-10pm Mar-
Sep, 10am-8pm Oct-Feb, last entry 30min prior;
Ⓜ Brown, Orange, Purple, Pink Line to Quincy)
It's Chicago's tallest building, and the
103rd-floor Skydeck puts you high into the
heavens. Take the ear-popping, 70-second
elevator ride to the top and then step onto
one of the glass-floored ledges jutting out
into mid-air for a knee-buckling perspective straight down. On clear days the view
sweeps over four states. The entrance is
on Jackson Blvd. Queues can take up to
an hour on busy days (peak times are in
summer, between 11am and 4pm Friday
through Sunday).

Chicago Cultural
Center   Notable Building
(☎312-744-6630; www.chicagoculturalcenter.
org; 78 E Washington St; ☺10am-7pm Mon-Fri, to
5pm Sat & Sun; Ⓜ Brown, Orange, Green, Purple,
Pink Line to Washington/Wabash) **FREE** This

exquisite, beaux-arts building began its life
as the Chicago Public Library in 1897. Today
the block-long structure houses terrific art
exhibitions (especially the 4th-floor Yates
Gallery), as well as classical concerts at
lunchtime every Wednesday (12:15pm). It
also contains the world's largest Tiffany
stained-glass dome, on the 3rd floor where
the library circulation desk used to be.

InstaGreeter (www.chicagogreeter.com/insta-
greeter; 77 E Randolph St; ☺10am-3pm Fri & Sat,
11am-2pm Sun) tours of the Loop depart from
the Randolph St lobby, as do Millennium
Park tours. And it's all free!

Rookery   Architecture
(☎312-994-4000; www.flwright.org; 209 S
LaSalle St; ☺9am-5pm Mon-Fri; Ⓜ Brown,
Orange, Purple, Pink Line to Quincy) The famed
firm of Burnham and Root built the Rookery
– named for the site's previous building, a
temporary city hall that was popular with
roosting pigeons – in 1888; Frank Lloyd
Wright remodeled the two-story lobby
atrium 19 years later. It's renowned for its
contrast in styles: though it may look hulking and fortress-like outside, it's light and

Navy Pier

airy inside. You can walk in and look around for free. Tours ($10 to $15) are available weekdays at 11am, noon and 1pm.

◎ Near North

Navy Pier Waterfront
(📞312-595-7437; www.navypier.com; 600 E Grand Ave; ⊘10am-10pm Sun-Thu, to midnight Fri & Sat Jun-Aug, 10am-8pm Sun-Thu, to 10pm Fri & Sat Sep-May; 🚹; 🚌65) **FREE** Half-mile-long Navy Pier is one of Chicago's most-visited attractions, sporting a 196ft **Ferris wheel** (adult/child $18/15) and other carnival rides ($9 to $18 each), an **IMAX theater** (📞312-595-5629; www.amctheatres.com; 700 E Grand Aver; tickets $15-22), a beer garden and lots of chain restaurants. A renovation added public plazas, performance spaces and free cultural programming. Locals still groan over its commercialization, but its lakefront view and cool breezes can't be beat. The fireworks displays on summer Wednesdays (9:30pm) and Saturdays (10:15pm) are a treat too.

◎ Gold Coast

360° Chicago Observatory
(📞888-875-8439; www.360chicago.com; 875 N Michigan Ave, 94th fl; adult/child $22/15; ⊘9am-11pm, last tickets 10:30pm; Ⓜ️Red Line to Chicago) The views from the 94th-floor observatory of this iconic building (formerly known as the John Hancock Center) in many ways surpass those at the Willis Tower; there are informative displays and the 'Tilt' feature (floor-to-ceiling windows you stand in as they tip out over the ground), which costs $7.20 extra and is less exciting than it sounds. Or just shoot straight up to the 96th-floor **Signature Lounge** (www.signatureroom.com; ⊘11am-12:30am Sun-Thu, to 1:30am Fri & Sat), where the view is free if you buy a drink ($10 to $18).

Museum of Contemporary Art Museum

(MCA; 📞312-280-2660; www.mcachicago.org; 220 E Chicago Ave; adult/child $15/free; ⊘10am-9pm Tue & Fri, to 5pm Wed, Thu, Sat & Sun; Ⓜ️Red Line to Chicago) Consider it the Art Institute's

 Chicago for Children

For family-friendly events, see Chicago Kids (www.chicagokids.com). Top attractions include the following:

Chicago Children's Museum (📞312-527-1000; www.chicagochildrensmuseum.org; 700 E Grand Ave, Navy Pier; $15; ⊘10am-5pm, to 8pm Thu; 🚹; 🚌65) Designed to challenge the imaginations of toddlers to 10-year-olds, this colorful museum near Navy Pier's main entrance gives young visitors enough hands-on exhibits to keep them climbing and creating for hours. Among the favorites, Dinosaur Expedition explores the world of paleontology and lets kids excavate 'bones.' They can also climb a ropey schooner; get wet in Waterways (and learn about hydroelectric power); and use real tools to build things in the Tinkering Lab.

Maggie Daley Park (www.maggiedaleypark.com; 337 E Randolph St; ⊘6am-11pm; 🚹; Ⓜ️Brown, Orange, Green, Purple, Pink Line to Washington/Wabash) Families love this park's fanciful, free playgrounds in all their enchanted-forest and pirate-themed glory. There's also a rock-climbing wall, an 18-hole mini-golf course, a winding, in-line skating track called the Skating Ribbon (used for ice-skating in winter) and tennis courts; these features have various fees. Multiple picnic tables make the park an excellent spot to relax. It connects to Millennium Park via the pedestrian BP Bridge.

Maggie Daley Park
EVABAB/SHUTTERSTOCK ©

Downtown Chicago

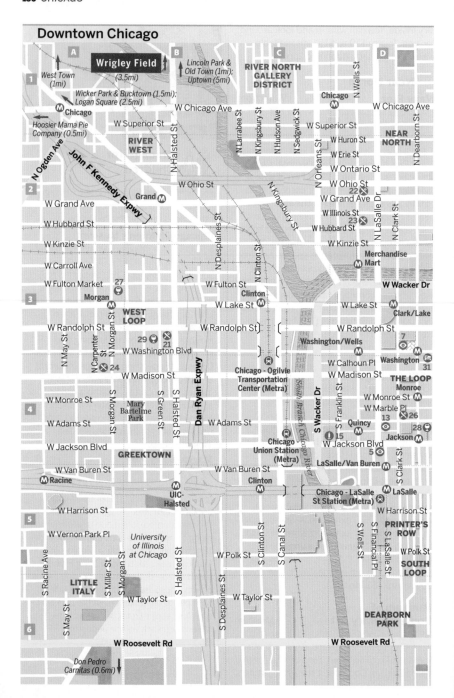

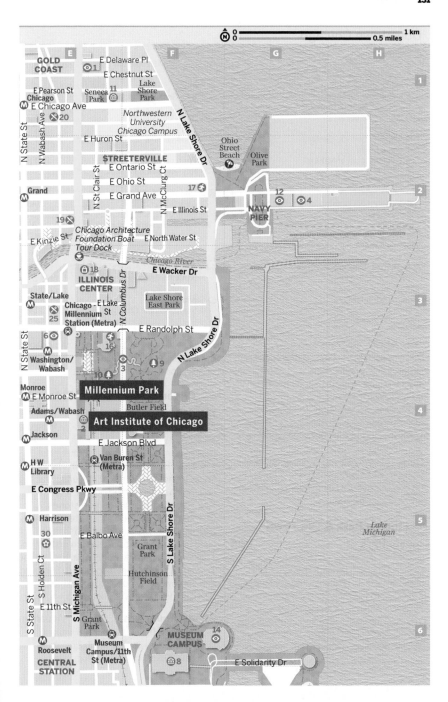

Downtown Chicago

brash, rebellious sibling, with especially strong minimalist, surrealist and conceptual photography collections, and permanent works by René Magritte, Cindy Sherman and Andy Warhol. Covering art from the 1920s onward, the MCA's collection spans the gamut, with displays arranged to blur the boundaries between painting, sculpture, video and other media. Exhibits change regularly so you never know what you'll see, but count on it being offbeat and provocative. Illinois residents get free admission on Tuesday.

◎ Lincoln Park & Old Town

Lincoln Park Park

(www.chicagoparkdistrict.com; ⊘6am-11pm; ▥; ▤22, 151, 156) The park that gave the neighborhood its name is Chicago's largest. Its 1200 acres stretch for 6 miles from North Ave north to Diversey Pkwy, where it narrows along the lake and continues on until the end of Lake Shore Dr. On sunny days locals come out to play in droves, taking advantage of the ponds, paths and

playing fields or visiting the zoo and beaches. It's a fine spot to while away a morning or afternoon (or both).

◎ Pilsen & Near South Side

**Field Museum of
Natural History** Museum

(☏312-922-9410; www.fieldmuseum.org; 1400 S Lake Shore Dr, Near South Side; adult/child $24/17; ⊘9am-5pm; ▥; ▤146, 130) The Field Museum houses some 30 million artifacts and includes everything but the kitchen sink – beetles, mummies, gemstones, Bushman the stuffed ape – all tended by a slew of PhD-wielding scientists, as the Field remains an active research institution. The collection's rock star is Sue, the largest *Tyrannosaurus rex* yet discovered. She even gets her own gift shop. Special exhibits, such as the 3-D movie, cost extra.

Shedd Aquarium Aquarium

(☏312-939-2438; www.sheddaquarium.org; 1200 S Lake Shore Dr, Near South Side; adult/child $40/30; ⊘9am-6pm Jun-Aug, 9am-5pm

Mon-Fri, to 6pm Sat & Sun Sep-May; 👶; 🚇146, 130) Top draws at the kiddie-mobbed Shedd Aquarium include the Wild Reef exhibit, where there's just 5in of Plexiglas between you and two-dozen fierce-looking sharks, and the Oceanarium, with its rescued sea otters. Note the Oceanarium also keeps beluga whales and Pacific white-sided dolphins, a practice that's increasingly frowned upon as captivity is stressful for these sensitive creatures.

🟢 ACTIVITIES

The flat, 18-mile Lakefront Trail is a beautiful route along the water, though on nice days it's jam-packed with runners and cyclists. It also connects the city's 26 beaches.

Bobby's Bike Hike   Cycling
(📞312-245-9300; www.bobbysbikehike.com; 540 N Lake Shore Dr, Streeterville; per hr/day from $8/27, tours $38-70; ⏰8:30am-8pm Mon-Fri, 8am-8pm Sat & Sun Jun-Aug, 9am-7pm Mar-May & Sep-Nov; Ⓜ Red Line to Grand) Locally based Bobby's earns rave reviews from riders. It rents bikes and has easy access to the Lakefront Trail (p133). It also offers cool tours of gangster sites, the lakefront, night-time vistas, and venues to indulge in pizza and beer. The Tike Hike caters to kids. Enter through the covered driveway to reach the shop. Call for winter hours.

Bike & Roll   Cycling
(📞312-729-1000; www.bikechicago.com; 239 E Randolph St; tours adult/child from $45/35; ⏰9am-7pm; Ⓜ Brown, Orange, Green, Purple, Pink Line to Washington/Wabash) Summer guided tours (adult/child from $45/35) cover themes such as lakefront parks, breweries and historic neighborhoods, or downtown's sights and fireworks at night (highly recommended). Prices include lock, helmet and map. Operates out of the McDonald's Cycle Center in Millennium Park; there's another branch on Navy Pier. It also rents out bikes for DIY explorations (per hour/day from $12.50/35).

🟢 TOURS

Chicago Architecture
Center Tours   Tours
(CAC; 📞312-922-3432; www.architecture.org; 111 E Wacker Dr; tours $20-55) Gold-standard boat tours ($47) sail from the **river dock** (Ⓜ Brown, Orange, Green, Purple, Pink Line to State/Lake) on the southeast side of the Michigan Ave Bridge. Also popular are the Historic Skyscrapers walking tours ($26) and tours exploring individual landmark buildings ($20). CAC sponsors bus, bike and L train tours, too. Buy tickets online or at the CAC's front desk; boat tickets can also be purchased at the dock.

🟢 SHOPPING

The main shopping vein is N Michigan Ave downtown, dubbed the Magnificent Mile and chock full of high-end, big-name retailers.

Chicago Architecture
Center Shop   Gifts & Souvenirs
(📞312-922-3432; http://shop.architecture.org; 111 E Wacker Dr; ⏰9am-5pm Mon, Wed & Fri-Sun, to 8pm Tue & Thu; 🚇151, Ⓜ Brown, Orange, Green, Purple, Pink Line to State/Lake) Browse through skyline T-shirts and posters, Frank Lloyd Wright note cards, skyscraper models and heaps of books that celebrate local architecture at this haven for anyone with an edifice complex; a children's section has books to pique the interest of budding builders. The items make excellent 'only in Chicago' souvenirs.

🟢 EATING

⚫ The Loop
Revival Food Hall   American $
(📞773-999-9411; www.revivalfoodhall.com; 125 S Clark St; mains $7-12; ⏰7am-7pm Mon-Fri; ; Ⓜ Blue Line to Monroe) The Loop needed a forward-thinking food court, and Revival Food Hall delivered. Come lunchtime, hip office workers pack the blond-wood tables of this ground-floor modern marketplace in the historic National building. The all-local

★ Top Five for Architecture

Chicago Architecture Center Tours (p133)

Willis Tower (p128)

Rookery (p128)

Chicago Cultural Center (p128)

360° Chicago (p129)

From left: Chicago Cultural Center (p128); Willis Tower (p128); 360° Chicago (p129)

dining concept brings 15 of Chicago's best fast-casual food outlets to the masses, from Antique Taco and Smoque BBQ to Furious Spoon ramen and HotChocolate Bakery.

Pastoral   Deli $

(☑312-658-1250; www.pastoralartisan.com; 53 E Lake St; sandwiches $8-11; ⊘10:30am-8pm Mon-Fri, 11am-6pm Sat & Sun; ☑; MBrown, Orange, Green, Purple, Pink Line to Randolph or State/Lake) Pastoral makes a mean sandwich. Fresh-shaved serrano ham, Calabrese salami and other carnivorous fixings meet smoky mozzarella, Gruyère and piquant spreads slathered on crusty baguettes. Vegetarians also have options. There's limited seating; most folks take away for picnics in Millennium Park (call in your order a few hours in advance to avoid a queue).

✪ Near North

Billy Goat Tavern   Burgers $

(☑312-222-1525; www.billygoattavern.com; 430 N Michigan Ave, lower level, Streeterville; burgers $4-8; ⊘6am-1am Mon-Thu, to 2am Fri, to 3am Sat, 9am-2am Sun; MRed Line to Grand) *Tribune* and *Sun Times* reporters have guzzled in the subterranean Billy Goat for decades. Order a 'cheezborger' and Schlitz beer, then look around at the newspapered walls to get the scoop on infamous local stories, such as the Cubs' Curse. This is a tourist magnet, but a deserving one. Follow the tavern signs leading below Michigan Ave to get here.

GT Fish & Oyster   Seafood $$

(☑312-929-3501; www.gtoyster.com; 531 N Wells St, River North; mains $17-30; ⊘5-10pm Mon-Thu, to 11pm Fri, 10am-2:30pm & 5-11pm Sat, 10am-2:30pm & 5-10pm Sun; MRed Line to Grand) Seafood restaurants can be fusty. Not so GT Fish & Oyster. The clean-lined room bustles with date-night couples and groups of friends drinking fizzy wines and slurping mollusks. Many of the dishes are shareable, which adds to the convivial, plate-clattering ambience. The sublime clam chowder arrives in a glass jar with housemade oyster crackers and bacon.

ALEX CIMBAL/SHUTTERSTOCK ©

🍴 Lincoln Park & Old Town

Alinea Gastronomy $$$
(📱312-867-0110; www.alinearestaurant.com;
1723 N Halsted St, Lincoln Park; 10-/16-course
menus from $205/290; ⏰5-10pm; Ⓜ Red Line
to North/Clybourn) One of the world's best
restaurants, the triple-Michelin-starred
Alinea purveys multiple courses of molecu-
lar gastronomy. Dishes may emanate from
a centrifuge or be pressed into a capsule,
à la duck served with a 'pillow of lavender
air.' There are no reservations; instead
Alinea sells tickets two to three months in
advance via its website. Check Twitter (@
Alinea) for last-minute seats.

🍴 Wicker Park & Bucktown

Irazu Latin American $
(📱773-252-5687; www.irazuchicago.com;
1865 N Milwaukee Ave, Bucktown; mains $7-16;
⏰11:30am-9:30pm Mon-Sat; 📷; Ⓜ Blue Line
to Western) Chicago's lone Costa Rican
eatery turns out burritos bursting with
chicken, black beans and fresh avocado,

and sandwiches dressed in a heavenly,
spicy-sweet vegetable sauce. Wash them
down with an *avena* (a slurpable milkshake
in tropical-fruit flavors). For breakfast, the
arroz con huevos (peppery eggs scrambled
into rice) relieves hangovers. Irazu is BYOB
with no corkage fee. Cash only.

Dove's Luncheonette Tex-Mex $$
(📱773-645-4060; www.doveschicago.com;
1545 N Damen Ave, Wicker Park; mains $13-22;
⏰9am-10pm Mon-Thu, to 11pm Fri, 8am-11pm
Sat, to 10pm Sun; Ⓜ Blue Line to Damen) Sit
at the retro counter for Tex-Mex plates of
pork-shoulder posole and buttermilk fried
chicken with chorizo-verde gravy. Dessert?
It's pie, of course – maybe horchata, lemon
cream or peach jalapeño, baked by **Hoosier
Mama** (📱312-243-4846; www.hoosiermamapie.
com; 1618 W Chicago Ave, East Village; slices $5-
6; ⏰8am-7pm Tue-Fri, 9am-5pm Sat, 10am-4pm
Sun; 🚌66, Ⓜ Blue Line to Chicago). Soul music
spins on a record player, tequila flows from
the 70 bottles rattling behind the bar, and
presto: all is right in the world.

🍴 Deep-Dish Pizza Icons

Lou Malnati's (📞312-828-9800; www.loumalnatis.com; 439 N Wells St, River North; small pizzas from $13; ⏰11am-11pm Sun-Thu, to midnight Fri & Sat; Ⓜ️Brown, Purple Line to Merchandise Mart) It's a matter of dispute, but some say Malnati is the innovator of Chicago's deep-dish pizza (Lou's father Rudy was a cook at Pizzeria Uno, which also lays claim to the title). Malnati's certainly concocted the unique 'butter-crust' and the 'sausage crust' to cradle its tangy toppings.

Pequod's Pizza (📞773-327-1512; www.pequodspizza.com; 2207 N Clybourn Ave, Lincoln Park; small pizzas from $12; ⏰11am-2am Mon-Sat, to midnight Sun; 🚌9 to Webster) Like the ship in *Moby Dick* from which this neighborhood restaurant takes its name, Pequod's pan-style (akin to deep-dish) pizza is a thing of legend – head and shoulders above chain competitors for its caramelized cheese, generous toppings and sweetly flavored sauce. Neon beer signs glow from the walls, and Blackhawks jerseys hang from the ceiling in the affably rugged interior.

Giordano's (📞312-951-0747; www.giordanos.com; 730 N Rush St, River North; small pizzas from $18; ⏰11am-11pm Sun-Thu, to midnight Fri & Sat; Ⓜ️Red Line to Chicago) Giordano's makes 'stuffed' pizza, a bigger, doughier version of deep dish. It's awesome. If you want a slice of heaven, order the 'special,' a stuffed pie containing sausage, mushroom, green pepper and onions.

🔵 West Loop

Monteverde Italian $$

(📞312-888-3041; www.monteverdechicago.com; 1020 W Madison St, West Loop; mains $18-24; ⏰5-10:30pm Tue-Fri, 11:30am-10:30pm Sat, 11:30am-9pm Sun; Ⓜ️Green, Pink Line to Morgan) Housemade pastas are the specialty here. They seem simple in concept, such as the *cacio whey pepe* (small tube pasta with pecorino Romano, ricotta whey and four-peppercorn blend), but the flavors are lusciously complex. That's why the light-wood tables in the lively room are always packed. Reserve ahead, especially for weekends, or try the bar or patio for walk-in seats.

Girl & the Goat American $$$

(📞312-492-6262; www.girlandthegoat.com; 809 W Randolph St, West Loop; small plates $12-19; ⏰4:30-11pm Sun-Thu, to midnight Fri & Sat; 📞; Ⓜ️Green, Pink Line to Morgan) ✔ Stephanie Izard's flagship restaurant rocks. The soaring ceilings, polished wood tables and cartoon-y art on the walls offer a convivial atmosphere where local beer and house-made wine hit the tables, along with unique small plates such as catfish with pickled persimmons. Reservations are difficult; try for walk-in seats before 5pm or see if anything opens up at the bar.

🔵 Pilsen & Near South Side

Don Pedro Carnitas Mexican $

(1113 W 18th St, Pilsen; tacos $2.50; ⏰6am-6pm Mon-Thu, 5am-5pm Fri-Sun; Ⓜ️Pink Line to 18th St) At this no-frills meat den, a man with a machete salutes you at the front counter. He awaits your command to hack off pork pieces and then wraps the thick chunks with onion and cilantro in a warm tortilla. You then devour the tacos at the tables in back. Goat stew and tripe add to the carnivorous menu. Cash only.

ILANA MATASHA/STOCKIMO/ALAMY ©

Berghoff beer flight

🍸 DRINKING & NIGHTLIFE

🍺 The Loop

Berghoff   Bar

(📞312-427-3170; www.theberghoff.com; 17 W
Adams St; 🕐11am-9pm Mon-Fri, from 11:30am
Sat; Ⓜ️Blue, Red Line to Jackson) The Berghoff
dates from 1898 and was the first Chicago
bar to serve a legal drink after Prohibition
(ask to see the liquor license stamped '#1').
Little has changed around the antique
wood bar since. Belly up for mugs of local
and imported beers and order sauerbraten,
schnitzel and pretzels the size of your head
from the adjoining German restaurant.

🍺 Lincoln Park & Old Town

Old Town Ale House   Bar

(📞312-944-7020; www.theoldtownalehouse.com;
219 W North Ave, Old Town; 🕐3pm-4am Mon-Fri,
noon-5am Sat, to-4am Sun; Ⓜ️Brown, Purple
Line to Sedgwick) Located near the Second
City (p138) comedy club and the scene of
late-night musings since the 1960s, this
unpretentious neighborhood favorite lets
you mingle with beautiful people and griz-
zled regulars, seated pint by pint under the
paintings of nude politicians (just go with
it). Classic jazz on the jukebox provides the
soundtrack for the jovial goings-on. Cash
only.

🍺 Wicker Park & Bucktown

Violet Hour   Cocktail Bar

(📞773-252-1500; www.theviolethour.com; 1520 N
Damen Ave, Wicker Park; 🕐6pm-2am Sun-Fri, to
3am Sat; Ⓜ️Blue Line to Damen) This nouveau
speakeasy isn't marked, so look for the
wood-paneled building with a full mural and
a yellow light over the door. Inside, high-
backed booths, chandeliers and long velvet
drapes provide the backdrop to elaborate-
ly engineered, award-winning seasonal
cocktails with droll names. As highbrow as
it sounds, friendly staff make Violet Hour
welcoming and accessible.

🍺 West Loop

RM Champagne Salon   Wine Bar

(📞312-243-1199; www.rmchampagnesalon.
com; 116 N Green St; 🕐5pm-midnight Mon-Wed
& Sun, to 2am Thu-Sat, plus 11am-2pm Sat &

Sun; Ⓜ Green, Pink Line to Morgan) This West Loop spot is a twinkling-light charmer for bubbles. Score a table in the cobblestoned courtyard and you'll feel transported to Paris. In winter, the indoor fireplace and plush seats provide a toasty refuge.

Aviary   Cocktail Bar

(www.theaviary.com; 955 W Fulton Market; ☺ 5pm-midnight Sun-Wed, to 2am Thu-Sat; Ⓜ Green, Pink Line to Morgan) The Aviary is a James Beard Award winner for best cocktails in the nation. The ethereal drinks are like nothing you've laid lips on before. Some arrive with Bunsen burners, others with a slingshot you use to break the ice. They taste terrific, whatever the science involved. It's wise to make reservations online. Drinks range between $21 and $29 each.

⭐ ENTERTAINMENT

Hot Tix (www.hottix.org) sells same-week drama, comedy and performing-arts tickets for half price (plus a $5 to $10 service charge). Book online or at the two Hot Tix outlets in the Loop. Check the Chicago Reader (www.chicagoreader.com) for listings.

Second City   Comedy

(☏ 312-337-3992; www.secondcity.com; 1616 N Wells St, Lincoln Park; tickets $35-55; Ⓜ Brown, Purple Line to Sedgwick) Bill Murray, Stephen Colbert, Tina Fey and more honed their wit at this slick venue with nightly shows. The Mainstage and ETC stage host sketch revues (with an improv scene thrown in); they're similar in price and quality. If you turn up around 10pm Monday through Thursday (or 1am Saturday or 9pm Sunday) you can watch a free improv set.

Hideout   Live Music

(☏ 773-227-4433; www.hideoutchicago.com; 1354 W Wabansia Ave, West Town; tickets $5-15; ☺ 4pm-midnight Mon-Thu, to 2am Fri, 6pm-3am Sat, hours vary Sun; 🚍 72) Hidden behind a factory past the edge of Bucktown, this two-room lodge of indie rock and alt-country is well worth seeking out. The owners

Jazz at the Green Mill

have nursed an outsider, underground vibe, and the place feels like your grandma's rumpus room. Music and other events (talk shows, literary readings, comedy etc) take place nightly. On Mondays at 9:30pm there's a great open-mike **poetry night** (www.facebook.com/WeedsPoetry;; by donation).

Buddy Guy's Legends Blues
(✆312-427-1190; www.buddyguy.com; 700 S Wabash Ave; cover charge Sun-Thu $10, Fri & Sat $20; ⏰5pm-2am Mon & Tue, from 11am Wed-Fri, noon-3am Sat, noon-2am Sun; Ⓜ Red Line to Harrison) Top local and national acts wail on the stage of local icon Buddy Guy. The man himself usually plays a series of shows in January; tickets go on sale in October. Free, all-ages acoustic shows are staged at lunch and dinner (the place doubles as a Cajun restaurant); note that you must pay to stay on for late-evening shows.

Green Mill Jazz
(✆773-878-5552; www.greenmilljazz.com; 4802 N Broadway, Uptown; ⏰noon-4am Mon-Fri, to 5am Sat, 11am-4am Sun; Ⓜ Red Line to Lawrence) The timeless – and notorious – Green Mill was Al Capone's favorite speakeasy (a trap door behind the bar accessed tunnels for running booze and escaping the feds). Sit in one of the curved booths and feel his ghost urging you on to another martini. Local and national jazz artists perform nightly; on Sunday is the nationally acclaimed **poetry slam** (www.greenmilljazz.com; 4802 N Broadway, Uptown; cover charge $7; ⏰7-10pm Sun; Ⓜ Red Line to Lawrence). Cash only.

Steppenwolf Theatre Theater
(✆312-335-1650; www.steppenwolf.org; 1650 N Halsted St, Lincoln Park; ⏰box office 11am-6:30pm Tue-Sat, from 1pm Sun; Ⓜ Red Line to North/Clybourn) Steppenwolf is Chicago's top stage for quality, provocative theater productions. The Hollywood-heavy ensemble includes Gary Sinise, John Malkovich, Martha Plimpton, Gary Cole, Joan Allen and Tracy Letts. A money-saving tip: the box office releases 20 tickets for $20 for each day's shows; they go on sale at 11am

🍽 Foodie Trip to Logan Square

Logan Square is the city's inventive foodie mecca, the neighborhood to go to for creative fare in casual digs. It's a 20-minute ride from downtown via the Blue Line L train. Hot spots:

Giant (✆773-252-0997; www.giantrestaurant.com; 3209 W Armitage Ave; small plates $14-19; ⏰5-10:30pm Tue-Sat; 🚌73) This wee storefront eatery produces huge flavors in its heady comfort food. Dishes like the king-crab tagliatelle, biscuits with jalapeño butter and sweet-and-sour eggplant have wowed the foodie masses, and rightfully so. The small plate portions mean you'll need to order a few dishes to make a meal. Well-matched cocktails and wine add luster to the spread. Reserve ahead.

Revolution Brewing (✆773-227-2739; www.revbrew.com; 2323 N Milwaukee Ave; ⏰11am-1am Mon-Fri, to 1am Sat, 10am-11pm Sun; Ⓜ Blue Line to California) Raise your fist to Revolution, an industrial-chic brewpub that fills glasses with heady beers such as the Eugene porter and Anti-Hero IPA. The brewmaster here led the way for Chicago's huge craft beer scene, and his suds are top-notch. Haute pub grub includes a pork belly and egg sandwich and bacon-fat popcorn with fried sage.

Tuesday to Saturday and at 1pm Sunday, and are available by phone.

Detour: Hyde Park

Hyde Park sits on Chicago's south side and holds a couple of top sights.

Museum of Science & Industry (MSI; ✆773-684-1414; www.msichicago.org; 5700 S Lake Shore Dr; adult/child $22/13; ⊗9:30am-5:30pm Jun-Aug, shorter hours Sep-May; 🚻; 🚌6 or 10, Ⓜ Metra Electric Line to 55th-56th-57th St) Geek out at the largest science museum in the Western Hemisphere. Highlights include a WWII German U-boat nestled in an underground display (adult/child $18/14 extra to tour it) and the Science Storms exhibit with a mock tornado and tsunami. Other popular exhibits include the baby chick hatchery, the minuscule furnishings in Colleen Moore's fairy castle and the life-size shaft of a coal mine (adult/child $12/9 extra to descend its workings).

Robie House (✆312-994-4000; www.flwright.org; 5757 S Woodlawn Ave; adult/child $18/15; ⊗10:30am-3pm Thu-Mon; 🚌6, Ⓜ Metra Electric Line to 59th St) Of the numerous buildings that Frank Lloyd Wright designed around Chicago, none is more famous or influential than Robie House. Because its horizontal lines resembled the flat landscape of the Midwestern prairie, the style became known as the Prairie style. Inside are 174 stained-glass windows and doors, which you'll see on the hour-long tours (frequency varies by season, but there's usually at least one tour per hour). Advance tickets are highly recommended.

Frederick C Robie House, 1910

ℹ INFORMATION

Choose Chicago (www.choosechicago.com) is the city's official tourism site, with loads of information online.

ℹ GETTING THERE & AROUND

TO/FROM THE AIRPORT

O'Hare International Airport (ORD; ✆800-832-6352; www.flychicago.com/ohare; 10000 W O'Hare Ave) Located 17 miles northwest of the Loop.

○ **Train** The Blue Line L train ($5) runs 24/7 and departs every 10 minutes or so. The journey to the city center takes 40 minutes.

○ **Shuttle** The GO Airport Express (www.airportexpress.com) shared-van service goes downtown for $35 per person. Vans run between 4am and 11:30pm, departing every 15 minutes. It takes an hour or more, depending on traffic.

○ **Taxi** Rides to the center take 30 minutes and cost around $50. Taxi queues can be lengthy, and the ride can take longer than the train, depending on traffic.

Midway International Airport (MDW; ✆773-838-0600; www.flychicago.com/midway; 5700 S Cicero Ave, Clearing) Located 11 miles southwest of the Loop.

○ **Train** The Orange Line L train ($3) runs between 4am and 1am, departing every 10 minutes or so. The journey takes 30 minutes to downtown.

○ **Shuttle** The GO Airport Express (www.airportexpress.com) door-to-door shuttle goes downtown for $28. Vans run between 4am and 10:30pm. The journey takes approximately 50 minutes.

○ **Taxi** Rides to the center take 20 minutes or longer (depending on traffic) and cost $35 to $40.

BICYCLE

Divvy (www.divvybikes.com) has some 5800 sky-blue bikes at 580 stations around Chicago. The $15 day pass allows unlimited rides in a 24-hour period, up to three hours each. Or opt for a $3 single-ride pass for 30 minutes. Both are available for purchase at station kiosks or via the Divvy app.

Bike rentals for longer rides (with accoutrements such as helmets and locks) start at around $8 per hour. Try Bike & Roll (p133) or Bobby's Bike Hike (p133).

CAR & MOTORCYCLE

Downtown garages cost about $40 per day. On-street, metered parking costs from $2 per hour (in outlying areas) to $6.50 per hour (in the Loop).

PUBLIC TRANSPORTATION

The **Chicago Transit Authority** (www.transit chicago.com) runs the transport system.

○ The L (a system of elevated and subway trains) is the main way to get around. Red and Blue Lines operate 24/7, others between 4am to 1am.

○ The standard fare is $3 (except from O'Hare airport, where it costs $5) and includes two transfers. Enter the turnstile using a Ventra Ticket, which is sold from vending machines at train stations.

○ You can also buy a Ventra Card, aka a rechargeable fare card, at stations. It has a one-time $5 fee that gets refunded once you register the card. It knocks around 75¢ off the cost of each ride.

○ Unlimited ride passes (one/three days $10/20) are another handy option.

○ Buses cover areas that the L misses. Most run at least from early morning until 10pm; some go later. Some don't run on weekends.

TAXI & RIDESHARE

Taxis are plentiful in the Loop, north to Lake View and northwest to Wicker Park/Bucktown. Fares are meter-based and start at $3.25 when you get into the cab, then it's $2.25 per mile. Try **Checker Taxi** (📞312-243-2537; www.checkertax-ichicago.com). The ridesharing companies Uber, Lyft and Via are also popular in Chicago.

TRAIN

Union Station (www.chicagounionstation.com; 225 S Canal St; Ⓜ Blue Line to Clinton) is the city's rail hub, located at the Loop's western edge. For public transportation onward, the Blue Line Clinton stop is a few blocks south (though not a good option at night). The Brown, Orange, Purple and Pink Line station at Quincy is about a half-mile east.

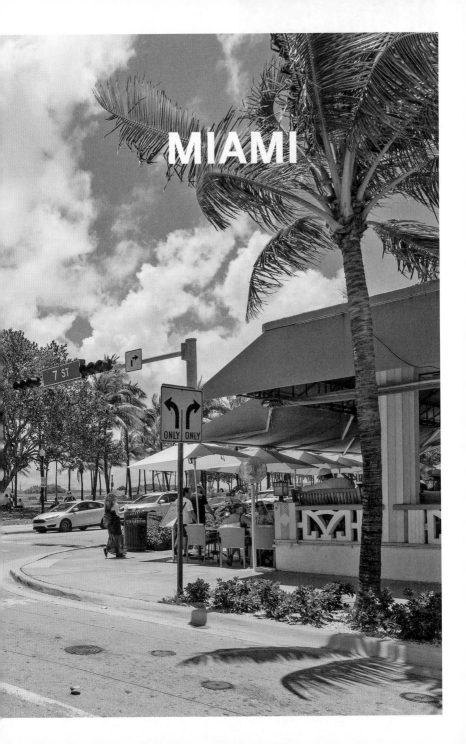

In This Chapter

Miami at a Glance...

Miami has so many different facets to its diverse neighborhoods that it's hard to believe it all fits in one place. By day you can admire incredible murals in Wynwood, then spend the evening immersed in Afro Cuban jazz in Little Havana, followed by rooftop drinks atop the city's latest skyscraper. Crossing town you can't help feeling like you've passed into another city. Over in Miami Beach, you can endlessly wander around deco masterpieces, each one bursting with personality – best followed by late-afternoon strolls along the sands, when the golden light is mesmerizing.

Two Days in Miami

Start your trip with a tour around the Miami Beach deco district with the **Design Preservation League** (p160), and consider a visit to the **Wolfsonian-FIU** (p149) and **New World Center** (p152). On your second day, head to downtown Miami and take in the **Pérez Art Museum** (p153) and **HistoryMiami** (p155), as well as **Bayfront Park** (p155).

Four Days in Miami

On your third day, go to Little Havana and watch the locals slap dominoes at **Máximo Gómez Park** (p157). Then go to Wynwood to peruse galleries and dine like royalty at **Alter** (p164) or **Kyu** (p164). On day four, witness the full opulent fantasy of Miami at sites such as the **Vizcaya Museum** (p158) and the **Biltmore Hotel** (p157), or head out to **Key Biscayne** (p150) for a nature fix.

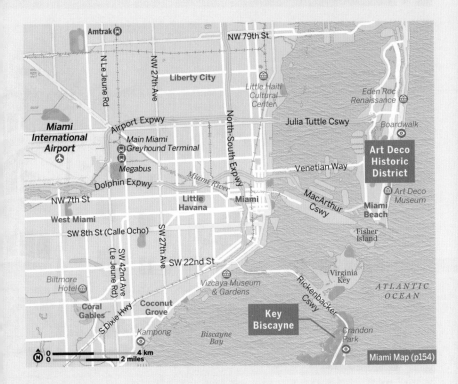

Map labels:
Amtrak · NW 79th St · N Le Jeune Rd · NW 27th Ave · Liberty City · Little Haiti Cultural Center · Eden Roc Renaissance · Miami International Airport · Airport Expwy · Main Miami Greyhound Terminal · North-South Expwy · Julia Tuttle Cswy · Boardwalk · Art Deco Historic District · Megabus · Venetian Way · Dolphin Expwy · Miami River · Art Deco Museum · NW 7th St · Little Havana · Miami · MacArthur Cswy · Miami Beach · West Miami · Fisher Island · SW 8th St (Calle Ocho) · SW 42nd Ave (Le Jeune Rd) · SW 27th Ave · SW 22nd St · Virginia Key · ATLANTIC OCEAN · Biltmore Hotel · Vizcaya Museum & Gardens · Rickenbacker Cswy · Coral Gables · S Dixie Hwy · Coconut Grove · **Key Biscayne** · Kampong · Biscayne Bay · Crandon Park

0 — 4 km / 0 — 2 miles

Miami Map (p154)

Arriving in Miami

Miami International Airport Flat-rate taxis go to Downtown ($22, 25 minutes) and South Beach ($35, 40 minutes); shared SuperShuttle vans make the trip for $17 to $22. The Miami Beach Airport Express 150 bus ($2.25) stops all along Miami Beach.

Fort Lauderdale-Hollywood International Airport GO Airport Shuttle runs shared vans to Miami (around $25). A taxi costs around $75.

Where to Stay

South Beach has all the name recognition with boutique hotels set in lovely art-deco buildings, but there are plenty of other options, from Downtown high-rises with sweeping views and endless amenities to historic charmers in Coral Gables and Coconut Grove to modern beauties along Biscayne Blvd.

Art Deco Historic District

The world-famous Art Deco Historic District of Miami Beach is pure exuberance: architecture of bold lines, whimsical tropical motifs and a color palette that evokes all the beauty of the Miami landscape.

Great For...

☑ Don't Miss

Strolling the 700 block of Ocean Dr at night to soak up the best of the deco neon.

Among the 800 deco buildings listed on the National Register of Historic Places, each design is different, and it's hard not to be captivated when strolling among these restored beauties from a bygone era.

Background

For much of its history, Miami Beach was little more than an empty landscape of swaying palm trees, scrubland and sandy shoreline. It wasn't until the early 20th century that a few entrepreneurs began to envision transforming the island into a resort. Beginning in the 1920s, a few hotels rose up, catering to an elite crowd of wealthy industrialists vacationing from the north. And then disaster struck. In 1926 a hurricane left a devastating swath across the island and much of South Florida.

Ocean Drive

FRANCISCO BLANCO/SHUTTERSTOCK ©

18th St

Lincoln Rd Mall

Art Deco ⊙
Historic District

Collins Ave
Ocean Dr

13th St

Biscayne
Bay

⊙ Need to Know

Many of the best deco buildings can be found between 11th and 14th Sts.

✕ Take a Break

Have your deco-district meal in the 11th St Diner (p162), set in a 1940s train car.

★ Top Tip

Miami Design Preservation League (p160) runs excellent walking tours of the deco district.

When it was time to rebuild, Miami Beach would undergo a dramatic rebirth. This is where art deco enters from stage left. As luck would have it, at exactly that moment, a bold new style of architecture was all the talk in America, having burst onto the scene at a renowned fair known as the Exposition Internationale des Arts Décoratifs et Industriels Modernes held in Paris in 1925.

Over the next few years developers arrived in droves, and the building boom was on. Miami Beach would become the epicenter of this groundbreaking new design (which incidentally was not called 'art deco' in those days, but simply 'art moderne' or 'modernistic'). Hundreds of new hotels were built during the 1930s to accommodate the influx of middle-class tourists flooding into Miami Beach for a

slice of sand and sun. And the golden era of deco architecture continued until it all came to an end during WWII.

Deco Style

The art-deco building style was very much rooted in the times. The late 1920s and 1930s was an era of invention – of new automobiles, streamlined machines, radio antennae and cruise ships. Architects manifested these elements in the strong vertical and horizontal lines, at times coupled with zigzags or sleek curves, all of which created the illusion of movement, of the bold forward march into the future.

In Miami Beach architects also incorporated more local motifs such as palm trees, flamingos and tropical plants. Nautical themes also appeared, with playful representations of ocean waves, sea horses, starfish and lighthouses. The style later became known as tropical deco.

Architects also came up with unique solutions to the challenges of building design in a hot, sun-drenched climate. Eyebrow-like ledges jutted over the windows, providing shade (and cooler inside temperatures), without obstructing the views. And thick glass blocks were incorporated into some building facades. These let in light while keeping out the heat – essential design elements in those days before air-conditioning.

The Best of Ocean Drive

One stretch of Ocean Dr has a collection of some of the most striking art-deco buildings in Miami Beach. Between 11th and 14th Sts, you'll see many of the classic deco elements at play in beautifully designed works – each bursting with individual personality. Close to 11th St, the **Congress Hotel** (1052 Ocean Dr) shows perfect symmetry in its three-story facade, with window-shading 'eyebrows' and a long marquee down the middle that's reminiscent of the grand movie palaces of the 1930s.

About a block north, the **Tides** (1220 Ocean Dr) is one of the finest of the nautical-themed hotels, with porthole windows over the entryway, a reception desk of Key limestone (itself imprinted with fossilized sea creatures), and curious arrows on the floor, meant to denote the ebb and flow of the tide (it's being reconstructed after hurricane Irma).

Near 13th St, the **Carlyle** (1250 Ocean Dr) comes with futuristic styling, triple parapets and a *Jetsons* vibe. Nearby the **Cavalier** (305-673-1199; www.cavaliersouth-beach.com; 1320 Ocean Dr) plays with the seahorse theme, in stylized depictions of the sea creatures and also has palm-tree-like iconography.

The art deco Carlyle on Ocean Drive

Art Deco Museum

This small **museum** (📞305-672-2014; www.
mdpl.org; 1001 Ocean Dr; ⊙10am-5pm Tue-Sun)
`FREE` is one of the best places in town for
an enlightening overview of the art-deco
district. Through videos, photography,
models and other displays you'll learn of
the pioneering work of Barbara Capitman,
who helped save these buildings from
certain destruction back in the 1970s, and
her collaboration with Leonard Horowitz,
the talented artist who designed the pastel
color palette that is an integral part of the
design visible today.

★ **Did You Know?**

The Birdcage, a 1996 comedy, was
filmed at the Carlyle.

LAZYLLAMA/SHUTTERSTOCK ©

The museum also touches on other key
architectural styles in Miami, including
Mediterranean Revival – typified by the **Villa Casa Casuarina** (📞786-485-2200; www.
vmmiamibeach.com; 1116 Ocean Dr) – and the
post-deco boom of MiMo (Miami Modern),
which emerged after WWII, and is particularly prevalent in North Miami Beach.

Wolfsonian-FIU

The imposing **Wolfsonian-FIU** (📞305-531-
1001; www.wolfsonian.org; 1001 Washington Ave;
adult/child $12/8, 6-9pm Fri free; ⊙10am-6pm
Mon, Tue, Thu & Sat, to 9pm Fri, noon-6pm Sun,
closed Wed), formerly the Washington Storage Company, is now an excellent design
museum. Wealthy snowbirds of the 1930s
stashed their pricey belongings here before
heading back up north. Visit early in your
stay to put the aesthetics of Miami Beach
into context. It's one thing to see how
wealth, leisure and the pursuit of beauty
manifests in Miami Beach, but it's another
to understand the roots and shadings of
local artistic movements. By chronicling
the interior evolution of everyday life, the
Wolfsonian reveals how these trends manifested architecturally in SoBe's exterior
deco.

Don't forget to take a look at the
Wolfsonian's own noteworthy architectural
features with its Gothic-futurist angles and
lion-head-studded grand elevator.

☑ **Don't Miss**

The **Art Deco Weekend** (www.art-
decoweekend.com; Ocean Dr, btwn 1st & 23rd
Sts; ⊙mid-Jan) features guided tours,
concerts, classic-auto shows, sidewalk
cafes, arts and antiques.

Key Biscayne

Key Biscayne is an easy getaway from Downtown Miami. But once you're here, you'll feel like you've been transported to a far-off tropical realm, with magnificent beaches, lush nature trails in state parks, and aquatic adventures aplenty.

Great For...

☑ Don't Miss

Join one of the monthly full-moon evening kayaking adventures offered by Virginia Key Outdoor Center (p159).

Start early in the day for the drive or bike ride out to this picturesque landscape, roughly 5 miles southeast of Downtown Miami (a 10-minute drive). Heading out along the Rickenbacker Causeway leads first to small Virginia Key, which has a few worthwhile sights – tiny beaches, a small mountain-bike park and pretty spots for kayaking.

The road continues to Key Biscayne, an island that's just 7 miles long with unrivaled views of the Miami skyline. As you pass over the causeway, note the small public beaches, picnic areas and fishing spots arranged on its margins.

Crandon Park

This 1200-acre **park** (☎305-365-2320; www.miamidade.gov/parks/crandon.asp; 6747 Crandon Blvd; per car weekday/weekend $5/7;

Crandon Park Beach

FOTOLUMINATE LLC/SHUTTERSTOCK ©

Miami ●

ATLANTIC OCEAN

Key Biscayne

🛈 Need to Know

Crandon Blvd is Key Biscayne's only real main road.

✕ Take a Break

There are several good places to dine in Bill Baggs state park, including **Boater's Grill** (🖉305-361-0080; www.boatersgrill. com; 1200 S Crandon Blvd, Bill Baggs Cape Florida State Park; mains $14-41; ⊘9am-8:30pm Sun-Wed, to 10pm Thu-Sat).

★ Top Tip

The area gets busy on the weekends. To escape the crowds, come on a weekday.

⊘sunrise-sunset; ℗🧒🏖) boasts Crandon Park Beach, a glorious stretch of sand that spreads for 2 miles. Much of the park consists of a dense coastal hammock (hardwood forest) and mangrove swamps. The beach here is clean and uncluttered by tourists, faces a lovely sweep of teal goodness and is regularly named one of the best beaches in the USA. Pretty cabanas at the south end of the park can be rented by the day ($40).

Bill Baggs Cape Florida State Park

If you don't make it to the Florida Keys, come to this **park** (🖉786-582-2673; www. floridastateparks.org/capeflorida; 1200 S Crandon Blvd; per car/person $8/2; ⊘8am-sunset, lighthouse 9am-5pm; ℗🧒🏖) ✿ for a taste of their unique island ecosystems. The 494-

acre space is a tangled clot of tropical fauna and dark mangroves, all interconnected by sandy trails and wooden boardwalks, and surrounded by miles of pale ocean. A concession shack rents out kayaks, bikes, in-line skates, beach chairs and umbrellas.

At the state recreation area's southernmost tip, the 1845 brick Cape Florida Lighthouse is the oldest structure in Florida (it replaced another lighthouse that was severely damaged in 1836 during the Second Seminole War). Free tours run at 10am and 1pm Thursday to Monday.

Water Sports

One of the best reasons to visit this tropical hot spot is to get out on the water, whether on a kayak, stand up paddle board or sailboat. With special guided excursions out here, it pays to plan ahead. Be sure to check out if Virginia Key Outdoor Center (p159) has any trips planned while you're in the area.

SIGHTS

Miami's major sights aren't concentrated in one neighborhood. The most frequently visited area is South Beach, home to hot nightlife, beautiful beaches and art-deco hotels, but you'll find historic sites and museums in the Downtown area, street art in Wynwood and galleries in the Design District, old-fashioned hotels and eateries in Mid-Beach (in Miami Beach), more beaches on Key Biscayne, and peaceful neighborhood attractions in Coral Gables and Coconut Grove.

◎ South Beach

South Beach   Beach
(Ocean Dr; ⊙5am-midnight) When most people think of Miami Beach, they're envisioning South Beach (SoBe). This area is rife with clubs, bars, restaurants, models and a distinctive veneer of art deco architecture. The beach itself encompasses a lovely stretch of golden sands, dotted with colorful deco-style lifeguard stations. The shore gathers a wide mix of humanity, including suntanned locals and plenty of tourists, and gets crowded in high season (December to March) and on weekends when the weather is warm.

New World Center   Notable Building
(⊡305-680-5866, tours 305-428-6776; www.nws.edu/new-world-center; 500 17th St; tours $5; ⊙tours 4pm Tue & Thu, 1pm Fri, 3pm Sat) Designed by Frank Gehry, this performance hall rises majestically out of a manicured lawn just above Lincoln Rd. Not unlike the ethereal power of the music within, the glass-and-steel facade encases characteristically Gehry-esque sail-like shapes within that help create the magnificent acoustics and add to the futuristic quality of the concert hall. The grounds form a 2.5-acre public park aptly known as SoundScape Park.

SoundScape Park   Park
(www.nws.edu; 500 17th St) Outside of the New World Center, this park is one of the best places for open-air screenings in Miami Beach. During some New World Symphony performances, the outside wall of the Frank Gehry–designed concert hall features a 7000-sq-ft projection of the concert within.

Bring a picnic and enjoy the free show. In addition, there are free once-monthly yoga sessions on the lawns. Check the website for dates.

World Erotic Art Museum   Museum
(⊡305-532-9336; www.weam.com; 1205 Washington Ave; over 18yr $15; ⊙11am-10pm Mon-Thu, to midnight Fri-Sun) The World Erotic Art Museum celebrates its staggering but artful erotica collection, including pieces by Rembrandt and Picasso. Back in 2005, 70-year-old Naomi Wilzig turned her 5000-piece collection into a South Beach attraction.

Miami Beach Botanical Garden   Gardens
(www.mbgarden.org; 2000 Convention Center Dr; suggested donation $2; ⊙9am-5pm Tue-Sat) This lush but little-known 2.6 acres of plantings is operated by the Miami Beach Garden Conservancy, and is a veritable green haven in the midst of the urban jungle – an oasis of palm trees, flowering hibiscus trees and glassy ponds. It's a great spot for a picnic.

◎ North Beach

Oleta River State Park   State Park
(⊡305-919-1844; www.floridastateparks.org/oletariver; 3400 NE 163rd St; vehicle/pedestrian & bicycle $6/2; ⊙8am-sunset; P🖐) Tequesta people were boating the Oleta River estuary as early as 500 BC, so you're following a long tradition if you canoe or kayak in this park. At almost 1000 acres, this is the largest urban park in the state and one of the best places in Miami to escape the madding crowd. Boat out to the local mangrove island, watch the eagles fly by, or just chill on the pretension-free beach.

Boardwalk   Beach
(www.miamibeachboardwalk.com; 21st St–46th St) Posing is what many people do best

in Miami, and there are plenty of skimpily dressed hotties on the Mid-Beach board-walk, but there are also middle-class folks, who walk their dogs and play with their kids here, giving the entire place a laid-back, real-world vibe that contrasts with the nonstop glamour of South Beach.

Eden Roc Renaissance
Historic Building

(www.nobuedenroc.com; 4525 Collins Ave) The Eden Roc was the second groundbreaking resort from Morris Lapidus, and it's a fine example of the architecture known as MiMo (Miami Modern). It was the hangout for the 1960s Rat Pack – Sammy Davis Jr, Dean Martin, Frank Sinatra and crew. Extensive renovation has eclipsed some of Lapidus' style, but with that said, the building is still an iconic piece of Miami Beach architecture, and an exemplar of the brash beauty of Millionaire's Row.

Haulover Beach Park
Park

(☑305-947-3525; www.miamidade.gov/parks/haulover.asp; 10800 Collins Ave; per car Mon-Fri $5, Sat & Sun $7; ☺sunrise-sunset; ℗) Speedos are optional at this 40-acre beach park hidden behind vegetation from the sight of condos, highways and prying passers-by. You don't have to get into your birthday suit if you don't fancy it; however, most of the beach is clothed and there's even a dog park. It is one of the nicer spots for sand in the area. It's on Collins Ave about 4.5 miles north of 71st St.

◎ Downtown Miami

Pérez Art Museum Miami
Museum

(PAMM; ☑305-375-3000; www.pamm.org; 1103 Biscayne Blvd; adult/senior & student $16/12, 1st Thu & 2nd Sat of month free; ☺10am-6pm Fri-Tue, to 9pm Thu, closed Wed; ℗) One of Miami's most impressive spaces, designed by Swiss architects Herzog & de Meuron, integrates tropical foliage, glass, concrete and wood – a melding of tropical vitality and fresh modernism that fits perfectly in Miami. PAMM stages some of the best contemporary exhibitions in the city, with established artists and impressive newcomers. The

 Miami for Children

Miami has loads of attractions for young travelers.

Zoo Miami (Metrozoo; ☑305-251-0400; www.zoomiami.org; 12400 SW 152nd St; adult/child $23/19; ☺10am-5pm; ℗🖐) Miami's tropical weather makes strolling around the Metrozoo almost feel like a day in the wild. Look for Asian and African elephants, rare and regal Bengal tigers prowling an evocative Hindu temple, pygmy hippos, Andean condors, a pack of hyenas, cute koalas, colobus monkeys, black rhinoceroses and a pair of Komodo dragons from Indonesia. For a quick overview (and because the zoo is so big), hop on the Safari Monorail; it departs every 20 minutes.

Miami Children's Museum (☑305-373-5437; www.miamichildrensmuseum.org; 980 MacArthur Causeway; $20; ☺10am-6pm; 🖐) This museum, located between South Beach and Downtown Miami, isn't exactly a museum but more like an uberplayhouse, with areas for kids to practice all sorts of adult activities – banking and food shopping, caring for pets, and acting as a local cop or firefighter. Adults must go accompanied by children, and vice versa.

Zoo Miami
IMAGEMD/SHUTTERSTOCK ©

permanent collection rotates through unique pieces every few months – drawing from a treasure trove of work spanning the last 80 years. Don't miss.

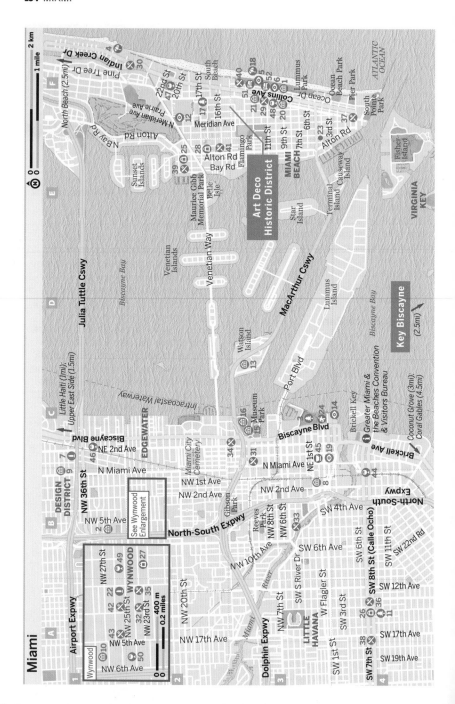

Miami

Art Deco
Historic District

Key Biscayne
(2.5mi)

Miami

Sights

1 Art Deco Museum ... F3
2 Bakehouse Art Complex ... B1
3 Bayfront Park ... C3
4 Boardwalk ... F1
5 Carlyle ... F3
6 Congress Hotel ... F3
7 Fly's Eye Dome ... C1
8 HistoryMiami ... B3
9 Institute of Contemporary Art ... B1
10 Margulies Collection at the Warehouse ... A1
11 Máximo Gómez Park ... A4
12 Miami Beach Botanical Garden ... F2
13 Miami Children's Museum ... C3
14 Miami Riverwalk ... C4
New World Center ... (see 17)
15 Patricia & Phillip Frost Museum of Science ... C3
16 Pérez Art Museum Miami ... C3
17 SoundScape Park ... F2
18 South Beach ... F3
19 Void Projects ... C3
20 Wolfsonian-FIU ... F3
21 World Erotic Art Museum ... F3
22 Wynwood Walls ... A1

Activities, Courses & Tours

Bike & Roll ... (see 1)
Miami Design Preservation League ... (see 1)
23 Miami Food Tours ... F3
24 Tina Hills Pavilion ... C3

Shopping

25 Consign of the Times ... E2
26 Guantanamera ... A4
Havana Collection ... (see 26)
27 Nomad Tribe ... B2
28 Taschen ... E2

Eating

29 11th Street Diner ... F3
30 27 Restaurant ... F2
31 All Day ... C3
32 Alter ... A2
33 Casablanca ... B3
34 Chef Allen's Farm-to-Table Dinner ... C3
35 Coyo Taco ... A2
36 El Nuevo Siglo ... A4
37 Joe's Stone Crab Restaurant ... F4
Kyu ... (see 22)
38 Lung Yai Thai Tapas ... A4
Panther Coffee ... (see 39)
Panther Coffee ... (see 32)
39 Pubbelly ... E2
40 Taquiza ... F3
Verde ... (see 16)
41 Yardbird ... E2
42 Zak the Baker ... A1
43 Zak the Baker ... A1

Drinking & Nightlife

Ball & Chain ... (see 26)
44 Blackbird Ordinary ... B4
Bodega ... (see 41)
Broken Shaker ... (see 30)
45 Galleria ... C3
46 Lagniappe ... C1
47 Sweet Liberty ... F2
48 Twist ... F3
49 Wood Tavern ... B1
50 Wynwood Brewing Company ... A2

Entertainment

Adrienne Arsht Center for the Performing Arts ... (see 34)
Colony Theater ... (see 28)
Cubaocho ... (see 26)
Klipsch Amphitheater ... (see 3)
New World Symphony ... (see 17)
Tower Theater ... (see 11)

Sleeping

51 Cavalier South Beach ... F3
Freehand Miami ... (see 30)
52 Villa Casa Casuarina ... F3

Bayfront Park — Park

(☎305-358-7550; www.bayfrontparkmiami.com; 301 N Biscayne Blvd) Few American parks can claim to front such a lovely stretch of turquoise (Biscayne Bay), but Miamians are lucky like that. Notable park features are two performance venues: the **Klipsch Amphitheater** (www.klipsch.com/klipsch-amphitheater-at; 301 N Biscayne Blvd), which boasts excellent views over Biscayne Bay and is a good spot for live-music shows, and the smaller 200-seat (lawn seating can accommodate 800 more) Tina Hills Pavilion, which hosts free springtime performances.

HistoryMiami — Museum

(☎305-375-1492; www.historymiami.org; 101 W Flagler St; adult/child 6-12 yr $10/5; ⌚10am-5pm Tue-Sat, from noon Sun; 👪) South Florida – a land of escaped slaves, guerrilla Native

Americans, gangsters, land grabbers, pirates, tourists, drug dealers and alligators – has a special history, and it takes a special kind of museum to capture that narrative. This highly recommended place, located in the Miami-Dade Cultural Center, does just that, weaving together the stories of the region's successive waves of population, from Native Americans to Nicaraguans.

Void Projects   Arts Center

(www.voidprojects.org; 60 SE 1st St; ☺11am-6pm) FREE If you'd like to meet local artists and see how life is lived on a smaller, more modest scale in Miami's creative pockets, visit this arts collective – run by artist Axel Void – where resident artists paint and hold exhibitions (by visiting artists) and organise free life drawing classes for the public (Thursdays from 6:30pm) and movie screenings.

Patricia & Phillip Frost
Museum of Science   Museum

(✆305-434-9600; www.frostscience.org; 1101 Biscayne Blvd; adult/child $30/21; ☺9am-6pm; P⛟) This sprawling new Downtown museum spreads across 250,000 sq ft that includes a three-level aquarium, a 250-seat, state-of-the-art planetarium and two distinct wings that delve into the wonders of science and nature. Exhibitions range from weather phenomena to creepy crawlies, feathered dinosaurs and vital-microbe displays, while Florida's fascinating Everglades and biologically rich coral reefs play starring roles.

Miami Riverwalk   Waterfront

This pedestrian walkway follows along the northern edge of the river as it bisects Downtown, and offers some peaceful vantage points of bridges and skyscrapers dotting the urban landscape. You can start the walk at the south end of Bayfront Park and follow it under bridges and along the waterline till it ends just west of the SW 2nd Ave Bridge.

◉ Wynwood & the
Design District

Margulies Collection at the
Warehouse   Gallery

(✆305-576-1051; www.margulieswarehouse. com; 591 NW 27th St; adult/student $10/5; ☺11am-4pm Tue-Sat mid-Oct–Apr) Encompassing 45,000 sq ft, this vast not-for-profit exhibition space houses one of the best art collections in Wynwood – Martin Margulies' awe-inspiring 4000-piece collection includes sculptures by Isamu Noguchi, George Segal, Richard Serra and Olafur Eliasson, among many others, plus sound installations by Susan Philipsz and jaw-dropping room-sized works by Anselm Kiefer. Thought-provoking, large-format installations are the focus at the Warehouse, and you'll see works by some leading 21st-century artists here.

Wynwood Walls   Public Art

(www.thewynwoodwalls.com; NW 2nd Ave, btwn 25th & 26th Sts) FREE In the midst of rusted warehouses and concrete blah, there's a pastel-and-graffiti explosion of urban art. Wynwood Walls is a collection of murals and paintings laid out over an open courtyard that invariably bowls people over with its sheer color profile and unexpected location. What's on offer tends to change with the coming and going of major arts events, such as **Art Basel** (www.artbasel. com/miami-beach; ☺early Dec), but it's always interesting stuff.

Bakehouse Art Complex   Gallery

(BAC; ✆305-576-2828; www.bacfl.org; 561 NW 32nd St; ☺noon-5pm; P) FREE One of the pivotal art destinations in Wynwood, the Bakehouse has been an arts incubator since well before the creation of the Wynwood Walls. Today this former bakery houses galleries and some 60 studios, and the range of works is quite impressive. Check the schedule for upcoming artist talks and other events.

Institute of Contemporary Art   Museum

(ICA; www.icamiami.org; 61 NE 41st St; ⊘11am-7pm Tue-Sun) FREE An excellent contemporary arts museum, the ICA sits in the midst of the Design District, and hosts a fantastic range of contemporary exhibitions alongside its permanent collection pieces. The building, designed in 2017 by Aranguren & Gallegos architects, is especially beautiful, with its sharp geometric lines and large windows overlooking the back garden. The metallic grey facade is simultaneously industrial and elegant.

Fly's Eye Dome   Sculpture

(140 NE 39th St, Palm Court) Installed during Art Basel (p156) in 2014, Buckminster Fuller's striking geodesic dome looks otherworldly as it appears to float in a small reflecting pool surrounded by slender, gently swaying palm trees. The 24ft-tall sculpture was dubbed an 'autonomous dwelling machine' by Fuller when he conceived it back in 1965.

◎ Little Havana

Máximo Gómez Park   Park

(cnr SW 8th St & SW 15th Ave; ⊘9am-6pm) Little Havana's most evocative reminder of Cuba is Máximo Gómez Park ('Domino Park'), where the sound of elderly men trash-talking over games of dominoes is harmonized with the quick clack-clack of slapping tiles – though the tourists taking photos all the while does take away from the authenticity of the place somewhat. The heavy cigar smell and a sunrise-bright mural of the 1994 Summit of the Americas add to the atmosphere.

◎ Coral Gables

Biltmore Hotel   Historic Building

(☏855-311-6903; www.biltmorehotel.com; 1200 Anastasia Ave; ⊘tours 1:30pm & 2:30pm Sun; P) In the most opulent neighborhood of one of the showiest cities in the world, the Biltmore is the greatest of the grand hotels of the American Jazz Age. If this joint were

Cruising down Ocean Drive

Ocean Dr is the great cruising strip of Miami: an endless parade of classic cars, testosterone-sweating young men, peacock-like young women, street performers, vendors, those guys who yell unintelligible nonsense at everyone, celebrities pretending to be tourists, tourists who want to play celebrity, beautiful people, not-so-beautiful people, people people and the best ribbon of art-deco preservation on the beach. Say 'Miami.' That image in your head? Probably Ocean Dr.

FRANK FELL MEDIA/SHUTTERSTOCK ©

a fictional character from a novel, it'd be, without question, Jay Gatsby. Al Capone had a speakeasy on-site, and the Capone Suite is said to be haunted by the spirit of Fats Walsh, who was murdered here.

Fairchild Tropical Garden   Gardens

(☏305-667-1651; www.fairchildgarden.org; 10901 Old Cutler Rd; adult/child/senior $25/12/18; ⊘9:30am-4:30pm; P🚼) If you need to escape Miami's madness, consider a green day in one of the country's largest tropical botanical gardens. A butterfly grove, tropical plant conservatory and gentle vistas of marsh and keys habitats, plus frequent art installations from artists like Roy Lichtenstein, are all stunning. In addition to easy-to-follow, self-guided walking tours, a free 45-minute tram tours the entire park on the hour from 10am to 3pm (till 4pm weekends).

◎ Coconut Grove

Vizcaya Museum & Gardens　　Historic Building

(⏀305-250-9133; www.vizcaya.org; 3251 S Miami Ave; adult/child 6-12yr/student & senior $22/10/15; ⏱9:30am-4:30pm Wed-Mon; ⓟ) If you want to see something that is 'very Miami', this is it – lush, big, over the top, a patchwork of all that a rich US businessperson might want to show off to friends. Which is essentially what industrialist James Deering did in 1916, starting a Miami tradition of making a ton of money and building ridiculously grandiose digs. He employed 1000 people (then 10% of the local population) and stuffed his home with Renaissance furniture, tapestries, paintings and decorative arts.

Kampong　　Gardens

(⏀305-442-7169; https://ntbg.org/gardens/ kampong; 4013 Douglas Rd; adult/child $20/5; ⏱tours by appointment only 9:30am-3pm Tue-Fri, from 10:15am Sat) David Fairchild, the Indiana Jones of the botanical world and founder of Fairchild Tropical Garden, would rest at the Kampong (Malay/Indonesian for 'village') in between journeys in search of beautiful and economically viable plant life. Today this lush garden is listed on the National Register of Historic Places and the lovely grounds serve as a classroom for the National Tropical Botanical Garden. Self-guided tours (allow at least an hour) are available by appointment, as are $25 one-hour guided tours.

◎ Little Haiti & the Upper East Side

Little Haiti Cultural Center　　Gallery

(⏀305-960-2969; www.littlehaiticulturalcenter. com; 212 NE 59th Tce; ⏱10am-9pm Mon-Fri, to 4pm Sat) FREE This cultural center hosts an art gallery with often thought-provoking exhibitions from Haitian painters, sculptors and multimedia artists. You can also find dance classes, drama productions and a Caribbean-themed market during special events. The building itself is quite a confection of bold tropical colors, steep A-framed roofs and lacy decorative elements. Don't miss the mural in the palm-filled courtyard.

Vizcaya Museum & Gardens

ROBERTO MICHEL/SHUTTERSTOCK ©

⊕ ACTIVITIES

Virginia Key Outdoor
Center   Outdoors

(VKOC; ☏786-224-4777; www.vkoc.net; 3801
Rickenbacker Causeway, Virginia Key; kayak or
bike hire 1st hour $25, each additional hour $10;
⊙9am-6pm Mon-Fri, 8am-7pm Sat & Sun Mar-
Aug, reduced hours other months) This highly
recommended outfitter will get you out
on the water in a hurry with kayaks and
stand-up paddle boards, which you can put
in the water just across from its office. The
small mangrove-lined bay (known as Lamar
Lake) has manatees, and makes for a great
start to the paddle before you venture
further out.

One of the highlights is partaking in one
of VKOC's guided sunset and full moon
paddles, which happen several times a
month. You can also hire mountain bikes
for the nearby Virginia Key North Point
Trails (p160).

Venetian Pool   Swimming

(☏305-460-5306; www.coralgables.com/venetian-
pool; 2701 De Soto Blvd; adult/child Sep-May
$15/10, Jun-Aug $20/15; ⊙11am-5:30pm Tue-Fri,
til 6:30pm Jun-Aug, 10am-4:30pm Sat & Sun, closed
Dec-Feb, reduced hours Nov; 👪) One of the
few pools listed on the National Register of
Historic Places, this is a wonderland of rock
caves, cascading waterfalls, a palm-fringed
island and Venetian-style moorings. Back in
1923, rock was quarried for one of the most
beautiful Miami neighborhoods leaving an
ugly gash – cleverly, it was laden with mosaic
and tiles, and filled up with water.

Citi Bike   Cycling

(☏305-532-9494; www.citibikemiami.com; rental
per 30min $4.50, 1/2/4hr $6.50/10/18, day $24)
This bike-sharing program, modeled after
similar initiatives in New York, London and
Paris, makes getting on a bike a relative
breeze. Just rock up to a solar-powered Citi
Bike station (a handy map can be found on
the website), insert a credit card and ride
away. You can return your bike at any Citi
Bike location.

 **Little Haiti's
Botanicas**

If you pay a visit to Little Haiti, you might
notice a few storefronts emblazoned
with 'botanica' signs. Not to be confused
with a plant store, a *botanica* is a *vodou*
shop. *Botanicas* are perhaps the most
'foreign' sight in Little Haiti. Storefronts
promise to help in matters of love, work
and sometimes 'immigration services,'
but trust us, there are no marriage
counselors or INS guys in here. As you
enter you'll probably get a funny look,
but be courteous, curious and respect-
ful and you should be welcomed.

Before you browse, forget stereotypes about pins and dolls. Like many
traditional religions, *vodou* recognizes
supernatural forces in everyday objects,
and powers that are both distinct from
and part of one overarching deity.
Ergo, you'll see shrines to Jesus next
to altars to traditional *vodou* deities.
Notice the large statues of what look
like people; these actually represent *loa*
(pronounced lwa), intermediary spirits
that form a pantheon below God in the
vodou religious hierarchy. Drop a coin
into a *loa* offering bowl before you leave,
especially to Papa Legba, spirit of crossroads and, by our reckoning, travelers.

Libreri Mapou (p162)
ROSAIRENEBETANCOURT 14/ALAMY ©

Tina Hills Pavilion   Yoga

(Biscayne Blvd, Bayfront Park) **FREE** This small
open-air pavilion hosts free events, including
free 75-minute yoga sessions, suitable for all
levels on Mondays and Wednesdays at 6pm,
and 9am Saturday morning.

 ## Miami Specialties

Cuban Sandwich

The traditional Cuban sandwich, also known as a *sandwich mixto,* is not some slapdash creation. It's a craft best left to the experts – but here's some insight into how they do it. Correct bread is crucial – it should be Cuban white bread: fresh, soft and easy to press. The insides (both sides) should be buttered and layered (in the following order) with sliced pickles, slices of roast Cuban pork, ham (preferably sweet-cured ham) and baby Swiss cheese. Then it all gets pressed in a hot *plancha* (sandwich press) until the cheese melts.

Arepas

The greatness of a city can be measured by many yardsticks. The arts. Civic involvement. Infrastructure. What you eat when you're plowed at 3am. In Miami, the answer is often enough *arepas,* delicious South American corn cakes that can be stuffed (Venezuelan-style) or topped (Colombian-style) with any manner of deliciousness; generally, you can't go wrong with cheese.

Stone Crabs

The first reusable crustacean: only one claw is taken from a stone crab – the rest is tossed back in the sea (the claw regrows in 12 to 18 months, and crabs plucked again are called 'retreads'). The claws are so perishable that they're always cooked before selling.

Cuban sandwich
MARIDAV/SHUTTERSTOCK ©

SoBe Surf　　　　　　　　Surfing
(📞786-216-7703; www.sobesurf.com; group/private lessons from $70/100) Offers surf lessons both in Miami Beach and in Cocoa Beach, where there tends to be better waves. Instruction on Miami Beach usually happens around South Point. All bookings are done by phone or email.

Virginia Key North Point Trails　　Mountain Biking
(📞786-224-4777; 3801 Rickenbacker Causeway, Virginia Key Beach North Point Park; ⊙10am-5pm Mon-Fri, 8am-6pm Sat & Sun) FREE In a wooded section at the north end of the Virginia Key Beach North Point Park, you'll find a series of short mountain-bike trails, color coded for beginner, intermediate and advanced. It's free to use the trails, though you'll have to pay for parking at the Virginia Key Beach North Point Park to get here.

🕐 TOURS

Miami Design Preservation League　　　　　　Walking
(MDPL; 📞305-672-2014; www.mdpl.org; 1001 Ocean Dr; guided tours adult/student $30/25; ⊙10:30am daily & 6:30pm Thu) Tells the stories and history behind the art-deco buildings in South Beach, with a lively guide from the Miami Design Preservation League. Tours last 90 minutes. Also offers tours of Jewish Miami Beach, Gay & Lesbian Miami Beach and a once-monthly tour (first Saturday at 9:30am) of the MiMo district in the North Beach area. Check website for details.

Miami Food Tours　　　Food & Drink
(📞786-361-0991; www.miamifoodtours.com; 429 Lenox Ave; South Beach tour adult/child $58/35, Wynwood tour $75/55, Swooped with Forks $129/109; ⊙tours South Beach 11am & 4:30pm daily, Wynwood 10:30am Mon-Sat) This highly rated tour explores various facets of the city – culture, history, art and of course cuisine – while making stops at restaurants and cafes along the way. It's a walking tour, though distances aren't great, and happens in South Beach and Wynwood. There is

also the Swooped with Forks food tour that takes you places in a golf cart.

History Miami Tours   History
(☑305-375-1492; www.historymiami.org/city-tour; tours $30-60) Historian extraordinaire Dr Paul George leads fascinating walking tours, including culturally rich strolls through Little Haiti, Little Havana, Downtown and Coral Gables at twilight, plus the occasional boat trip to Stiltsville and Key Biscayne. Tours happen once a week or so. Get the full menu and sign up online.

Bike & Roll   Cycling
(☑305-604-0001; www.bikemiami.com; 210 10th St; hire per 2/4hr from $15/20, per day from $25, tours $40; ⊘9am-7pm) This well-run outfit offers a good selection of bikes, including single-speed cruisers, geared hybrids and speedy road bikes; all rentals include helmets, lights, locks and maps. Staff move things along quickly, so you won't have to waste time waiting to get out and riding. Bike tours are also available (daily at 10am).

🔒 SHOPPING

🔒 South Beach

Taschen   Books
(☑305-538-6185; www.taschen.com; 1111 Lincoln Rd; ⊘11am-9pm Mon-Thu, to 10pm Fri & Sat, noon-9pm Sun) An incredibly well-stocked collection of art, photography, design and coffee-table books from this high-quality picture books publisher. Check out David Hockney's color-rich art books, the *New Erotic Photography* (always a great conversation starter) and Sebastião Salgado's lushly photographed human-filled landscapes.

Consign of the Times   Vintage
(☑305-535-0811; www.consignofthetimes. com; 1935 West Ave; ⊘10am-7pm Mon-Sat, noon-6pm Sun) Cute vintage boutique that carries labels from Gucci (ballerina shoes, little leather bags), Diana Von Furstenberg (leather slingbacks), Versace (silver bustier!) or Valentino (colorful trainers).

🔒 Wynwood & the Design District

Nomad Tribe   Clothing
(☑305-364-5193; www.nomadtribeshop. com; 2301 NW 2nd Ave; ⊘noon-8pm) 🌱 This boutique earns high marks for carrying only ethically and sustainably produced merchandise. You'll find cleverly designed jewelry from Miami-based Kathe Cuervo, Osom brand socks (made of upcycled thread), ecologically produced graphic T-shirts from Thinking MU, and THX coffee and candles (which donates 100% of profits to nonprofit organizations), among much else.

🔒 Little Havana

Guantanamera   Cigars
(☑786-618-5142; www.guantanameracigars. com; 1465 SW 8th St; ⊘10:30am-8pm Sun-Wed, to 10pm Thu, to 3am Fri & Sat) In a central location in Little Havana, Guantanamera sells high-quality hand-rolled cigars, plus strong Cuban coffee. It's an atmospheric shop, where you can stop for a smoke, a drink (there's a bar here) and some friendly banter. There's also some great live music most nights of the week. The rocking chairs in front are a fine perch for people-watching.

Havana Collection   Clothing
(☑786-717-7474; 1421 SW 8th St; ⊘10am-6pm) One of the best and most striking collections of the classic traditional *guayaberas* (Cuban dress shirts) in Miami can be found in this shop. Prices are high (plan on spending about $85 for a shirt), but so is the quality, so you can be assured of a long-lasting product.

🔒 Little Haiti & the Upper East Side

Upper East Side Farmers Market   Market
(cnr Biscayne Blvd & 66th St, Legion Park; ⊘9am-2pm Sat) For a taste of local culture, stop by this small farmers market held each Saturday in the Upper East Side's Legion Park. Here you can meet some of the farmers

producing delectable fresh fruits and veggies, plus stock up on breads and crackers, pastries, cheeses, jams, honeys and fresh juices. In short, everything you need for a great picnic. It's open year-round.

Libreri Mapou   Books

(☑305-757-9922; http://mapoubooks.com; 5919 NE 2nd Ave; ☺noon-7pm Fri, Sat & Mon-Wed, to 5pm Sun, closed Thu) If you're interested in Haitian culture, this Haitian bookshop specializes in English, French and Creole titles and periodicals, with thousands of great titles and live events – the owner, Jan Mapou, a writer and political thinker, has made this place a local hotspot.

Sweat Records   Music

(☑786-693-9309; www.sweatrecordsmiami. com; 5505 NE 2nd Ave; ☺noon-10pm Mon-Sat, to 5pm Sun) Sweat's almost a stereotypical indie record store – there's art and graffiti on the walls, it sells weird Japanese toys, there are tattooed staff with thick glasses arguing over LPs and EPs you've never heard of and, of course, there's coffee and vegan snacks.

EATING

Miami has tons of immigrants – mainly from Latin America, the Caribbean and Russia – and it's a sucker for food trends. Thus you get a good mix of cheap ethnic eateries and high-quality top-end cuisine, alongside some poor-value dross in touristy zones like Miami Beach. Downtown, Wynwood and Upper East Side have excellent offerings; for great classics, head to Coral Gables.

🌴 South Beach

Taquiza   Mexican $

(☑305-203-2197; www.taquizatacos.com; 1351 Collins Ave; tacos $3.50-5; ☺noon-midnight) Taquiza has acquired a stellar reputation among Miami's street-food lovers. The takeout stand with a few outdoor tables serves delicious perfection in its steak, pork, shrimp or veggie tacos (but no fish options) served on handmade blue-corn tortillas. They're small, so order a few.

11th Street Diner   Diner $

(☑305-534-6373; www.eleventhstreetdiner.com; 1065 Washington Ave; mains $10-20; ☺7am-midnight Sun-Wed, 24hr Thu-Sat) A gorgeous slice of Americana, this Pullman-car diner trucked down from Wilkes-Barre, PA, is where you can replicate Edward Hopper's *Nighthawks* – if that's something you've always wanted to do. The food is as classic as the architecture, with oven-roasted turkey, baby back ribs and mac 'n' cheese among the hits – plus breakfast at all hours.

Yardbird   Southern US $$

(☑305-538-5220; www.runchickenrun.com; 1600 Lenox Ave; mains $18-38; ☺11am-midnight Mon-Fri, from 9am Sat & Sun; ☑) Yardbird has earned a die-hard following for its delicious haute Southern comfort food. The kitchen churns out some nice shrimp and grits, St Louis–style pork ribs, charred okra, and biscuits with smoked brisket, but it's most famous for its supremely good plate of fried chicken, spiced watermelon and waffles with bourbon maple syrup.

Pubbelly   Fusion $$

(☑305-532-7555; http://pubbellyglobal.com; 1424 20th St; plates $9-24; ☺6pm-11pm Sun-Thu, to midnight Fri & Sat; ☑) A mix of Asian and Latin flavors, Pubbelly serves delicacies such as grilled miso black cod with spring onions, beef tartare rolls with mustard and truffle poached egg, and Japanese fried chicken with kimchi. Super popular and decently priced, it's a real treat on South Beach.

Joe's Stone Crab
Restaurant   American $$$

(☑305-673-0365; www.joesstonecrab.com; 11 Washington Ave; mains lunch $14-30, dinner $19-60; ☺11:30am-2:30pm Tue-Sat, 5-10pm daily) The wait is long and the prices for iconic dishes can be high. But if those aren't deal breakers, queue to don a bib in Miami's most famous restaurant (around since 1913!) and enjoy deliciously fresh stone-crab claws. Aside from tender stone crab (which can top $60 for half-a-dozen jumbo claws), you'll find excellent blackened codfish sandwiches and creamy lobster mac 'n' cheese.

North Beach

27 Restaurant
Fusion $$

(📞786-476-7020; www.freehandhotels.com; 2727 Indian Creek Dr, Freehand Miami Hotel; mains $17-30; ⏰6-11:30pm Mon-Sat, 11am-3pm Sat & Sun; 🚗) Part of Freehand Miami Hotel and the very popular Broken Shaker (p166), 27 has a lovely setting – akin to dining in an old tropical cottage, with worn floorboards, candlelit tables, and various rooms slung with artwork and curious knickknacks, plus a lovely terrace. Try the braised octopus, crispy pork shoulder, kimchi fried rice and yogurt-tahini-massaged kale. Book ahead.

Cafe Prima Pasta
Italian $$

(📞305-867-0106; www.cafeprimapasta.com; 414 71st St; mains $17-28; ⏰5-11:30pm Mon-Thu, to midnight Fri & Sat, 4-11pm Sun) We're not sure what's better at this Argentine-Italian place: the much-touted pasta, which deserves every one of the accolades heaped on it, or the atmosphere, which captures the dignified sultriness of Buenos Aires. You can't go wrong with the small, well-curated menu, with standouts including gnocchi formaggi, baked branzino, and squid-ink linguine with seafood in a lobster sauce.

Downtown Miami

All Day
Cafe $

(📞305-699-3447; www.alldaymia.com; 1035 N Miami Ave; coffee from $3.50, breakfast $10-14; ⏰7am-5pm Mon-Fri, from 9am Sat & Sun; 🛜) All Day is positively Miami's best cafe – with locally sourced ingredients forming the basis of its simple menu, as well as excellent coffees, teas, beer and wine, and an airy, light Scandinavian-style decor, this is a winner all-around. Stylish chairs, wood-and-marble tables, friendly staff and an always enticing soundtrack lend it an easygoing vibe.

Casablanca
Seafood $$

(📞305-371-4107; www.casablancaseafood.com; 400 N River Dr; mains $17-37; ⏰11am-10pm Mon-Thu, to 11pm Fri, 8am-11pm Sat, to 10pm Sun) Perched over the Miami River, Casablanca serves some of the best seafood in town.

★ Top Five Cheap Eats

Versailles (p164)

Zak the Baker

Taquiza

El Nuevo Siglo (p164)

Chef Creole (p165)

The setting is a big draw – with tables on a long wooden deck just above the water, and the odd seagull winging past. But the fresh fish is the real star here.

Verde
American $$

(📞786-345-5697; www.pamm.org/dining; 1103 Biscayne Blvd; mains $15-25; ⏰11am-4pm Mon, Tue & Fri, to 9pm Thu, to 5pm Sat & Sun, closed Wed; 🚗) Inside the Pérez Art Museum Miami (p153), Verde is a local favorite for its tasty market-fresh dishes and great setting – with outdoor seating on a terrace overlooking the bay. Crispy mahi-mahi tacos, pizza with squash blossoms and goat cheese, and grilled endive salads are among the temptations. The service can be quite slow at busy times.

Chef Allen's Farm-to-Table Dinner
Vegetarian $$$

(📞786-405-1745; 1300 Biscayne Blvd; dinner $40, with wine pairing $60; ⏰6:30pm Mon; 🚗) A great way to get to know some locals, this Monday-night feast is served family-style at outdoor tables in front of the Arsht Center, with live music and plenty of chatting between the diners. The vegetarian menu is inspired by the farmers market held on the same day. Call ahead to reserve a spot or book online.

Wynwood & the Design District

Zak the Baker
Bakery $

(📞786-294-0876; www.zakthebaker.com; 295 NW 26th St; pastries from $3.50; ⏰7am-7pm Sun-Fri, closed Sat) Everyone's favorite bakery has become a Miami icon, and for good reason. The fresh baked breads, croissants and pastries are fabulous. For something more filling, don't miss ZTB's **Deli** (📞786-347-7100; www.zakthebaker.com; 405 NW 26th St; sandwiches $14-18; ⏱8am-5pm Sun-Fri) up the street.

Coyo Taco   Mexican $

(📞305-573-8228; www.coyo-taco.com; 2300 NW 2nd Ave; mains $7.5-12; ⏱11am-3am Mon-Sat, to 11pm Sun; 🖉) If you're in Wynwood and craving tacos, this is the place to be. You'll have to contend with lines day or night, but those beautifully turned-out tacos are well worth the wait – and come in creative varieties such as chargrilled octopus, marinated mushrooms or crispy duck, along with the usual array of steak, grilled fish and roasted pork.

Panther Coffee   Cafe $

(📞305-677-3952; www.panthercoffee.com; 2390 NW 2nd Ave; coffees $3-6; ⏱7am-9pm Sun-Thu, to 1am Fri & Sat; 🛜) Miami's best independent coffee shop specializes in single-origin, small-batch roasts, fired up to perfection. Aside from sipping on a zesty brewed-to-order Chemex-made coffee (or a creamy latte), you can enjoy microbrews, wines and sweet treats. The front patio is a great spot for people-watching.

Panther also hosts cupping classes and occasional nights of live music, performance art and other events. There's also a Miami Beach location in **Sunset Harbour** (1875 Purdy Ave; coffees $3-6; ⏱7am-9pm).

Kyu   Fusion $$

(📞786-577-0150; www.kyumiami.com; 251 NW 25th St; sharing plates $22-44; ⏱noon-11:30pm Mon-Sat, 11am-10:30pm Sun, bar till 1am Fri & Sat; 🖉) 🌿 Kyu has been dazzling locals and food critics alike with its creative Asian-inspired dishes, most of which are cooked over the open flames of a wood-fired grill. Try the Florida red snapper, beef tenderloin and a magnificent head of cauliflower. There's also grilled octopus, soft-shell-crab steamed buns and smoked beef brisket.

Alter   Modern American $$$

(📞305-573-5996; www.altermiami.com; 223 NW 23rd St; set menu 5/7 courses $79/99; ⏱7-11pm Tue-Sun) Alter brings creative high-end cooking via its award-winning young chef Brad Kilgore. The changing menu showcases Florida's high-quality ingredients from sea and land in seasonally inspired dishes with Asian and European-flavoured haute cuisine. Expect dishes such as eggs with sea scallop foam, truffle pearls and Siberian caviar, or lamb neck, forest consommé, toasted apple miso and shaved kombu. Reserve well ahead.

🚫 Little Havana

Versailles   Cuban $

(📞305-444-0240; www.versaillesrestaurant.com; 3555 SW 8th St; mains $6-21; ⏱8am-1am Mon-Thu, to 2:30am Fri & Sat, 9am-1am Sun) Versailles (ver-*sigh*-yay) is an institution – one of the mainstays of Miami's Cuban gastronomic scene. Try the excellent black-bean soup or the fried yucca before moving onto heartier meat and seafood plates. Older Cubans and Miami's Latin political elite still love coming here, so you've got a real chance to rub elbows with Miami's most prominent Latin citizens.

El Nuevo Siglo   Latin American $

(📞305-854-1916; 1305 SW 8th St; mains $8-12; ⏱7am-9pm) An unusual location for an eatery, this place is hidden inside a supermarket (El Nuevo Siglo). Foodie-minded locals come for delicious cooking at excellent prices – and the unfussy ambience. Grab a seat at the shiny black countertop and nibble on roast meats, fried yucca, tangy Cuban sandwiches, grilled snapper with rice, beans and plantains, and other daily specials.

Lung Yai Thai Tapas   Thai $

(📞786-334-6262; 1731 SW 8th St; mains $10-15; ⏱noon-3pm & 5pm-midnight) This tiny gem in Little Havana has some excellent Thai cooking – and provides a nice change of palate in the area. Chef and owner Bas Trisransi produces a menu ideal for sharing – hence the 'tapas' in the name – try the perfectly spiced fried chicken wings, tender duck salad or a much-revered Kaho Soi Gai (a rich noodle curry).

El Carajo
Spanish $$

(📞305-856-2424; www.el-carajo.com; 2465 SW 17th Ave; tapas $5-15; ⊘noon-10pm Sun-Wed, to 11pm Thu-Sat; 📶) Walk past the motor oil inside the Citgo gas station on SW 17th Ave (yes, really!) into this Granadan wine cellar and get yourself a seat at the bar. Order the divine bacon-wrapped stuffed dates, fluffy tortilla of patata (thick Spanish omelets) and don't miss the sardines – cooked with a bit of salt and olive oil till they're dizzyingly delicious.

Coral Gables
Threefold
Cafe $$

(📞305-704-8007; www.threefoldcafe.com; 141 Giralda Ave; mains $10-16; ⊘7:30am-3pm Mon, to 4pm Tue-Fri, 7am-4pm Sat & Sun; 📶📶) Coral Gables' most talked-about cafe is a buzzing, Aussie-run charmer that serves perfectly pulled espressos (and a good flat white), along with creative breakfast and lunch fare. Start the morning with waffles and berry compote, smashed avocado toast topped with feta, or a slow-roasted leg of lamb with fried eggs.

Coconut Grove
Last Carrot
Vegetarian $

(📞305-445-0805; http://lastcarrot.com; 3133 Grand Ave; mains $5-9; ⊘10:30am-6pm Mon-Sat, 11am-5pm Sun; 📶📶) Going strong since the 1970s, and set in a decidedly unglamorous part of Coconut Grove, the Last Carrot serves fresh juices, delicious pita sandwiches, avocado melts, veggie burgers and rather famous spinach pies. The Carrot's endurance is testament to the quality of its good-for-your-body food served in a good-for-your-soul setting.

Bianco Gelato
Ice Cream $

(📞786-717-5315; 3137 Commodore Plaza; ice cream $3.50-7) A much-loved spot in the neighborhood that's been around a long time, Bianco whips up amazing gelato

that's all made from organic milk and natural ingredients. Flavors change regularly, but a few hits include guava and cheese, avocado with carmelized nuts, hazelnut and vegan chocolate.

Spillover
Modern American $$

(📞305-456-5723; www.spillovermiami.com; 2911 Grand Ave; mains $13-25; ⊘11:30am-10pm Sun-Thu, to 11pm Fri & Sat; 📶📶) Tucked down a pedestrian strip near the CocoWalk, the Spillover serves locally sourced seafood and creative bistro fare in an enticing vintage setting (cast-iron stools and recycled doors around the bar, suspenders-wearing staff, brassy jazz playing overhead). Come for crab cakes, buffalo shrimp tacos, spear-caught fish and chips, or a melt-in-your-mouth lobster Reuben.

✖ Little Haiti & the Upper East Side
Chef Creole
Haitian $

(📞305-754-2223; www.chefcreole.com; 200 NW 54th St; mains $10-22; ⊘11am-10pm Mon-Wed, to 11pm Thu-Sat) When you need Caribbean food on the cheap, head to the edge of Little Haiti and this excellent takeout shack. Order up fried conch, oxtail or fish, ladle rice and beans on the side, and you'll be full for a week. Enjoy the food on nearby picnic benches while Haitian music blasts out of tinny speakers – as island an experience as they come.

Phuc Yea
Vietnamese $$

(📞305-602-3710; www.phucyea.com; 7100 Biscayne Blvd; mains $12-29; ⊘6pm-10pm Mon-Thu, to 11pm Fri & Sat, 11:30am-3:30pm & 6-9pm Sun) Phuc Yea started as a pop up and went wildly popular with its delicious Cajun-Vietnamese cooking. The name got about as much attention – but 'phuc', says Urban Dictionary, stands for 'blessing and prosperity.' Get yourself some lobster summer rolls, the excellent fish curry, octopus with lime and sweet chili, spicy chicken wings and other great sharing plates.

Andiamo
Pizza $$

(☏305-762-5751; www.andiamopizzamiami.com; 5600 Biscayne Blvd; pizzas $12-20; ☺11am-11pm Sun-Thu, to midnight Fri & Sat; ☝) Miami's best thin-crust pizzas come from the brick oven at this converted industrial space (once a tire shop). With over 30 varieties, it's a lively setting to start off the night, with flickering tiki torches scattered around the outdoor tables and large screens showing sports on big-game nights.

🍸 DRINKING & NIGHTLIFE

Miami has an intense variety of bars, ranging from grotty jazz and punk dives (with excellent music) to beautiful – and laid-back – lounges and nightclubs. There is a great live-music scene across the city. Miami's nightlife reputation for being all about wealth, good looks and phoniness is thankfully mostly isolated to the South Beach scene.

🍸 South Beach

Sweet Liberty
Bar

(☏305-763-8217; www.mysweetliberty.com; 237 20th St; ☺4pm-5am Mon-Sat, from noon Sun) A much-loved local haunt near Collins Park, Sweet Liberty has all the right ingredients for a fun night out: friendly, easygoing bartenders who whip up excellent cocktails (try a mint julep), great happy-hour specials (including 75¢ oysters) and a relaxed, pretension-free crowd. The space is huge, with flickering candles, a long wooden bar and the odd band adding to the cheer.

Bodega
Cocktail Bar

(☏305-704-2145; www.bodegasouthbeach.com; 1220 16th St; ☺noon-5am) Bodega looks like your average hipster Mexican joint – serving delicious tacos ($3 to $5) from a converted Airstream trailer to a party-minded crowd. But there's actually a bar hidden behind that blue porta-potty door on the right. Head inside (or join the long line on weekends) to take in a bit of old-school glam in a sprawling drinking den.

Twist
Gay

(☏305-538-9478; www.twistsobe.com; 1057 Washington Ave; ☺1pm-5am) There's never a dull moment at this two-story gay club – it has some serious staying power and a little bit of something for everyone: six different bars; go-go dancers; drag shows; lounging areas; and a small dance floor.

🍸 North Beach

Broken Shaker
Bar

(☏305-531-2727; www.freehandhotels.com; 2727 Indian Creek Dr, Freehand Miami Hotel; ☺5:30pm-2am Mon-Thu, 4:30pm-3am Fri, 1pm-3am Sat, to 2am Sun) A single small room with a well-equipped bar produces expert cocktails, which are mostly consumed in the beautiful, softly lit garden – all of it part of the Freehand Miami hotel (p163). There's a great soundtrack at all times, and the drinks are excellent. The clientele is a mix of hotel guests (young and into partying) and hip locals.

🍸 Downtown Miami

Galleria
Cafe

(http://galleriadowntown.com; 69 SE 1st St; ☺11am-4pm) ☝ Galleria is a tiny spot of beauty, with its tiled benches and coral walls. The owner, Jeremy Sapienza, makes all his own nut milks, and everything here, including the pastries, is vegan. There are also vintage ceramics on sale – if you'd like an alternative Miami souvenir.

Blackbird Ordinary
Bar

(☏305-671-3307; www.blackbirdordinary.com; 729 SW 1st Ave; ☺3pm-5am Mon-Fri, from 5pm Sat & Sun) The Blackbird is an excellent bar, with great cocktails (the London Sparrow, with gin, cayenne, lemon juice and passion fruit, goes down well) and an enormous courtyard. The only thing 'ordinary' about the place is the sense that all are welcome for a fun and pretension-free night out.

> *Miami has an intense variety of bars...*

🚇 Wynwood & the Design District

Lagniappe
Bar

(☎305-576-0108; www.lagniappehouse.com; 3425 NE 2nd Ave; ⏲7pm-2am Sun-Thu, to 3am Fri & Sat) A touch of New Orleans in Miami, Lagniappe has an old-fashioned front-room bar, packed with art, faded vintage furnishings and weathered walls. The vibe is just right: with great live music (nightly from 9pm to midnight) and an easygoing crowd, plus there's a sprawling back garden with palm trees and fairy lights.

Wynwood Brewing Company
Microbrewery

(☎305-982-8732; www.wynwoodbrewing.com; 565 NW 24th St; ⏲noon-10pm Sun-Tue, to midnight Wed-Sat) The first craft brewery in Wynwood still produces the best beer, even though craft breweries are quite popular in Miami nowadays. The family-owned 15-barrel brewhouse has friendly and knowledgeable staff, excellent year-round brews (including a blonde ale, a robust porter and a top-notch IPA) and seasonal beers, and there's always a food truck parked outside.

Wood Tavern
Bar

(☎305-748-2828; www.facebook.com/wood-tavern; 2531 NW 2nd Ave; ⏲5pm-3am Tue-Sat, 3pm-midnight Sun, 5pm-2am Mon) The crowd here is local kids who want something stylish, but don't want South Beach – Wood Tavern has both atmosphere and aesthetic. Food specials are cheap, the beer selection is excellent and the crowd is friendly. The outdoor space has picnic benches, a wooden stage complete with bleachers and a giant Jenga game, and an attached art gallery with rotating exhibits.

🚇 Little Havana

Ball & Chain
Bar

(www.ballandchainmiami.com; 1513 SW 8th St; ⏲11am-midnight Mon-Wed, to 2am Thu, to 3am Fri & Sat, to 1am Sun) The Ball & Chain has survived several incarnations over the years. Back in 1935, when 8th St was

Where Nightlife Meets Art

The **Wynwood Art Walk Block Party** (www.wynwoodartwalkblockparty.com; ⏲12pm-3am 2nd Sat of month) has become an incredibly popular (free) nightlife option where a big party of people wander around murals and galleries with food trucks, ever-flowing drinks (not always free), live music and special markets.

IMAGE PROFESSIONALS GMBH/ALAMY ©

more Jewish than Latino, it was the sort of jazz joint Billie Holiday would croon in. That iteration closed in 1957, but today's Ball & Chain is still dedicated to music and good times – specifically, Latin music and tropical cocktails.

🚇 Little Haiti & the Upper East Side

Vagabond Pool Bar
Bar

(☎305-400-8420; www.thevagabondhotelmiami.com; 7301 Biscayne Blvd; ⏲5-11pm Sun-Thu, to midnight Fri & Sat) Tucked behind the Vagabond Hotel, this is a great spot to start the evening, with perfectly mixed cocktails, courtesy of pro bartenders (the kind who will shake your hand and introduce themselves). The outdoor setting overlooking the palm-fringed pool and eclectic crowd pairs nicely with elixirs like the Lost in Smoke (mezcal, amaro, amaretto and orange bitters).

Churchill's
Bar

(☎305-757-1807; www.churchillspub.com; 5501 NE 2nd Ave; ⏲3pm-3am Sun-Thu, to 5am Fri &

Sat) A Miami icon that's been around since 1979, Churchill's is a Brit-owned pub in the midst of what could be Port-au-Prince. There's a lot of live music here, mainly punk, indie and more punk, plus jazz on Monday nights.

ENTERTAINMENT

Adrienne Arsht Center for the Performing Arts
Performing Arts

(📞305-949-6722; www.arshtcenter.org; 1300 Biscayne Blvd; ⏰box office noon-5pm Mon-Fri, plus 2hr before performances) This magnificent venue manages to both humble and enthrall visitors. Today the Arsht is where the biggest cultural acts in Miami come to perform; a show here is a must-see on any Miami trip. There's an Adrienne Arsht Center stop on the Metromover.

Cubaocho
Live Performance

(📞305-285-5880; www.cubaocho.com; 1465 SW 8th St; ⏰11am-3am) Jewel of the Little Havana Art District, Cubaocho is renowned for its concerts, with excellent bands from across the Spanish-speaking world. It's also a community center, art gallery and research outpost for all things Cuban. The interior resembles an old Havana cigar bar, yet the walls are decked out in artwork that references both the classical past of Cuban art and its avant-garde future.

New World Symphony
Classical Music

(NWS; 📞305-680-5866; www.nws.edu; 500 17th St, Miami Beach) Housed in the New World Center (p152) – a funky explosion of cubist lines and geometric curves, fresh white against the blue Miami sky – the acclaimed New World Symphony holds performances from October to May. The deservedly heralded NWS serves as a three- to four-year preparatory program for talented musicians from prestigious music schools.

Colony Theater
Performing Arts

(📞305-674-1040, box office 800-211-1414; www.colonymb.org; 1040 Lincoln Rd) The Colony was built in 1935 and was the main cinema in upper South Beach before it fell into

disrepair in the mid-20th century. It was renovated and revived in 1976 and now boasts 465 seats and great acoustics. It's an absolute art-deco gem, with a classic marquee and Inca-style crenellations, and now serves as a major venue for performing arts.

Tower Theater
Cinema

(📞305-237-2463; www.towertheatermiami.com; 1508 SW 8th St) This renovated 1926 landmark theater has a proud deco facade and a handsomely renovated interior, thanks to support from the Miami-Dade Community College. In its heyday, it was the center of Little Havana social life and, via the films it showed, served as a bridge between immigrant society and American pop culture. Today it frequently shows independent and Spanish-language films (sometimes both).

ℹ INFORMATION

Greater Miami & the Beaches Convention & Visitors Bureau (📞305-539-3000; www.miamiandbeaches.com; 701 Brickell Ave, 27th fl; ⏰8:30am-6pm Mon-Fri) Offers loads of info on Miami and keeps up-to-date with the latest events and cultural offerings.

ℹ GETTING THERE & AWAY

AIR

Miami International Airport (MIA; 📞305-876-7000; www.miami-airport.com; 2100 NW 42nd Ave) Located 6 miles west of Downtown. Transport options to/from the city:

○ **Taxi** Flat rate that varies depending on what zone you travel to. It's $22 to Downtown, Coconut Grove or Coral Gables; $35 to South Beach; and $44 to Key Biscayne. Count on 40 minutes to South Beach, and about 25 minutes to Downtown.

○ **SuperShuttle** (📞305-871-8210; www.supershuttle.com) Shared van service to hotels in Downtown (one way $17), South Beach (one way $22) and more; drive time varies.

○ **Bus** Miami Beach Airport Express (bus 150) costs $2.25 and makes stops all along Miami Beach; about 35 minutes.

○ **Train** Metrorail goes to downtown (Government Center) for $2.25 (15 minutes).

Fort Lauderdale-Hollywood International Airport (FLL; www.broward.org/airport) Located 21 miles north of Downtown Miami. Shared van service is available from the airport with **GO Airport Shuttle** (773-363-0001; https://goairportshuttle.com). Prices are around $25 to South Beach.

BUS

For bus trips, **Greyhound** (www.greyhound.com) is the main long-distance operator. **Megabus** (https://us.megabus.com; Miami International Center, 3801 NW 21st St) offers service to Tampa and Orlando.

Greyhound's **main bus terminal** (305-871-1810; 3801 NW 21st) is near the airport, though additional services also depart from the company's **Cutler Bay terminal** (Cutler Bay; 305-296-9072; 10801 Caribbean Blvd) and **North Miami terminal** (305-688-7277; 16000 NW 7th Ave).

TRAIN

The main Miami terminal of **Amtrak** (305-835-1222; www.amtrak.com; 8303 NW 37th Ave, West Little River), about 9 miles northwest of Downtown, connects the city with several other points in Florida (including Orlando and Jacksonville) on the Silver Service line that runs up to New York City. The Miami Amtrak station is connected by Tri-rail to Downtown Miami and has a left-luggage facility.

ⓘ GETTING AROUND

Bus Extensive system, though slow for long journeys. Metrobus fare is $2.25; must be paid in exact change or with an Easy Card (available from Metrorail stations).

Citi Bike Bike-sharing network in both Miami and Miami Beach. With heavy traffic, however, take care riding long distances – it can be hazardous.

Metromover Elevated, electric monorail that is a great (and free!) way to see central Miami from a height.

Metrorail Elevated line running from Hialeah through Downtown Miami and south to Kendall/Dadeland. Trains run every five to 15 minutes. Fare is $2.25. Pay with either the reloadable Easy Card or single-use Easy Ticket (sold from vending machines at Metrorail stations).

Rental Car Convenient for zipping around town, but parking can be expensive.

Taxi & Ride-Sharing Services Best for getting between destinations if you don't want to drive, but can be pricey for long distances. Difficult to hail on the street; call or use an app (Lyft or Uber are the most popular) for a pick-up.

Trolley Free service with various routes in Miami Beach, Downtown, Wynwood, Coconut Grove, Coral Gables, Little Havana and other neighborhoods.

Clockwise from top left: Miami architecture (p146); South Beach skyline (p152); Classic car; South Beach (p152) with its exercise park.

Clockwise from top left: Ocean Drive (p157); Cape Florida Lighthouse (p151); Venetian Pool (p159), Miami food stalls

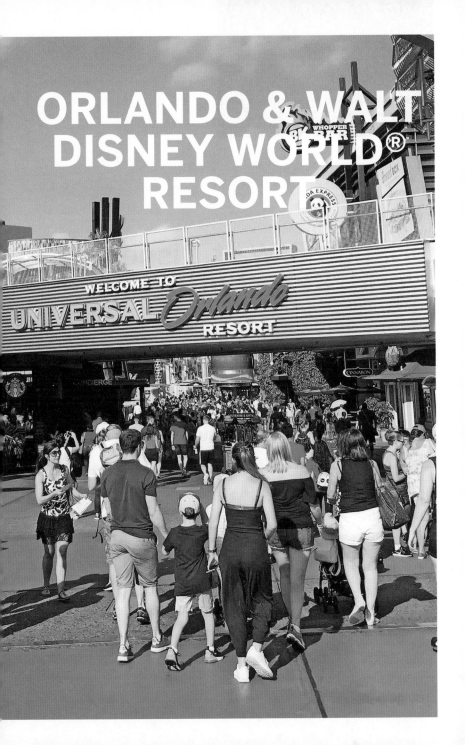

ORLANDO & WALT DISNEY WORLD® RESORT

Orlando & Walt Disney World®Resort at a Glance...

It's so easy to get caught up in Greater Orlando – in the isolated, fabricated worlds of Disney or Universal Orlando (for which, let's face it, you're probably here) – that you forget all about the downtown city of Orlando itself. It has a lot to offer: lovely tree-lined neighborhoods; a rich arts scene; several fantastic gardens and nature preserves; fabulous cuisine; and a delightfully slower pace devoid of manic crowds. So, sure, enjoy the theme parks and the sparkles, but also take time to explore the quieter, gentler side of the city.

Two Days in Orlando

Assuming you're here for some theme-park fun, you can easily kill two days at either Walt Disney World® Resort or Universal Orlando Resort. If you're at the former, pick two out of these three: **Magic Kingdom** (p178), **Epcot** (p179) or the **Animal Kingdom** (p180). At **Universal** (p185), everywhere is fun, but don't miss the Wizarding World of Harry Potter.

Four Days in Orlando

If you still want another world of imagination, head to **Legoland** (p191). Otherwise, spend day three hitting up the **Mennello Museum of American Art** (p190) and **Orlando Museum of Art** (p190), and make sure you have a slice at **P Is for Pie** (p191). On the fourth day, go to Winter Park and enjoy the **Charles Hosmer Morse Museum** (p195).

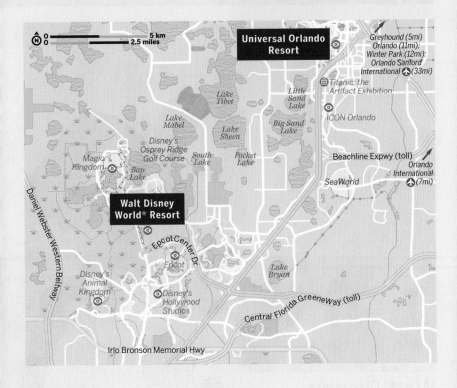

Arriving in Orlando

Orlando lies 285 miles from Miami; the fastest and most direct route is a 4½-hour road trip via Florida's Turnpike.

Orlando International Airport Handles more passengers than any other airport in Florida. Serves Walt Disney World® Resort, the Space Coast and the Orlando area.

Orlando Sanford International Airport Small airport around 25 miles northeast of downtown Orlando and 45 miles northeast of Walt Disney World® Resort.

Where to Stay

Downtown Orlando has some lovely privately owned options, which can be a relief from the resorts. Walt Disney World® Resort and Universal Orlando both offer on-site resort hotels with all kinds of enticing perks. While the town itself is a nice escape, Winter Park's accommodation is limited. Kissimmee has chain hotels within easy driving of the theme parks, but note those in Historic Downtown Kissimmee are too far away to be useful.

Walt Disney World® Resort

It proclaims itself the 'Happiest Place on Earth,' and who's to argue? The Magic Kingdom, Epcot, Animal Kingdom and Hollywood Studios are the four realms that make up Walt Disney World® Resort, and together they work their enchantment.

Great For...

☑ Don't Miss

Waving to all of your favorite characters during the Festival of Fantasy parade each afternoon in the Magic Kingdom.

Magic Kingdom

When most people think of Walt Disney World® Resort, they're thinking of just one of the four theme parks – the **Magic Kingdom** (1180 Seven Seas Dr; $109-129, prices vary daily; ☺9am-11pm, hours vary). This is the Disney of commercials, of princesses and pirates, of dreams come true; this is quintessential old-school Disney with classic rides such as It's a Small World and Space Mountain.

At its core is Cinderella's Castle, the iconic image (this overused phrase is used correctly here) of the television show. Remember when Tinkerbell dashed across the screen as fireworks burst across the castle turrets?

You'll see it as soon as you enter the park and emerge onto Main Street, USA. A horse-drawn carriage and an old-fashioned car run for the first hour from the park

HELEN SESSIONS/ALAMY ©

HELEN SESSIONS/ALAMY ©

ℹ Need to Know

📞407-939-5277; www.disneyworld.disney.
go.com; prices & hours vary; 🚈Disney,
🚌Disney

✕ Take a Break

Epcot's World Showcase brings visitors
food from multiple continents in one
pavilion.

★ Top Tip

If you're staying at a Disney hotel and
are arriving at Orlando International
Airport, arrange in advance for deluxe
bus transportation with **Disney's
Magical Express** (📞866-599-0951; www.
disneyworld.disney.go.com).

entrance to the castle (most people walk),
and from there paths lead to the four
'lands' – Fantasyland, Tomorrowland,
Adventureland and Frontierland, as well as
two other areas: Liberty Square and Main
Street, USA.

Epcot

With no roller coasters screeching overhead, no parades, no water rides and plenty
of water, things run a bit slower in **Epcot**
(200 Epcot Center Dr; $109-129, prices vary daily;
⊙9am-9pm, hours vary) than in the rest of
Walt Disney World® Resort. Slow down and
enjoy. Smell the incense in Morocco, listen
to the Beatles in the UK and sip miso in
Japan.

The park is divided into two sections
situated around a lake. Future World has
Epcot's only two thrill rides plus several
pavilions with attractions, restaurants and
character greeting spots. World Showcase
comprises 11 re-created nations featuring country-specific food, shopping and
entertainment.

There are two entrances (though only
one is shown on the official map). The main
entrance, next to the bus and monorail stations, sits at the landmark geodesic dome
of Spaceship Earth in Future World. The
back entrance ('International Gateway')
is for those catching a boat from Disney's
BoardWalk, Hollywood Studios and Disney
Epcot resort hotels.

Spaceship Earth

Inside what people joke is a giant golf ball
landmark at the front entrance, Spaceship
Earth is a bizarre, kitschy slow-moving
ride past animatronic scenes depicting
the history of communication from cave
painting to computers. Yes, it sounds
boring, and yes, it sounds weird. But it's

surprisingly funny and a cult favorite. In recent years they've tried to modernize it with an interactive questionnaire about your travel interests, but we like the retro aspects better.

World Showcase

Who needs the hassle of a passport and jet lag when you can travel the world right here at Walt Disney World® Resort? World Showcase comprises 11 countries arranged around a lagoon. Watch belly dancing in Morocco, eat pizza in Italy, and buy personally engraved bottles of perfume in France, before settling down to watch fireworks about world peace and harmony.

Disney's Animal Kingdom

Set apart from the rest of Disney both in miles and in tone, **Animal Kingdom**

(2901 Osceola Pkwy; $109-129, prices vary daily; ◎9am-7pm, hours vary) attempts to blend theme park and zoo, carnival and African safari, with a healthy dose of Disney characters, storytelling and transformative magic.

Short trails around Animal Kingdom's Discovery Island lead to quiet spots along the water, where a handful of benches make a great place to relax with a snack. Keep an eye out for animals such as tortoises and monkeys.

Pandora – The World of Avatar

The much-awaited Pandora – The World of Avatar is now open, with highlights that include Flight of Passage, where you get to soar on the back of the Mountain Banshees; the Na'vi River Journey, a boat ride through the bioluminescent rain forest; and

Disney's Animal Kingdom

Valley of Mo'ara, a walk-through extravaganza comprising floating mountains, Na'vi totems and a drum circle.

Finding Nemo: The Musical

Arguably the best show at Walt Disney World® Resort, this sophisticated 40-minute musical theater performance features massive and elaborate puppets on stage and down the aisles, incredible set design and great acting. The music was composed by Robert Lopez and Kristen Anderson-Lopez, who also wrote *Frozen's* Academy Award–winning 'Let It Go,' and

★ **Top Tip**

Call ☏407-939-3463 to make reservations at table-service restaurants throughout Walt Disney World® Resort, or use the My Disney Experience app.

SONGQUAN DENG/SHUTTERSTOCK ©

the spectacular puppets were created by Michael Curry, the creative and artistic force behind the puppets in Broadway's *The Lion King*.

Kilimanjaro Safaris

Board a jeep and ride through the African Savannah, pausing to look at zebras, lions, giraffes, alligators and more, all seemingly roaming free. Sometimes you'll have to wait to let an animal cross the road, and if you're lucky, you'll see babies or some raucous activity. These are not classic Disney auto-animatronic creatures, but real, live animals.

Disney's Hollywood Studios

Hollywood Studios (351 S Studio Dr, Walt Disney World® Resort; $109-129, prices vary daily; ◷9am-8pm, hours vary) is the least-charming of Disney's four parks, but it is home to a couple of WDW's most exciting rides: the plunging elevator in the Twilight Zone Tower of Terror and the Aerosmith-themed Rock 'n' Roller Coaster. Kids can join the Jedi Training Academy, and various programs present Walt Disney himself and how Disney's movies are made. The nighttime spectacular is a Star Wars–themed light and firework extravaganza. Newly added are Toy Story Mania and the Slinky Dog Dash.

Best Restaurants

Jiko – The Cooking Place (☏407-938-4733; 2901 Osceola Pkwy, Disney's Animal Kingdom Lodge; mains $40-57; ◷5:30-10pm; 🅿🍷), with plenty of grains, vegetables and creative twists, a tiny bar, and rich African surrounds is a Disney favorite for both quality and theming. You can relax with a glass of wine on the hotel's back deck, alongside the giraffes and other African beasts.

☑ **Don't Miss**

Build a Better Mousetrip (www.buildabettermousetrip.com) has planning advice and a schedule of free outdoor screenings of Disney movies.

The Polynesian's signature restaurant **'Ohana** (📞407-939-3463; 1600 Seven Seas Dr, Disney's Polynesian Resort; feast adult/child breakfast $40/25, dinner $56/31; ⏰7:30am-noon & 3:30-10pm; 🚸) evokes a South Pacific feel with rock-art animals, a huge oak-burning grill cooking up massive kebabs of meat, and demonstrations of hula and limbo dancing, plus other Polynesian-themed shenanigans. The only thing on the menu is the all-you-can-eat family-style kebabs and veggies, slid off skewers directly onto the giant wok-like platters on the table.

Tips for a Successful Visit

Buy tickets that cover more days than you think you'll need It's less expensive per day, and it gives the freedom to break up time at the theme parks with downtime in the pool or at low-key attractions beyond theme-park gates.

Stay at a Walt Disney World® resort hotel While it's tempting to save money by staying elsewhere, the value of staying at a Walt Disney World® Resort lies in the convenience offered. They do vary in standards, however, and are divided by budget, midrange and deluxe.

Download the Disney app 'My Disney Experience' You can make reservations, reserve Fast-Pass+ attractions, view listings and programs as well as your own schedule.

Take advantage of 'My Disney Experience' Reserve your three FastPass+ attractions per day (www.disneyworld.disney.go.com) up to 60 days in advance (30 days for nonresort guests) – this will give you three guaranteed short lines each day. You can redeem additional FastPasses after you use the first three.

Stock up on snacks Even if it's nothing more than some snack packets and some bananas, you'll save the irritation of waiting in line for bad, overpriced food. Or, to avoid the lines, buy a sandwich early on the way in.

Arrive at the park at least 30 minutes before gates open Don't window shop or dawdle – just march quickly to the rides and then kick back for the afternoon. If you can only manage this on one day of your trip, make it the day you're going to Magic Kingdom. Factor in the time to get here

from the Transportation & Ticket Center (this can take up to an hour).

Speed up, slow down Yes, there's a time to hurry, as 10 minutes of pushing the pedal to the metal could save two hours waiting in line, but allow days to unfold according to the ebbs and flows of your children's moods.

Program 'Disney Dining' into your cell phone While you'll want to make some plans well in advance, once you have a sense of where you'll be at meal time, call 407-939-3463 to make reservations at table-service restaurants at all four theme parks, Disney resort hotels and at Disney's two shopping districts, Disney Springs and Disney Boardwalk (or go online). Also, check

Visitors at Disney's Animal Kingdom (p180)

for last-minute cancellations to dinner shows or character meals.

Transport and accommodation When booking accommodation it's worth considering your transport options. All Disney resorts offer bus transportation, but those offering boat and monorail transportation are far more convenient.

Go with the flow This is about managing expectations. If you build up the idea that your child will definitely hug Belle in a so-called 'character meet,' only to see the line is ridiculous, then recalibrate. Suggest initially that you're going

★ **Top Tip**

Avoid the lunchtime queues: buy a sandwich on the way and picnic at your leisure.

to spot, rather than visit, a character. Believe us, you'll end up spotting them in parades or by chance. In addition to your three FastPass+ experiences, you can head to any of the activities listed in the daily schedule/map.

Popeye & Bluto's Bilge-Rat Barges

Universal Orlando Resort

Pedestrian-friendly Universal Orlando Resort has got spunk, spirit and attitude. It's comparable to Walt Disney World® Resort, but Universal does everything just a bit more smoothly, as well as being smaller and easier to navigate.

Great For...

☑ Don't Miss

The Wizarding World of Harry Potter – likely to be the best theme-park experience you'll ever encounter.

The Universal Orlando Resort consists of three theme parks: Islands of Adventure, with the bulk of the thrill rides; Universal Studios, with movie-based attractions and shows; and Volcano Bay, a state-of-the-art water park.

Islands of Adventure

Islands of Adventure is just plain fun. Scream-it-from-the-rooftops, no-holds-barred, laugh-out-loud kind of fun. Superheroes zoom by on motorcycles, roller coasters whiz overhead and plenty of rides will get you soaked. The park is divided into distinct areas, including the dinosaur-themed Jurassic Park and the cartoon-heavy Toon Lagoon.

Despicable Me Minion Mayhem

ℹ Need to Know

☎407-363-8000; www.universalorlando.com; 1000 Universal Studios Plaza; single park from adult/child $115/110, both parks from adult/child $170/165; ⊙daily, hours vary; ▣Lynx 21, 37 & 40, ⛟Universal

✕ Take a Break

Each Universal resort has high-quality bars and restaurants that you can enjoy even if you're not a guest.

★ Top Tip

If possible, visit during low season; avoid Christmas through early January, March and summer.

Wizarding World of Harry Potter – Hogsmeade

Poke along the cobbled streets and impossibly crooked buildings of Hogsmeade, sip frothy Butterbeer, munch on Cauldron Cakes and mail a card via Owl Post, all in the shadow of Hogwarts Castle. The detail and authenticity tickle the fancy at every turn, from the screeches of the mandrakes in the shop windows to the groans of Moaning Myrtle in the bathroom – keep your eyes peeled for magical happenings.

Harry Potter and the Forbidden Journey Feel the cold chill of Dementors and soar over the castle in a Quidditch match on this simulated masterpiece.

Flight of the Hippogriff Family-friendly coaster passes over Hagrid's Hut – don't forget to bow to Buckbeak!

Hagrid's Magical Creatures Motorbike Adventure Visitors buckle in and 'fly' through the Forbidden Forest.

The Incredible Hulk Coaster

Follow the screams to this massive loop-dee-loop coaster. There's no clickity-clackity building of suspense on this beast – you climb in, buckle up, and zoom, off you launch, from zero to 67mph. Climb up 150ft and fly down through a zero-gravity roll. It was reopened in 2016 with new 'enhancements,' including a new vehicle and a high-tech scientific facility with a 'Gamma Core' as the entrance.

Seuss Landing

Drink Moose Juice or Goose Juice and peruse shelves of Dr Seuss books before riding through The Cat in the Hat or around and around on an elephant-bird from *Horton Hears a Who*. In Seuss Landing, the Lorax guards his truffula trees, Thing One and Thing Two make trouble and creatures from all kinds of Seuss favorites adorn the shops and the rides. There are four rides, a storytelling performance and the wonderful If I Ran the Zoo interactive splash play area.

Universal Studios

Divided geographically by film-inspired and region-specific architecture and ambience, and themed as a Hollywood backlot, Universal Studios has shows and magnificently designed, simulation-heavy rides dedicated to silver-screen and TV icons. Drink Duff beer, a Homer favorite, in Springfield; ride the Hogwarts Express into Diagon Alley; and challenge the host of *The Tonight Show* to a scavenger hunt.

And even folks who don't know anything about he Transformers franchise will enjoy the mind-blowing, Universal-styled 3D simulation of the Transformers ride.

Wizarding World of Harry Potter – Diagon Alley

Diagon Alley, lined with magical shops selling robes, Quidditch supplies, wands, scaly creatures and more, leads to the massive Gringotts Bank. Detour through the blackness of Knockturn Alley, where only dark wizards go to buy their supplies, hydrate with an elixir of Fire Protection Potion poured into Gilly Water, try a scoop of Butterbeer ice cream and, when you hear the grumblings of the bank's ferocious dragon, perched on the top, be prepared for his fiery roar.

Hogwarts Express, linking Hogwarts and Diagon Alley, Wizarding World of Harry Potter

The massive Harry Potter landmarks of Hogwarts and Gringotts house the lines for the respective rides, but are also in and of themselves marvelously themed in great detail. In Hogwarts, the queue winds through the corridors of the school, past talking portraits and Dumbledore's office, and at Gringotts the towering goblin bank tellers look you in the eye. Note: there is a route, too, for those who want to enter without doing the ride, so nobody misses out!

© 2017 UNIVERSAL ORLANDO RESORT. ALL RIGHTS RESERVED

Escape from Gringotts Wind through the bank, with its massive marble columns and goblin tellers, and hop on a combination coaster and simulation ride through Gringotts.

Ollivander's Wand Shop Floor-to-ceiling shelves crammed with dusty wand boxes set the scene for a 10-minute show in which the wand chooses the wizard (note that there is also an Ollivander's show in Hogsmeade).

To enter the Wizarding World of Harry Potter, you must, of course, start in London. Like the rest of Universal Studios, it's themed with great detail to create a sense of place – and it isn't just any London, it's the London of JK Rowling's imagination, the London shared by wizards and muggles alike. There are no traditional rides, but you catch the *Hogwarts Express* from King's Cross Station here.

The Simpsons Ride

The Simpsons creators James Brooks and Matt Groening helped create a simulated extravaganza into Krusty the Clown's techno-colored theme park, Krustyland. Sideshow Bob, escaped from prison, is chasing you and the Simpsons through the park, and you must zip down coasters, spin on kiddie rides and cruise down water slides as you try to escape.

Revenge of the Mummy

A high-thrill indoor coaster combines roller-coaster speed and twists with in-your-face special effects. Head deep into ancient Egyptian catacombs in near pitch black, but don't anger Imhotep the mummy – in his wrath he flings you past fire, water and more. The deep growl of the mummy, screeching of bats and unexpected twists add to the creepy thrills to take this several notches beyond your classic coaster.

Themed Bars at Universal Orlando

Hog's Head Pub (Islands of Adventure; drinks $4-8, theme-park admission required; ☼park opening-park closing) Butterbeer, frozen or frothy, real beer on tap, pumpkin cider and more. Keep an eye on that hog over the bar – he's more real than you think!

Duff Brewery (Springfield; snacks $5-12, theme-park admission required; ☼11am-park closing; 📶) Outdoor lagoonside bar serving Homer Simpson's beer of choice, on tap or by the bottle, and Springfield's signature Flaming Moe.

Moe's Tavern (Springfields; drinks $3-9, theme-park admission required; ☼11am-park closing; 📶) Brilliantly themed Simpsons bar with Isotopes memorabilia, the Love Tester and Bart Simpson crank-calling the red rotary phone; it's as if you walked straight into your TV to find yourself at Homer's favorite neighborhood joint.

Volcano Bay

This is Universal Orlando Resort's third theme park – a water park – launched in 2017. Modeled on a Pacific island, the main feature of this tropical oasis is a colossal volcano through and down which, you guessed it, run watery thrills and spills. Among the attractions are winding rivers with family raft rides, pools and two intertwining slides, but the main attraction is the Ko'okiri Body Plunge. At a hair-raising 125ft, it's the tallest trap-door body plunge ride in North America.

Express Pass

Avoid lines at designated Islands of Adventure and Universal Studios rides by flashing your Express Pass for entry to a separate, shorter line. The standard Express Pass (from $70) allows you to bypass the regular lines one time per participating attraction. The Unlimited Express Pass (from $90) allows you to bypass the regular lines an unlimited number of times per participating attraction.

Most of the Universal Orlando Resort hotels provide Unlimited Express Pass access to guests as part of their package. A limited number of passes per day are available at the park gates, but they do sell out. Check www.universalorlando.com for a calendar of prices and black-out dates.

Jimmy Buffet's Margaritaville, Universal CityWalk

☑ **Don't Miss**

For some downtime or a picnic, a fenced-in grassy area with shade trees and views across the lagoon sits just across from the entrance to Universal Studios' Woody Woodpecker's KidZone.

CityWalk

Across the canal from the three theme parks is CityWalk, Universal's entertainment district comprising a pedestrian mall with restaurants, clubs, bars, a multiplex movie theater, miniature golf and shops. Live music and *mucho* alcohol sums up the entertainment options here. Although nights can be packed with partying 20-somethings, there's a distinct family-friendly vibe and several bars have reasonable food. Oh, and although it feels like a partying theme park in its own right, you can come here even if you're not visiting the Universal theme parks.

Delancy Street Preview Center

Some Universal Orlando visitors could be pulled from the crowds and asked to go to the Delancy Street Preview Center (in the New York section of Universal Studios) to watch clips from a TV pilot or movie and to give their opinions. It's a way of testing potential new shows – and the best part is participants are compensated for their time. As in money. They're looking for a particular demographic based on the material, and it's not always open, but if you stop by and ask you just may be what they want.

★ Top Tip

Pick up a free map at each park entrance. The maps also list the attractions, with a schedule outlining events, shows and locations of free character interactions.

SOLARISYS/SHUTTERSTOCK ©

Orlando

Many visitors never reach downtown Orlando, distracted by the hype and sparkle of Cinderella and Hogwarts, but those who do discover a pretty, leafy city, blessed with a great field-to-fork eating scene and world-class museums.

◎ SIGHTS & ACTIVITIES

Mennello Museum of American Art   Museum

(☏407-246-4278; www.mennellomuseum.org; 900 E Princeton St, Loch Haven Park, Downtown; adult/child 6-18yr $5/1; ⊘10:30am-4:30pm Tue-Sat, from noon Sun; ☐Lynx 125, ☒Florida Hospital Health Village) Tiny but excellent lakeside art museum featuring the work of Earl Cunningham, whose brightly colored images, a fusion of pop and folk art, leap off the canvas. Visiting exhibits often feature American folk art. Every four months there's a new exhibition, everything from a Smithsonian collection to a local artist. The mystical live oak in front makes even parking beautiful.

Orlando Museum of Art   Museum

(☏407-896-4231; www.omart.org; 2416 N Mills Ave, Loch Haven Park, Downtown; adult/child $15/5; ⊘10am-4pm Tue-Fri, from noon Sat & Sun; ☖; ☐Lynx 125, ☒Florida Hospital Health Village) Founded in 1924, Orlando's grand center for the arts boasts a fantastic collection – both permanent and temporary – and hosts an array of adult and family-friendly art events and classes. The popular First Thursday ($15), from 6pm to 9pm on the first Thursday of the month, celebrates local artists with regional work, live music and food from Orlando restaurants.

Titanic: the Artifact Exhibition   Museum

(☏407-248-1166; www.premierexhibitions.com; 7324 International Dr, International Drive; adult/child 6-11yr $24/17; ⊘10am-6pm Fri-Sat, to 8pm Sun-Thu; ☖; ☐Lynx 8, 38, 42, ☐I-Ride Trolley Red Line Stop 9) Full-scale replicas of the doomed ship's interior and artifacts found at the bottom of the sea, 170 in all, including one of only two pieces of the actual ship's hull. Kids especially love the dramatic and realistic interpretation of

ICON Orlando

history – each passenger receives a boarding pass, with the name of a real passenger, and at the end of the experience (once the ship has sunk) you learn your fate.

ICON Orlando   Amusement Park

(www.iconorlando.com; I-Drive 360, 8401 International Dr, International Drive; from $24; ◷10am-10pm Sun-Thu, to midnight Fri & Sat) Orlando has got everything else that goes up and down, so why not round and around? Opened in 2017, ICON Orlando is one of International Drive's latest landmarks. Orlando is flat, but a trip in this, especially at night, affords views of theme parks and the greater area. Check ahead as it sometimes closes for private events.

Combination tickets are available with the Madame Tussauds and Sea Life.

EATING

The 5-mile stretch of Sand Lake Rd from I-4 (at Whole Foods) west to Apopka-Vineland Rd, and including Dr Philips Blvd, is known as Restaurant Row. Here you'll find a concentration of restaurants and high-end chains more popular with locals than tourists, with everything from wine bars to cigar bars, sushi to burgers.

P Is for Pie   Bakery $

(☑407-745-4743; www.crazyforpies.com; 2806 Corrine Dr, Audubon Park; from $2; ◷7:30am-4:30pm Mon-Sat) Clean-lined with an artisan twist to classic pies (as in sweet tarts with a biscuit base), offering mini and specialty options. Flavors include a sublime key lime and tiramisu. Sublime.

Dandelion Communitea Café   Vegetarian $

(☑407-362-1864; www.dandelioncommunity. com; 618 N Thornton Ave, Thornton Park; mains $9-12; ◷11am-10pm Mon-Sat, to 5pm Sun; ☑⚕) 🍃 Unabashedly crunchy and definitively organic, this pillar of the sprouts and tempeh and green-tea dining scene serves up creative and excellent plant-based fare in a refurbished old house that invites folks to sit down and hang out.

👪 Worth a Trip: Legoland

In Winter Haven, about 50 miles southwest of Orlando, **Legoland** (☑863-318-5346; www.legoland.com/florida; 1 Legoland Way; 1-/2-day tickets adult $96/116, child 3-12yr $91/111; ◷10am-5pm, sometimes later; ⚕; ☐Legoland Shuttle) is a joy. With manageable crowds, and no bells and whistles, this lakeside theme park maintains an old-school vibe – you don't have to plan like a general to enjoy a day here, and it's strikingly stress-free. This is about fun (and yes, education) in a colorful and interactive environment. Rides and attractions, including the attached water park, are best for children aged two to 12 years.

Highlights include Flight School, a coaster that zips you around with your feet dangling free, Miniland, a Lego re-creation of iconic American landmarks and cities, and Ninjago, the park's new martial arts–themed section. There are a few remnants from the park's history as the site of Cypress Gardens (c 1936), including lovely botanical gardens. The water-ski show centers on a bizarre and rather silly pirate theme.

Don't miss the Imagination Zone, a wonderful interactive learning center heavily staffed with skilled Lego makers happy to help children of all ages create delights with their blocks. Legoland Shuttle ($5; booking 24 hours ahead is essential) runs daily from I-Drive 360 (near the ICON Orlando).

Celebration town
VIAVAL/SHUTTERSTOCK ©

🍽 Good Eats Near Disney

There are plenty of restaurants catering to Walt Disney World® Resort visitors in Lake Buena Vista and Kissimmee, but it's mostly chains and overhyped disappointments. If you're looking for a quiet evening away from the spinning wheel of Disney, head to nearby Celebration. Several restaurants and bars line the small lake, and they all have patio dining.

There's a 'Little Library,' a drum circle, tables in the yard, and craft and local beers; check the website for details on art openings, poetry readings and live music.

East End Market   Market $
(📋231-236-3316; www.eastendmkt.com; 3201 Corrine Dr, Audubon Park; ⏰8am-7pm Mon-Thu, to 9pm Fri & Sat, 11am-6pm Sun; 🖧🚻) 🍴 Look for the raised vegetable beds and picnic tables outside this hip, earthy little organic collection of locally sourced places to eat and markets. Inside there's Lineage, a fabulous coffee stand; a bar offering Florida beer and wine; Gideon's Bakehouse, with fabulous cakes and cookies; the excellent raw-vegan bar Skybird Juicebar & Experimental Kitchen; Olde Hearth Bread Company; and more.

Stardust Video & Coffee   Cafe $
(📋407-623-3393; www.stardustvideoandcoffee. wordpress.com; 1842 E Winter Park Rd, Audubon Park; mains $7-14; ⏰7am-midnight Mon-Fri, from 8am Sat & Sun; 🅿🛜🖧) 'Don't use the word

hipster to describe this place,' says Tess, the server. She prefers 'weirdo eclectic.' Whatever you call it, you get the picture. This, er, hipster-hippie hangout has folks hiding behind laptops munching on veggie treats or sipping on freshly squeezed juices by day. It's an atmospheric craft cocktail and artisan-beer hot spot by night.

Pho 88   Vietnamese $
(📋407-897-3488; www.pho88orlando.com; 730 N Mills Ave, Mills 50; mains $9-17; ⏰10am-10pm; 🖧) A flagship in Orlando's thriving Vietnamese district (known as Little Saigon), just northeast of downtown in an area informally referred to as Mills 50, this authentic, no frills, *pho* (noodle soup) specialist is always packed. Big bowls of noodles are cheap and tasty, as are the popular potstickers. Many of the items are, or can be done, vegetarian.

DoveCote   French $$
(📋407-930-1700; www.dovecoteorlando.com; 390 N Orange Ave, Suite 110; lunch mains $9-24, dinner mains $16-29; ⏰11:30am-2:30pm & 5-10pm Mon-Sat, 10:30am-2:30pm Sun) With walls painted in vivid blue, gold, and other colors that might come from a Klimt painting close-up, this restaurant, one of the hottest tickets in Orlando, sits within the city's Bank of America building. It's an all-things-to-all-people spot with a brasserie and a coffee stop, plus plenty of excellent cocktails. 'Comfort French' is often used to describe the cuisine.

Melting Pot   European $$
(📋407-903-1100; www.meltingpot.com; 7549 W Sand Lake Rd, Restaurant Row; mains $11-48; ⏰5-10pm Mon-Thu, to 11pm Fri, noon-11pm Sat, to 10pm Sun; 🚻) Kids in particular love the novelty of a fondue dinner (cheese, beef, chicken, seafood and, of course, chocolate). Having said that, it's an elegant spot and a popular date-night place.

La Luce   Italian $$$
(📋407-597-3675; www.laluceorlando.com; 14100 Bonnet Creek Resort Ln; mains $26-44; ⏰6-11pm; 🅿) La Luce is a gem – whether it's a quiet corner table with a special someone or a friendly chat with folks at the bar – and

feels like that place you've been going to for years even if it's your first time here. Meals are fantastic, sometimes quirky, always tasty. Duck *ragu* (meat sauce), crisp salads, melt-in-your-mouth desserts. Just a world of yum. Their butterscotch pudding is so good it even has its own Facebook fan page.

🍷 DRINKING & NIGHTLIFE

Icebar   Bar

(📞407-426-7555; www.icebarorlando.com; 8967 International Dr; entry at door/advance online $20/15; ⏱5pm-midnight Sun-Wed, to 1am Thu, to 2am Fri & Sat; 🚍I-Trolley Red Line Stop 18 or Green Line Stop 10) More classic Orlando gimmicky fun. Step into the 22°F (-5°C) ice house, sit on the ice seat, admire the ice carvings and sip the icy drinks. Coat and gloves are provided at the door (or upgrade to the photogenic faux fur for $10), and the fire room, bathrooms and other areas of the bar are kept at normal temperature.

Adults over 21 welcome anytime; folks aged between eight and 20 are allowed between 5pm and 9pm only.

Hanson's Shoe Repair   Cocktail Bar

(📞407-476-9446; www.facebook.com/hansonsshoerepair; 3rd fl, 27 E Pine St, Downtown; cocktails $15; ⏱8pm-2am Tue-Thu & Sat, from 5pm Fri, from 3pm Sun) In a city saturated with over-the-top theming from Beauty and the Beast to Harry Potter, it shouldn't be surprising that you can walk from 21st-century Downtown Orlando into a Prohibition-era speakeasy, complete with historically accurate cocktails (among others) and a secret daily password for entry. Call for the password. Sure, the cocktails are pricey, but this is Orlando, capital of the gimmicky and pricey. There's a dress code – no sloppy gear. Once inside, it's a cozy nest of folks having a quiet good time.

Redlight, Redlight   Bar

(📞407-893-9832; www.redlightredlightbeerparlour.com; 2810 Corrine Dr, Audubon Park; beers $5-10; ⏱3:30pm-midnight Mon-Thu, to 2am Fri, 1pm-2am Sat, to 11pm Sun; 🛜) Beer aficionados will love the impressive offerings of craft beers on draft at this contemporary local hangout housed in a former Weathermasters repair shop.

Street cafe, Celebration

Independent Bar Club

(407-839-0457; 70 N Orange Ave, Downtown; varies, often $10; ⊙10pm-2:30am Sat-Thu, from 9:30pm Fri) Known to locals as simply the 'I-Bar,' it's hip, crowded and loud, with DJs spinning underground dance and alternative rock into the wee hours.

Woods Cocktail Bar

(407-203-1114; www.thewoodsorlando.com; 49 N Orange Ave, Downtown; cocktails $10; ⊙5pm-2am Mon-Fri, from 7pm Sat, from 4pm Sun) Craft cocktails and craft beers hidden in a cozy, smoke-free, 2nd-floor setting (in the historic Rose Building), with exposed brick, a tree-trunk bar and an earthy feel.

ℹ INFORMATION

Official Visitor Center – Visit Orlando

(407-363-5872; www.visitorlando.com; 8102 International Dr; ⊙8am-8pm; 🚋I-Ride Trolley Red Line 11) Seeming almost like a theme park itself, this vast info center has giant plasma screens, Minions on the walls, and (the reason you came, right?) legitimate discount attraction tickets (also available through its website). It's a great source for information on theme parks, accommodations, outdoor activities, performing arts and more.

ℹ GETTING THERE & AWAY

Amtrak (www.amtrak.com; 1400 Sligh Blvd) Offers daily trains south to Miami (from $47) and north to New York City (from $150).

Greyhound (407-292-3424; www.greyhound. com; 555 N John Young Pkwy) Serves numerous cities from Orlando.

Orlando International Airport (MCO; 407-825-8463; www.orlandoairports.net; 1 Jeff Fuqua Blvd) About 10 miles south of town.

Orlando Sanford International Airport (407-585-4000; www.flysfb.com; 1200 Red Cleveland Blvd) Situated around 25 miles northeast of town.

ℹ GETTING AROUND

LYMMO (www.golynx.com; free; ⊙6am-10:45pm Mon-Fri, from 10am Sat, to 10pm Sun) circles downtown Orlando for free with stops near

Charles Hosmer Morse Museum of American Art, Winter Park

JAMES SCHWABEL/ALAMY ©

Lynx Central Station, near SunRail's Church St Station, at Central and Magnolia, Jefferson and Magnolia and outside the Westin Grand Bohemian.

Winter Park

Founded in the mid-19th century and home to the small liberal-arts school Rollins College, bucolic Winter Park concentrates some of Orlando's best-kept secrets – including several of the city's most talked about restaurants and field-to-fork favorites – within a few shaded, pedestri-an-friendly streets. Shops, wine bars and sidewalk cafes line Park Ave.

◎ SIGHTS

Charles Hosmer Morse Museum of American Art   Museum

(☏407-645-5311; www.morsemuseum.org; 445 N Park Ave; adult/child $6/free; ◎9:30am-4pm Tue-Sat, from 1pm Sun, to 8pm Fri Nov-Apr; 👪) Internationally famous, this stunning and delightful museum houses the world's most comprehensive collection of Louis Comfort Tiffany art. Highlights include the chapel interior designed by the artist for the 1893 World's Columbian Exhibition in Chicago; 10 galleries filled with architec-tural and art objects from Tiffany's Long Island home, Laurelton Hall; and an instal-lation of the Laurelton's Daffodil Terrace.

Cornell Fine Arts Museum   Museum

(www.rollins.edu/cfam; Rollins College, 1000 Holt Ave; ◎10am-7pm Tue, to 4pm Wed-Fri, noon-5pm Sat & Sun) **FREE** This tiny lakeside museum (accredited by the American Alliance of Museums) sits on the campus of Rollins College and houses US, European and Latin American art. Among the highlights are some exquisite old European Master works, as well as a good-sized contempo-rary collection. The collection is on display both here at the museum and at the nearby **Alfond Inn** (☏407-998-8090; www.thealfond-inn.com; 300 E New England Ave; r from $309; 🅿❄@🛜♿🐾), a college-owned boutique hotel. Both have guided tours for visitors, and the museum hosts many other events throughout the year.

❶ GETTING THERE & AWAY

From downtown Orlando, take I-4 to Fairbanks Ave and head east for about 2 miles to Park Ave.

Orlando's **SunRail** (www.sunrail.com) stops at downtown Winter Park.

NEW ORLEANS

New Orleans at a Glance...

New Orleans is something, and somewhere, else. Founded by the French and administered by the Spanish (and then by the French again), it is, with its sidewalk cafes and iron balconies, one of America's most European cities. But it is also, with its vodou (voodoo), Mardi Gras Indians, brass bands and gumbo, the most African and Caribbean city in the country.

However you see it, one fact is certain: the things that make life worth living – eating, drinking and the making of merriment – are the air that New Orleans breathes.

Two Days in New Orleans

Spend day one in the French Quarter. Wander around **Jackson Square** (p206) and explore the **Cabildo** (p206). Grab dinner and drinks in the area, followed by live music at **Preservation Hall** (p215). On day two, head to Uptown and shop along Magazine St. Then check out the Garden District, popping into **Lafayette Cemetery No 1** (p209) and hopping onto the **St Charles Avenue Streetcar** (p204).

Four Days in New Orleans

On day three, soak up the Marigny's vibe. Gape at the Mississippi River from **Crescent Park** (p209) and peruse cool crafts at the **Frenchmen Art Market** (p209). On day four meander around the Tremé – don't miss the **Backstreet Cultural Museum** (p207) or **Willie Mae's** (p212) fried chicken. Head up Esplanade Ave to **City Park** (p206) and wander around the **New Orleans Museum of Art** (p207).

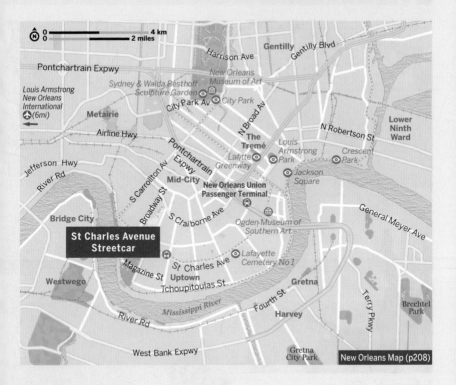

New Orleans Map (p208)

Arriving in New Orleans

Louis Armstrong New Orleans International Airport Located 13 miles west of New Orleans. A taxi to the CBD costs $36, or $15 per passenger for three or more passengers. Shuttles to the CBD cost $24/44 per person one way/return. The E2 bus takes you to Carrollton and Tulane Ave in Mid-City for $2. It's about a five-minute walk to the airport rental-car facility from the main terminal.

Where to Stay

Big hotels are found in the French Quarter and CBD; they tend to have a more boutique, historical feel in the French Quarter, while CBD properties are more modern. Intimate (and quirky) guesthouses and B&Bs are the norm in the Garden District, Uptown, Faubourg Marigny and the Bywater.

Mardi Gras

Weird pageantry, West African rituals, Catholic liturgy and massive parade floats, all culminating in the single-most exhausting and exhilarating day of your life – happy Mardi Gras!

Great For...

☑ **Don't Miss**

The all-female Muses krewe, who take over St Charles Ave in one of the best early parades.

Pagan Beginnings

Carnival's pagan origins are deep. Pre-spring festivals of unabashed sexuality and indulgence of appetite are not a rarity around the world, and neither is the concept of denying these appetites as a means of reasserting human forbearance in the face of animalistic cravings. After trying unsuccessfully to suppress these traditions, the early Catholic Church co-opted the spring rite and slotted it into the Christian calendar. Carnival kickoff is rife with costuming, cross-dressing, mistaken identities and satirical, often crude, pokes at people in power. This attitude persists into Fat Tuesday (Mardi Gras).

Modern Mardi Gras

During the mid-19th century, a growing number of krewes (a deliberately quirky

Krewe member from Mardi Gras Indians

SUZANNE C GRIM/SHUTTERSTOCK ©

❶ Need to Know

Mardi Gras New Orleans (www.mardi-grasneworleans.com) has parade and krewe information and tips on visiting the spectacle.

✗ Take a Break

Coop's Place (p211) cooks up terrific local dishes near the parade action.

★ Top Tip

Bring the kids: Mardi Gras is surprisingly family-friendly outside of the debauch in the French Quarter.

spelling of 'crews,' or clubs) supplied Mardi Gras with both structure and spectacle; the former made the celebration easily accessible, while the latter gave it popularity and notoriety outside of New Orleans. **Rex** first appeared in 1872, **Momus** a year later, and **Proteus** in 1882. Mythological and sometimes satirical themes defined the parades, making these processions coherent theatrical works on wheels. These old-line krewes were (and for the most part remain) highly secretive societies comprising the city's wealthiest, most powerful men.

Many enduring black traditions emerged around the turn of the 20th century. The spectacular **Mardi Gras Indians** began to appear in 1885; today their elaborate feathered costumes, sewn as a tribute to Native American warriors, are recognized as pieces of folk art. The black krewe of

Zulu appeared in 1909, with members initially calling themselves the Tramps and parading on foot. By 1916, when the Zulu Social Aid & Pleasure Club was incorporated, the krewe brought floats, and its antics deliberately spoofed the pomposity of elite white krewes.

Today's 'superkrewes' began forming in the 1960s. **Endymion** debuted as a modest neighborhood parade in 1967; now its parades and floats are the largest around, with nearly 2000 riders and with one of its immense floats measuring 240ft in length.

Throw Me Something!

During Mardi Gras, enormous floats crowded with riders representing the city's Carnival krewes proceed up and down thoroughfares such as St Charles Ave and Canal St. The float riders toss 'throws' to the waiting crowds; throws range from strings of beads to plastic cups, blinking baubles and stuffed animals. Here are some locally recognized rules for throw-catching:

○ First: Locals never bare their breasts for beads. Most find it crude, and there are kids around.

○ Second: If there's a young kid near you, move, or be prepared to give the kid whatever you catch.

○ Third: Many locals will say they'd never touch a throw that hit the street, but we've seen more than a few sneakily bend over to scoop up a cup or a unique string of beads. Rest assured it's not the done thing – even if it is occasionally, well, done.

Twelve Days of Parades

The parade season is a 12-day period beginning two Fridays before Fat Tuesday. Early parades are charming, neighborly processions that whet your appetite for the later parades, which increase in size and grandeur.

Krewe du Vieux By parading before the official parade season and marching on foot, Krewe du Vieux is permitted to pass through the French Quarter. Notoriously bawdy and satirical. Usually held three Saturdays before Fat Tuesday.

Le Krewe d'Etat The name is a clever, satirical pun: d'Etat is ruled by a dictator rather than a king.

Muses An all-women's krewe that parades down St Charles Ave with thousands of members and some imaginative, innovative floats; their throws include coveted hand-decorated shoes.

Mardi Gras weekend is lit up by the entrance of the superkrewes, who arrive with their monstrous floats and endless processions of celebrities, as flashy as a Vegas revue.

Endymion On Saturday night this megakrewe stages its spectacular parade and 'Extravaganza,' in the Superdome.

Revelers during the Bacchus Parade

Bacchus On Sunday night the Bacchus superkrewe wows an enraptured crowd along St Charles Ave with its celebrity monarch and a gorgeous fleet of crowd-pleasing floats.

Zulu On Mardi Gras morning Zulu rolls along Jackson Ave, where folks set up barbecues and krewe members distribute their prized hand-painted coconuts.

Rex The 'King of Carnival,' waits further Uptown; it's a much more restrained affair, with the monarch himself looking like he's been plucked from a deck of cards.

> ★ **Top Tip**
>
> For Mardi Gras or Jazz Fest, reserve accommodations six months to a year in advance.

Walking Krewe Review

Some of the best parades of Carnival Season are put on by DIY bohemian walking krewes, groups of friends who create a grassroots show. Casual observers are always welcome to participate: bring a costume!

Barkus Dress up your furry friends for this all-pet parade (www.barkus.org).

Box of Wine Crazily costumed revelers march up St Charles Ave ahead of the Bacchus (god of wine) parade, distributing free wine from boxes along the way.

Intergalactic Krewe of Chewbacchus Dress up as your favorite sci-fi character at this wonderful parade for geeks, nerds and other people we might hang out with on weekends (www.chew-bacchus.org).

Red Beans & Rice On Lundi Gras, folks dress up in costumes made from dry beans or as Louisiana food items (www.redbeansparade.com).

Society of St Anne Traditionally made up of artists and bohemians, St Anne marches on Mardi Gras morning from the Bywater to the Mississippi and features the best costumes of Carnival Season.

Costume Contests

Mardi Gras is a citywide costume party, and many locals take a dim view of visitors who crash the party without one. For truly fantastic outfits, march with the Society of St Ann on Mardi Gras morning. This collection of artists and misfits prides itself on its DIY outfits, which seem to have marched out of a collision between a David Bowie video and a '60s acid trip. The creativity and pageantry on display needs to be seen to be believed.

SUZANNE C GRIM/SHUTTERSTOCK ©

> ★ **Did You Know?**
>
> The Presbytère (p206) has a permanent exhibit on the Mardi Gras where you can learn everything you ever wanted to know about the festival.

St Charles Avenue Streetcar

Clanging through this bucolic corridor comes the St Charles Avenue Streetcar, a mobile bit of urban transportation history, bearing tourists and commuters along a street as important to American architecture as Frank Lloyd Wright.

Great For...

☑ Don't Miss

Tulane and Loyola Universities and several historic churches and synagogues on the streetcar route.

The Streetcar

The clang and swoosh of the St Charles Avenue Streetcar is as essential to Uptown and the Garden District as live oaks and mansions. New Orleanians are justifiably proud of their moving monument, which began life as the nation's second horse-drawn streetcar line, the New Orleans & Carrollton Railroad, in 1835.

In 1893 the line was among the first streetcar systems in the country to be electrified. Now it is one of the few streetcars in the USA to have survived the automobile era. Millions of passengers utilize the streetcar every day despite the fact the city's bus service tends to be faster. In many ways, the streetcar is the quintessential vehicle for New Orleans public transportation: slow, pretty and, if not entirely efficient, extremely atmospheric.

EQROY/SHUTTERSTOCK ©

St Charles Avenue Streetcar

St Charles Ave

Mississippi River

❶ Need to Know

Streetcars arrive every 15 minutes or so, 24 hours a day. The cost per ride is $1.25.

✕ Take a Break

Surrey's Juice Bar (p212) sits a few blocks away from the streetcar's route, prime for a meaty pit stop.

★ Top Tip

The Jazzy Pass provides unlimited rides on streetcars for one ($3) or three ($9) days; see www.norta.com.

The fleet of antique cars survived the hurricanes of 2005 and today full service has been restored all the way to South Carrollton Ave. In recent times the line has carried more than 3 million passengers a year.

St Charles Avenue

It's only slightly hyperbolic to claim St Charles Ave is the most beautiful street in the USA. Once you enter the Garden District, the entire street is shaded under a tunnel of grand oak trees that look like they could have wiped the floor with an orc army in a Tolkien novel (ie they're old, and they're big).

Gorgeous houses, barely concealed behind the trees, belong to the most aristocratic elite of the city. Those same elite often ride in the floats that proceed along St Charles during Carnival season; look up to the tree branches and you'll see many are laden with shiny beads tossed from Mardi Gras floats. Within the Neutral Ground, or median space that houses the streetcar tracks, you'll often see joggers and families passing through the verdant corridor. By far the best way of experiencing this cityscape is via the slow, antique rumble of the streetcar; freed from driving, you can gaze on all the beauty.

Some of the most elegant buildings to keep an eye out for:

Elms Mansion (3029 St Charles Ave)
Smith House (4534 St Charles Ave)
'Wedding Cake' House (5807 St Charles Ave)
Milton Latter Memorial Library (5120 St Charles Ave)

◉ SIGHTS

◉ French Quarter

Jackson Square Square

(Decatur & St Peter Sts) Sprinkled with lazing loungers, surrounded by sketch artists, fortune tellers and traveling performers, and watched over by cathedrals, offices and shops plucked from a Parisian fantasy, Jackson Sq is one of America's great town greens and the heart of the Quarter. The identical, block-long Pontalba Buildings overlook the scene, and the nearly identical Cabildo and Presbytère structures flank the impressive St Louis Cathedral, which fronts the square.

Cabildo Museum

(☑504-568-6968; https://louisianastatemuseum. org/museum/cabildo; 701 Chartres St; adult/ student/child under 6yr $9/7/free; ☺10am-4:30pm Tue-Sun) The former seat of government in colonial Louisiana now serves as the gateway to exploring the history of the state in general, and New Orleans in particular. It's also a magnificent building in its own right; the elegant Cabildo marries elements of Spanish Colonial architecture and French urban design better than most buildings in the city. The diverse exhibits include Native American tools, 'Wanted' posters for escaped slaves, and a gallery's worth of paintings of stone-faced old New Orleanians.

St Louis Cathedral Cathedral

(☑504-525-9585; www.stlouiscathedral.org; Jackson Sq; donations accepted, audio guide $8; ☺8:30am-4pm, Mass 12:05pm Mon-Fri, 5pm Sat, 9am & 11am Sun) One of the best examples of French architecture in the country, this triple-spired 18th-century cathedral is dedicated to Louis IX, the French king sainted in 1297. It's an attractive bit of Gallic heritage in the heart of an American city. In addition to hosting black, white and Creole Catholic congregants, St Louis has also attracted those who, in the best New Orleanian tradition, mix their influences, such as voodoo queen Marie Laveau.

Historic New Orleans Collection Museum

(THNOC; ☑504-523-4662; www.hnoc.org; 533 Royal St; admission free, tours $5; ☺9:30am-4:30pm Tue-Sat, from 10:30am Sun, tours 10am, 11am, 2pm & 3pm Tue-Sat, 11am, 2pm & 3pm Sun) A combination of preserved buildings, museums and research centers all rolled into one, the Historic New Orleans Collection is a good introduction to the history of the city. The complex is anchored by its Royal St campus, which presents a series of regularly rotating exhibits and occasional temporary exhibits. Artifacts on display include an original Jazz Fest poster, transfer documents of the Louisiana Purchase and utterly disturbing slave advertisements.

Presbytère Museum

(☑504-568-6968; https://louisianastatemuseum. org/museum/presbytere; 751 Chartres St; adult/ student/child $6/5/free; ☺10am-4:30pm Tue-Sun) ✐ The lovely Presbytère building, designed in 1791 as a rectory for the St Louis Cathedral, serves as New Orleans' Mardi Gras museum. You'll find there's more to the city's most famous celebration than wanton debauchery – or, at least, discover the many levels of meaning behind the debauchery. There's an encyclopedia's worth of material on the krewes (parade marching clubs), secret societies, costumes and racial histories that comprise the complex Mardi Gras tapestry, all intensely illuminating and easy to follow.

◉ Mid-City, Bayou St John & City Park

City Park Park

(☑504-482-4888; www.neworleanscitypark. com; Esplanade Ave & City Park Ave; ☺dawn-dusk; P⛽⛲) FREE Live oaks, Spanish moss and lazy bayous frame this masterpiece of urban planning. Three miles long and 1 mile wide, dotted with gardens, waterways and bridges and home to a captivating art museum, City Park is bigger than Central Park in NYC and it's New Orleans' prettiest green space.

New Orleans
Museum of Art
Museum

(NOMA; ☏504-658-4100; www.noma.org; 1
Collins Diboll Circle, City Park; adult/student/
child 7-17yr $15/8/6; ⏱10am-6pm Tue-Fri, to
5pm Sat, 11am-5pm Sun) Inside City Park,
this elegant museum was opened in 1911
and is well worth a visit for its special
exhibitions, gorgeous marble atrium and
top-floor galleries of African, Asian, Native
American and Oceanic art. Its **sculpture
garden** (www.noma.org/sculpture-garden;
⏱10am-6pm Apr-Sep, to 5pm Oct-Mar) FREE
contains a cutting-edge collection in lush,
meticulously planned grounds. Other
specialties include Southern painters and
an ever-expanding collection of modern
and contemporary art. Open until 9pm on
select Friday nights.

◎ Tremé-Lafitte

Backstreet Cultural
Museum
Museum

(☏504-657-6700; www.backstreetmuseum.
org; 1116 Henriette Delille St; $10; ⏱11am-5pm
Mon-Fri, 10am-3pm Sat) Mardi Gras Indian
suits grab the spotlight with dazzling flair –
and finely crafted detail – in this inform-
ative museum examining the distinctive
elements of African American culture in
New Orleans. The museum isn't terribly big
(it's the former Blandin's Funeral Home),
but if you have any interest in the suits
and rituals of Mardi Gras Indians, as well
as second-line parades and Social Aid and
Pleasure Clubs (the local African American
community version of civic associations),
you should stop by.

Louis Armstrong Park
Park

(701 N Rampart St; ⏱sunrise-sunset) The
entrance to this massive park has got to be
one of the greatest gateways in the US, a
picturesque arch that ought rightfully to be
the final set piece in a period drama about
Jazz Age New Orleans. The original Congo
Sq is here, as well as a Louis Armstrong
Statue and a bust of Sidney Bechet. The
Mahalia Jackson Theater (☏504-287-0350;
www.mahaliajacksontheater.com; 1419 Basin St)
hosts opera and Broadway productions.
The park often hosts live-music festivals
throughout the year.

St Louis Cathedral

VESPERSTOCK/SHUTTERSTOCK ©

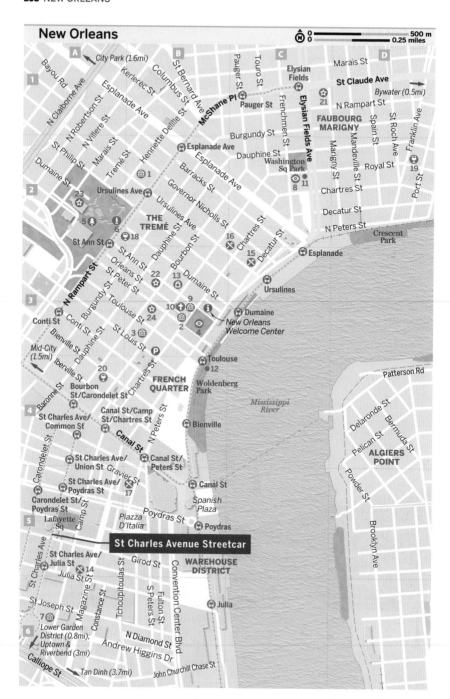

New Orleans

City Park (1.6mi)
Bayou Rd
N Claiborne Ave
Kerlerec St
Esplanade Ave
N Robertson St
St Bernard Ave
Columbus St
McShane Pl
Pauger St
Touro St
Elysian Fields
Marais St
St Claude Ave
Bywater (0.5mi)
21
N Rampart St
N Villere St
Marais St
Tremé St
St Philip St
Henriette Delille St
Pauger St
Frenchmen St
FAUBOURG MARIGNY
Spain St
St Roch Ave
Franklin Ave
Dumaine St
Esplanade Ave
Burgundy St
Dauphine St
Washington Sq Park
Marigny St
Mandeville St
Royal St
19
Esplanade Ave
Barracks St
8
11
Chartres St
Port St
Ursulines Ave
23
Governor Nicholls St
Decatur St
THE TREMÉ
Ursulines Ave
Chartres St
N Peters St
Crescent Park
St Ann St
5
6
18
Dauphine St
16
15
Decatur St
Esplanade
N Rampart St
Orleans St
St Peter St
22
Bourbon St
13
Dumaine St
Ursulines
9
Conti St
Burgundy St
Toulouse St
St Louis St
24
10
2
4
Dumaine New Orleans Welcome Center
Mid-City (1.5mi)
Conti St
Dauphine St
Bienville St
3
Iberville St
20
Toulouse
12
Bourbon St/Carondelet St
FRENCH QUARTER
Woldenberg Park
Patterson Rd
St Charles Ave/Common St
Batonne St
Canal/Camp St/Chartres St
Chartres St
N Peters St
Mississippi River
Delaronde St
Bermuda St
ALGIERS POINT
Canal St
Bienville
St Charles Ave/Union St
Gravier St
Canal St/Peters St
Pelican St
Carondelet St
St Charles Ave/Poydras St
17
Canal St
Powder St
Carondelet St/Poydras St
Spanish Plaza
Camp St
Lafayette Sq
Piazza D'Italia
Poydras St
Poydras
Brooklyn Ave

St Charles Avenue Streetcar

St Charles Ave
St Charles Ave/Julia St
Girod St
WAREHOUSE DISTRICT
St Charles Ave/Julia St
14
Julia St
Magazine St
Tchoupitoulas St
S Peters St
Fulton St
Convention Center Blvd
Julia
St Joseph St
Constance St
7
Lower Garden District (0.8mi); Uptown & Riverbend (3mi)
N Diamond St
Andrew Higgins Dr
Calliope St
Tan Dinh (3.7mi)
John Churchill Chase St

0 500 m
0 0.25 miles
N

New Orleans

Lafitte Greenway   Park
(☎504-462-0645; www.lafittegreenway.org; N
Alexander & St Louis Sts to Basin & St Louis Sts;
☉24hr; ⛺☀) ♦ FREE This 2.6-mile green
corridor connects the Tremé to City Park
via Bayou St John, traversing the length of
the Tremé and Mid-City along the way. It's
a bicycle- and pedestrian-friendly trail that
follows the course of one of the city's oldest
transportation paths – this was originally a
canal and, later, a railroad.

⊙ Faubourg Marigny & Bywater

Crescent Park   Park
(☎504-636-6400; www.crescentparknola.org;
Piety, Chartres & Mazant Sts; ☉6am-7:30pm;
P⛺☀) ♦ This waterfront park is our
favorite spot in the city for taking in the
Mississippi. Enter over the enormous
arch at Piety and Chartres Sts, or at the
steps at Marigny and N Peters Sts, and
watch the fog blanket the nearby skyline.
A promenade meanders past an angular
metal-and-concrete conceptual 'wharf'
(placed next to the burned remains of the
former commercial wharf). A dog park is
located near the Mazant St entrance.

Palace Market   Market
(☎504-249-9003; www.palacemarketnola.com;
619 Frenchmen St, Faubourg Marigny; ☉7pm-mid-
night Sun-Wed, to 1am Thu & Fri, 2pm-1am Sat)

Independent artists and artisans line this
alleyway market, which has built a reputation as one of the better spots in town to
find a unique gift to take home as your New
Orleans souvenir. The selections include
T-shirts with clever New Orleans puns, hand-
crafted jewelry, trinkets and a nice selection
of prints and original artwork.

⊙ CBD & Warehouse District

**Ogden Museum of
Southern Art**   Museum
(☎504-539-9650; www.ogdenmuseum.org; 925
Camp St, Warehouse District; adult/child 5-17yr
$13.50/6.75; ☉10am-5pm Fri-Wed, to 8pm Thu)
The South has one of the most distinctive
aesthetic cultures in the US artistic uni-
verse, a creative vision indelibly influenced
by the region's complicated history and
deep links to the land. Few museums
explore the throughlines of Southern art
like the Ogden, which boasts lovely gallery
spaces, an awesome gift shop and kicking
after-hours performances.

⊙ Garden, Lower Garden & Central City

Lafayette Cemetery No 1   Cemetery
(☎504-658-3781; Washington Ave, at Prytania
St, Garden District; ☉7am-3pm) FREE Of all
the cemeteries in New Orleans, Lafayette

exudes the strongest sense of subtropical Southern Gothic. The stark contrast of moldering crypts and gentle decay with the forceful fertility of the fecund greenery is incredibly jarring. It's a place filled with stories – of German and Irish immigrants, deaths by yellow fever, social societies doing right by their dead – that pulls the living into New Orleans' long, troubled past.

⊙ TOURS

Confederacy of Cruisers   Cycling
(📞504-400-5468; www.confederacyofcruisers.com; 634 Elysian Fields Ave, Faubourg Marigny; tours $49-89) This company sets you up on cruiser bikes that come with fat tires and padded seats for Nola's flat, potholed roads. The 'Creole New Orleans' tour takes in the best architecture of Marigny, Bywater, Esplanade Ave and the Tremé. Confederacy also does a 'History of Drinking' tour (for those 21 and over) and a tasty culinary tour.

Steamboat Natchez   Boating
(📞504-586-8777; www.steamboatnatchez.com; 600 Decatur St) The closest thing to an authentic steamboat running out of New Orleans today, the Natchez is both steam-powered and has a bona-fide calliope on board. The evening dinner-and-jazz cruise (adult/teenager/child $85/40/19.25, without dinner $49/24.50/free) departs at 7pm nightly. There are also brunch-and-jazz cruises at 11:30am and 2:30pm ($53/27.50/10.50, without brunch $36/15.50/free) and a two-hour sightseeing cruise ($48/24/10.50, without brunch $36/15.50/free).

🔒 SHOPPING

Trashy Diva   Clothing
(📞504-299-8777; www.trashydiva.com; 2048 Magazine St, Lower Garden District; ⊙noon-6pm Mon-Fri, from 11am Sat, 1-5pm Sun) It isn't really as scandalous as the name suggests, except by Victorian standards. Diva's specialty is sassy 1940s- and '50s-style cinched, hourglass dresses and belle-epoque undergarments – lots of corsets, lace and such. The shop also features Kabuki-inspired dresses with embroidered dragons, and retro tops, skirts and shawls reflecting styles plucked from just about every era.

ANDRIY BLOKHIN/SHUTTERSTOCK ©

Boutique du Vampyre
Gifts & Souvenirs

(☑504-561-8267; www.feelthebite.com; 709 St Ann St; ☉10am-9pm) This dungeon-esque store stocks all kinds of vampire-themed gifts. Come here for books, curses, spells, souvenirs and witty banter with the awesome clerks who oversee this curious crypt. Among the items is a deck of tarot cards with truly surreal, somewhat disturbing artwork. If your fangs have chipped, their on-call fangsmith can even shape you a new custom pair.

🍽 EATING

🍽 French Quarter

Croissant D'Or Patisserie
Bakery $

(☑504-524-4663; www.croissantdornola.com; 615-617 Ursulines Ave; mains $3-7; ☉6am-3pm Wed-Mon) Bring a paper, order coffee and a croissant – or a tart, quiche or sandwich topped with béchamel sauce – and bliss out. Check out the tiled sign on the threshold that says 'ladies entrance' – a holdover from earlier days. While the coffee is bland,

the pastries are perfect, and the shop is well-lit, friendly and clean.

Coop's Place
Cajun $$

(☑504-525-9053; www.coopsplace.net; 1109 Decatur St; mains $10-20; ☉11am-midnight Sun-Thu, to 1am Fri & Sat) Coop's is an authentic Cajun dive, but more rocked out. Make no mistake: it can be grotty and chaotic, the servers have attitude and the layout is annoying. But it's worth it for the food: rabbit jambalaya or chicken with shrimp and tasso (smoked ham) in a cream sauce – there's no such thing as 'too heavy' here.

🍽 Mid-City, Bayou St John & City Park

Parkway Tavern
Sandwiches $

(☑504-482-3047; www.parkwaypoorboys.com; 538 Hagan Ave, Bayou St John; po'boys $8-14; ☉11am-10pm Wed-Mon; P🚲) Who makes the best po'boy in New Orleans? Honestly, who can say? But tell a local you think the top sandwich comes from Parkway and you will get, at the least, a nod of respect. The roast beef in particular – a craft some would say is dying among the great po'boy makers – is messy as hell and twice as good.

★ Top Five for Eating

Marjie's Grill (p212)

Bacchanal (p212)

Commander's Palace (p213)

Coop's Place

Parkway Tavern

From left: Palace Market (p209); Commander's Palace restaurant (p213); Steamboat Natchez

SUZANNE C GRIM/SHUTTERSTOCK ©

RUBENS ALARCON/ALAMY ©

Marjie's Grill
Asian $$

(☏504-603-2234; www.marjiesgrill.com; 320 S Broad St, Mid-City; mains $8-26; ⊗11am-2:30pm & 5-10pm Mon-Fri, 4-10pm Sat) In one word: brilliant. Marjie's is run by chefs who were inspired by Southeast Asian street food, but rather than coming home and doing pale imitations of the real thing, they've turned an old house on Broad St into a corner in Hanoi, Luang Prabang or Chiang Mai. With that said, there's a hint of New Orleans at work.

🟠 Tremé-Lafitte

Gabrielle
Cajun $$

(☏504-603-2344; 2441 Orleans Ave; mains $16-32; ⊗5:30-10pm Tue-Sat, plus 11:30am-2pm Fri) This old school, high-end Cajun spot has been refurbished into a lovely little blue-and-yellow cottage doling out sumptuous, rich plates of braised rabbit, slow-roasted duck and other favorites. The wine list is deep and, all in all, this is a perfect spot for a date.

Willie Mae's Scotch House
Southern US $$

(☏504-822-9503; www.williemaesnola.com; 2401 St Ann St; fried chicken $15; ⊗10am-5pm Mon-Sat) Willie Mae's has been dubbed the best fried chicken in the world by the James Beard Foundation, the Food Network and other media, and in this case, the hype isn't far off – this is superlative fried bird. The white beans are also amazing. The drawback is everyone knows about it, so expect long lines, sometimes around the block.

🟠 Faubourg Marigny & Bywater

Red's Chinese
Chinese $

(☏504-304-6030; www.redschinese.com; 3048 St Claude Ave, Bywater; mains $5-18; ⊗noon-11pm; 🅿) Red's has upped the Chinese cuisine game in New Orleans in a big way. The chefs aren't afraid to add lashings of Louisiana flavor, yet this isn't what we'd call 'fusion' cuisine. The food is grounded deeply in spicy Szechuan flavors, which pair well with the occasional dash of cayenne.

Bacchanal
American $$

(☏504-948-9111; www.bacchanalwine.com; 600 Poland Ave, Bywater; mains $8-21, cheese from $6; ⊗11am-midnight Sun-Thu, to 1am Fri & Sat) From the outside, Bacchanal looks like a leaning Bywater shack; inside are racks of wine and stinky-but-sexy cheese. Musicians play in the garden, while cooks dispense delicious meals on paper plates from the kitchen in the back; on any given day you may try chorizo-stuffed dates or seared diver scallops that will blow your gastronomic mind.

🟠 CBD & Warehouse District

Carmo
Vegetarian $

(☏504-875-4132; www.cafecarmo.com; 527 Julia St, Warehouse District; lunch $9-12, dinner $9-16; ⊗9am-10pm Mon-Sat; 🅿) 🍃 Carmo isn't just an alternative to the fatty, carnivorous New Orleans menu – it's an excellent restaurant by any gastronomic measuring stick. Both the aesthetic and the food speak to deep tropical influences, from Southeast Asia to South America. Dishes range from pescatarian to full vegan; try Peruvian-style sashimi or Burmese tea-leaf salad and walk away happy.

Restaurant August
Creole $$$

(☏504-299-9777; www.restaurantaugust.com; 301 Tchoupitoulas St, CBD; lunch fixed menu $29, dinner mains $34-50; ⊗5-10pm daily, 11am-2pm Mon-Fri; 🅿) For a little romance, reserve a table at Restaurant August. This converted 19th-century tobacco warehouse, with its flickering candles and warm, soft shades, earns a nod for most aristocratic dining room in New Orleans, but somehow manages to be both intimate and lively. Delicious meals take you to another level of gastronomic perception.

🟠 Garden, Lower Garden & Central City

Surrey's Juice Bar
American $

(☏504-524-3828; www.surreysnola.com; 1418 Magazine St, Garden District; mains $6.50-13; ⊗8am-3pm; 🅿) Surrey's makes a simple bacon-and-egg sandwich taste – and look –

like the most delicious breakfast you've ever been served. And you know what? It probably *is* the best. Boudin biscuits; eggs scrambled with salmon; biscuits swimming in salty sausage gravy; and a shrimp, grits and bacon dish that should be illegal. And the juice, as you might guess, is blessedly fresh.

Commander's Palace   Creole $$$

(📞504-899-8221; www.commanderspalace.com; 1403 Washington Ave, Garden District; dinner mains $28-46; ⏰11:30am-1pm & 6:30-10:30pm Mon-Fri, from 11am Sat, from 10am Sun) Commander's Palace is a dapper host who wows with white-linen dining rooms, decadent dishes and attentive Southern hospitality. The nouveau Creole menu shifts, running from crispy oysters with brie-cauliflower fondue to pecan-crusted gulf fish. The dress code adds to the charm: no shorts or T-shirts, and jackets preferred at dinner. It's a *very* nice place – and lots of fun.

Uptown & Riverbend

Avo   Sicilian $$

(📞504-509-6550; http://restaurantavo. com; 5908 Magazine St, Uptown; mains $17-32; ⏰5-10pm Mon-Sat) Avo is a new kid on the Magazine St block, serving pastas cooked to perfection – as one would expect, with the owner-chef hailing from Sicily. It's clean, cozy and convenient – a perfect stop if you're strolling along shopping and need a bite. It also offers impressive takes on classic cocktails and a 4pm-to-6pm happy hour (cocktails $6, wine half price).

Jacques-Imo's Café   Louisianan $$$

(📞504-861-0886; http://jacques-imos.com; 8324 Oak St, Riverbend; mains $22-36; ⏰5-10pm Mon-Thu, to 10:30pm Fri & Sat) Ask locals for restaurant recommendations in New Orleans, and almost everybody mentions Jacques-Imo's. We understand why: cornbread muffins swimming in butter, steak smothered in blue-cheese sauce, and the insane yet wickedly brilliant shrimp and alligator-sausage cheesecake. That's the attitude at Jack Leonardi's exceedingly popular restaurant: die, happily, with butter and heavy sauces sweating out of your pores.

🍴 Detour: Gretna & Tan Dinh

It may look like a bog standard strip-mall Vietnamese joint when you walk in, but we'd happily contend that **Tan Dinh** (📞504-361-8008; 1705 Lafayette St, Gretna; mains $8-19; ⏰9am-8pm Wed-Mon; 🅿️🍴) is one of the best restaurants in greater New Orleans. The garlic butter chicken wings could be served in heaven's pub, and the Korean short ribs are mouthwatering. It's also a contender for high-quality *pho*. It's popular with families, office workers, as well as some of New Orleans's best chefs, who often come here to indulge their own foodie fantasies. Tan Dinh is located in Gretna, which is across the river from the city center.

Gretna ferry
CRAIG LOVELL/EAGLE VISIONS PHOTOGRAPHY/ALAMY ©

🍷 DRINKING & NIGHTLIFE

🍸 French Quarter

Bar Tonique   Cocktail Bar

(📞504-324-6045; www.bartonique.com; 820 N Rampart St; ⏰noon-2am) 'Providing shelter from sobriety since 08/08/08', Tonique is a bartender's bar. Seriously, on a Sunday night, when the weekend rush is over, we've seen no fewer than three of the city's top bartenders arrive here to unwind. This gem mixes some of the best drinks in the city, offering a spirits menu as long as a Tolstoy novel.

Patrick's Bar Vin   Wine Bar

(📞504-200-3180; http://patricksbarvin.com; 730 Bienville St; ⏰4pm-midnight Mon-Thu, noon-1am Fri, 2pm-1am Sat, 2pm-midnight Sun) With its carpets, plush chairs, nooks and shelves upon shelves of wine, you'll feel like you're visiting a rich friend's house when you have a glass or two here. Along with its own extensive collection, Patrick's Bar Vin offers a limited number of personal, temperature-controlled wine lockers to keep your precious bottles safely stored.

Mid-City, Bayou St John & City Park

Twelve Mile Limit   Bar
(📞504-488-8114; www.facebook.com/twelve.mile.limit; 500 S Telemachus St, Mid-City; ⏰5pm-2am Mon-Fri, 10am-2am Sat, to midnight Sun) Twelve Mile is simply a great bar. It's staffed by people who have the skill, both behind the bar and in the kitchen, to work in four-star spots, but who chose to set up shop in a neighborhood, for a neighborhood. The mixed drinks are excellent, the match of any mixologist's cocktail in Manhattan, and the vibe is super-accepting.

Second Line Brewing   Brewery
(📞504-248-8979; www.secondlinebrewing.com; 433 N Bernadotte St, City Park; ⏰4-8pm Mon, to 10pm Wed & Thu, 2-10pm Fri, noon-10pm Sat, to 8pm Sun; 🚼) Located at the end of some old railroad tracks, Second Line has turned a light industrial warehouse into a kicking brewery with a courtyard and kid-friendly play accoutrements. The frequent presence of food trucks makes this outdoor suds spot a popular place with families and those seeking beer and bites alfresco.

Faubourg Marigny & Bywater

Mimi's in the Marigny   Bar
(📞504-872-9868; www.mimismarigny.com; 2601 Royal St, Faubourg Marigny; ⏰11am-late) The name of this bar could justifiably change to 'Mimi's *is* the Marigny' – it's impossible to imagine the neighborhood without this institution. It's an attractively disheveled place, with comfy furniture, pool tables, an upstairs dance hall decorated like a Creole mansion gone punk, and dim lighting like a fantasy in sepia. The bar closes when the bartenders want it to.

BJ's   Bar
(www.facebook.com/bjs.bywater; 4301 Burgundy St, Bywater) This Bywater dive attracts a neighborhood crowd seeking cheap beers, chilled-out banter and frequent events, from blues-rock gigs to sci-fi readings by local authors. How great is this place? Robert Plant felt the need to put on an impromptu set here when he visited town. Cash only.

★ ENTERTAINMENT

Tipitina's   Live Music
(📞504-895-8477; www.tipitinas.com; 501 Napoleon Ave, Uptown; cover $5-20; ⏰8pm-2am) 'Tips,' as locals call it, is one of New Orleans' great musical icons. The legendary Uptown nightclub, which takes its name from Professor Longhair's 1953 hit single, is the site of some of the city's most memorable shows, particularly when big names such as Dr John come home to perform. Outstanding music from local talent packs 'em in year-round.

AllWays Lounge   Theater, Live Music
(📞504-218-5778; www.theallwayslounge.net; 2240 St Claude Ave; cover $5-10; ⏰6pm-2am Sun-Thu, to 4am Fri & Sat) In a city full of funky music venues, AllWays stands out as one of the funkiest. On any given night of the week you may see experimental guitar, local theater, thrash-y rock, live comedy, burlesque or a '60s-inspired shagadelic dance party. Also, the drinks are super-cheap. A cover fee applies only during shows.

Spotted Cat   Live Music
(www.spottedcatmusicclub.com; 623 Frenchmen St, Faubourg Marigny; cover $5-10; ⏰2pm-2am Mon-Fri, noon-2am Sat & Sun) The Cat might just be your sexy dream of a New Orleans jazz club, a thumping sweatbox where drinks are served in plastic cups, impromptu dances break out at the drop of a feathered hat and the music is always exceptional. Fair warning, though, it can get crowded.

Fritzel's European Jazz Pub   Jazz

(📞504-586-4800; www.fritzelsjazz.net; 733 Bourbon St; ⊙noon-2am) There's no cover charge at this awesome venue for live jazz, which is so small that you really can't have a bad seat. The seating is kind of rustic: benches and chairs so tightly packed that you'll be apologizing for disturbing people each time you go to the bathroom. But the music is great, so come in for a set.

Preservation Hall   Jazz

(📞504-522-2841; www.preservationhall.com; 726 St Peter St; cover Sun-Thu $15, Fri & Sat $20, reserved seats $40-50; ⊙showtimes 5pm, 6pm, 8pm, 9pm & 10pm; ♿) Preservation Hall, housed in a former art gallery dating from 1803, is one of New Orleans' most storied live-music venues. The resident performers, the Preservation Hall Jazz Band, are ludicrously talented, and regularly tour the world. 'The Hall' dates from 1961, when Barbara Reid and Grayson 'Ken' Mills formed the Society for the Preservation of New Orleans Jazz.

❶ INFORMATION

New Orleans Welcome Center (📞504-568-5661; www.crt.state.la.us/tourism; 529 St Ann St; ⊙8:30am-5pm) In the heart of the French Quarter; offers maps, events listings and a variety of brochures for sights, restaurants and hotels.

❶ GETTING THERE & AROUND

TO/FROM THE AIRPORT

Louis Armstrong New Orleans International Airport (MSY; 📞504-303-7500; www.flymsy. com; 900 Airline Hwy, Kenner; 🛜) is located 13 miles west of the city.

⦿ **Taxi** A taxi ride downtown costs a flat rate of $36 for one or two passengers, or $15 per person for three or more passengers.

⦿ **Shuttle** The **Airport Shuttle** (📞504-522-3500; www.airportshuttleneworleans.com; one

way/return $24/44) offers frequent service between the airport and downtown hotels, although it can be time-consuming.

⦿ **Bus** If your baggage is not too unwieldy and you're in no hurry, **Jefferson Transit** (www. jeffersontransit.org) offers the cheapest ride downtown aboard its E2 Airport Downtown Express ($2). On weekdays, until 6:14pm, the bus goes all the way to Tulane and Loyola Ave, at the edge of downtown and the French Quarter; on weekends it will only get you as far as the corner of Tulane St and Carrollton Ave.

BICYCLE

Flat New Orleans is easy to cycle – you can cross the entirety of town in 45 minutes.

The city rents its fleet of **Blue Bikes** (📞504-608-0603; www.bluebikesnola.com; sign-up $5, then per minute 10¢) from kiosks around town. Register for a plan online or via the app to use the service. You can also find private bicycle-rental outfits across town, such as friendly **Alex's Bikes** (📞504-327-9248; www.alexsbikes. com; 607 Marigny St, Faubourg Marigny; per hour/ day $5/30; ⊙10am-6pm Tue-Fri, to 5pm Sat, noon-5pm Sun) in the heart of Marigny.

PUBLIC TRANSPORTATION

Streetcars (aka trolleys or trams) have made a comeback in New Orleans, with four lines serving key routes in the city. They are run by the **Regional Transit Authority** (www.norta.com). Fares cost $1.25 – have exact change – or purchase a Jazzy Pass (one-/three-day unlimited rides $3/9), which is also good on buses. Streetcars run about every 15 to 20 minutes, leaning toward every 30 minutes later at night.

Bus service is decent, but limited. Most visitors only use buses when venturing uptown or out to City Park. Fares are $1.25 plus 25¢ per transfer.

TAXI & RIDESHARE

Uber and Lyft are popular in the city. For a taxi, call **United Cabs** (📞504-522-9771).

AUSTIN

Austin at a Glance...

A big city with a small-town heart, Austin earns the love with great music, culinary prowess, whip-smart locals and a sociable streak that's impossible to resist.

The city easily merits its 'Live Music Capital of the World' title – quality live performances go down every night in its countless bars and clubs. The laid-back food scene is awesome, with busted-up food trucks, down-home barbecue joints and whimsical farm-to-table restaurants cooking up glory. There's heaps of outdoor action on the lakes and trails. And it's all wrapped in an artsy, eccentric package. Austin keeps on keeping it weird.

Two Days in Austin

Start at the **Bob Bullock Texas State History Museum** (p222). Wander Guadalupe St for lunch and groovy murals, then cool off at **Barton Springs Pool** (p229). After dark, plug into Austin's live-music scene downtown. On day two, explore the **Texas State Capitol** (p226). Head to South Congress for lunch and shopping. If it's summer, don't miss the **bat colony** (p220) at dusk. End the night two-steppin' at **Broken Spoke** (p235).

Four Days in Austin

On day three, visit the **Lyndon Baines Johnson (LBJ) Library & Museum** (p227), go paddling at **Lady Bird Lake** (p229) and chow in one of the city's many barbecue joints. Check out the **Lady Bird Johnson Wildflower Center** (p227) on day four, followed by more South Congress action at **Güero's Taco Bar** (p233) and the **Continental Club** (p235).

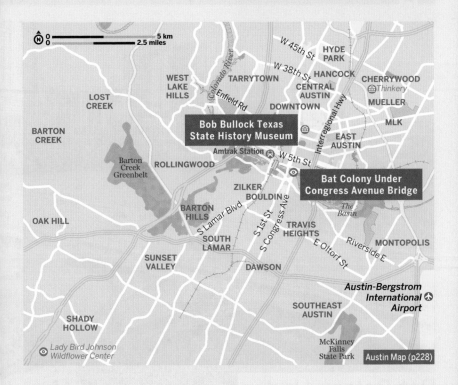

Map labels:
5 km / 2.5 miles

HYDE PARK
W 45th St
W 38th St
HANCOCK
WEST LAKE HILLS
TARRYTOWN
CENTRAL AUSTIN
CHERRYWOOD
Thinkery
LOST CREEK
Colorado River
Enfield Rd
MUELLER
DOWNTOWN
MLK
BARTON CREEK
Bob Bullock Texas State History Museum
Interregional Hwy
EAST AUSTIN
Amtrak Station
W 5th St
ROLLINGWOOD
Barton Creek Greenbelt
ZILKER
BOULDIN
Bat Colony Under Congress Avenue Bridge
The Basin
OAK HILL
BARTON HILLS
S Lamar Blvd
S 1st St
S Congress Ave
TRAVIS HEIGHTS
SOUTH LAMAR
Riverside E
MONTOPOLIS
SUNSET VALLEY
DAWSON
E Oltorf St
SHADY HOLLOW
SOUTHEAST AUSTIN
Austin-Bergstrom International Airport
Lady Bird Johnson Wildflower Center
McKinney Falls State Park
Austin Map (p228)

Arriving in Austin

Austin-Bergstrom International Airport A taxi to or from downtown costs around $30 (Uber and Lyft are typically a bit less), while Capital Metro bus 20 connects the airport with downtown for just $1.25, with departures every 15 minutes.

Where to Stay

Most lodgings are in South Austin, Downtown and the UT & Central Austin area. South Austin holds the mother lode, with excellent boutique hotels. Artsy B&Bs cluster around UT & Central Austin. For budgeteers, a handful of hostels dot the city. Prices skyrocket during SXSW (mid-March), the Formula 1 Grand Prix (late October or November) and Austin City Limits Festival (October).

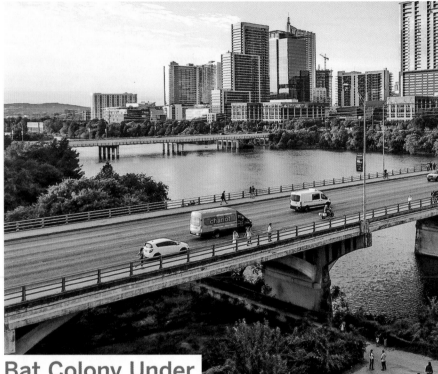

Bat Colony Under Congress Avenue Bridge

Looking like a special effect from a B movie, a funnel cloud of up to 1.5 million Mexican free-tailed bats swarms from under the Congress Avenue Bridge nightly from April to November.

Great For...

☑ **Don't Miss**

Bat Conservation International (www. batcon.org) runs programs throughout the bat season.

Bat Story

The Congress Avenue Bridge was built in 1910. After improvements to the bridge in 1980, a colony of Mexican free-tailed bats moved in. Apparently the bats like the bridge's nooks and crannies for roosting. These tiny winged mammals live in Mexico in the winter then migrate north when Austin warms up. They typically emerge at twilight to feed. The colony is made up entirely of female and young animals. In June, each female gives birth to one pup, and such is the density as the families take to the skies that bat radars have detected bat columns up to 10,000 bat feet (3050m) high.

Congress Avenue Bridge

Lady Bird Lake

Congress Ave Bridge

◉ **Bat Colony**

❶ Need to Know

Congress Ave; ⊘sunset Apr-Nov

✖ Take a Break

Many good restaurants line S Congress Ave south of the bridge. Try Hopdoddy Burger Bar (p232).

★ Top Tip

The best viewing is in August, which is the peak bat migrating season.

Bat Viewing from Land

It's an Austin tradition to sit on the grassy banks of Lady Bird Lake and watch the bats swarm out as dusk approaches, like a fast-moving, black, chittering river. Each night, they feed on an estimated 30,000lb (13,500kg) of insects. Best places on land for viewing? One easy spot is the sidewalk on the eastern side of the bridge. You can also try the lawn behind the Austin-American Statesman building at 305 S Congress Ave, on the southeast end of the bridge. Parking in the Statesman lot is $6 for four hours. Don't miss this nightly show.

Bat Cruises & Kayak Tours

To add a little adventure to your bat watching, view the bats from a boat or kayak on Lady Bird Lake. During bat season, **Lone Star Riverboat** (☏512-327-1388; www. lonestarriverboat.com; adult/child $10/7; ⊘Mar–mid-Dec) offers nightly sunset bat-watching trips on its 32ft electric cruiser. The company's dock is on the south shore of Lady Bird Lake near the Hyatt; **Capital Cruises** (☏512-480-9264; www.capitalcruises.com; adult/child $10/5) also runs tours that depart from behind the Hyatt. **Live Love Paddle** (www.livelovepaddle.com) and **Congress Avenue Kayaks** (www.congresskayaks.com) offer guided evening bat tours.

Bob Bullock Texas State History Museum

This is no dusty historical museum. Big and glitzy, it shows off the Lone Star State's history, from when it used to be part of Mexico up to the present.

Great For...

☑ **Don't Miss**

The not-so-pretty Goddess of Liberty in her display.

La Belle: The Ship That Changed History

The museum's highlight is this exhibit on the 1st floor that showcases the history – and the recovered hull – of *La Belle,* a French ship that sank off the Gulf Coast in the 1680s, changing the course of Texas history. Exhibits explore the ship's remarkable story: sent by King Louis XIV of France under the command of René-Robert Cavelier, Sieur de la Salle, *La Belle* was one of four vessels carrying 400 passengers to the new world, where they were to establish a colony and trade routes. All four ships were eventually lost, with *La Belle* sinking off the Texas coast in 1686. Archaeologists have recovered 1.4 million artifacts; muskets, glass beads and farming tools are currently on display.

ARCHITECT VERNER JOHNSON. IMAGE: KUMAR SRISKANDAN/ALAMY ©

❶ Need to Know

📞512-936-8746; www.thestoryoftexas. com; 1800 Congress Ave; adult/child $13/9; ⊙9am-5pm Mon-Sat, noon-5pm Sun

✕ Take a Break

Grab at beer at **Scholz Garten** (📞512-474-1958; www.scholzgarten.com; 1607 San Jacinto Blvd; ⊙11am-10pm Mon-Sat, noon-8pm Sun).

★ Top Tip

Don't waste too much time driving around looking for parking. The lot beneath the building is convenient and costs a flat $10.

Story of Texas

The Texas History galleries are the core of the museum, and more than 700 artifacts are displayed across three floors. The 1st floor focuses on *La Belle,* while exhibits on the 2nd floor trace Texas history from 1821 to 1936. A statue of Texas statesman and hero Sam Houston marks the entrance. As you explore, you'll discover more about Texas booster Stephen F Austin (check out his pine desk) and learn more about the Alamo and Texas Comanches. The 3rd floor covers the state's economic expansion into oil drilling and space exploration. Special

features cover John Wayne's 1960 movie *The Alamo*, and home-grown music from Bob Wills to Buddy Holly. Allow a few hours for your visit.

IMAX & The Star of Destiny

The museum also houses an IMAX theater (check website for listings; adult/child four to 17 years $9/7), and the Texas Spirit Theater (adult/child four to 17 years $6/5), which shows *The Star of Destiny*, a 'multi-sensory' 15-minute film that's simultaneously high-tech and hokey fun.

South Congress Stroll

You won't find any chain stores along S Congress Ave, and the indie shops here are truly unique. People-watching is superb.

Start Lucy in Disguise
Distance 0.1 mile
Duration 1 hour

6 Colorful and unique arts and crafts, many with a Latin influence, stock **Tesoros Trading Co** (1500 S Congress Ave, ⏱11am-6pm Sun-Fri, 10am-6pm Sat).

W Monroe St

Classic Photo Allens Boots

3 Towering aisles of men's and women's cowboy boots beckon at **Allens Boots** (p230).

W Milton St

4 Willy Wonka would be impressed by **Big Top Candy Shop** (1706 S Congress Ave), filled with sweet delights.

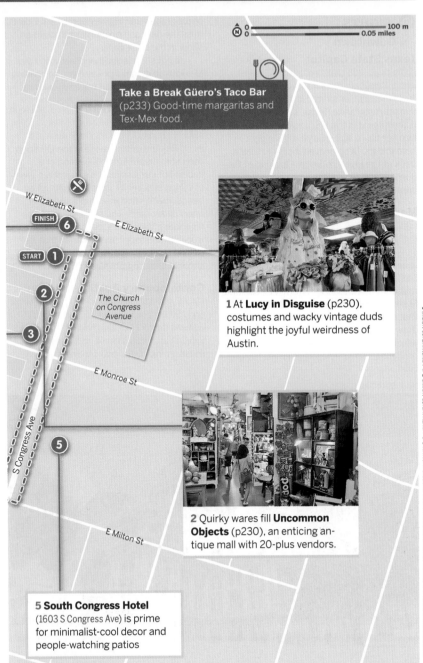

N

0 ——— 100 m
0 ——— 0.05 miles

Take a Break Güero's Taco Bar
(p233) Good-time margaritas and
Tex-Mex food.

W Elizabeth St

FINISH 6

E Elizabeth St

START 1

2

3

The Church
on Congress
Avenue

E Monroe St

S Congress Ave

5

E Milton St

1 At **Lucy in Disguise** (p230),
costumes and wacky vintage duds
highlight the joyful weirdness of
Austin.

2 Quirky wares fill **Uncommon
Objects** (p230), an enticing antique mall with 20-plus vendors.

5 South Congress Hotel
(1603 S Congress Ave) is prime
for minimalist-cool decor and
people-watching patios

⊙ SIGHTS

◉ Downtown

Texas State Capitol   Historic Building
(tours 512-305-8402; cnr 11th St & Congress Ave; ⊘7am-10pm Mon-Fri, 9am-8pm Sat & Sun; 🚹) **FREE** Completed in 1888 using sunset-red granite, Texas' state capitol is the largest in the US, backing up the familiar claim that everything's bigger hereabouts. Drop in even if only to take a peek at the lovely rotunda – look up at the dome – and try out the whispering gallery created by its curved ceiling.

Mexic-Arte Museum   Museum
(512-480-9373; www.mexic-artemuseum. org; 419 Congress Ave; adult/child under 12yr/ student $7/1/4, free Sun; ⊘10am-6pm Mon-Thu, to 5pm Fri & Sat, noon-5pm Sun, closed during SXSW) This wonderful, eclectic downtown museum features works from Mexican and Mexican American artists in exhibitions that change every two months. Many are drawn from the permanent collection, which includes carved wooden masks, modern Latin American paintings, historic photographs and contemporary art. Don't miss the new and experimental talent on show in the back gallery.

The gift shop is another draw, with killer Mexican stuff that's pricey if you're heading south of the border, but reasonable if not.

Museum of the Weird   Museum
(512-476-5493; www.museumoftheweird.com; 412 E 6th St; adult/child $12/8; ⊘10am-midnight) Pay the entrance fee in the gift shop, then step inside Austin's version of a cabinet of curiosities. It's more of a hallway of curiosities, really, lined with shrunken heads, malformed mammals and other unusual artifacts. The show stealer? The legendary Minnesota Ice Man – is that a frozen prehistoric man under all that ice? See for yourself, then grab a seat for a live show of amazing physical derring-do.

Contemporary Austin   Museum
(512-453-5312; www.thecontemporaryaustin. org; 700 Congress Ave; adult/child $10/free; ⊘Jones Center 11am-7pm Tue-Sat, noon-5pm Sun, Laguna Gloria 10am-4pm Tue-Sun) This museum operates two separate sites.

Texas State Capitol building

The Jones Center, downtown, features rotating exhibits representing new artists, spreading through two gallery floors plus the two-tier Moody Rooftop, an open-air event space with great city views. The Laguna Gloria (3809 W 35th St) is a 1916 Italianate villa on the shores of Lake Austin that holds temporary exhibits plus an engaging sculpture park.

◎ East Austin
Thinkery   Museum
(📞512-469-6200; www.thinkeryaustin.org; 1830 Simond Ave; adult/child under 2yr $12/ free; ⏰10am-5pm Tue, Thu & Fri, to 8pm Wed, to 6pm Sat & Sun; 🚼) This huge, red, box-like building north of downtown inspires young minds with hands-on activities in the realms of science, technology and the arts. Kids can get wet learning about fluid dynamics, build LED light structures and explore chemical reactions in the Kitchen Lab, among other attractions. A spectacular outdoor play area holds nets and climbing toys. Closed Monday except for Baby Bloomers and other special events.

◎ UT & Central Austin
Lyndon Baines Johnson (LBJ) Library & Museum   Museum
(📞512-721-0200; www.lbjlibrary.org; 2313 Red River St; adult/child 13-17yr $10/3; ⏰9am-5pm) Devoted to the 36th US president, who launched his political career in Austin, this museum is still attracting the crowds more than 50 years since he left office. Beyond the hokey, animatronic LBJ that regales visitors with the president's favourite anecdotes, the displays are fascinating and comprehensive, covering such major 1960s events as the assassination of President Kennedy, Johnson's subsequent role in pushing through Civil Rights legislation, and the role played by the Vietnam War in his eventual downfall.

Personal mementos include LBJ's presidential limo and assorted gifts from heads of state (including two terracotta horseback riders from Chiang Kai-shek). Don't

Lady Bird Johnson Wildflower Center

Anyone with an interest in Texas' flora and fauna should make the 20-minute drive to the wonderful gardens of the **Lady Bird Johnson Wildflower Center** (📞512-232-0100; www.wildflower.org; 4801 La Crosse Ave; adult/child 5-17yr/student & senior $10/4/8; ⏰9am-5pm Tue-Sun), southwest of downtown Austin. The center, founded in 1982 with the assistance of Texas' beloved former first lady, has a display garden featuring every type of wildflower and plant that grows in Texas, separated by geographical region, with an emphasis on Hill Country flora. Spring is the best time to visit, but there's something in bloom all year.

The Wildflower Center hosts a variety of events during National Wildflower Week in May.

miss the 8th floor, for a replica of Johnson's Oval Office, and an exhibit on Lady Bird Johnson, the president's wife.

University of Texas at Austin   University
(www.utexas.edu; cnr University Ave & 24th St) Whatever you do, don't call it 'Texas University' – them's fightin' words, usually used derisively by Texas A&M students to take their rivals down a notch. Sorry, A&M, but the main campus of the University of Texas is kind of a big deal. Established in 1883, UT has the largest enrollment in the state, with over 50,000 students.

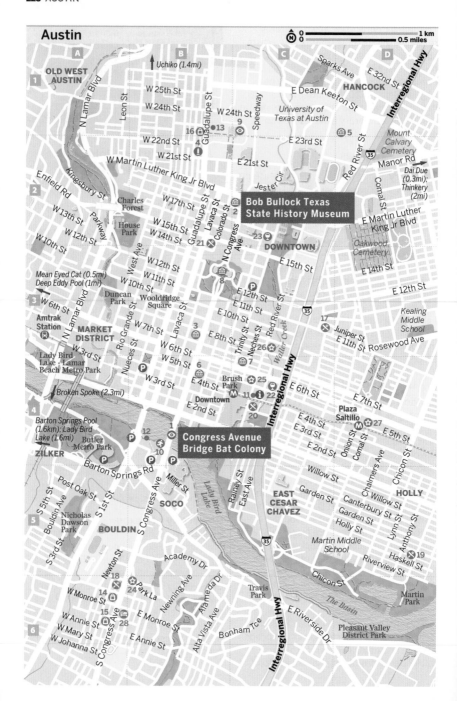

Austin

0 ———— 1 km
0 ———— 0.5 miles

A

OLD WEST
AUSTIN

Uchiko (1.4mi) ↑

N Lamar Blvd

Leon St

W 25th St

W 24th St

B

Guadalupe St

W 24th St

Speedway

Sparks Ave

C

E Dean Keeton St

HANCOCK

E 32nd St

D

Interregional Hwy

University of
Texas at Austin

E 23rd St

Mount
Calvary
Cemetery

16 🅰 ● 13
4 🅰
W 22nd St

9 �“
2

Red River St

Manor Rd →

Dai Due
(0.3mi);
Thinkery
(2mi)

Comal St

W 21st St

W Martin Luther King Jr Blvd

E 21st St

Jester Cir

🏛 5

Kingsbury St

Enfield Rd

1

2

W 13th St

W 12th St

W 10th St

Charles
Forest

House
Park

Parkway

W 17th St

W 15th St
W 14th St

Guadalupe St

Lavaca St

Colorado St

N Congress Ave

**Bob Bullock Texas
State History Museum**

E Martin Luther
King Jr Blvd

Comal St

23 🍴

DOWNTOWN

Oakwood
Cemetery

E 14th St

West Ave

W 12th St
W 11th St
W 10th St

21 🍴

8

E 15th St

E 12th St

Mean Eyed Cat (0.5mi)
Deep Eddy Pool (1mi)

3

W 6th St

N Lamar Blvd

Duncan
Park

Rio Grande St

Wooldridge
Square

Lavaca St

E 12th St
E 11th St
E 10th St

Red River St

🅿

17
🍴 Juniper St
E 11th St Rosewood Ave

Kealing
Middle
School

Amtrak
Station
🚉

MARKET
DISTRICT

W 7th St

Nueces St

W 6th St

W 5th St

E 8th St

Trinity St

Neches St

3
🏛

26 🍴

7 🏛

Walter Creek

E 7th St

Lady Bird
Lake - Lamar
Beach Metro Park

W 3rd St

🅿

W 3rd St

6

E 4th St
Brush
Park

Downtown
Ⓜ 11 ℹ 22

E 6th St

Interregional Hwy

Broken Spoke (2.3mi) ↓

Barton Springs Pool
(1.6km); Lady Bird
Lake (1.6mi)

ZILKER

4

Butler
Metro Park

🅿

12
🅿

10 🅰

1 �“

🅿

🍴 25

20 🍴

Downtown
E 2nd St

E 4th St
E 3rd St

E 2nd St

Plaza
Saltillo
Ⓜ 27 🍴

Onion St

Comal St

Chalmers Ave

E 5th St

Chicon St

HOLLY

**Congress Avenue
Bridge Bat Colony**

Willow St

Rainey St

East Ave

Garden St

Canterbury St

Willow St

EAST
CESAR
CHAVEZ

Garden St

Holly St

Lynn St

Anthony St

Barton Springs Rd

Miller St

SOCO

Lady Bird Lake

Post Oak St

Bouldin Ave

S 5th St

S 3rd St

Nicholas
Dawson
Park

1st St

BOULDIN

S Congress Ave

5

Newton St

18 🍴

14 🅰

15 🍴

28 ℹ

Park La

24 🍴

E Monroe St

Academy Dr

Newning Ave

Alameda Dr

Alta Vista Ave

Martin Middle
School

35

Riverview Ave

Chicon St

Haskell St

19 🍴

Martin
Park

W Monroe St

6

W Annie St

W Mary St

W Johanna St

S Congress Ave

E Annie St

Bonham Tce

Travis
Park

The Basin

Pleasant Valley
District Park

E Riverside Dr

Interregional Hwy

Austin

Hi, How Are You Mural   Public Art

(cnr 21st & Guadalupe Sts) Created by songwriter and artist Daniel Johnston, this iconic bug-eyed frog greets passersby near the University of Texas. Also known as Jeremiah the Innocent, the mural covers the south wall of a Thai restaurant known as Thai, How Are You – which changed its name from the less pun-tastic Thai Spice.

 ACTIVITIES

Barton Springs Pool   Swimming

(512-974-6300; 2201 Barton Springs Rd; adult/ child $9/5; 5am-10pm) Hot? Not for long. Even when the temperature hits 100, you'll be shivering in a jiff after you jump into this icy-cold natural-spring pool. Draped with century-old pecan trees, the area around the pool is a social scene in itself, and the place gets packed on hot summer days.

Lady Bird Lake   Canoeing

(512-459-0999; www.rowingdock.com; 2418 Stratford Dr; 9am-8pm) Named after former first lady 'Lady Bird' Johnson, Lady Bird Lake looks like a river. And no wonder:

it's actually a dammed-off section of the Colorado River. Get on the water at the rowing dock, which rents kayaks, stand-up paddleboards and canoes from $10 to $20 per hour Monday to Thursday, and slightly higher prices on weekends.

Deep Eddy Pool   Swimming

(512-472-8546; www.deepeddy.org; 401 Deep Eddy Ave; adult/child/12-17/ under 11yr $9/5/4; 8am-10pm Mon-Fri, to 9pm Sat & Sun) Complete with vintage 1930s bathhouse, built by the Works Progress Administration, Texas' oldest swimming pool is fed by cold springs and surrounded by cottonwood trees. Separate areas accommodate waders and lap swimmers.

TOURS

Texpert Tours   Tours

(512-383-8989; www.texperttours.com; per hour from $100, minimum 3hr) For an interesting alternative to your stereotypical, run-of-the-mill bus and van tour, contact affable public-radio host Howie Richey (aka the 'Texas Back Roads Scholar'). Historical

Detour: Barbecue Trail

They call it the **Texas Barbecue Trail** (www.texasbbqtrails.com): 80 artery-clogging miles worth of the best brisket, ribs and sausage Texas has to offer, stretching from Taylor (36 miles northeast of Austin) down to Luling, passing through Elgin and Lockhart along the way. Marketing gimmick? Perhaps. Do our stomachs care? They do not. If your schedule or limited appetite make driving two hours and eating at 12 different barbecue restaurants unfeasible, make a beeline for brisket in Lockhart, or, if it's hot sausage you crave, Elgin is your best bet.

Smitty's Market barbecue restaurant
STEPHEN SAKS PHOTOGRAPHY/ALAMY ©

anecdotes, natural history and environmental tips are all part of the educational experience. A three-hour tour of central Austin takes visitors to the state capitol, the Governor's Mansion and the top of Mt Bonnell.

Downtown Walking Tours   Walking
([📞]512-478-0098; www.austintexas.org; 602 E 4th St; $10; ⊙schedules vary) The Austin Visitor Center (p235) runs a program of three different downtown walking tours. Each lasts 1½ hours, costs $10, and starts either from the capitol steps or the visitor center itself, nearby. Check schedules online, and reserve 48 hours in advance if possible.

UT Tower Tours   Tours
([📞]512-475-6636; www.tower.utexas.edu; $6; ⊙hours vary seasonally) Student escorts accompany visitors to the observation deck of the landmark tower, where they provide information about its history and background. Guests can walk around the deck on their own, before the escort takes the group back down. The tour includes an elevator ride to the 27th floor followed by a climb up three short flights of stairs (auxiliary elevator available for those with restricted mobility). Reserve your ticket in advance; pick it up at the Texas Union.

No bags or purses are permitted. You cannot leave the tour early.

🅂 SHOPPING

Uncommon Objects   Vintage
([📞]512-442-4000; 1512 S Congress Ave; ⊙11am-7pm Sun-Thu, to 8pm Fri & Sat) 'Curious oddities' is what they advertise at this quirky antique store that sells all manner of fabulous knickknacks, all displayed with an artful eye. More than 20 different vendors scour the state to stock their stalls, so there's plenty to look at.

Lucy in Disguise   Vintage
([📞]512-444-2002; www.lucyindisguise.com; 1506 S Congress Ave; ⊙11am-7pm Mon-Thu, to 8pm Fri-Sun) Colorful and over the top, this South Congress staple has been outfitting Austinites for years. You can rent or buy costume pieces, which is this place's specialty, but you can also find everyday vintage duds as well.

Allens Boots   Fashion & Accessories
([📞]512-447-1413; www.allensboots.com; 1522 S Congress Ave; ⊙9am-8pm Mon-Sat, noon-6pm Sun) In hip South Austin, family-owned Allens sells row upon row of traditional cowboy boots for ladies, gents and kids. A basic pair costs from $100 or so, while somethin' fancy runs a few hundred dollars.

Barton Springs Pool (p229)

University Co-op   Gifts & Souvenirs
(📞512-476-7211; www.universitycoop.com; 2246 Guadalupe St; ⏰9am-8pm Mon-Fri, to 7pm Sat, 11am-6pm Sun) Stock up on souvenirs sporting the Longhorn logo at this store brimming with school spirit. It's amazing the sheer quantity of objects that come in burnt orange and white.

EATING

🔵 Downtown

Texas Chili Parlor   Tex-Mex $
(📞512-472-2828; 1409 Lavaca St; mains $4-10; ⏰11am-2am Mon-Sat, to 1am Sun) Ready for an X-rated meal? Venture into the large dining room that lurks behind the frankly unenticing facade of this Austin institution. When ordering your chili, keep in mind that 'X' is mild, 'XX' is spicy and 'XXX' is melt-your-face-off hot. Of course there's more than just chili here; there's Frito pie, which is chili over Fritos.

Moonshine Patio
Bar & Grill   American $$
(📞512-236-9599; www.moonshinegrill.com; 303 Red River St; dinner mains $14-25; ⏰11am-10pm Mon-Thu, to 11pm Fri & Sat, 9am-2pm & 5-10pm Sun) A remarkable relic from Austin's early days, this historic mid-1850s building now houses a large and deservedly popular restaurant, serving upscale Southern-flavored comfort food like shrimp and grits or chicken-fried steak. Happy hour sees half-price appetizers, and there's a lavish Sunday brunch buffet ($20). Dine indoors or beneath the pecan trees on the patio.

🔵 East Austin

Franklin Barbecue   Barbecue $
(📞512-653-1187; www.franklinbbq.com; 900 E 11th St; sandwiches $7-12.50, ribs/brisket per lb $19/25; ⏰11am-2pm Tue-Sun) This famous BBQ joint only serves lunch, and only until it runs out – usually well before 2pm. To avoid missing out, join the line – and there will be a line – by 10am (9am on weekends). Treat it as a tailgating party: bring beer or

mimosas to share and make friends. And yes, you do want the fatty brisket.

A few tips? Look for handy fold-out chairs near the front of the line. While you wait, you can buy beer from a cooler-toting server. And when your moment of glory arrives, go for the two-meat plate, or nab all you can for a feast to enjoy later. (Just be quick about it. The people behind you are starving.)

Launderette   Modern American $$

(☑512-382-1599; www.launderetteaustin.com; 2115 Holly St; mains $18-42; ⊙11am-2:30pm daily, 5-10pm Sun-Thu, to 11pm Fri & Sat) A brilliant repurposing of a former washeteria, Launderette has a stylish, streamlined design that provides a fine backdrop to the delicious Mediterranean-inspired cooking. Among the hits: crab toast, wood-grilled octopus, brussels sprouts with apple-bacon marmalade, a perfectly rendered brick chicken and whole grilled branzino.

Dai Due   American $$$

(☑512-719-3332; www.daidue.com; 2406 Manor Rd; breakfast & lunch $13-22, dinner $21-69;

⊙11am-3pm & 5-10pm Tue-Fri, from 10am Sat & Sun) Even an eggs-and-sausage breakfast is a meal to remember at this lauded East Austin favorite. All ingredients come from Texas farms, rivers and hunting grounds, as well as the Gulf of Mexico. Supper Club dinners spotlight items like wild game and foraged treats. Like your cut of meat? See if the attached butcher shop has a few pounds to go.

⊗ South Austin

Hopdoddy Burger Bar   Burgers $

(☑512-243-7505; www.hopdoddy.com; 1400 S Congress Ave; burgers $7-13; ⊙5pm-3am Sun-Thu, to 4am Fri & Sat; 🖘) Folks line up around the block for burgers, fries and shakes – and it's not because they're hard to come by in Austin. It's because the Hopdoddy chain's flagship outlet slathers love into everything it makes, from the humanely raised beef to the locally sourced ingredients to the fresh-baked buns. The sleek, modern building is pretty sweet, too.

Güero's Taco Bar

Güero's Taco Bar   Tex-Mex $$

(☎512-447-7688; www.gueros.com; 1412 S Congress Ave; breakfast $5-7, lunch & dinner $9-38; ⏰11am-10pm Mon-Wed, to 11pm Thu & Fri, 8am-11pm Sat, to 10pm Sun; 🛜) Set in a sprawling former feed-and-seed store from the late 1800s, this Austin classic always draws a crowd. Güero's may not serve the best Tex-Mex in town, but with its free chips and salsa, refreshing margaritas and convivial vibe, we can almost guarantee a fantastic time. And the food? Try the homemade corn tortillas and chicken tortilla soup.

Market District, Clarksville & North Austin

Uchiko   Japanese $$$

(☎512-916-4808; www.uchikoaustin.com; 4200 N Lamar Blvd; small plates $4-28, sushi rolls $10-16; ⏰5-10pm Sun-Thu, to 11pm Fri & Sat) Not content to rest on his Uchi laurels, chef Tyson Cole opened this bustling North Lamar restaurant, which describes itself as 'Japanese farmhouse dining.' All we can say is, if these fantastic and unique delicacies are anything to go by, you'll soon be yearning to visit a few Japanese farmhouses. Reservations are highly recommended.

DRINKING & NIGHTLIFE

Little Longhorn Saloon   Bar

(www.thelittlelonghornsaloon.com; 5434 Burnet Rd; ⏰5pm-midnight Tue & Wed, to 1am Thu-Sat, 2-10pm Sun) This funky little cinder-block building, 5 miles north of downtown, is one of those dive bars that Austinites love so very much. They did even before it became nationally famous for Chicken Shit Bingo on Sunday night, when it's so crowded you can barely see the darn chicken – but, hey, it's still fun. There's live music most other nights.

Easy Tiger   Beer Garden

(☎512-614-4972; www.easytigeraustin.com; 709 E 6th St; ⏰11am-midnight Sun-Wed, to 2am Thu-Sat) The one bar on Dirty 6th that all locals love? Easy Tiger, an inside-outside beer

Big-Time Music Fests

Austin hosts a couple of world-renowned music bashes, but be prepared for massive crowds.

South by Southwest (SXSW; www.sxsw.com; single festival $825-1325, combo pass $1150-1650; ⏰mid-Mar) The American music industry's major annual gathering has expanded to include film, interactive media and comedy. Austin is absolutely besieged with visitors during this two-week window; many a new resident first came to the city to hear a little live music. Admission to festival events is by badge only, but many bands also play free shows.

Austin City Limits Music Festival (www.aclfestival.com; Zilker Park; 1-/3-day pass $100/255; ⏰Oct) What do music lovers do in the fall? They head to the Austin City Limits Festival, which, though not as big as SXSW (what is?), seems to grow larger every year. Spreading through the first two weekends in October, in Zilker Park, it books more than 100 impressive acts – Paul McCartney, say – and sells out months in advance.

MACH PHOTOS/SHUTTERSTOCK ©

garden overlooking Waller Creek, which welcomes all comers with an upbeat communal vibe. Craft beers like local favorite Electric Jellyfish are listed on the chalkboard, while the artisanal sandwiches use tasty bread from the bakery upstairs (7am to 2am). The meat is cooked in-house.

Continental Club

Mean Eyed Cat
Bar

(☎512-920-6645; www.themeaneyedcat.com; 1621 W 5th St; ⏰11am-2am) We're not sure if this watering hole is a legit dive bar or a calculated dive bar (it opened in 2004). Either way, a bar dedicated to Johnny Cash has our utmost respect. Inside this former chainsaw repair shop, *Man in Black* album covers, show posters and other knick-knackery adorn the walls. A 300-year-old live oak anchors the lively patio.

✪ ENTERTAINMENT

Music is the town's leading nighttime attraction, and a major industry. You can get heaps of information on the scene from the *Austin Chronicle* (www.austinchronicle.com) or from the *Austin American-Statesman's* Austin 360 website (www.austin360.com).

✪ Downtown

Stubb's Bar-B-Q
Live Music

(☎512-480-8341; www.stubbsaustin.com; 801 Red River St; ⏰11am-10pm Mon-Thu, to 11pm Fri & Sat, 10:30am-9pm Sun) Stubb's puts on live music almost every night, with a great mix of premier local and touring acts from across the musical spectrum. Many warm-weather shows are held out back along Waller Creek. It has two stages, a smaller stage indoors and a larger back-yard venue. Every Sunday, there's a gospel brunch at 10:30am and 12:30pm.

Esther's Follies
Comedy

(☎512-320-0198; www.esthersfollies.com; 525 E 6th St; reserved seating/general admission $30/25; ⏰shows 8pm Thu-Sat, plus 10pm Fri & Sat) Drawing from current events and pop culture, this long-running satire show has a vaudevillian slant, thanks to musical numbers and, yep, even a magician. Good, harmless fun.

⊙ East Austin

White Horse   Live Music

(www.thewhitehorseaustin.com; 500 Comal
St; ⊘3pm-2am) Ladies, you will be asked
to dance at this East Austin honky-tonk,
where two-steppers and hipsters mingle
like siblings in a diverse but happy family.
Play pool, take a dance lesson or step
outside to sip a microbrew on the patio.
Live music nightly – only on weekends is
a (small) cover charged – and whiskey on
tap. We like this place.

⊙ South Austin

Broken Spoke   Live Music

(☑512-442-6189; www.brokenspokeaustintx.net;
3201 S Lamar Blvd; ⊘4-11:30pm Tue, to midnight
Wed & Thu, 11am-1:30am Fri & Sat) George Strait
once hung from the wagon-wheel chandeliers at the wooden-floored Broken Spoke,
a true Texas honky-tonk. Not sure of your
dance moves? Join a lesson, offered from
8pm to 9pm ($8). As the sign inside says:
'Please do Not!!!! Stand on the Dance Floor.'

Continental Club   Live Music

(☑512-441-2444; www.continentalclub.com; 1315
S Congress Ave; ⊘4pm-2am Mon-Fri, from 1pm
Sat, from 3pm Sun) No passive toe-tapping
here; the dance floor at this 1950s-era
lounge is always swinging with some of
the city's best local acts. On most Monday
nights you can catch local legend Dale
Watson and his Lone Stars (10:15pm).

ⓘ INFORMATION

Austin Visitor Center (☑512-478-0098; www.
austintexas.org; 602 E 4th St; ⊘9am-5pm Mon-
Sat, from 10am Sun) Maps, brochures and gift
shop downtown.

ⓘ GETTING THERE & AROUND

TO/FROM THE AIRPORT

Austin-Bergstrom International Airport (AUS;
☑512-530-2242; www.austintexas.gov/airport;
3600 Presidential Blvd) is about 10 miles southeast of downtown. A taxi to or from downtown
costs around $30 (Uber and Lyft are usually a
bit less), while Capital Metro bus 20 connects
the airport with downtown for just $1.25, with
departures every 15 minutes.

BICYCLE

Austin B-cycle (www.austin.bcycle.com) is the
city's bike-sharing scheme. It has well over 50
self-checkout bike stations scattered around
town. Rates are $12 for 24-hour access or $18
for three consecutive days. The first 60 minutes
of each use is free; each additional half hour
costs $4.

CAR & MOTORCYCLE

Downtown, the best parking deal is at the **Capitol Visitors Parking Garage** (1201 San Jacinto
Blvd). It's free for the first two hours, and only $1
per half-hour after that, maxing out at $12.

PUBLIC TRANSPORTATION

Austin's handy public-transit system is run by
Capital Metro (CapMetro; ☑512-474-1200,
transit store 512-389-7454; www.capmetro.org;
⊘transit store 7:30am-5:30pm Mon-Fri). Regular
city buses – not including the more expensive
express routes – cost $1.25. Children under six
years of age are free.

RIDESHARE

Both Uber and Lyft operate in Austin. A typical
ride between the airport and downtown costs
around $22.

TAXI

You'll usually need to call for a cab instead of just
flagging one down on the street, except at the
airport, at major hotels, around the state capitol
and at major entertainment areas. Companies
include **Yellow Cab** (☑512-452-9999) and
Austin Cab (☑512-478-2222).

Las Vegas at a Glance...

Vegas, baby! An oasis of indulgence dazzling in the desert. This is the only place you can spend the night partying in ancient Rome, wake up for brunch beneath the Eiffel Tower, watch an erupting volcano at sunset and get married in a pink Cadillac. Double down with the high rollers, browse couture or sip a frozen vodka martini from a bar made of ice – it's all here for the taking.

So, is Vegas America's dirty little secret or its dream factory? It is, of course, both – and remains a bastion of hangover-inducing weekends for people from all walks of life.

Two Days in Las Vegas

It's all about the Strip. On day one, check out Hollywood theatrics at the **MGM Grand** (p243), sky-high views at the **Stratosphere** (p243), the unmissable fountains at the **Bellagio** (p242), and **Caesars Palace** (p242) for a show. On day two, visit the futuristic **Aria** (p246) and the marbled **Venetian** (p243); at night see **O** (p251) or **Aces of Comedy** (p251).

Four Days in Las Vegas

Explore Downtown Vegas on day three, taking in the **Mob Museum** (p247) and **Neon Museum – Neon Boneyard** (p247). Sip at retro-kitschy **ReBAR** (p250). On day four, seek out the **Pinball Hall of Fame** (p247). Afterward, head back to the Strip for more action at the casinos, shows and cocktail bars.

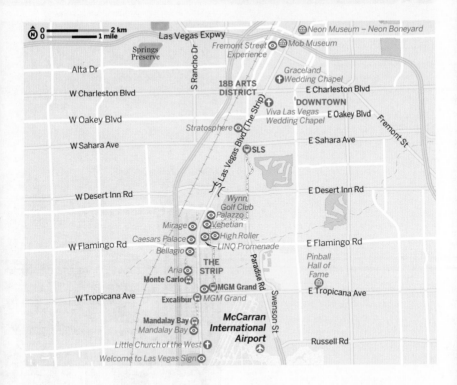

Neon Museum – Neon Boneyard

Las Vegas Expwy

Springs Preserve

Fremont Street Experience
Mob Museum

Alta Dr

S Rancho Dr

18B ARTS DISTRICT

Graceland
Wedding Chapel

E Charleston Blvd

W Charleston Blvd

DOWNTOWN

W Oakey Blvd

Viva Las Vegas
Wedding Chapel
E Oakey Blvd

Fremont St

Stratosphere

S Las Vegas Blvd (The Strip)

E Sahara Ave

W Sahara Ave

SLS

W Desert Inn Rd

E Desert Inn Rd

Wynn
Golf Club
Palazzo
Venetian
High Roller
LINQ Promenade

Mirage
Caesars Palace
Bellagio

E Flamingo Rd

W Flamingo Rd

Pinball
Hall of
Fame

Aria
THE STRIP
Monte Carlo

Paradise Rd

MGM Grand
MGM Grand
E Tropicana Ave

W Tropicana Ave

Excalibur

Swenson St

Mandalay Bay
Mandalay Bay

McCarran
International
Airport

Little Church of the West

Russell Rd

Welcome to Las Vegas Sign

Arriving in Las Vegas

McCarran International Airport

Shuttle buses run to Strip hotels from $6 one way, from $8 to Downtown and off-Strip hotels. You'll pay from $13 for a rideshare to the Strip, from $20 for a taxi.

Driving Most travelers approach the Strip (Las Vegas Blvd) off the I-15 Fwy. Try to avoid exiting onto busy Flamingo Rd; opt for quieter Tropicana Ave or Spring Mountain Rd.

Where to Stay

Downtown is cheaper, but the Strip is where the action is. Properties east and west of the Strip have their merits, though you'll need wheels to get around. Always ask whether the hotel will be undergoing renovations during your visit and whether or not the swimming pool will be open. Reserve well ahead, especially during March, April and May.

The Strip viewed from the Cosmopolitan Hotel

Cruising the Strip

The Strip, a 4.2-mile stretch of S Las Vegas Blvd lined with hulking casino hotels and mega amusements, is so hypnotizing that few visitors venture beyond it – this is where Vegas is at.

Great For...

ℹ Need to Know

See www.vegas.com for the lowdown on restaurants, bars and events.

★ Top Tip

Rideshare services offered by a glut of eager drivers are the cheapest and most efficient way to get around.

LUCKY-PHOTOGRAPHER/SHUTTERSTOCK ©

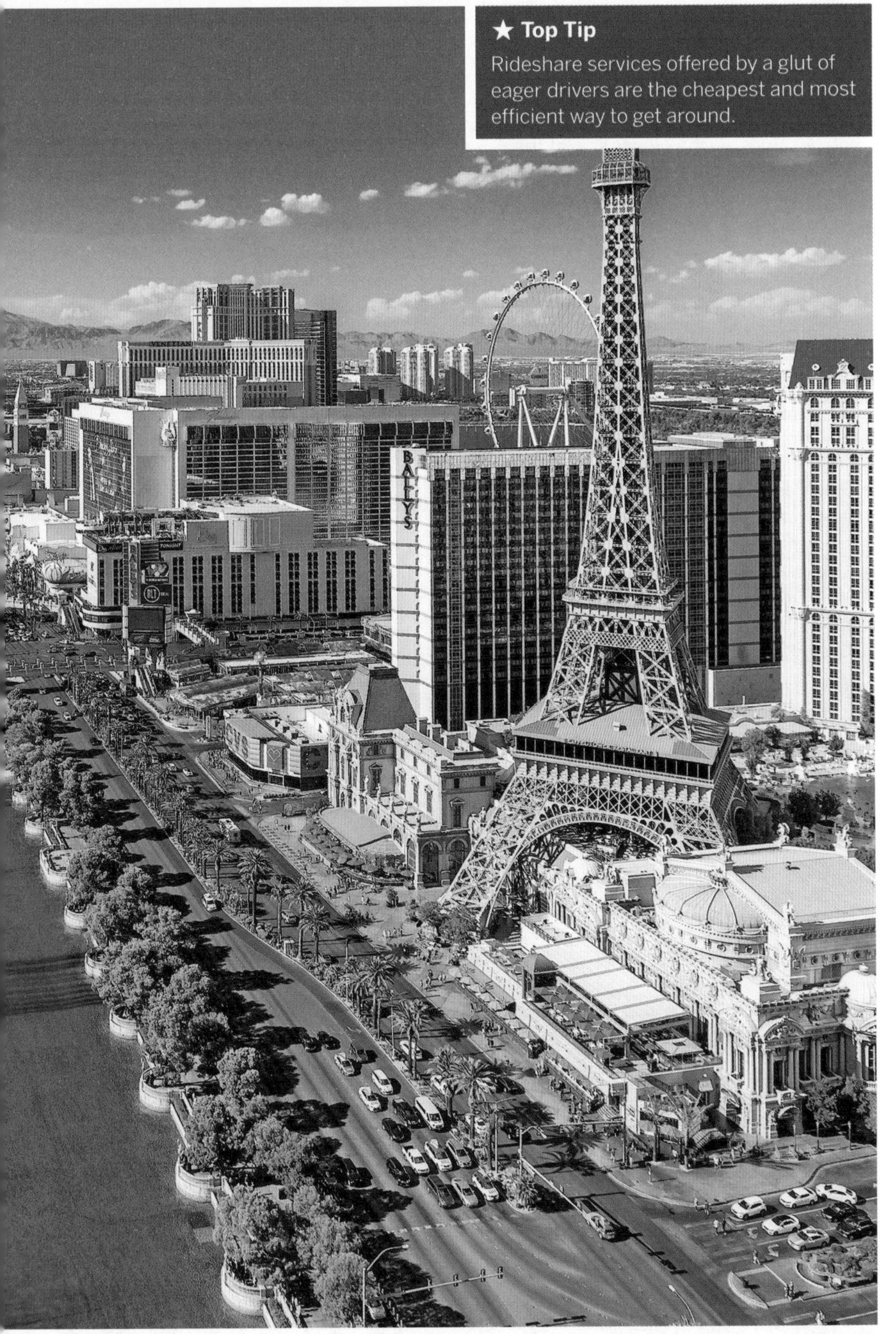

The Strip is what happens when you take the ideals of freedom and abundance to their extremes. It's Vegas' entertainment central, the epicenter in a vortex of limitless potential, where *almost* anything goes and time becomes elastic. Heads spin at the endless sales pitches: some get lucky, many have such an unspeakably good time they don't seem to mind incinerating their hard-earned cash. Magic dwells in this garden of earthly delights, but finding *yours* can be tricky: the Strip excels at distraction.

Casinos

Bellagio (☏702-693-7111; www.bellagio.com; 3600 S Las Vegas Blvd; ⊙24hr; P) The Bellagio experience transcends its decadent casino floor of high-limit gaming tables and in excess of 2300 slot machines; locals say odds here are less than favorable. A stop on the World Poker Tour,

Bellagio's tournament-worthy poker room offers kitchen-to-gaming-table delivery around-the-clock. Most come for the property's stunning architecture, interiors and amenities, including the **Conservatory & Botanical Gardens** (⊙24hr; P ⚧) **FREE**, **Gallery of Fine Art** (☏702-693-7871; adult/child under 12yr $18/free; ⊙10am-8pm, last entry 7:30pm; P ⚧) and unmissable **Fountains of Bellagio** (⊙shows every 30min 3-8pm Mon-Fri, noon-8pm Sat, 11am-7pm Sun, every 15min 8pm-midnight Mon-Sat, from 7pm Sun; P ⚧) **FREE**.

Caesars Palace (☏866-227-5938; www.caesars.com/caesars-palace; 3570 S Las Vegas Blvd; ⊙24hr; P) Caesars Palace claims that its smartly renovated casino floor has more million-dollar slots than anywhere in the world, but its claims to fame are far more numerous than that. Entertainment heavyweights Celine Dion

Caesars Palace

and Elton John 'own' its custom-built **Colosseum theater** (tickets $55-500), fashionistas saunter around **The Forum Shops** (⌖702-893-4800; www.simon.com/mall/the-forum-shops-at-caesars-palace; ⊙10am-11pm Sun-Thu, to midnight Fri & Sat), while Caesars' hotel guests quaff cocktails in the Garden of the Gods Pool Oasis.

Venetian (⌖702-414-1000; www.venetian. com; 3355 S Las Vegas Blvd; ⊙24hr; P) The Venetian's regal 120,000-sq-ft casino has marble floors, hand-painted ceiling frescoes and 120 table games, including a high-limit lounge and an elegant nonsmoking poker room. When combined with its younger, neighboring sibling **Palazzo** (⌖702-607-7777; www.palazzo.com;

☑ **Don't Miss**

The Bellagio's dancing fountains (free shows take place at least twice hourly) and its blockbuster Gallery of Fine Art.

3325 S Las Vegas Blvd; ⊙24hr; P), the properties claim the largest casino space in Las Vegas. Unmissable on the Strip, a highlight of this miniature replica of Venice is to take a **gondola ride** (⌖877-691-1997; www.venetian.com/resort/attractions/gondola-rides.html; shared ride per person $29, child under 3yr free, private 2-passenger ride $116; ⊙indoor rides 10am-11pm Sun-Thu, to midnight Fri & Sat, outdoor rides 11am-10pm, weather permitting; ♿) down its Grand Canal.

MGM Grand (⌖877-880-0880; www.mgmgrand. com; 3799 S Las Vegas Blvd; ⊙24hr; P♿) Owned by the eponymous Hollywood studio, the Grand liberally borrows Hollywood themes. Flashing LED screens and computerized fountains add extra theatrics to the 100,000lb, 45ft-tall bronze lion statue at the casino's entrance. Inside the labyrinthine casino bedecked with giant screens, you can get table-side massages or take free Texas hold'em lessons in the poker room.

Stratosphere (⌖702-380-7777; www.stratospherehotel.com; 2000 S Las Vegas Blvd; tower adult/child $20/10, all-day pass incl unlimited thrill rides $40; ⊙casino 24hr, tower & thrill rides 10am-1am Sun-Thu, to 2am Fri & Sat, weather permitting; P♿) Vegas has many buildings more than 20 stories tall, but only Stratosphere exceeds 100 and features the nation's highest thrill rides. Atop the 1149ft-high tapered tripod tower, vertiginous indoor and outdoor viewing decks afford Vegas' best 360-degree panoramas. There you'll also find the jazzy 107 SkyLounge (p250) cocktail bar, while below is a casino with 1200 slots and video poker machines.

✕ Take a Break
You can't get any higher for views and cocktails than at 107 SkyLounge (p250).

Vegas Shows

Whether you hanker for Celine Dion, Journey, feats of underwater acrobatics or erotic burlesque, you can bet it's on stage in Vegas. Larger-than-life production shows are the main stock-in-trade.

All Kinds of Shows

The whirling **Cirque du Soleil** (☎877-924-7783; www.cirquedusoleil.com/las-vegas; discount tickets from $49, full price from $69) empire keeps expanding, with the addition of two musical-themed spectaculars – *Beatles LOVE* and *Michael Jackson ONE*. The much-ballyhooed invasion of the Strip by Broadway showstoppers has slowed, although big productions like *Jersey Boys* and *Mamma Mia!* still sweep through town for limited runs.

This is Vegas, so there's first-rate comedy, too, as well as heavyweight rock stars in constant rotation. Resident shows of late have included Lady Gaga, Gwen Stefani, Aerosmith and Journey. Megaresort venues host a veritable who's-who of famous faces and voices throughout the year.

Great For...

☑ Don't Miss

With a cast performing in, on and above water, Cirque du Soleil's *O* (p251) tells the tale of theater through the ages.

Cirque du Soleil's *Beatles LOVE*

DIEGO GRANDI/ALAMY ©

Old-school production shows at smaller casinos feature a variety of hokey song, dance and magic numbers that often don't follow a storyline. Capitalizing on Sin City's reputation, there's also a grab-bag of erotically themed shows, from rock musicals to late-night pin-up revues, all featuring topless showgirls.

Sin City's new breed of bawdy, hilarious variety shows are staged cabaret-style in unusual venues, mostly on the Strip: **Absinthe** (☎855-234-7469; www.absinthevegas.com; Caesars Palace; tickets $99-199; ☻8pm & 10pm) lights up a big-top circus tent outside Caesars Palace.

Ticket Outlets

Be aware that most Vegas ticket outlets apply a surcharge for each ticket sold.

Tix 4 Tonight (www.tix4tonight.com) All but the biggest-ticket shows are up for grabs at these same-day, discount ticket outlets, but you must show up in person (no online or phone sales). Get in line before 10am for the best selection of shows and seats. Check the website for a list of handy outlet locations around town.

Vegas.com (www.vegas.com) Sells tickets to a variety of high-profile and low-budget shows, special events and touring exhibitions, as well as nightclub VIP and front-of-the-line passes.

Ticketmaster (www.ticketmaster.com) A broker for megaconcerts and sporting events.

◉ SIGHTS

◉ The Strip

Aria   Landmark

(CityCenter; www.aria.com; 3780 S Las Vegas Blvd; P) We've seen this symbiotic relationship before (think giant hotel anchored by a mall 'concept'), but the way that this futuristic-feeling complex places a small galaxy of hypermodern, chichi hotels in orbit around the glitzy **Shops at Crystals** (www.simon.com/mall/the-shops-at-crystals; 3720 S Las Vegas Blvdr; ◷10am-11pm Mon-Thu, to midnight Fri-Sun) is a first. The upscale spread includes the subdued, stylish **Vdara** (☏702-590-2111; www.vdara.com; 2600 W Harmon Ave) ✦, the hush-hush opulent **Waldorf Astoria** (www.waldorfastorialasvegas.com; 3752 S Las Vegas Blvd) and the dramatic architectural showpiece **Aria** (☏702-590-7111; www.aria.com; 3730 S Las Vegas Blvd, CityCenter; ◷24hr; P), whose sophisticated casino provides a fitting backdrop to its many gorgeous restaurants!

LINQ Promenade   Street

(☏800-634-6441; www.caesars.com/linq; ◷24hr; P♿) You'll be delighted by the fun vibe of the Strip's newest outdoor pedestrian promenade, where you can browse the latest LA fashions, gorge yourself on cupcakes, jaburritos (where sushi rolls meet burritos!) and fish and chips, go bowling, ride the **High Roller** (☏702-777-2782; www.caesars.com/linq/high-roller; adult/child from $22/9, after 5pm $32/19; ◷11:30am-1:30am; P♿; 🚇Flamingo or Harrah's/Linq), rock out to live music, or sip pints on lazy patios beneath the desert sun.

Welcome to Las Vegas Sign   Landmark

(5200 S Las Vegas Blvd; ◷24hr; ♿) **FREE** In a city famous for neon signs, one reigns supreme: the 'Welcome to Fabulous Las Vegas Nevada' sign, facing north and straddling Las Vegas Blvd just south of **Mandalay Bay** (☏702-632-7700; www.mandalaybay.com; 3950 S Las Vegas Blvd; ◷24hr; P♿), the unofficial beginning of the Strip. Designed by Betty Willis at the end of the 'Fabulous Fifties,' this sign is a classic photo op and a

Welcome to Las Vegas sign

PAGE LIGHT STUDIOS/SHUTTERSTOCK ©

reminder of Vegas' past. Only southbound traffic can enter the parking lot, greeted by its flip-side reminder to 'Drive Carefully' and 'Come Back Soon.'

◎ Downtown

Neon Museum – Neon Boneyard　　Museum

(☏702-387-6366; www.neonmuseum.org; 770 N Las Vegas Blvd; 1hr tour adult/child $28/24; ☉tours daily, schedules vary; 🚌113) This non-profit project is doing what almost no one else does: saving Las Vegas' history. Book ahead for a fascinating guided walking tour of the 'Neon Boneyard,' where irreplaceable vintage neon signs – Las Vegas' original art form – spend their retirement. Start exploring at the visitor center inside the salvaged La Concha Motel lobby, a mid-century modern icon designed by African American architect Paul Revere Williams. Tours are usually given throughout the day, but are most spectacular at night.

Mob Museum　　Museum

(☏702-229-2734; www.themobmuseum.org; 300 Stewart Ave; adult/child $27/17; ☉9am-9pm; P; 🚌Deuce) It's hard to say what's more impressive: the museum's physical location in a historic federal courthouse where mobsters sat for federal hearings in 1950–51, the fact that the board of directors is headed up by a former FBI special agent, or the thoughtfully curated exhibits telling the story of organized crime in America. The museum features hands-on FBI equipment and mob-related artifacts, as well as interviews with real-life Tony Sopranos.

◎ East of the Strip

Pinball Hall of Fame　　Museum

(☏702-597-2627; www.pinballmuseum.org; 1610 E Tropicana Ave; per game 25¢-$1; ☉11am-11pm Sun-Thu, to midnight Fri & Sat; 🚻; 🚌201) You may have more fun at this no-frills arcade than playing slot machines back on the Strip. Tim Arnold shares his collection of 200-plus vintage pinball and video games with the public. Take time to read the handwritten curatorial cards explaining

🏛 Gambling Terms

All in To bet everything you've got.

Ante A starting wager required to play table games.

Comps Freebies (eg buffet passes, show tickets, hotel rooms) given to players.

Cooler An unlucky gambler who makes everyone else lose.

Double down In blackjack, to double your bet after getting your first two cards.

Eye in the sky High-tech casino surveillance systems.

Fold To throw in your cards and stop betting.

High roller A gambler who bets big (aka 'whale').

Let it ride To roll over a winning wager into the next bet.

Low roller A small-time gambler (eg who likes penny slot machines).

Marker Credit-line debt owed to a casino.

One-armed bandit Old-fashioned nickname for a slot machine.

Pit boss A card dealer's supervisor on the casino floor.

Sucker bet A gamble on nearly impossible odds.

Toke A tip or gratuity.

the unusual history behind these restored machines.

Going to the Chapel

If you're thinking of officially tying the knot in Las Vegas and want to know what's required, contact Clark County's **Marriage License Bureau** (☎702-671-0600; 201 E Clark Ave; marriage license $77; ⊗8am-midnight), which gets jammed during crunch times such as weekends, holidays and 'lucky number' days. For an inexpensive, no-fuss civil ceremony, make an appointment with the county's **Office of Civil Marriages** (☎702-671-0577; www.clarkcountynv.gov/depts/clerk/services/pages/civilmarriages.aspx; 330 S 3rd St, 6th fl; wedding ceremonies from $75; ⊗2-6pm Mon-Thu, 9:30am-8:45pm Fri, 12:30-8:45pm Sat, 9am-5pm Sun).

Expect to pay at least $200 for a basic ceremony at an old-school Vegas wedding chapel. Operating for more than 50 years, **Graceland Wedding Chapel** (☎702-382-0091; www.gracelandchapel.com; 619 S Las Vegas Blvd; ⊗9am-11pm) created the original Elvis wedding. **Little Church of the West** (☎702-739-7971; www.littlechurchlv.com; 4617 S Las Vegas Blvd; ⊗8am-11pm) features a quaint, quiet little wooden chapel built in 1942 and pictured in *Viva Las Vegas*. At zany **Viva Las Vegas Wedding Chapel** (☎702-384-0771; www.vivalasvegasweddings.com; 1205 S Las Vegas Blvd; [P]), you can invite your family and friends to watch your wacky themed ceremony broadcast live online.

Little Church of the West

🔒 SHOPPING

Planet 13   Dispensary
(☎702-815-1313; www.planet13lasvegas.com; 2548 W Desert Inn Rd; ⊗24hr; 🅟) File this under only-in-Vegas: this self-described 'cannabis superstore and entertainment complex' is an emporium the size of several city blocks devoted to all things weed. Your personal concierge walks you through the myriad products, from flower, seeds, edibles, CBD products and accessories. Even if you're not partial to a toke, this totally unprecedented shopping experience is worth a visit.

EATING

🍴 The Strip

Tacos El Gordo   Mexican $
(☎702-982-5420; www.tacoselgordobc.com; 3049 S Las Vegas Blvd; small plates $3-12; ⊗10am-2am Sun-Thu, to 4am Fri & Sat; [P][⌖][♿]; 🚌Deuce, SDX) This Tijuana-style taco shop from SoCal is just the ticket when it's way late, you've got almost no money left and you're desperately craving *carne asada* (beef) or *adobada* (chili-marinated pork) tacos in hot, handmade tortillas. Adventurous eaters will be lured by the authentic *sesos* (beef brains), *cabeza* (roasted cow's head) or tripe (intestines) variations.

Twist by Pierre Gagnaire   French $$$
(☎702-590-8888; www.waldorfastorialasvegas.com; Waldorf Astoria, CityCenter; mains $67-76, tasting menus $170-295; ⊗5:30-10pm Tue-Thu, from 6pm Fri & Sat) If romantic Twist's sparkling nighttime Strip views don't make you gasp, the modern French cuisine by this three-star Michelin chef just might. Seasonal tasting menus may include squid-ink *gnocchetti* topped with carrot gelée or langoustine with grapefruit fondue, finished off with bubblegum ice cream with marshmallow and green-tea crumbles. Reservations essential; dress code is business casual.

MAURICE SAVAGE/ALAMY ©

Mob Museum (p247)

Restaurant Guy Savoy   French $$$

(☎702-731-7286; www.caesars.com/caesars-palace; Caesars Palace; mains $80-110, tasting menus $120-350; ⊗5:30-9:30pm Wed-Sun) With Strip-view picture windows, this exclusive dining room is the only US restaurant by three-star Michelin chef Guy Savoy. Both the culinary concepts and the prices reach heavenly heights. If you just want a small taste, perhaps of artichoke black-truffle soup or crispy-skinned sea bass, sit in the Cognac Lounge for drinks and nibbles. Dinner reservations are essential.

Wicked Spoon Buffet   Buffet $$$

(☎702-698-7870; www.cosmopolitanlasvegas.com; Cosmopolitan; per person $28-49; ⊗8am-9pm Sun-Thu, to 10pm Fri & Sat; ☎ 🏵) Wicked Spoon makes casino buffets seem cool again, with freshly prepared temptations served on individual plates for you to grab and take back to your table. The spread has all the expected meat, sushi, seafood and desserts, but with global upgrades – think roasted bone marrow and a gelato bar. Add unlimited champagne mimosas or Bloody Marys (surcharge $17).

⊗ Downtown

VegeNation   Vegan $

(☎702-366-8515; www.vegenationlv.com; 616 E Carson Ave; mains $13; ⊗8am-9pm Sun-Thu, to 10pm Fri & Sat; ☎🖉) 🖉 Faced with a health crisis, veteran chef Donald Lemperle adopted a plant-based diet, and used his learnings to open Downtown's most exciting new cafe. His kitchen sends out insanely delicious plant-based tacos, sandwiches, pizzas and desserts sourced from local products and community gardens to an adoring local fan base. You can even get CBD kombucha. Welcome to the new Vegas.

Esther's Kitchen   Italian $$

(☎702-570-7864; www.estherslv.com; 1130 S Casino Center Blvd; pasta from $15; ⊗11am-3pm & 5-10pm Mon-Fri, from 10am Sat & Sun; ❋☎) Locals are justifiably mad for the housemade seasonal pasta and heritage sourdough at this little Arts District bistro. Everything is extremely delicious, but we're partial to the anchovy-garlic butter you can order with the sourdough, and a kale-cauliflower salad that has no right to be as delectable as it is.

East of the Strip

Lotus of Siam   Thai $$

(📞702-735-3033; www.lotusofsiamlv.com; 953
E Sahara Ave; mains $9-30; ⊙11am-2:30pm
Mon-Fri, 5:30-10pm daily; 🅿; 🖥SDX) Saipin
Chutima's authentic northern Thai cooking
has won almost as many awards as her
distinguished, geographically diverse wine
cellar. Critics have suggested this might be
America's best Thai restaurant and we're
sure it's at least very close. Although the
strip-mall hole-in-the-wall may not look
like much, those in the know flock here.
Reservations essential.

🍷 DRINKING & NIGHTLIFE

Hakkasan   Club

(📞702-891-3838; www.hakkasannightclub.com;
MGM Grand; cover $20-75; ⊙10:30pm-4am Thu-
Sun) At this lavish Asian-inspired nightclub,
international jet-set DJs such as Tiësto and
Steve Aoki rule the jam-packed main dance
floor bordered by VIP booths and floor-to-
ceiling LED screens. More offbeat sounds
spin in the intimate Ling Ling Club, revealing
leather sofas and backlit amber glass.

107 SkyLounge   Lounge

(📞702-380-7711; www.stratospherehotel.com;
2000 S Las Vegas Blvd, 107th fl, Stratosphere
Tower; ⊙4pm-3am) There's no place to get
any higher in Las Vegas – in terms of altitude, at least – than the lounge overlooking
the revolving **Top of the World** (📞702-380-
7711; www.topoftheworldlv.com; Stratosphere;
mains from $44; ⊙11am-11pm) restaurant.
Come during happy hour (4pm to 7pm
daily) for two-for-one cocktails, half-price
appetizers and striking sunset views.

ReBAR   Bar

(📞702-349-2283; www.rebarlv.com; 1225 S
Main St; ⊙1pm-midnight Sun-Wed, to 1am Thu,
to 2am Fri & Sat) Las Vegas definitely revels
in kitsch, and it absolutely loves drinking
spots. ReBAR unites both. Located in the
Arts District, it's a temple of nutty craft
items, vintage bar signs, outrageous beer
steins and one-of-a-kind doohickeys.
Peruse the walls for that perfect retro
souvenir, then sit down for a respectable
selection of beers and spirits. Bask in the
vintage glow.

Hakkasan nightclub

Double Down Saloon
Bar

(📞702-791-5775; www.doubledownsaloon.com; 4640 Paradise Rd; ⊗24hr; 🚌108) This dark, psychedelic gin joint appeals to the lunatic fringe. It never closes, there's never a cover charge, the house drink is called 'ass juice' and it claims to be the birthplace of the bacon martini. When live bands aren't terrorizing the crowd, the jukebox vibrates with New Orleans jazz, British punk, Chicago blues and the late, great surf-guitar king Dick Dale.

NoMad Bar
Cocktail Bar

(📞702-730-6785; www.mgmresorts.com; NoMad Hotel; cocktails $17; ⊗5-11pm Mon-Thu, to 1am Fri & Sat, 11am-5pm Sun) You have to walk across the restaurant to check in with the hostess at this bar – all the better for checking out the gorgeous decor (and people) at this sumptuous new addition to Vegas' craft cocktail scene. This place isn't just beautiful though – the drinks are truly out of this world, and well worth the hefty price tag.

⭐ ENTERTAINMENT

O
Theater

(📞702-693-8866; www.cirquedusoleil.com/o; Bellagio; tickets $99-212; ⊗7pm & 9:30pm Wed-Sun) Phonetically speaking, it's the French word for water (eau). With a lithe international cast performing in, on and above water, Cirque du Soleil's O tells the tale of theater through the ages. It's a spectacular feat of imagination and engineering, and you'll pay dearly to see it – it's one of the Strip's few shows that rarely sells discounted tickets.

Aces of Comedy
Comedy

(📞702-792-7777; www.mirage.com; 3400 S Las Vegas Blvd, Mirage; tickets $40-100; ⊗schedules vary, box office 10am-10pm Thu-Mon, to 8pm Tue & Wed) You'd be hard pressed to find a better A-list collection of famous stand-up comedians than this year-round series of appearances at the **Mirage** (📞702-791-7111; ⊗24hr; 🅿), which delivers the likes of Jay Leno, Joe Rogan and George Lopez to the Strip. Buy tickets in advance online or by phone, or go in person to the Mirage's Cirque du Soleil (p244) box office.

ℹ INFORMATION

Las Vegas Convention & Visitors Authority (LVCVA; 📞702-892-7575; www.lasvegas.com; 3150 Paradise Rd; ⊗8am-5pm Mon-Fri; 🚌Las Vegas Convention Center) The hotline provides up-to-date information about shows, attractions, activities and more; staff may help with finding last-minute accommodations.

ℹ GETTING THERE & AWAY

McCarran International Airport (LAS; 📞702-261-5211; www.mccarran.com; 5757 Wayne Newton Blvd; 🛜) sits near the south end of the Strip.

The easiest and cheapest way to get to your hotel is by airport shuttle (one way to Strip/Downtown hotels from $6/8) or a rideshare service (from $13). As you exit baggage claim, look for shuttle-bus kiosks lining the curb; prices and destinations are clearly marked.

ℹ GETTING AROUND

Rideshare By far the best way to get around Vegas in most circumstances, and even cheaper when traveling with others.

Bus Day passes on the 24-hour Deuce and faster (though not 24-hour and not servicing all casinos) SDX buses are an excellent way to get around.

Taxi Expensive. Tips are expected.

Monorail Expensive, inconveniently located on the east side of the Strip and with a limited route, but great views and regular services.

Tram Operates between some casinos. Free and slow.

GRAND CANYON
NATIONAL PARK

Grand Canyon National Park at a Glance...

No matter how much you read about the Grand Canyon or how many photographs you've seen, nothing really prepares you for the sight of it. One of the world's seven natural wonders, it's so startlingly familiar and iconic you can't take your eyes off it. The canyon's immensity, the sheer intensity of light and shadow at sunrise or sunset, even its very age, scream for superlatives.

Snaking along its floor are 277 miles of the Colorado River, which has carved the canyon over the past six million years and exposed rocks up to two billion years old.

Two Days at Grand Canyon South Rim

On day one, see the sun rise at **Yaki Point** (p256). Stroll the **Rim Trail** (p259) and have lunch at **El Tovar Dining Room** (p260). Later, catch the sunset at **Hopi Point** (p256). The next day, hike on the **South Kaibab Trail** (p259). Wrap up with a drive east along Desert View Dr, stopping at **viewpoints** (p256) and **Desert View Watchtower** (p258).

Two Days at Grand Canyon North Rim

On day one, arrive early and get your first canyon eyeful at **Bright Angel Point** (p262). Bring a picnic, then hike along the **Widforss Trail** (p262). In the afternoon check out the killer view at Cape Royal. Have dinner at **Grand Canyon Lodge Dining Room** (p263). On day two hike along the **North Kaibab Trail** (p262) or saddle up with **Canyon Trail Rides** (p263).

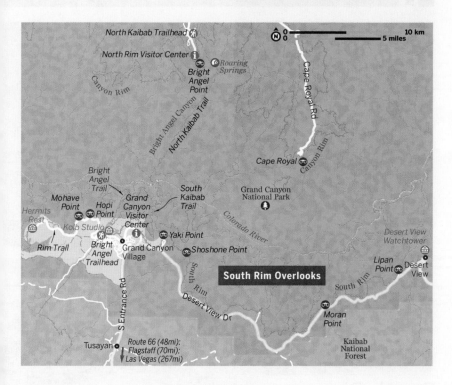

North Kaibab Trailhead

North Rim Visitor Center

Bright Angel Point

Roaring Springs

Canyon Rim

Cape Royal Rd

Bright Angel Canyon

North Kaibab Trail

Cape Royal

Canyon Rim

Bright Angel Trail

Grand Canyon National Park

South Kaibab Trail

Colorado River

Mohave Point

Hopi Point

Grand Canyon Visitor Center

Hermits Rest

Kolb Studio

Yaki Point

Desert View Watchtower

Rim Trail

Bright Angel Trailhead

Grand Canyon Village

Shoshone Point

Lipan Point

Desert View

South Rim Overlooks

S Entrance Rd

South Rim

South Rim

Desert View Dr

Moran Point

Tusayan

Route 66 (48mi);
Flagstaff (70mi);
Las Vegas (267mi)

Kaibab National Forest

10 km
5 miles

Arriving in Grand Canyon National Park

South Rim The more accessible entry point, an easy 60-mile drive north of I-40 at Williams. Shuttles arrive from Sedona, Williams, Flagstaff and airports in Phoenix (230 miles south) and Las Vegas (273 miles west).

North Rim Access is via Hwy 67. It's a 215-mile, four- to five-hour drive to the South Rim; or take the Trans-Canyon Shuttle. Vegas has the closest airport.

Where to Stay

South Rim Has three campgrounds and six lodges. Xanterra (www.grandcanyon-lodges.com) and Delaware North (www.visitgrandcanyon.com) operate the lodges. Reserve well ahead. If everything is booked up, consider Tusayan (7 miles south), Valle (30 miles south) or Williams (60 miles south).

North Rim There's one lodge and one campground. More options are another 60 miles north in Kanab, UT.

South Rim Overlooks

The views from the South Rim are stunners. Each overlook has its individual beauty – a dizzyingly sheer drop, a view of river rapids or a felicitous arrangement of jagged temples and buttes.

Great For...

☑ Don't Miss

Mohave and Hopi Points: these are the two to view if you're short on time.

Top Five Overlooks

Mohave Point (www.nps.gov/grca; Rim Trail, Hermit Rd; P; ⬚Hermits Rest; Mar 1-Nov 30) Overlooks the river and three rapids; great for sunrise or sunset.

Hopi Point (www.nps.gov/grca; Rim Trail, Hermit Rd; P; ⬚Hermits Rest west-bound; Mar 1-Nov 30) Juts further into the canyon than any other South Rim overlook, offering magnificent east–west views; beautiful at dawn and dusk, but gets very crowded.

Lipan Point (www.nps.gov/grca; Desert View Dr; P⬚) Offers expansive views and an excellent perch for sunset.

Moran Point (www.nps.gov/grca; Desert View Dr; P⬚⬚) Striking, dramatic river views and an excellent panorama of the canyon's geologic history.

Yaki Point (www.nps.gov/grca; Desert View Dr; ⬚; ⬚Kaibab/Rim) A favorite spot for watch-

DEEP DESERT PHOTOGRAPHY/SHUTTERSTOCK ©

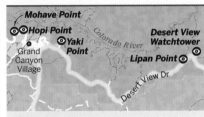

ⓘ Need to Know

Park entry (vehicle $35, shuttle-bus passenger $20) is valid for seven days at both rims.

✕ Take a Break

Fuel up on pancakes, fresh trout and more at El Tovar Dining Room (p260).

★ Top Tip

Hermit Road offers nine overlooks; Desert View Dr leads to seven overlooks.

---

ing the sunrise; it's accessible year-round by shuttle or bicycle only, so it tends to be quieter.

Reading the Formations

Many visitors are eager to identify the formations that layer the canyon. The distinctive sequence of color and texture is worth learning, as you'll see it from each viewpoint.

Kaibab limestone Starting at the top, a layer of creamy white Kaibab limestone caps the rim on both sides of the canyon.

Toroweap formation The vegetated slope between the cliffs of Kaibab limestone above and the massive Coconino cliffs below.

Coconino sandstone Note how sandstone erodes differently from limestone when you see these sheer 350ft cliffs.

Hermit shale Next lies a slope of crumbly red Hermit shale; today it supports a distinctive band of shrubs and trees.

Supai Group Just below the Hermit shale are the red cliffs and ledges of the Supai Group, similar in composition and color, but differing in hardness.

Redwall limestone This next layer is one of the canyon's most prominent features; the huge red cliff forms a dividing line between forest habitats above and desert habitats below. Finally comes the small slope of **Muav limestone**, followed by the soft greenish **Bright Angel shale** and **Tapeats sandstone**, the last and oldest layer.

South Rim

Easily accessible, well developed and open year-round, the South Rim offers iconic canyon views, almost two dozen official overlooks, historic buildings, multiple trails, museums and ranger talks. Infrastructure is abundant: you'll find several lodgings, restaurants, cafeterias, bookstores, libraries and a supermarket. Grand Canyon Village is the hub.

◉ SIGHTS

Desert View Watchtower
Historic Building, Viewpoint

(📞928-638-8960; www.nps.gov; Desert View, Desert View Dr; ⊗8am-7pm Apr-Sep, to 6pm Oct-Mar; stairs close 30min before closing; 🅿️🚻) The marvelously worn winding staircase of Mary Colter's 70ft stone tower, built in 1932, leads to one of the highest spots on the rim. From here, slats in the tower wall offer unparalleled views of not only the canyon and a long swath of the Colorado River, but also the San Francisco Peaks, the Navajo Reservation and the Painted Desert. Hopi artist Fred Kabotie's murals depicting Hopi origin stories grace the interior walls of the 1st floor.

Shoshone Point
Viewpoint

(📞park headquarters 928-638-7888; www.nps.gov/grca; Desert View Dr; 🚹) Walk about 1 mile along the mostly level and shaded dirt road to marvelously uncrowded Shoshone Point, a rocky promontory with some of the canyon's best views. Just before reaching the canyon rim, there's a grassy area with picnic tables and grills (advanced permit from NPS required). If you come for sunset, bring a flashlight for the walk back to your car. This viewpoint is unmarked; look for the small dirt parking lot about 1.2 miles east of Yaki Point.

Kolb Studio
Museum

(📞928-638-2771; www.nps.gov/grca/planyour-visit/art-exhibits.htm; Rim Trail, Grand Canyon Village Historic District; ⊗8am-7pm Mar-May & Sep-Nov, to 6pm Dec-Feb, to 8pm Jun-Aug; 🚌Village; Hermits Rest Route Transfer stop), 🚌Hermits Rest; Mar 1-Nov 30; Village Route Transfer) **FREE** In 1905 Ellsworth and Emery

Desert View Watchtower

CHR OFFENBERG/SHUTTERSTOCK ©

Kolb built a small photography studio on the edge of the rim, which has since been expanded and now holds a bookstore and a museum. An original Kolb brothers 1911 silent film runs continuously, and shows incredible footage of their early explorations of the Colorado River, and the museum displays mementos and photographs from their careers. In January and February, the NPS offers tours of their original Craftsman home, in a lower level of the studio.

ACTIVITIES

South Kaibab Trail   Hiking

(www.nps.gov/grca; South Kaibab Trailhead, off Desert View Dr; Kaibab/Rim) The maintained South Kaibab is one of the park's prettiest trails, combining stunning scenery and unobstructed 360-degree views with every step. Steep, rough and wholly exposed, this ridgeline descent plummets 4470ft along 6.4 miles to the Colorado River; from here, it is 0.5 miles to **Bright Angel Campground** (Backcountry Information Center 928-638-7875; www.nps.gov/grca; bottom of canyon, 9.5 miles below South Rim on Bright Angel, 7 miles below South Rim on South Kaibab, 14 miles below North Rim on North Kaibab; backcountry permit $10, plus per person per night $8; year-round) . Rangers warn against all but the shortest day hikes during the summer.

Bright Angel Trail   Hiking

(www.nps.gov/grca; Rim Trail, Grand Canyon Village Historic District; Village, Hermits Rest; Mar 1-Nov 30) The most popular and accessible of the corridor trails is the beautiful Bright Angel Trail, a spectacularly scenic 7.8-mile descent to the Colorado River with several logical day-hike destinations. Though steep, long stretches wind down without precarious drops along the edge, making this an excellent choice for families.

Rim Trail   Hiking

(www.nps.gov/grca; Hermits Rest to South Kaibab Trailhead; Village, Kaibab/Rim, Hermits Rest; Mar 1-Nov 30) Stretching along the rim from the South Kaibab Trailhead 13 miles west to **Hermits Rest** (928-638-

Hermit Road Scenic Drive

Hermit Rd, roughly paralleling the rim and dotted with nine incredible canyon overlooks, stretches west from Grand Canyon Village Historic District 7 miles to **Hermits Rest**, an amazing, century-old stone building that is the South Rim's westernmost scenic overlook. Accessible by bus tour, taxi, bike, or hiking the Rim Trail year-round, it is open to private vehicles December through February only. From March 1 through November 30, a shuttle services all overlooks.

One of the best ways to experience Hermit Rd is by bike; rent one at Bright Angel Bicycles (p260), at the Visitor Center Complex.

Entrance to Herman's Rest
 MANIVANNAN T/SHUTTERSTOCK ©

2351; www.nps.gov/grca; Hermit Rd; 8am-8pm May-Sep, 9am-5pm Oct-Mar, to 6:30pm Apr; ; Hermits Rest; Mar 1-Nov 30), the paved and dirt Rim Trail connects museums, historic buildings, hotels and some of the South Rim's most spectacular overlooks. West and east of Grand Canyon Village, the trail dips in and out of scrubby pines, and it's easy to find a quiet spot.

TOURS

Grand Canyon Mule Rides   Tours

(888-297-2757, next-day reservations 928-638-2631; www.grandcanyonlodges.com/plan/mule-rides; Bright Angel Lodge, Grand Canyon Village Historic District; 2hr mule ride $143, 1-/2-night mule ride incl meals & accommodations

$606/875; per 2 people $1057/1440; ⊕rides available year-round, hours vary; 🚻) If you want to descend into the canyon, the only option is an overnight to **Phantom Ranch** (📞888-297-2757; www.grandcanyonlodges. com; bottom of canyon, 9.9 miles below South Rim on Bright Angel, 7.4 miles below South Rim on South Kaibab, 13.6 miles below North Rim on North Kaibab; dm $65, cabin d $169, available by lottery; 🚻). These 10-mule trains follow the Bright Angel Trail (p259) 10.5 miles (5½ hours) down, spend one or two nights at Phantom Ranch, and return 7.8 miles (five hours) along the South Kaibab Trail (p259). Alternatively, the 4-mile Canyon Vistas ride stays on the rim.

✖ EATING & DRINKING

Bright Angel Bicycles & Cafe at Mather Point   Sandwiches $

(📞928-638-3055; www.bikegrandcanyon.com; Grand Canyon Visitor Center Complex, Grand Canyon Village; mains under $10; ⊕6am-8pm May-Sep, shorter hrs rest of year; 🚻; 🚌Kaibab/ Rim, 🚌Village) Grab-and-go sandwiches, wraps, salads, snacks and coffee drinks from the bike-shop cafe – the best spot to pick up a last-minute lunch to throw in your backpack before a hike. The cafe doubles as a **bicycle rental** (📞bike shop 928-638-3055, reservations 928-679-0992; 24hr rental adult/child 16yr & under $47/31.50, 5hr rental $31.50/20, wheelchair $10.50, single/double stroller up to 8hr $18/31; ⊕8am-6pm May-mid-Sep, 9am-5pm mid-Sep–Oct, 8am-5pm Mar & Apr; 🚻), and offers bicycle tours.

El Tovar Dining Room   American $$$

(📞928-638-2631; www.grandcanyonlodges.com/ dine/el-tovar-dining-room-and-lounge; El Tovar, Grand Canyon Village Historic District; mains $20-30; ⊕restaurant 6:30-10:30am, 11:15am-2pm & 4:30-9:30pm, lounge 11:30am-11pm; 🅿🚻; 🚌Village) Classic national park dining at its best. Dark-wood tables are set with china and white linen, eye-catching murals spotlight American Indian tribes and huge windows frame views of the Rim Trail and canyon beyond. Breakfast options include El Tovar's pancake trio (buttermilk, blue cornmeal and buckwheat pancakes with pine-nut butter and prickly-pear syrup), and blackened trout with two eggs.

El Tovar Lounge   Bar

(📞928-638-2631; www.grandcanyonlodges.com/ dine/el-tovar-dining-room-and-lounge/; El Tovar, Grand Canyon Village Historic District; ⊕11am-11pm; 🚌Village) Though the bar inside the historic El Tovar offers basics like nachos and sliders, the real draw is the canyon views from the back porch. Pop in for a post-hike Grand Canyon IPA or a prickly pear margarita, and watch the comings and goings along the Rim Trail, with the canyon vista stretched beyond.

ℹ INFORMATION

Grand Canyon Visitor Center (📞park headquarters 928-638-7888; www.nps.gov/ grca/planyourvisit/visitorcenters.htm; Grand Canyon Visitor Center Plaza, Grand Canyon Village; ⊕9am-5pm; 🚌Village, 🚌Kaibab/Rim, 🚌Tusayan (Mar 1-Sep 30)) The South Rim's main visitor center; on the plaza here, bulletin boards and kiosks display information about ranger programs, the weather, tours and hikes. Inside is a ranger-staffed information desk, a lecture hall and a theater screening a 20-minute movie *Grand Canyon: A Journey of Wonder*.

ℹ GETTING THERE & AWAY

Car Grand Canyon Village, the tourist hub, is accessed via Hwy 64 north from Williams (60 miles) or from Flagstaff (79 miles, partly on Hwy 180).

Air Phoenix (230 miles south) has the closest airport, from which travelers can rent a car or make connections by shuttle.

Bus Shuttles service the South Rim from Flagstaff, Williams, Sedona and Phoenix.

Train The historic **Grand Canyon Railway** (📞800-843-8724; www.thetrain.com; 233 N Grand Canyon Bvd, Railway Depot; return adult/child from $67/32; ⊕departs 9:30am) runs once daily from Williams.

ℹ️ GETTING AROUND

CAR
Grand Canyon Village is very congested from March through September. Several massive parking lots sit at the Visitor Center Complex, but it is easier and more pleasant to first try to find a spot in one the smaller lots by El Tovar or Bright Angel Lodge.

SHUTTLE
Free shuttle buses ply three routes along the South Rim. During the hour before sunrise and after sunset, shuttles run every half-hour or so, and from early morning until sunset they run every 15 minutes.

Hermits Rest Route Shuttle Bus (Red) March 1 to November 30

Hikers' Express Bus Year-round

Kaibab/Rim Route Shuttle Bus (Orange) Year-round

Tusayan Route Shuttle Bus (Purple) March 1 to September 30

Village Route Shuttle Bus (Blue) Year-round

North Rim

The North Rim is Grand Canyon plus. Here, the elevation is a little higher, the temperatures are a little cooler, the trails are a little steeper and the views...yeah, they're a little bigger. This part of the canyon is far less developed, and sees far fewer visitors than its southern counterpart. In part this is due to seasonal closure: at these altitudes (8000ft) the winter snows shut things down between October 15 and May 15.

◎ SIGHTS

Cape Royal   Viewpoint
(www.nps.gov/grca) Strategically located on the southernmost tip of the North Rim high above the great westward turn of the Colorado River, Cape Royal takes in almost every major part of the Grand Canyon with thousand-mile views. Imposing Wotan's

🛶 Rafting the Colorado River

Rafting the Colorado is an epic, adrenaline-pumping adventure.

OARS (209-736-4677, 800-346-6277; www.oars.com; 6 days from $1499, 10 days from $4408; ⌚6am-6pm) One of the most respected outfitters working in the canyon, OARS boasts the best guide-to-guest ratio in the business (1:4). Inflatable raft and dory trips are highly professional and comfortable, and the main office in Angels Camp, CA, runs entirely on solar power. See website for details on river running and four- to five-day rim-to-river and rim-to-rim hiking trips.

Arizona Raft Adventures (⌨800-786-7238, 928-526-8200; www.azraft.com; 4050 East Huntington Dr, Flagstaff, AZ 86004; 6-16-day raft trips $2305-4675, 8-/10-day motor trips $2945/3455) This multi-generational family-run outfit offers motor, oar and paddle (with opportunities for both paddling and floating) trips. Look online for details on photography, music, yoga and kayak 'specialty adventure' trips.

Rafting on the Colorado River
JIM MALLOUK/SHUTTERSTOCK ©

Throne fills the foreground to the southwest, while solitary Vishnu Temple to the south evokes a sacred shrine from a distant land. Tiny Desert View Watchtower can be seen to the southwest.

North Kaibab Trail

Toroweap Overlook   Viewpoint
(www.nps.gov/grca/planyourvisit/tuweep.htm;
Tuweep; ☾sunrise-30min past sunset) While
not the biggest, or highest, this is perhaps
the most dramatic viewpoint in the canyon:
you're literally on the edge of a 3000ft
drop.

Bright Angel Point   Viewpoint
(www.nps.gov/grca) An easily accessible
overlook that gives unfettered views down
into Bright Angel Canyon: a maze of mesas,
buttes, spires and side canyons. The South
Rim lodges are 11 miles across the canyon
as the crow flies – look for the switchbacks
of the Bright Angel Trail scaling the oppo-
site valley – and the distant San Francisco
Peaks towering over Flagstaff define the
horizon. Listen carefully and you can hear
Roaring Springs below: the source for all
your drinking water.

🏃 ACTIVITIES

North Kaibab Trail   Hiking
(www.nps.gov/grca; Inner Canyon) The North
Rim's most accessible inner-canyon trek
features strenuous switchbacks, raging waterfalls, a cottonwood-fringed campground
and long creekside stretches. It takes a few
days to complete – depending on how you
pace it – but the first few miles also make
for popular day hikes for those wanting a
peek inside the canyon.

Widforss Trail   Hiking
(www.nps.gov/grca; Point Sublime Rd) Meandering through shady forests of mixed conifer,
old growth ponderosa pine and quaking as-
pen punctuated by carpets of lupine, the Widforss Trail rolls past the head of The Transept
and out to Widforss Point. Numbered interp
signs provide some depth to your stroll while
the dramatic viewpoint at the end provides
an ideal place to have a picnic.

TOURS

Canyon Trail Rides Outdoors

(435-679-8665; www.canyonrides.com;
1/3hr mule ride $45/90; 🕗7:30am, 8:30am,
12:30pm, 1:30pm, 2:30pm mid-May–mid-Oct)
You can make reservations anytime for
the upcoming year, but, unlike mule trips
on the South Rim, you can usually book a
trip upon your arrival at the park; just duck
inside the Grand Canyon Lodge to the Mule
Desk. Rides don't reach the Colorado River,
but the North Kaibab Trail trip gives a taste
of life below the rim.

✖ EATING & DRINKING

**Grand Canyon Lodge
Dining Room** American $$

(🖉May-Oct 928-638-8560; www.grandcanyon-
forever.com/dining; breakfast $8-11, lunch $10-15,
dinner $18-35; 🕗6:30-10am, 11:30am-2:30pm
& 4:30-9:30pm May 15-Oct 15; 🅿🅷) While the
solid dinner menu includes buffalo steak,
western trout and several vegetarian op-
tions, don't expect great culinary memories
– the view is the thing. Lunch is just OK,
and the breakfast buffet is entirely forget-
table; order something prepared. Although
seats beside the window are wonderful,
views from the dining room are so huge it
really doesn't matter where you sit.

**Coffee Shop & Rough
Rider Saloon** Coffee, Bar

(🖉928-638-2611; www.grandcanyonforever.com;
Grand Canyon Lodge; 🕗5:30-10:30am & 11:30am-
10:30pm) If you're up for an early-morning
hike, stop for coffee and a breakfast burrito
at the Coffee Shop – a space that morphs
back into a saloon by noon, serving beer,
wine and mixed drinks, snacks and pizza.
Teddy Roosevelt memorabilia lines the
walls (and inspires the cocktails), honoring
his role in the history of the park.

ℹ INFORMATION

North Rim Visitor Center (🖉928-638-7888;
www.nps.gov/grca; 🕗8am-6pm May 15-Oct 15)
Beside Grand Canyon Lodge, this is the place to
get information on the park and it's the starting

point for ranger-led nature walks. A few hands-on
displays give a brief introduction to the region's
geology and wildlife.

ℹ GETTING THERE & AWAY

The only access road to the Grand Canyon North
Rim is Hwy 67, which closes with the first snow-
fall and reopens in spring after the snowmelt
(exact dates vary).

Although only 11 miles from the South Rim as
the crow flies, it's a grueling 215-mile, four- to
five-hour drive on winding desert roads between
here and Grand Canyon Village. You can drive
yourself or take the **Trans-Canyon Shuttle**
(🖉928-638-2820; www.trans-canyonshuttle.
com; one way $90). Reserve at least two weeks
in advance.

Flagstaff

Flagstaff's laid-back charms are many,
from a pedestrian-friendly historic down-
town crammed with eclectic vernacular
architecture to hiking and skiing in the
country's largest ponderosa pine forest.
Throw in a healthy appreciation for craft
beer, freshly roasted coffee beans and an
all-around good time, and you have the
makings of the perfect northern Arizonan
escape.

◎ SIGHTS & ACTIVITIES

Lowell Observatory Observatory

(🖉928-774-3358; www.lowell.edu; 1400 W Mars
Hill Rd; adult/senior/child $17/16/10; 🕗10am-
10pm Mon-Sat, to 5pm Sun) Astronomers, get
ready to geek out! Sitting atop a hill just
west of downtown, this national historic
landmark – famous for the first sighting of
Pluto in 1930 – was built by Percival Lowell
in 1894. Check out the solar telescope or
go on a tour during the day. Once evening
falls, visitors can stargaze through on-site
telescopes (weather permitting). A new
exhibit, the Giovale Open Deck Observa-
tory (GODO), which houses six telescopes
alongside interactive displays, opened in
October 2019.

Flagstaff Bicycle
Revolution   Mountain Biking
(☏928-774-3042; www.flagbikerev.com; 3 S
Mikes Pike; per 24hr hardtail/full suspension
$45/70; ⊘8am-6pm Mon-Fri, 9am-5pm Sat &
Sun) Flagstaff's best mountain-biking shop,
with both hardtail (no rear suspension) and
full-suspension bikes available to rent. You
can ride directly to the trails from the shop,
and it's sandwiched between great pizza
and beer for postride celebrations.

 EATING

Macy's   Cafe $
(☏928-774-2243; www.macyscoffee.net; 14 S
Beaver St; mains $6-9.50; ⊘6am-6pm; 🛜🍴)
The delicious coffee – house-roasted in the
original, handsome, fire-engine-red roaster
in the corner – at this Flagstaff institution has kept local students and caffeine
devotees buzzing since the 1980s. The
all-vegetarian menu includes many vegan
choices, along with traditional cafe grub
including pastries, steamed eggs, waffles,
yogurt and granola, salads and sandwiches.

Proper Meats + Provisions   Deli $
(☏928-774-9001; www.propermeats.com; 110
E Rte 66; sandwiches $12-14; ⊘10am-9pm) 🍴
Don't miss the sensational sandwiches
at this local butcher's shop, which sells
house-made salami and pancetta, local
grass-fed beef for the barbecue and other
meat-lovers' delights. The pastrami with
grilled onions and rye and the banh mi
with confit pork shoulder are both popular
choices, as is the charcuterie board, with
cheese, figs and olives.

Coppa Cafe   Cafe $$$
(☏928-637-6813; www.facebook.com/coppa
cafeaz; 1300 S Milton Rd; lunch $11-15, mains
$15-32; ⊘3-9pm Wed-Fri, 11am-3pm & 5-9pm
Sat, 10am-3pm Sun; 🛜) Brian Konefal and
Paola Fioravanti, who met at an Italian
culinary school, are the husband-and-wife
team behind this friendly, art-strewn bistro
with egg-yolk-yellow walls. Expect ingredients foraged from nearby woods (and
further afield in Arizona) in dishes such as
slow-roasted top loin with wildflower butter,

Mountain biking, Kaibab National Forest

or clay-baked duck's egg with a 'risotto' of Sonoran wheat and wild herbs.

🍸 DRINKING & NIGHTLIFE

Museum Club   Bar
(📞928-440-5214; www.museumclub.net; 3404 E Rte 66; ⏱11am-2am) This country-music roadhouse on Route 66 has been kicking up its heels since 1936. Inside what looks like a huge log cabin you'll find a large wooden dance floor, animal mounts and a sumptuous elixir-filled mahogany bar. The origins of the name? In 1931 it housed a taxidermy museum.

Hops on Birch   Pub
(📞928-440-5380; www.hopsonbirch.com; 22 E Birch Ave; ⏱noon-1:30am; 🐾) Simple and handsome, Hops on Birch has 34 rotating beers on tap, live music five nights a week and a friendly local-crowd vibe. In classic Flagstaff style, dogs are as welcome as humans.

Annex Cocktail Lounge   Cocktail Bar
(Tinderbox Kitchen; 📞928-226-8400; www. annexcocktaillounge.com; 34 S San Francisco St; ⏱4-11pm Mon-Thu, 3pm-midnight Fri & Sat, 4-10pm Sun) This slinky cocktail bar mixes up great originals and classics: the Moscow Mule with mint and cucumber might just be the best cocktail in Flagstaff. The outdoor patio, actually a handball court built by Basque immigrants in 1926, attracts a low-key local crowd. Annexed to the wonderful Tinderbox Kitchen (5pm to 10pm), it also does poutine and other top-notch drinking food.

ℹ GETTING THERE & AWAY

Hwy 180 is the most direct route northwest to Tusayan and the South Rim (80 miles), while Hwy 89 beelines north to Cameron (59 miles), where it meets Hwy 64 heading west to the canyon's East Entrance.

Groome Transportation (📞928-350-8466; www.groometransportation.com) has shuttles that run between Flagstaff, Grand Canyon National Park, Williams, Sedona and Phoenix's Sky Harbor International Airport.

LOS ANGELES

Los Angeles at a Glance...

Ruggedly good looking, deeply creative, with a sunny disposition to boot...if LA were on Tinder, the app would crash. This is a city of incredible energy, architectural riches and some of the best places to eat and drink in the nation. Despite the plastic clichés, LA is one of the world's great cultural cities, home to exceptional art collections, world-shaking architecture and an extraordinary melting pot of cultures. But it's the incomparable beauty of its setting that sets it apart. Here, the rat race comes with sweeping beaches, mountain vistas and bewitching sunsets.

Two Days in Los Angeles

Start in Hollywood by walking all over your favorite stars on the **Hollywood Walk of Fame** (p275), snapping pics of the iconic **Capitol Records Tower** (p274) and pressing up against famous hands outside **TCL Chinese Theatre** (p275). On day two, hit the streets of rapidly evolving Downtown LA. Check out the stunning **Broad** (p280) art museum and the **Grammy Museum** (p280).

Four Days in Los Angeles

With two more days in town, you'll want to get a taste of beach life, by walking around Santa Monica, a hip and eccentric enclave of surfers and tourists surrounding its world-famous **pier** (p271). Get a dose of nature at **Griffith Park** (p277). Finally, explore the incredible **Getty Center** (p280), a spectacular synergy of art, architecture, landscaping and views.

Previous page: Rodeo Drive (p286)

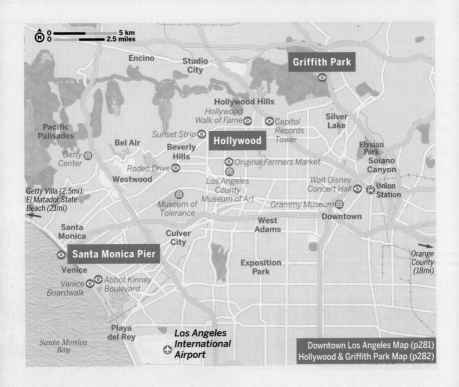

5 km
2.5 miles

Encino

Studio
City

Griffith Park

Pacific
Palisades

Hollywood Hills
Hollywood
Walk of Fame

Capitol
Records
Tower

Silver
Lake

Sunset Strip

Hollywood

Bel Air

Beverly
Hills

Getty
Center

Rodeo Drive

Original Farmers Market

Elysian
Park

Solano
Canyon

Westwood

Los Angeles
County
Museum of Art

Walt Disney
Concert Hall

Union
Station

Getty Villa (2.5mi);
El Matador State
Beach (21mi)

Museum of
Tolerance

Grammy Museum

Downtown

West
Adams

Santa
Monica

Culver
City

Orange
County
(18mi)

 Santa Monica Pier

Venice

Exposition
Park

Venice
Boardwalk

Abbot Kinney
Boulevard

Playa
del Rey

Santa Monica
Bay

*Los Angeles
International
Airport*

Downtown Los Angeles Map (p281)
Hollywood & Griffith Park Map (p282)

Arriving in Los Angeles
Los Angeles International Airport
Door-to-door shuttles run by Super
Shuttle cost $24, $29 and $19 for trips
to Santa Monica, Hollywood and Downtown, respectively. Taxi and rideshare
services cost around $50 to Downtown.
LAX FlyAway Buses (one way $9.75)
travel nonstop to Downtown's Union
Station (45 minutes) and Hollywood
(one to 1½ hours).

Where to Stay
LA is huge, and your interests will
determine where you want to stay, from
rock-and-roll Downtown digs to fabled
Hollywood hideaways to Santa Monica
beachside escapes. Plan well ahead, and
consider visiting between January and
April, when room rates and occupancy
are usually at their lowest (Oscars week
aside).

Santa Monica Pier

Santa Monica is LA's cute, alluring, hippie-chic little sister, its karmic counterbalance and, to many, its salvation. This is where you'll encounter the picturesque oceanside California you've seen in the movies.

Surrounded by LA on three sides and the Pacific on the fourth, SaMo is a place where real-life Lebowskis sip white Russians next to martini-swilling Hollywood producers, while celebrity chefs dine at family-owned taquerias and farmers markets. All the while, kids, out-of-towners and those who love them flock to wide beaches and the pier, where the landmark Ferris wheel and roller coaster welcome one and all.

Once the very end of the mythical Route 66, and still the object of a tourist love affair, the Santa Monica Pier dates back to 1908 and is the city's most compelling landmark. There are arcades and carnival games, and the pier comes alive with free concerts (Twilight Concert Series) and outdoor movies in the summertime.

Great For...

☑ **Don't Miss**

The beautiful, hand-painted horses of the historic carousel at the entrance to Santa Monica Pier.

Pacific Park

BONANBON/SHUTTERSTOCK ®

Santa Monica Bay · *Santa Monica Pier* ◎ · Ocean Ave · Santa Monica State Beach

❶ Need to Know

☎310-458-8901; www.santamonicapier.org; ♿

✕ Take a Break

Try The Godmother, the Queen of All Sandwiches, at **Bay Cities** (☎310-395-8279; www.baycitiesitaliandeli.com; 1517 Lincoln Blvd; sandwiches $5.50-13.30; ☺9am-6pm Tue-Sun; Ⓟ), the best Italian deli in LA.

★ Top Tip

The best way to get around is by bicycle; you'll find rentals by the day or hour.

Pacific Park

Kids get their kicks at **Pacific Park** (☎310-260-8744; www.pacpark.com; 380 Santa Monica Pier; per ride $5-10, all-day pass adult/child under 8yr $35/19; ☺daily, seasonal hours vary; ♿; ⓂExpo Line to Downtown Santa Monica), a small amusement park with a solar-powered Ferris wheel, kiddy rides, midway games and food stands. Check the website for discount passes.

Aquarium

If you peer under the pier – just below the carousel – you'll find Heal the Bay's **Santa Monica Pier Aquarium** (☎310-393-6149; www.healthebay.org; 1600 Ocean Front Walk; adult/child $5/free; ☺2-6pm Mon-Thu, 12:30-6pm Fri-Sun; ♿; ⓂExpo Line to Downtown Santa Monica) ☞. Sea stars, crabs, sea urchins and other critters and crustaceans scooped from the bay are on display in their adopted touch-tank homes. For a fin-filled frenzy, stop by the shark tanks for feedings of those multifanged beasts.

South of the Pier

South of the pier is the **Original Muscle Beach** (www.santamonica.com/original-muscle-beach-santa-monica; 1800 Ocean Front Walk; ☺sunrise-sunset), where the Southern California exercise craze began in the mid-20th century. New equipment now draws a fresh generation of fitness fanatics. Close by, the search for the next Bobby Fischer is on at the **International Chess Park** (☎310-458-8450; www.smgov.net; 1652 Ocean Front Walk; ☺sunrise-sunset). Anyone can join in. Following the **South Bay Bicycle Trail**, a paved bike and walking path, south for about 1.5 miles takes you straight to Venice Beach. Bikes or in-line skates are available to rent on the pier and at beachside kiosks.

TCL Chinese Theatre (p275)

Hollywood

No other corner of LA is steeped in as much mythology as Hollywood. You'll find the Walk of Fame, Capitol Records and TCL Chinese Theatre, where the entertainment deities have been immortalized in concrete.

Great For...

ℹ️ Need to Know

Many of Hollywood's tourist attractions gravitate around the intersection of Hollywood Blvd and Highland Ave.

★ **Top Tip**

Take the metro (Red Line); if driving, park at the Hollywood & Highland mall.

FIIPHOTO/SHUTTERSTOCK ©

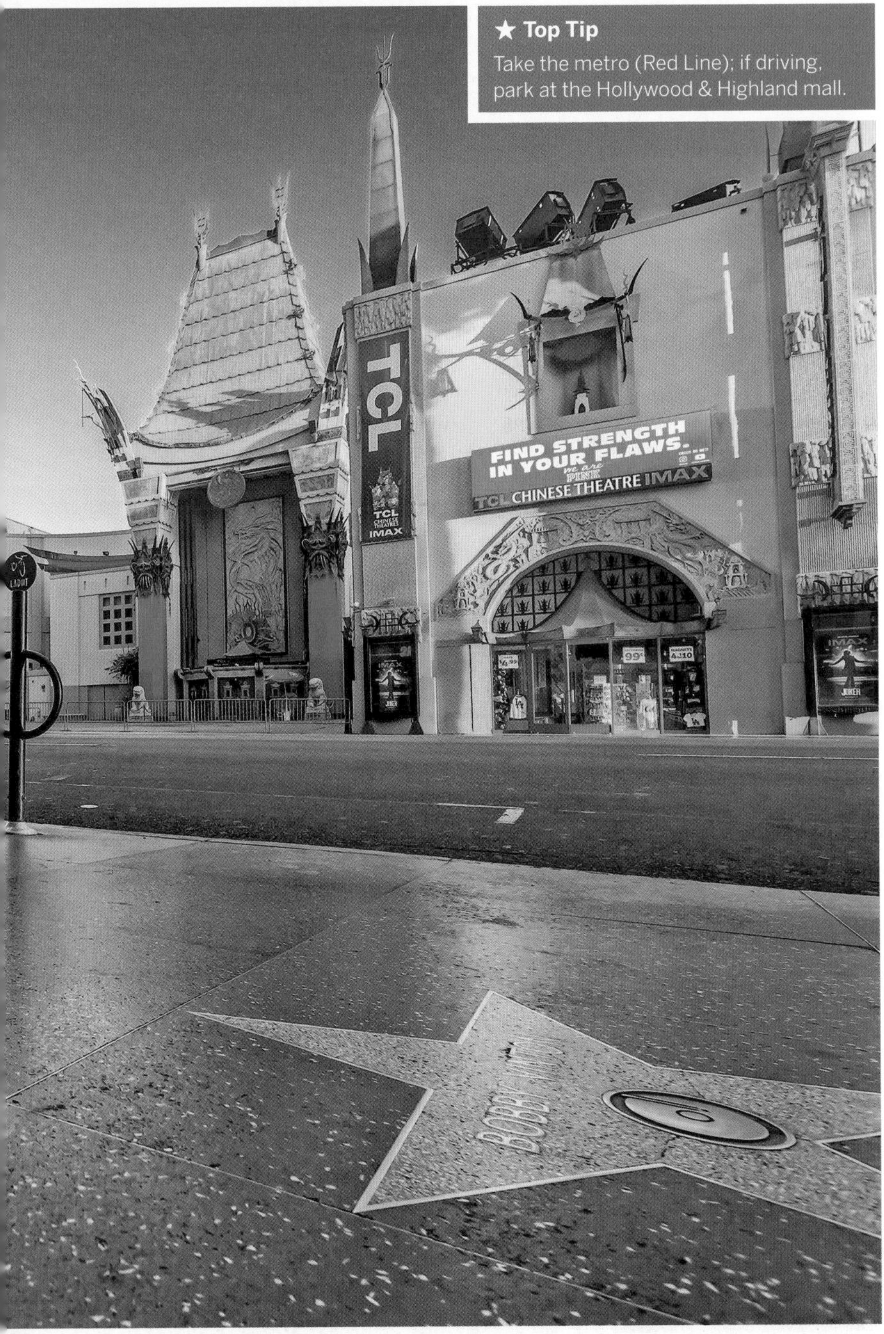

Most of Hollywood's main tourist attractions are steps away from the intersection of Hollywood Blvd and Highland Ave (serviced by metro Red Line).

Capitol Records Tower

Vine St is where you'll find the **Capitol Records Tower** (Map p282; 1750 Vine St) FREE. You'll have no trouble recognizing this iconic 1956 structure, one of LA's great mid-century buildings. Designed by Welton Becket, it resembles a stack of records topped by a stylus blinking out 'Hollywood' in Morse code. Some of music's biggest stars have recorded hits in the building's basement studios, among them Nat King Cole, Frank Sinatra, the Beatles, Katy Perry and Sam Smith. Outside on the sidewalk, Garth Brooks and John Lennon have their stars.

Hollywood Museum

For a taste of Old Hollywood, do not miss this musty temple to the stars, its four floors crammed with movie and TV costumes and props. The **museum** (Map p282; 323-464-7776; www.thehollywoodmuseum.com; 1660 N Highland Ave; adult/senior & student/child $15/12/5; 10am-5pm Wed-Sun; Red Line to Hollywood/Highland) is housed inside the Max Factor Building, built in 1914 and relaunched as a glamorous beauty salon in 1935. At the helm was Polish-Jewish entrepeneur Max Factor, Hollywood's leading authority on cosmetics. And it was right here that he worked his magic on Hollywood's most famous screen queens. The makeup rooms, complete with custom hues and lighting to complement the ladies' varying complexions and hair colors, are still located on the ground floor,

Hollywood Walk of Fame

along with personal items from the likes of Joan Crawford, Judy Garland and Marilyn Monroe.

TCL Chinese Theatre

Ever wondered what it's like to be in George Clooney's shoes? Find his foot- and handprints alongside dozens of other stars', forever set in the concrete forecourt of this world-famous **movie palace** (Grauman's Chinese Theatre; Map p282; 323-461-3331; www.tclchinesetheatres.com; 6925 Hollywood Blvd; ; MRed Line to Hollywood/Highland)

> ### ✗ Take a Break
> One of the oldest dive bars in Hollywood, the **Frolic Room** (Map p282; 323-462-5890; 6245 Hollywood Blvd; 11am-2am; MRed Line to Hollywood/Vine) remains a hit.

FREE, opened in 1927 and styled after an exotic pagoda complete with temple bells and stone heaven dogs from China. Join the throngs to find out how big Arnold's feet really are, or search for Betty Grable's legs, Whoopi Goldberg's braids, Daniel Radcliffe's wand or R2-D2's wheels.

Hollywood Walk of Fame

The **Hollywood Walk of Fame** (Map p282; www.walkoffame.com; Hollywood Blvd; MRed Line to Hollywood/Highland) runs along Hollywood Blvd, as well as along Vine St a mile to the east. Big Bird, Bob Hope, Marilyn Monroe and Aretha Franklin are among the 2600 stars being sought out, worshipped, photographed and stepped on along the path. They've been adding the brass and pink-marble stars since 1960, with yet another ceremony once or twice monthly.

Paramount Studios

Star Trek, Indiana Jones and the *Iron Man* series are among the blockbusters that originated at Paramount, the country's second-oldest movie studio and the only one still in Hollywood proper. Two-hour **tours** (Map p282; 323-956-1777; www.paramount studiotour.com; 5555 Melrose Ave; regular/VIP tours $60/189, After Dark tours $99; tours 9:30am-5pm, last tour 3pm) of the studio complex are offered year-round, taking in the back lots and sound stages. Passionate, knowledgeable guides offer fascinating insights into the studio's history and the movie-making process in general.

> ### ☑ Don't Miss
> Stepping into the shoe prints of your favorite movie star at TCL Chinese Theatre.

Griffith Park

A gift to the city in 1896 by mining mogul Griffith J Griffith, and five times the size of New York's Central Park, Griffith Park is one of the country's largest urban green spaces.

It's easy to spend a whole day in this sprawling park, which contains a major outdoor theater, the city zoo, an observatory, two museums, golf courses, playgrounds, 53 miles of hiking trails, Batman's caves and the Hollywood sign.

Griffith Observatory

LA's landmark 1935 **observatory** (📞213-473-0890;www.griffithobservatory.org; 2800 E Observatory Rd;admission free, planetarium shows adult/student & senior/child $7/5/3; ⊘noon-10pm Tue-Fri, from 10am Sat & Sun) opens a window onto the universe from its perch on the southern slopes of Mt Hollywood. Its planetarium claims the world's most advanced star projector, while its astronomical touch displays explore some mind-bending topics, from the evolution of the telescope and the ultraviolet X-rays

Great For...

☑ Don't Miss

The observatory's rooftop viewing platform has prime-time views of LA and the Hollywood Hills.

Griffith Observatory

ARCHITECT: JOHN C AUSTIN; IMAGE: TREKANDSHOOT/SHUTTERSTOCK ©

❶ Need to Know

Map p282; ☎323-644-2050; www.laparks.org/griffithpark; 4730 Crystal Springs Dr; ◷5am-10:30pm, trails sunrise-sunset; P⛽ FREE

✕ Take a Break

Follow the signposted 0.6-mile hike to Fern Dell Dr for lunch at **Trails** (Map p282; ☎323-871-2102; 2333 Fern Dell Dr, Los Feliz; pastries $3-8, meals $5-9; ◷8am-5pm; 🛜⛽), an outdoor cafe with made-from-scratch treats.

★ Top Tip

Parking is plentiful and free here – unlike most sights in LA.

used to map our solar system to the cosmos itself. Then, of course, there are the views (on clear days) of the entire LA basin, surrounding mountains and Pacific Ocean.

You can peer into the Zeiss Telescope on the east side of the roof where sweeping views of the Hollywood Hills and the gleaming city below are especially spectacular at sunset. After dark, staff wheel additional telescopes out to the front lawn for stargazing.

Inside the building, grab a seat in the Planetarium – the aluminum-domed ceiling becomes a massive screen where lasers are projected to offer a tour of the cosmos, while another laser-projection show allows you to search for water, and life, beyond earth. Downstairs, the Leonard Nimoy Event Horizon Theater screens a fascinating 24-minute documentary about the observatory's history, including an extraordinary engineering feat that saw the entire

building lifted from its foundations during its expansion in the early 2000s.

If relying on public transit, reach the observatory by hopping on the DASH Observatory shuttle bus, which runs between Vermont/Sunset metro station on the Red Line and the observatory. Buses run every 20 minutes from noon to 10pm on weekdays and from 10am to 10pm on weekends.

Hollywood Sign

LA's most famous landmark first appeared in the hills in 1923 as an advertising gimmick for a real-estate development called 'Hollywoodland.' Each letter is 50ft tall and made of sheet metal. In 1932 a struggling young actress named Peggy Entwistle leapt her way into local lore from the letter 'H.' The last four letters were lopped off in the '40s as the sign started to crumble. In the late '70s Alice Cooper and Hugh Hefner joined forces with fans to save the famous symbol In 2010 when the hills behind the sign became slated for a housing development.

Los Angeles Architectural Masterpieces

Filled with amazing buildings, eateries and museums, Downtown LA is one of the most exciting neighborhoods for a stroll.
Start Verve
Distance 2.5 miles
Duration Three hours

4 Step inside for a look at the opulent interiors of **Millennium Biltmore Hotel** (www.thebiltmore.com; 506 S Grand Ave), which has appeared in *Ghostbusters, Fight Club* and *Mad Men*.

3 Pershing Square, LA's first public park, was recently redone by French landscape architecture firm Agence Ter.

5 Gape in wonder at **Broad** (p280), Downtown's most extraordinary building.

2 Architect Claud Beelman's extraordinary 1929 **Eastern Columbia Building** (849 S Broadway) is a masterpiece of art moderne architecture.

Take a Break Grand Park (www.grandparkla.org; 227 N Spring St) is a great place to catch your breath and post some pics using the free wi-fi.

Classic Photo A selfie outside the glittering facade of the **Walt Disney Concert Hall** (p280).

6 Frank Gehry's showstopping masterpiece, **Walt Disney Concert Hall** (p280), is home to the LA Philharmonic.

N Broadway

N Spring St

M Civic Center/ Grand Park

S Broadway

W 3rd St

E Temple St

E 1st St

E 2nd St

101

7 Grand Central Market (p284) is in a beaux-arts building that's been satisfying appetites since 1917.

1 Start the tour with a steaming cup from Santa Cruz microroastery **Verve** (213-455-5991; www.grandparkla.org; 227 N Spring St; 7am-7pm).

4 USA-PYON/SHUTTERSTOCK © 6 ALISIA LUTHER/SHUTTERSTOCK © 7 TUPUNGATO/SHUTTERSTOCK ©

0 500 m
0 0.25 miles

⊙ SIGHTS

⊙ Downtown Los Angeles & Boyle Heights

Broad   Museum
(Map p281; ☎213-232-6200; www.thebroad. org; 221 S Grand Ave; ⊗11am-5pm Tue & Wed, to 8pm Thu & Fri, 10am-8pm Sat, to 6pm Sun; P⊞; MRed/Purple Lines to Civic Center/Grand Park) FREE From the instant it opened in September 2015, the Broad (rhymes with 'road') became a must-visit for contemporary-art fans. It houses the world-class collection of local philanthropist and billionaire real-estate honcho Eli Broad and his wife Edythe, with more than 2000 postwar pieces by dozens of heavy hitters, including Cindy Sherman, Jeff Koons, Andy Warhol, Roy Lichtenstein, Robert Rauschenberg, Keith Haring and Kara Walker.

Grammy Museum   Museum
(Map p281; ☎213-765-6800; www.grammymuse um.org; 800 W Olympic Blvd; adult/child, senior & student $15/13; ⊗10:30am-6:30pm Sun, Mon, Wed & Thu, 10am-8pm Fri & Sat; P⊞; MBlue/ Expo Lines to Pico Station) The highlight of **LA Live** (☎213-763-5483; www.lalive.com), this museum's interactive exhibits define, differentiate and link musical genres. Spanning three levels, the rotating exhibitions might include threads worn by the likes of Michael Jackson, Whitney Houston and Beyoncé, scribbled words from the hands of Count Basie and Taylor Swift, and instruments once used by world-renowned rock deities. Inspired? Interactive sound chambers allow you to try your own hand at singing.

Walt Disney Concert Hall   Notable Building
(Map p281; ☎323-850-2000; www.laphil.org; 111 S Grand Ave; P; MRed/Purple Lines to Civic Center/Grand Park) FREE A molten blend of steel, music and psychedelic architecture, this iconic concert venue is the home base of the Los Angeles Philharmonic, but has also hosted contemporary bands such as Phoenix, and classic jazz musicians such as Sonny Rollins. The 2003 concert hall's visionary architect, Frank Gehry,

pulled out all the stops for this building, a gravity-defying sculpture of heaving and billowing stainless steel.

⊙ Beverly Hills, Bel Air, Brentwood & Westwood

Getty Center   Museum
(☎310-440-7300; www.getty.edu; 1200 Getty Center Dr, off I-405 Fwy; ⊗10am-5:30pm Tue-Fri & Sun, to 9pm Sat; P⊞; ⊒734, 234) FREE In its billion-dollar, in-the-clouds perch, high above the city grit and grime, the Getty Center presents triple delights: a stellar art collection (everything from medieval triptychs to baroque sculpture and impressionist brushstrokes), Richard Meier's cutting-edge architecture, and the visual splendor of seasonally changing gardens. Admission is free, but parking is $20 ($15 after 3pm).

Museum of Tolerance   Museum
(☎reservations 310-772-2505; www.museumof-tolerance.com; 9786 W Pico Blvd; adult/senior/ student $15.50/12.50/11.50, Anne Frank Exhibit $15.50/13.50/12.50; ⊗10am-5pm Sun-Wed & Fri, to 9:30pm Thu, to 3:30pm Fri Nov-Mar; P) Run by the Simon Wiesenthal Center, this powerful, deeply moving museum uses interactive technology to engage visitors in discussion and contemplation around racism and bigotry. Particular focus is given to the Holocaust, with a major basement exhibition that examines the social, political and economic conditions that led to the Holocaust as well as the experience of the millions persecuted. On the museum's 2nd floor, another major exhibition offers an intimate look into the life and impact of Anne Frank.

⊙ West Hollywood & Mid-City

Los Angeles County Museum of Art   Museum
(LACMA; Map p282; ☎323-857-6000; www.lacma. org; 5905 Wilshire Blvd, Mid-City; adult/senior & student/child $25/21/free, 2nd Tue each month free, some holidays free; ⊗11am-5pm Mon, Tue & Thu, to 8pm Fri, 10am-7pm Sat & Sun; P; ⊒Metro lines 20, 217, 720, 780 to Wilshire & Fairfax)

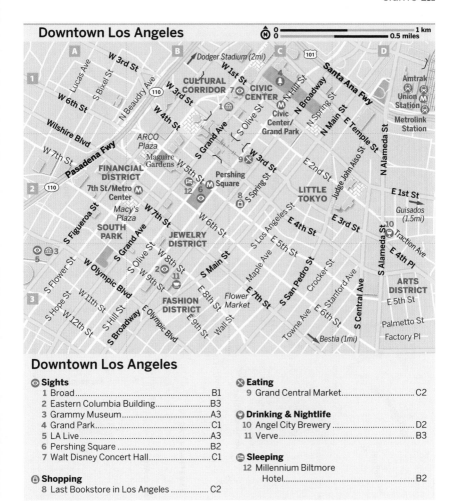

Downtown Los Angeles

The depth and wealth of the collection at the largest museum in the western US is stunning. LACMA holds all the major players – Rembrandt, Cézanne, Magritte, Mary Cassatt, Ansel Adams – plus millennia's worth of Chinese, Japanese, pre-Columbian and ancient Greek, Roman and Egyptian sculpture. Recent acquisitions include massive outdoor installations such as Chris Burden's *Urban Light* (a surreal selfie backdrop of hundreds of vintage LA street-lamps) and Michael Heizer's *Levitated Mass,* a surprisingly inspirational 340-ton boulder perched over a walkway.

Original Farmers Market   Market
(Map p282; ☎323-933-9211; www.farmers-marketla.com; 6333 W 3rd St, Fairfax District; ⊙9am-9pm Mon-Fri, to 8pm Sat, 10am-7pm Sun; 🅿👪) Long before the city was flooded with farmers markets, there was *the* farmers market. Fresh produce, roasted nuts, doughnuts, cheeses, blini – you'll find them

Hollywood & Griffith Park

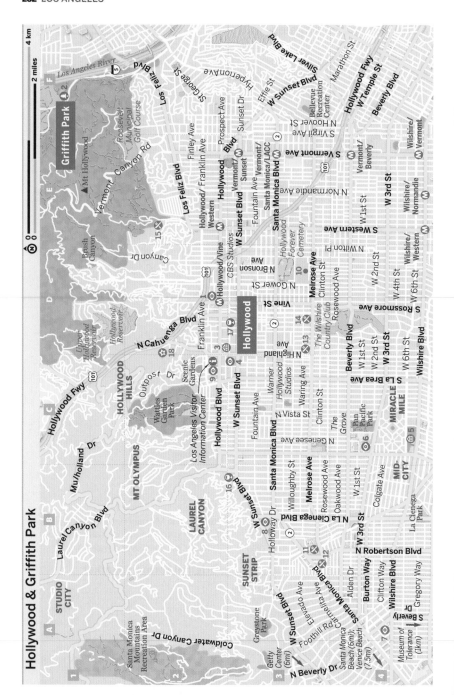

Hollywood & Griffith Park

all at this 1934 landmark. Casual and kid friendly, it's a fun place for a browse, snack or for people-watching.

Sunset Strip   Street

(Map p282; Sunset Blvd) A visual cacophony of billboards, giant ad banners and neon signs, the sinuous stretch of Sunset Blvd running between Laurel Canyon and Doheny Dr has been nightlife central since the 1920s.

◎ Venice, Marina Del Rey & Playa del Rey

Venice Boardwalk   Waterfront

(Ocean Front Walk; Venice Pier to Rose Ave) Life in Venice moves to a different rhythm and nowhere more so than on the famous Venice Boardwalk, officially known as Ocean Front Walk. It's a freak show, a human zoo and a wacky carnival alive with Hula-Hoop magicians, old-timey jazz combos, solo distorted garage rockers and artists (good and bad) – as far as LA experiences go, it's a must.

Abbot Kinney Boulevard   Area

(⊠Big Blue Bus line 18) Abbot Kinney, who founded Venice in the early 1900s, would probably be delighted to find that one of Venice's best-loved streets bears his name. Sort of a seaside Melrose with a Venetian flavor, the mile-long stretch of Abbot Kinney Blvd between Venice Blvd and Main St is full of upscale boutiques, galleries, lofts

and sensational restaurants. Some years back, GQ named it America's coolest street, and that cachet has only grown since.

◎ Malibu & Pacific Palisades

El Matador State Beach   Beach

(☎818-880-0363; 32215 Pacific Coast Hwy, Malibu; ℙ) Arguably Malibu's most stunning beach, where you park on the bluffs and stroll down a trail to sandstone rock towers that rise from emerald coves. Topless sunbathers stroll through the tides, and dolphins breech the surface beyond the waves. It's been impacted by coastal erosion, but you can still find a sliver of dry sand tucked against the bluffs.

Getty Villa   Museum

(☎310-430-7300; www.getty.edu; 17985 Pacific Coast Hwy, Pacific Palisades; ◷10am-5pm Wed-Mon; ℙ⊕; ⊠line 534 to Coastline Dr) **FREE** Stunningly perched on an ocean-view hillside, this museum in a replica 1st-century Roman villa is an exquisite, 64-acre showcase for Greek, Roman and Etruscan antiquities. Dating back 7000 years, they were amassed by oil tycoon J Paul Getty. Galleries, peristiles, courtyards and lushly landscaped gardens ensconce all manner of friezes, busts and mosaics, along with millennia-old cut, blown and colored glass and brain-bending geometric configurations in the Hall of Colored Marbles. Other highlights include the Pompeii fountain and Temple of Herakles.

Exposition Park & South LA

Watts Towers Landmark

(☏213-847-4646; www.wattstowers.org; 1761-1765 E 107th St, Watts; ☺tours 11am-3pm Thu & Fri, 10:30am-3pm Sat, noon-3pm Sun; ℗; Ⓜ Blue Line to 103rd St) The three 'Gothic' spires of the fabulous Watts Towers rank among the world's greatest monuments of folk art. In 1921 Italian immigrant Simon Rodia set out 'to make something big' and then spent 33 years cobbling together this whimsical free-form sculpture from concrete, steel and a motley assortment of found objects: green 7Up bottles to sea shells, tiles, rocks and pottery.

✖ EATING

🍴 Downtown Los Angeles & Boyle Heights

Grand Central Market Market

(Map p281; www.grandcentralmarket.com; 317 S Broadway; ☺8am-10pm; ☎; Ⓜ Red/Purple Lines to Pershing Sq) Designed by prolific architect John Parkinson and once home to an office occupied by Frank Lloyd Wright, LA's beaux arts market hall has been satisfying appetites since 1917 and today is Downtown LA's gourmet hotspot. Lose yourself in its bustle of neon signs, stalls and counters, peddling everything from fresh produce and nuts, to sizzling Thai street food, hipster breakfasts, modern deli classics, artisanal pasta and specialty coffee.

Guisados Tacos $

(☏323-264-7201; www.guisados.co; 2100 E Cesar Chavez Ave, Boyle Heights; tacos from $2.95; ☺9am-8pm Mon-Fri, to 9pm Sat, to 5pm Sun; Ⓜ Gold Line to Mariachi Plaza) Guisados' citywide fame is founded on its *tacos de guisados*: warm, thick, nixtamal tortillas made to order and topped with smoky, slow-cooked stews. Do yourself a favor and order the sampler plate ($7.25), a democratic mix of six mini tacos. The *chiles torreados* (blistered, charred chili) taco is a must for serious spice-lovers.

Bestia Italian $$$

(☏213-514-5724; www.bestiala.com; 2121 7th Pl; pizzas $18-21, pasta $19-31, mains $38-130; ☺5-11pm Sun-Thu, to midnight Fri & Sat; ℗) In a

Grand Central Market

once-abandoned Arts District corner, this loud, buzzing, industrial dining space is one of the most sought-after reservations in town; book at least a week ahead. The draw remains Chef Ori Menashe's clever, produce-driven take on Italian flavors, from charred pizzas topped with house-made 'nduja (spicy Calabrian paste), to sultry stinging-nettle raviolo with egg, mixed mushrooms, hazelnut and ricotta.

Hollywood

Petit Trois French $$

(Map p282; 323-468-8916; www.petittrois. com; 718 N Highland Ave; mains $18-39; ⊗noon-10pm Sun-Thu, to 11pm Fri & Sat; P) Good things come in small packages...like tiny, no-reservations Petit Trois! Owned by acclaimed TV chef Ludovic Lefebvre, its two long counters (the place is too small for tables) are where food-lovers squeeze in for smashing, honest, Gallic-inspired grub, from a ridiculously light Boursin-stuffed omelette to a showstopping 'Big Mec' double cheeseburger served with a standout foie gras–infused red-wine Bordelaise.

Providence Modern American $$$

(Map p282; 323-460-4170; www.providencela. com; 5955 Melrose Ave; lunch mains $38-48, dinner tasting menus $120-240; ⊗noon-2pm & 6-10pm Mon-Fri, 5:30-10pm Sat, to 9pm Sun; P) Consistently near the top of every list of great LA restaurants, chef Michael Cimarusti's James Beard–winning, two-Michelin-starred darling turns superlative seafood into arresting, nuanced dishes that might see abalone paired with eggplant, turnip and nori, or spiny lobster conspire decadently with macadamia nut and earthy black truffle. À la carte options are available at lunch only.

Movie-Star Tours

Warner Bros Studio Tour (877-492-8687, 818-972-8687; www.wbstudiotour.com; 3400 Warner Blvd, Burbank; tours adult/child 8-12yr from $72/62; ⊗8:30am-3:30pm, extended hours Jun-Aug; 155, 222, 501 stop about 400yd from tour center) This tour offers the most fun, yet authentic, look behind the scenes of a major movie studio. The two-hour standard tour kicks off with a video of WB's greatest film hits (*Rebel Without a Cause, Harry Potter,* etc), before a tram whisks you around 110 acres of sound stages, backlot sets and technical departments, including props, costumes and the paint shop, and a collection of Batmobiles.

TMZ Celebrity Tour (Map p282; 844-869-8687; www.tmz.com/tour; 6822 Hollywood Blvd; adult/child $52/32; ⊗tours depart 10am-5pm most days, check website for additional hours; MRed Line to Hollywood/Highland) Cut the shame; we know you want to spot celebrities, glimpse their homes and laugh at their dirt. Super-fun tours by open-sided bus run for two hours, and you'll likely meet some of the TMZ stars...and perhaps even celebrity guests on the bus.

Warner Bros Studio

Shopaholic Essentials

It might be pricey and unapologetically pretentious, but no trip to LA would be complete without a saunter along **Rodeo Drive** (Map p282), the famous three-block ribbon of style where sample-size fembots browse for Gucci and Dior. Fashion retailer Fred Hayman opened the strip's first luxury boutique, Giorgio Beverly Hills, at No 273 back in 1961. Famed for its striped white-and-yellow awning, the store allowed its well-heeled clients to sip cocktails while shopping and have their purchases home delivered in a Rolls-Royce.

Downtown, what started as a single storefront is now **Last Bookstore in Los Angeles** (Map p281; ☑213-488-0599; www.lastbookstorela.com; 453 S Spring St; ☉10am-10pm Mon-Thu, to 11pm Fri & Sat, to 9pm Sun), California's largest new-and-used bookstore, spanning two levels of an old bank building. Eye up the cabinets of rare books before heading upstairs, home to a horror- and crime-book den, a book tunnel and a few art galleries to boot. The store also houses a terrific vinyl collection.

Rodeo Drive
V_E/SHUTTERSTOCK ©

Santa Monica
Milo & Olive   Italian $$
(☑310-453-6776; www.miloandolive.com; 2723 Wilshire Blvd; dishes $12-23; ☉7am-11pm) We

love this place for its small-batch wines, incredible pizzas, terrific breakfasts (creamy polenta and poached eggs anyone?), breads and pastries, all of which you may enjoy at the marble bar or shoulder to shoulder with new friends at one of two common tables. It's a cozy neighborhood joint so it doesn't take reservations.

Cassia   Southeast Asian $$$
(☑310-393-6699; www.cassiala.com; 1314 7th St; appetizers $12-18, mains $19-76; ☉5-10pm Sun-Thu, to 11pm Fri & Sat; P) Ever since it opened in 2015, open, airy Cassia has made about every local and national 'best' list of LA restaurants. Chef Bryant Ng draws on his Chinese-Singaporean heritage in dishes such as *kaya* toast (with coconut jam, butter and a slow-cooked egg), 'sunbathing' prawns, and the encompassing Vietnamese pot-au-feu: short-rib stew, veggies, bone marrow and delectable accompaniments.

🍴 West Hollywood & Mid-City
Gracias Madre   Vegan, Mexican $$
(Map p282; ☑323-978-2170; www.gracias madreweho.com; 8905 Melrose Ave, West Hollywood; mains lunch $12-17, dinner $12-18; ☉11am-11pm Mon-Fri, from 10am Sat & Sun; 🌱) Gracias Madre shows just how tasty – and chichi – organic, plant-based Mexican cooking can be. Sit on the gracious patio or in the cozy interior and feel good as you eat healthily: sweet-potato flautas, coconut 'bacon,' plantain 'quesadillas,' plus salads and bowls. We're consistently surprised at innovations like cashew 'cheese,' mushroom 'chorizo' and heart-of-palm 'crab cakes.'

Catch LA   Fusion $$$
(Map p282; ☑323-347-6060; www.catchrest aurants.com/catchla; 8715 Melrose Ave, West Hollywood; shared dishes $8-39, dinner mains $34-79; ☉11am-3pm Sat & Sun, 5pm-2am daily; P) An LA-scene extraordinaire. You may well find sidewalk paparazzi stalking celebrity guests and a doorman to check your reservation, but all that's forgotten once

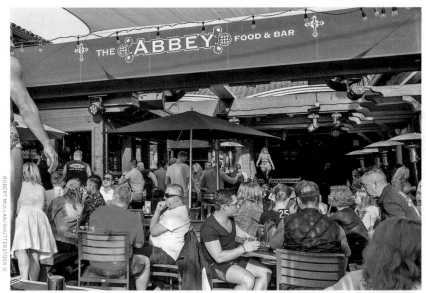

Abbey

you're in this 3rd-floor rooftop restaurant/ bar above WeHo. The Pacific Rim–inspired menu features supercreative cocktails and shared dishes such as truffle sashimi, black-cod lettuce wraps, and scallop and cauliflower with tamarind brown butter.

🍸 DRINKING & NIGHTLIFE

Abbey   Gay & Lesbian
(Map p282; ☏310-289-8410; www.theabbeyweho. com; 692 N Robertson Blvd, West Hollywood; ⏰11am-2am Mon-Thu, from 10am Fri, from 9am Sat & Sun) It's been called the best gay bar in the world, and who are we to argue? Once a humble coffeehouse, the Abbey has expand- ed into the bar/club/restaurant of record in WeHo. It has so many different-flavored martinis and mojitos that you'd think they were invented here, plus a menu of upscale pub food (mains $14 to $21).

Bar Marmont   Bar
(Map p282; ☏323-650-0575; www.chateau- marmont.com; 8171 Sunset Blvd, Hollywood; ⏰6pm-2am) Elegant, but not stuck up; been around, yet still cherished. With high ceilings, molded walls and terrific martinis, the famous and the wish-they-weres still flock here. If you time it right you might see celebs – the Marmont doesn't share who. Come midweek. Weekends are for amateurs.

Angel City Brewery   Microbrewery
(Map p281; ☏213-622-1261; www.angelcity- brewery.com; 216 S Alameda St; ⏰4pm-1am Mon-Thu, to 2am Fri, noon-2am Sat, to 1am Sun) Where suspension cables were once manufactured, craft brews are now made and poured. Located on the edge of the Arts District, this is a popular spot to knock back an India pale ale or chai-spiced Impe- rial stout, listen to some tunes and chow down some food-truck tacos.

KELTON GALE/SHUTTERSTOCK ©

LA Dodgers in action

Rooftop Bar at Mama Shelter   Bar
(Map p282; 323-785-6600; www.mamashelter. com/en/los-angeles/restaurants/rooftop; 6500 Selma Ave; noon-1am Mon-Thu, 11am-2am Fri & Sat, to 1am Sun; Red Line to Hollywood/Vine) Less a hotel rooftop bar and more lush, tropical-like oasis with killer views of the Hollywood sign and LA skyline, multicolored daybeds and tongue-in-cheek bar bites like 'boujee fries' and outré tacos. Pulling everyone from hotel guests to locals from the nearby Buzzfeed offices, it's a winner for languid cocktail sessions, landmark spotting and a game of giant Jenga.

⭐ ENTERTAINMENT

Hollywood Bowl   Concert Venue
(Map p282; 323-850-2000; www.hollywood-bowl.com; 2301 N Highland Ave; rehearsals free, performance costs vary; Jun-Sep) Summers in LA just wouldn't be the same without alfresco melodies under the stars at the Bowl, a huge natural amphitheater in the Hollywood Hills. Its annual season – which usually runs from June to September – includes symphonies, jazz bands and iconic acts such as Blondie, Bryan Ferry and Angélique Kidjo. Bring a sweater or blanket as it gets cool at night.

Off the 405   Live Music
(www.getty.edu; Getty Center; 6-9pm Sat May-Sep) FREE On selected Saturdays from May to September, the Getty Center (p280) courtyard fills with evening crowds for a delicious collision of art, brilliant live acts and beat-pumping DJ sets.

Dodger Stadium   Baseball
(866-363-4377; www.dodgers.com; 1000 Vin Scully Ave) Few clubs can match the Dodgers' history (Jackie Robinson, Sandy Koufax, Kirk Gibson and sportscaster Vin Scully), success and fan loyalty, and this 1950s-era stadium is still considered one of baseball's most beautiful, framed by views of palm trees and the San Gabriel Mountains. Best views are from behind home plate, or gorge in the all-you-can-eat pavilion in right field.

ℹ INFORMATION

Los Angeles Visitor Information Center (Map p282; ☏323-467-6412; www.discoverlosangeles. com; Hollywood & Highland, 6801 Hollywood Blvd; ⊙9am-10pm Mon-Sat, 10am-7pm Sun; ☾Red Line to Hollywood/Highland) The main tourist office for Los Angeles, located in Hollywood.

ℹ GETTING THERE & AROUND

TO/FROM THE AIRPORT

Los Angeles International Airport (LAX; www. lawa.org/welcomeLAX.aspx; 1 World Way) is 17 miles from Downtown LA.

Door-to-door shuttles Two companies offer service from the airport: **Prime Time** (☏800-733-8267; www.primetimeshuttle.com) charges $18, $23 and $12 for trips to Santa Monica, Hollywood and Downtown, respectively. **Super Shuttle** (☏800-258-3826; www.supershuttle. com) charges $24, $29 and $19 for trips to Santa Monica, Hollywood and Downtown, respectively.

Bus Coaches from **LAX FlyAway Buses** (☏866-435-9529; www.lawa.org/FlyAway) travel nonstop (one way $9.75) to Downtown's Patsaouras Transit Plaza at Union Station (45

minutes), Hollywood (one to 1½ hours) and Long Beach (50 minutes).

Taxi & Rideshare Cost is around $50 to Downtown LA (25 to 50 minutes). Note there are no curbside pick-ups. Instead travelers take a shuttle bus to a designated lot to catch their ride.

BICYCLE

Metro Bike Share (https://bikeshare.metro. net) allows you to hire bikes around-the-clock from more than 60 bike kiosks in the Downtown area, including Chinatown, Little Tokyo and the Arts District. Pay using your debit or credit card ($3.50 per 30 minutes).

CAR & MOTORCYCLE

Unless time is no factor – or money is extremely tight – you're going to want to spend some time behind the wheel, although this means contending with some of the worst traffic in the country. Avoid rush hour (7am to 9am and 3:30pm to 6:30pm).

PUBLIC TRANSPORTATION

Most public transportation is handled by **Metro** (☏323-466-3876; www.metro.net), which operates bus, subway and light rail lines. Metro offers trip-planning help through its website.

SAN FRANCISCO

In This Chapter

San Francisco at a Glance...

Grab your coat and a handful of glitter, and enter a wonderland of fog and fabulousness. So long, inhibitions; hello, San Francisco!

San Francisco is a 7-by-7-mile peninsula that looks like California's thumb, pointed optimistically upwards. Take this as a hint to look up: you'll notice San Francisco's crooked Victorian rooflines, wind-sculpted treetops, and fog tumbling over the Golden Gate Bridge. Heads are perpetually in the clouds atop San Francisco's 48 hills. Cable cars provide easy access to Russian and Nob Hills, and splendid panoramas reward the slog up to Coit Tower.

Two Days in San Francisco

On day one, hop aboard the Powell-Mason **cable car** (p296) and hold on for hills and thrills. Have lunch in the **Ferry Building** (p302), then catch your prebooked ferry to **Alcatraz** (p298). On day two, get the camera ready for vistas of the **Golden Gate Bridge** (p294). Walk across, or visit Golden Gate Park and the **California Academy of Sciences** (p308).

Four Days in San Francisco

Start day three in **Chinatown** (p304). Hit **Fisherman's Wharf** (p297) in the afternoon; take the Powell-Hyde cable car past zigzagging **Lombard Street** (p312). On day four have a taco in the **Mission** (p315), explore hippie-historic **Haight Street** (p313), and end the evening at **Specs** (p319) or another North Beach bar.

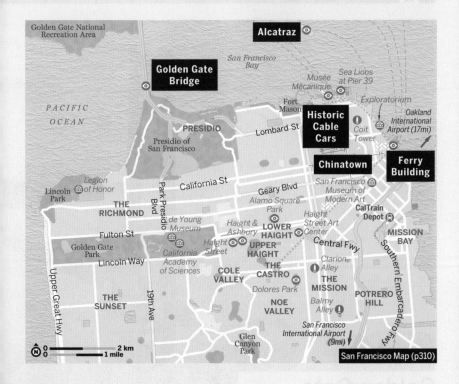

Golden Gate National Recreation Area

PACIFIC OCEAN

San Francisco Bay

Alcatraz

Golden Gate Bridge

Fort Mason

Musée Mécanique

Sea Lions at Pier 39

Exploratorium

PRESIDIO

Lombard St

Historic Cable Cars

Coit Tower

Oakland International Airport (17mi)

Presidio of San Francisco

Chinatown

Ferry Building

Legion of Honor

Lincoln Park

California St

Geary Blvd

San Francisco Museum of Modern Art

THE RICHMOND

Park Presidio Blvd

Alamo Square Park

CalTrain Depot

Fulton St

de Young Museum

Haight & Ashbury

Haight Street Art Center

LOWER HAIGHT

Central Fwy

MISSION BAY

Golden Gate Park

Lincoln Way

California Academy of Sciences

Haight Street

UPPER HAIGHT

Clarion Alley

Southern Embarcadero Fwy

Upper Great Hwy

19th Ave

COLE VALLEY

THE CASTRO

THE MISSION

POTRERO HILL

THE SUNSET

Dolores Park

NOE VALLEY

Balmy Alley

Glen Canyon Park

San Francisco International Airport (9mi)

San Francisco Map (p310)

2 km
1 mile

Arriving in San Francisco

San Francisco International Airport
Fast rides to downtown SF on BART cost $9.65; ride-share $30 to $50, plus tip; door-to-door shuttle vans $19 to $23, plus tip; or taxi $45 to $60, plus tip.

Oakland International Airport Catch BART from the airport to downtown SF ($10.95, 25 minutes). Taxis cost $70 to $90 (plus tip) to SF; ride-share $40 to $60 (plus tip) off-peak to SF.

Where to Stay

San Francisco hotel rates are among the world's highest. Plan ahead – well ahead – and grab bargains when you see them. Given the choice, San Francisco's boutique properties beat chains for a sense of place – but take what you can get at a price you can afford. Apartment rental options are limited in the city. For more detailed information, check out Where to Stay (p323).

Golden Gate Bridge

The city's most spectacular icon towers 80 stories above the roiling waters of the Golden Gate, the narrow entrance to San Francisco Bay. When the fog clears it reveals magnificent views.

Great For...

☑ **Don't Miss**

There's a cross-section of suspension cable behind the Bridge Pavilion Visitor Center..

San Franciscans have passionate perspectives on every subject, especially their signature landmark, though everyone agrees it's a good thing the Navy didn't get its way over the bridge's design – naval officials preferred a hulking concrete span, painted with caution-yellow stripes, over the soaring art-deco design of architects Gertrude and Irving Murrow and engineer Joseph B Strauss, which, luckily, won the day.

Construction

Nobody thought it could happen. Not until the early 1920s did the City of San Francisco seriously investigate building a bridge over the treacherous, windblown strait. The War Department owned the land on both sides and didn't want to take chances with ships: safety and solidity were its goals. But the green light was given to the counter-

ROSCHETZKY PHOTOGRAPHY/SHUTTERSTOCK ©

PACIFIC
OCEAN

San Francisco Bay

Golden Gate Bridge

101

❶ Need to Know

☏ toll information 877-229-8655; www.
goldengatebridge.org/visitors; Hwy 101;
northbound free, southbound $7-8; 🚌 28, all
Golden Gate Transit buses

✕ Take a Break

You'll find refreshments only at the SF
end of the bridge by the Bridge Pavilion.
Otherwise, there's nothing nearby.

★ Top Tip

For on-site information, drop into the
Bridge Pavilion Visitor Center (☏ 415-
426-5220; www.ggnpc.org; Golden Gate
Bridge toll plaza; ⊙ 9am-6pm).

proposal by Strauss and the Murrows for
a subtler suspension span, economic in
form, that harmonized with the natural
environment.

Before the War Department could insist
on an eyesore, laborers dove into the
treacherous riptides of the bay and got the
bridge under way in 1933. Just four years
later workers balancing atop swaying cables completed what was then the world's
longest suspension bridge – nearly 2 miles
long, with 746ft suspension towers, higher
than any construction west of New York.

Which View?

As far as best views go, cinema buffs
believe Hitchcock had it right: seen from
below at Fort Point, the 1937 bridge induces
a thrilling case of *Vertigo*. Fog aficionados
prefer the north-end lookout at Marin's
Vista Point, to watch gusts billow through
bridge cables like dry ice at a Kiss concert.

To see both sides of the Golden Gate
debate, hike or bike the 1.7-mile span. Muni
bus 28 runs to the parking lot, and pedestrians and cyclists can cross the bridge on
sidewalks. For drivers, bridge tolls are billed
electronically to your vehicle's license plate;
for details, see www.goldengate.org/tolls.

Walking & Cycling Over the Bridge

Pedestrians take the eastern sidewalk.
Dress warmly! From the parking area and
bus stop (off Lincoln Blvd), a pathway leads
past the toll plaza, then it's 1.7 miles across.
If 3.4 miles round-trip seems too much,
take a bus to the north side via Golden Gate
Transit, then walk back. By bicycle, from
the toll-plaza parking area ride toward the
Roundhouse, then follow signs to the western sidewalk, reserved for bikes only.

Historic Cable Cars

Offering million-dollar vistas and the promise of adventure, cable cars are the way to explore San Francisco. These ratcheting wonders bring you lurching into the heart of the city's best neighborhoods.

Carnival rides can't compare to cable cars, San Francisco's steampunk public transit. Novices slide into strangers' laps – cable cars were invented in 1873, long before seat belts – but regulars just grip the leather hand straps, lean back and ride the down-hill plunges like pro surfers. On this trip, you'll master the San Francisco stance and conquer SF hills without breaking a sweat.

Powell-Hyde Cable Car

At the **Powell Street Cable Car Turna-round**, you'll see operators turn the car atop a revolving wooden platform and a vintage kiosk where you can buy an all-day Muni Passport for $23, instead of paying $7 per ride. Board the red-signed Powell-Hyde cable car and begin your 338ft ascent of Nob Hill.

Great For...

☑ Don't Miss

The California St cable car rumbles through Chinatown and past Old St Mary's Cathedral.

Powell Street Cable Car Turnaround

ℹ **Need to Know**

Powell-Mason cars are quickest to reach Fisherman's Wharf, but Powell-Hyde cars are more scenic.

🍴 **Take a Break**

After the ride, visit the Ferry Building (p303), where champagne-and-oyster happy hour awaits.

★ **Top Tip**

If you're planning to stop en route, get a Muni Passport for $23 per day.

Nob Hill

As your cable car lurches uphill, you can imagine horses struggling up this slippery crag. Nineteenth-century city planners were skeptical of inventor Andrew Hallidie's 'wire-rope railway' – but after more than a century of near-continuous operation, his wire-and-hemp cables have seldom broken. Hallidie's cable cars even survived the 1906 earthquake and fire that destroyed 'Snob Hill' mansions, returning the faithful to the rebuilt Grace Cathedral (p309) – hop off to say hello to SF's gentle patron St Francis, carved by sculptor Beniamino Bufano.

Lombard Street

Back on the Powell-Hyde car, enjoy bay views as you careen past crooked, flower-lined Lombard Street (p312) toward Fisherman's Wharf. The waterfront terminus is named for Friedel Klussmann, who saved cable cars from mayoral modernization plans in 1947. She did the math: cable cars brought in more tourism dollars than they cost in upkeep. The mayor reluctantly agreed to a vote – and lost to 'the Cable Car Lady' by a landslide. For her funeral in 1986, cable cars citywide were draped in black.

Fisherman's Wharf

At the wharf, emerge from the submarine *USS Pampanito* to glimpse SF as sailors used to. Witness Western saloon brawls in vintage arcade games at the Musée Mécanique (p314).

Alcatraz

From its 19th-century founding to detain Civil War deserters and Native American dissidents until its closure by Bobby Kennedy in 1963, Alcatraz was America's most notorious jail.

Alcatraz: for more than 150 years the name has given the innocent chills and the guilty cold sweats. Over the decades it's been a military prison, a forbidding maximum-security penitentiary and disputed territory between Native American activists and the FBI.

It all started innocently enough back in 1775, when Spanish lieutenant Juan Manuel de Ayala sailed the *San Carlos* past the 22-acre island he called Isla de Alcatraces (Isle of the Pelicans). In 1859 a new post on Alcatraz became the first US West Coast fort, and soon proved handy as a holding pen for Civil War deserters, insubordinates and those who had been court-martialed. By 1902 the four cell blocks of wooden cages were rotting, unsanitary and otherwise ill-equipped for the influx of US soldiers convicted of war crimes in the Philippines.

Great For...

☑ Don't Miss

The D-Block solitary-confinement cells, which raise goosebumps.

Alcatraz

San Francisco Bay

Pier 33

❶ Need to Know

Alcatraz Cruises 415-981-7625; www.alcatrazcruises.com; tours adult/child 5-11yr day $38.35/23.50, night $45.50/27.05; call center 8am-7pm, ferries depart Pier 33 half-hourly 8:45am-3:50pm, night tours 5:55pm & 6:30pm;

✕ Take a Break

Codmother Fish & Chips (415-606-9349; www.codmother.com; 496 Beach St; mains $7-13; 11am-5pm Mon & Wed-Fri, 11:30am-6pm Sat & Sun; 47, Powell-Mason, MF) is a little food truck right by the Alcatraz departure docks.

★ Top Tip

For Alcatraz Cruises, book a month ahead for day visits, two to three months for night tours.

The army began building a new concrete military prison in 1909, but upkeep was expensive and the US soon had other things to worry about: WWI, financial ruin and flappers.

In 1922, when the 18th Amendment to the Constitution declared selling liquor a crime, rebellious Jazz Agers weren't prepared to give up their tipple – and gangsters kept the booze coming. Authorities were determined to make a public example of criminal ringleaders, and in 1934 the Federal Bureau of Prisons took over Alcatraz as a prominent showcase for its crime-fighting efforts. 'The Rock' averaged only 264 inmates, but its roster read like a list of America's Most Wanted. A-list criminals doing time on Alcatraz included Chicago crime boss Al 'Scarface' Capone, dapper kidnapper George 'Machine Gun' Kelly,

hot-headed Harlem mafioso and sometime poet 'Bumpy' Johnson, and Morton Sobell, the military contractor found guilty of Soviet espionage along with Julius and Ethel Rosenberg.

Today, first-person accounts of daily life in the Alcatraz lockup are included on the excellent self-guided audio tour provided by Alcatraz Cruises. But take your headphones off for just a moment and notice the sound of carefree city life traveling across the water: this is the torment that made perilous escapes into riptides worth the risk. Though Alcatraz was considered escape-proof, in 1962 the Anglin brothers and Frank Morris floated away on a makeshift raft and were never seen again. Security and upkeep proved prohibitively expensive, and finally the island prison was abandoned to the birds in 1963.

Alcatraz

A HALF-DAY TOUR

Book a ferry from Pier 33 and ride 1.5 miles across the bay to explore America's most notorious former prison. The trip itself is worth the money, providing stunning views of the city skyline. Once you've landed at the ❶ **Ferry Dock & Pier**, you begin the 580yd walk to the top of the island and prison; if you need assistance to reach the top, there's a twice-hourly tram.

As you climb toward the ❷ **Guardhouse**, notice the island's steep slope; before it was a prison, Alcatraz was a fort. In the 1850s, the military quarried the rocky shores into near-vertical cliffs. Ships could then only dock at a single port, separated from the main buildings by a sally port (a drawbridge and moat in what became the guardhouse). Inside, peer through floor grates to see Alcatraz's original prison.

Volunteers tend the brilliant ❸ **Officers' Row Gardens**, an orderly counterpoint to the overgrown rose bushes surrounding the burned-out shell of the ❹ **Warden's House**. At the top of the hill, by the front door of the ❺ **Main Cellhouse**, beautiful shots unfurl all around, including a view of the ❻ **Golden Gate Bridge**. Above the main door of the administration building, notice the ❼ **historic signs & graffiti**, before you step inside the dank, cold prison to find the ❽ **Frank Morris cell**, former home to Alcatraz's most notorious jail-breaker.

TOP TIPS

➡ Book at least one month prior for self-guided daytime visits, longer for ranger-led night tours. For info on garden tours, see www.alcatraz gardens.org.

➡ Be prepared to hike; a steep path ascends from the ferry landing to the cell block. Most people spend two to three hours on the island. You need only reserve for the outbound ferry; take any ferry back.

➡ There's no food (just water) but you can bring your own; picnicking is allowed at the ferry dock only. Dress in layers as weather changes fast and it's usually windy.

Historic Signs & Graffiti
During their 1969–71 occupation, Native Americans graffitied the water tower: 'Home of the Free Indian Land.' Above the cellhouse door, examine the eagle-and-flag crest to see how the red-and-white stripes were changed to spell 'Free.'

Warden's House
Fires destroyed the warden's house and other structures during the Indian Occupation. The government blamed the Native Americans; the Native Americans blamed agents provocateurs acting on behalf of the Nixon administration to undermine public sympathy.

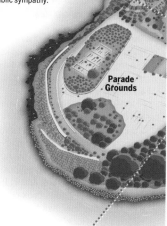

Parade Grounds

Officers' Row Gardens
In the 19th century soldiers imported topsoil to beautify the island with gardens. Well-trusted prisoners later gardened – Elliott Michener said it kept him sane. Historians, ornithologists and archaeologists choose today's plants.

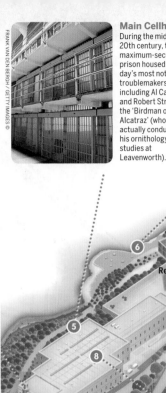

Main Cellhouse
During the mid-20th century, the maximum-security prison housed the day's most notorious troublemakers, including Al Capone and Robert Stroud, the 'Birdman of Alcatraz' (who actually conducted his ornithology studies at Leavenworth).

View of the Golden Gate Bridge
The Golden Gate Bridge stretches wide on the horizon. Best views are from atop the island at Eagle Plaza, near the cellhouse entrance, and at water level along the Agave Trail (September to January only).

Power House

Recreation Yard

Water Tower

Officers' Club

Guardhouse
Alcatraz's oldest building dates to 1857 and retains remnants of the original drawbridge and moat. During the Civil War the basement was transformed into a military dungeon – the genesis of Alcatraz as a prison.

⑥ ⑤ ⑧ ⑦ ③ ④ ② ①

Lighthouse

Guard Tower

Frank Morris Cell
Peer into cell 138 on B-Block to see a recreation of the dummy's head that Frank Morris left in his bed as a decoy to aid his notorious – and successful – 1962 escape from Alcatraz.

Ferry Dock & Pier
A giant wall map helps you get your bearings. Inside nearby Building 64, short films and exhibits provide historical perspective on the prison and details about the Native American Occupation.

Ferry Building

Global food trends start in San Francisco. To sample tomorrow's menu today, wander through the city's monument to trailblazing local, sustainable food. The Ferry Building has Northern California's best bites.

Great For...

☑ Don't Miss

During the Saturday farmers markets top chefs jostle for first pick of rare heirloom varietals.

Other towns have gourmet ghettos, but San Francisco puts its love of food front and center at the Ferry Building. The once-grand port was overshadowed by a 1950s elevated freeway – until the overpass collapsed in 1989's Loma Prieta earthquake. The Ferry Building survived and became a symbol of San Francisco's reinvention, marking your arrival onto America's forward-thinking food frontier.

History

The trademark 240ft tower greeted dozens of ferries daily after its 1898 inauguration. But with the opening of the Bay and Golden Gate Bridges, ferry traffic subsided in the 1930s. An overhead freeway was built, obscuring the building's stately facade and turning it black with exhaust fumes. Only after the 1989 earthquake did city planners realize what they'd been missing: with its

ℹ Need to Know

☏415-983-8000; www.ferrybuildingmarket-place.com; cnr Market St & the Embarcadero; ⏰10am-7pm Mon-Fri, 8am-6pm Sat, 11am-5pm Sun; ♿; 🚌2, 6, 9, 14, 21, 31, Ⓜ Embarcadero, ⒷEmbarcadero

✕ Take a Break

Slurp the sea's bounty at **Hog Island Oyster Company** (☏415-391-7117; www.hogislandoysters.com; 1 Ferry Bldg, cnr Market St & the Embarcadero; 6 oysters $19-21; ⏰11am-9pm; 🚌2, 6, 9, 14, 21, 31, Ⓜ Embarcadero, ⒷEmbarcadero) 🌱

★ Top Tip

You can still catch a ferry here and crossing the sparkling bay is a great escape.

grand halls and bay views, this was the perfect place for a new public commons.

Foodie Hot Spot

Today the grand arrivals hall tempts commuters to miss the boat and get on board with SF's latest culinary trends instead. Indoor kiosks sell locally roasted espresso, artisan cheese and cured meats, plus organic ice-cream flavors to match – that's right, Vietnamese coffee, cheese and prosciutto. People-watching wine bars and award-winning restaurants are further enticements to stick around and raise a toast to San Francisco.

Ferry Building Farmers Market

Even before Ferry Building renovations were completed in 2003, the **Ferry Plaza Farmers Market** (☏415-291-3276; www.cuesa.org; cnr Market St & the Embarcadero; street food $3-12; ⏰10am-2pm Tue & Thu, from 8am Sat; ♿♿; 🚌2, 6, 9, 14, 21, 31, Ⓜ Embarcadero, ⒷEmbarcadero) 🌱 began operating out front on the sidewalk. Soon the foodie action spread to the bayfront plaza, with 50 to 100 local food purveyors catering to hometown crowds three times a week. While locals sometimes grumble that the prices are higher here than at other markets, there's no denying that the Ferry Plaza market offers seasonal, sustainable, handmade gourmet treats and specialty produce not found elsewhere.

Join SF's legions of professional chefs and semiprofessional eaters, and taste-test the artisan goat cheese, fresh-pressed California olive oil, wild boar and organic pluots for yourself. The Saturday morning farmers market offers the best people-watching – it's not uncommon to spot celebrities – but arrive early if you're shopping.

Chinatown

Dumplings and rare teas are served under pagoda roofs on Chinatown's main streets – but its historic back alleys are filled with temple incense, mah-jongg tile clatter and distant echoes of revolution.

Grant Avenue

Enter through the **Dragon's Gate**, donated by Taiwan in 1970, and you'll find yourself on the street formerly known as Dupont in its notorious red-light heyday. The pagoda-topped 'Chinatown deco' architecture beyond this gate was innovated by Chinatown merchants, led by Look Tin Ely, in the 1920s – a pioneering initiative to lure tourists with a distinctive modern look.

Now it's hard to believe that this souvenir-shopping strip was once lined with brothels – at least until you see the fascinating displays at the **Chinese Historical Society of America** (CHSA; ☑415-391-1188; www.chsa.org; 965 Clay St; ⊙noon-5pm Tue-Fri, 11am-4pm Sat & Sun; ♿; ☑1, 8, 30, 45, ⓖCalifornia, Powell-Mason, Powell-Hyde, Ⓜ️Ⓣ) FREE.

Great For...

☑ Don't Miss

Hearing mah-jongg tiles, temple gongs and Chinese orchestras as you wander the Chinatown alleyways.

Dragon's Gate

Stockton St
Ross Al
Washington St
Grant Ave
Portsmouth Square
Spofford Alley
Waverly Place
Clay St
Commercial St

❶ Need to Know

Key bus routes to Chinatown include 1, 8, 30 and 45. The California St cable car passes through the neighborhood's southern end.

✕ Take a Break

Pick up where Jack Kerouac left off at Li Po (p320), a historic Beat hangout.

★ Top Tip

Parking is tough. There's public parking underneath Portsmouth Sq and at the Good Luck Parking Garage.

Waverly Place

Grant Ave may be the economic heart of Chinatown, but its soul is Waverly Pl, lined with historic clinker-brick buildings and flag-festooned temple balconies. Due to 19th-century race-based restrictions, family associations and temples were built right on top of the barber shops, laundries and restaurants lining these two city blocks. Through good times and bad, Waverly Pl stood its ground, and temple services have been held here since 1852.

Chinatown Alleyways

The 41 historic alleyways packed into Chinatown's 22 blocks have seen it all since 1849: gold rushes and revolution, incense and opium, fire and icy receptions. In clinker-brick buildings lining these narrow backstreets, temple balconies jut out over

bakeries, laundries and barbers – there was nowhere to go but up in Chinatown after 1870, when laws limited Chinese immigration, employment and housing. **Chinatown Alleyway Tours** (☏415-984-1478; www.china-townalleywaytours.org; Portsmouth Sq; adult/student $26/16; ⏰tours 11am Sat; 🚹; 🚌1, 8, 10, 12, 30, 41, 45, 🚋California, Powell-Mason, Powell-Hyde) and **Chinatown Heritage Walking Tours** (☏415-986-1822; https://tour.cccsf.us; Chinese Culture Center, Hilton Hotel, 3rd fl, 750 Kearny St; adult $30-40, student $20-30; 🚹; 🚌1, 8, 10, 12, 30, 41, 45, 🚋California, Powell-Mason, Powell-Hyde) offer community-supporting, time-traveling strolls through defining moments in American history.

Sun Yat-sen once plotted the overthrow of China's Manchu dynasty at **Spofford Alley**, and, during Prohibition, this was the site of turf battles over local bootlegging and protection rackets. Around sundown a Chinese orchestra strikes up a tune and mah-jongg games begin with clicking tiles.

North Beach Beat

This tour of the North Beach hits all the literary hot spots from San Francisco's Beat scene.

Start City Lights Books
Distance 1.5 miles
Duration Two hours

3 Look for parrots in the treetops and octogenarians in tai chi stances on the lawn at **Washington Square**.

Columbus Ave

Union St

Green St

Vallejo St

Powell St

Broadway

Stockton St

Jasper Pl

2 With opera on the jukebox and potent espresso, **Caffe Trieste** (p320) is where Francis Ford Coppola allegedly drafted *The Godfather*.

Classic Photo Browsing the shelves at **City Lights** (p312)

CITY LIGHTS BOOKS

1 Pick up a copy of Allen Ginsberg's *Howl* at **City Lights Books** (p312), home of Beat poetry and free speech.

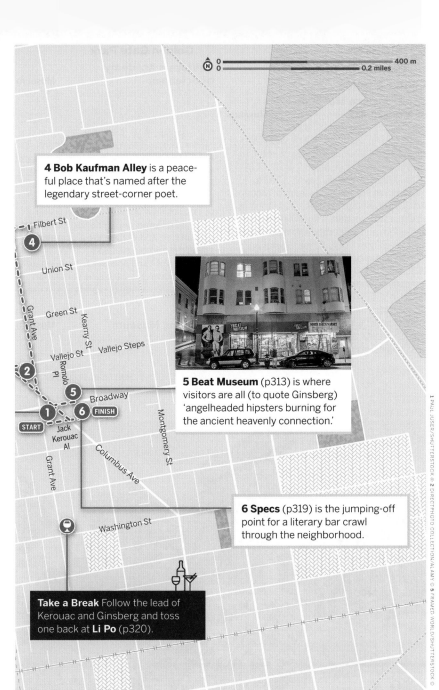

4 Bob Kaufman Alley is a peaceful place that's named after the legendary street-corner poet.

Filbert St

Union St

Grant Ave

Green St

Kearny St

Vallejo St Romolo Pl Vallejo Steps

Broadway

START

FINISH

Jack Kerouac Al

Grant Ave

Columbus Ave

Montgomery St

Washington St

5 Beat Museum (p313) is where visitors are all (to quote Ginsberg) 'angelheaded hipsters burning for the ancient heavenly connection.'

6 Specs (p319) is the jumping-off point for a literary bar crawl through the neighborhood.

Take a Break Follow the lead of Kerouac and Ginsberg and toss one back at **Li Po** (p320).

N 0 — 400 m
0 — 0.2 miles

⊙ SIGHTS

◎ Downtown, Civic Center & SoMa

San Francisco Museum of Modern Art　　Museum

(SFMOMA; ☑415-357-4000; www.sfmoma.org; 151 3rd St; adult/ages 19-24yr/under 18yr $25/19/free; ☺10am-5pm Fri-Tue, to 9pm Thu, atrium 8am Mon-Fri; ♿; ☐5, 6, 7, 14, 19, 21, 31, 38, ⓂMontgomery, ⒷMontgomery) The expanded San Francisco Museum of Modern Art is a mind-boggling feat, nearly tripling in size to accommodate a sprawling collection of modern and contemporary masterworks over seven floors of galleries – but then, SFMOMA has defied limits ever since its 1935 founding. The museum was a visionary early investor in then-emerging art forms including photography, installations, video, performance art, digital art and industrial design. Even during the Depression, SFMOMA envisioned a world of vivid possibilities, starting in San Francisco.

◎ Golden Gate Park

California Academy of Sciences　　Museum

(☑415-379-8000; www.calacademy.org; 55 Music Concourse Dr; adult/student/child $35.95/30.95/25.95; ☺9:30am-5pm Mon-Sat, from 11am Sun; ℗♿; ☐5, 6, 7, 21, 31, 33, 44, ⓂN) ✔ Architect Renzo Piano's 2008 landmark LEED-certified green building houses 40,000 animals in a four-story rainforest, split-level aquarium and planetarium, all under a 'living roof' of wildflowers. Inside, butterflies flit around in the glass Osher Rainforest Dome, penguins waddle in the African Hall, and Claude the albino alligator stalks the mezzanine swamp. Don't miss the Giants of Land and Sea exhibit, where you can brave an earthquake simulation, virtually climb a redwood and get lost in a fog room.

de Young Museum　　Museum

(☑415-750-3600; http://deyoung.famsf.org; 50 Hagiwara Tea Garden Dr; adult/child $15/free, 1st Tue of month free; ☺9:30am-5:15pm Tue-Sun; ☐5, 7, 44, ⓂN) Follow sculptor

de Young Museum

Andy Goldsworthy's artificial fault line in the sidewalk into Herzog & de Meuron's sleek, copper-clad building that's oxidizing green to blend into the park. Don't be fooled by the camouflaged exterior: shows here boldly broaden artistic horizons, from Oceanic ceremonial masks and trippy-hippie handmade fashion to James Turrell's domed *Skyspace* installation, built into a hill in the sculpture garden. Ticket includes free same-day entry to the **Legion of Honor** (☑415-750-3600; http://legionofhonor.famsf. org; 100 34th Ave; adult/child $15/free, 1st Tue of month free; ☺9:30am-5:15pm Tue-Sun; ☐1, 2, 18, 38); $2 discount with Muni, BART or Caltrain ticket.

◉ Nob Hill & Russian Hill

Cable Car Museum   Historic Site
(☑415-474-1887; www.cablecarmuseum.org; 1201 Mason St; donations appreciated; ☺10am-6pm Apr-Sep, to 5pm Oct-Mar; ⛨; ☐Powell-Mason, Powell-Hyde) **FREE** That clamor you hear riding cable cars is the sound of San Francisco's peak technology at work. Gears click and wire-hemp ropes whir as these vintage contraptions are hoisted up and over hills too steep for horses or buses – and you can inspect those cables close-up here, in the city's still-functioning cable-car barn. See three original 1870s cable cars stored here and browse a bonanza of SF memorabilia in the museum shop.

Grace Cathedral   Church
(☑415-749-6300; www.gracecathedral.org; 1100 California St; suggested donation adult/child $3/2; ☺8am-6pm Mon-Sat, to 7pm Sun, services 8:30am, 11am & 6pm Sun; ☐1, ☐California) San Francisco's Episcopal cathedral has been rebuilt three times since the gold rush and the current reinforced-concrete Gothic cathedral took 40 years to complete. Spectacular stained-glass windows include a 'Human Endeavor' series dedicated to science, depicting Albert Einstein uplifted in swirling nuclear particles. San Francisco history unfolds on murals covering the 1906 earthquake to the 1945 UN charter signing. People of all faiths wander indoor and outdoor inlaid-stone labyrinths, meant to guide

Active San Francisco

On sunny weekends, SF is out kite-flying, surfing or biking. Even on foggy days, don't neglect sunscreen: UV rays penetrate SF's thin cloud cover.

Coastal Trail (www.californiacoastaltrail. info; ☺sunrise-sunset; ☐1, 18, 38) Hit your stride on this 10.5-mile stretch, starting at Fort Funston, crossing 4 miles of sandy Ocean Beach and wrapping around the Presidio to the Golden Gate Bridge. Casual strollers can pick up the restored trail near Sutro Baths and head around the Lands End bluffs for end-of-the-world views and glimpses of shipwrecks at low tide.

Dandyhorse SF Bike Tours (☑415-890-2453; www.dandysftours.com; 33 Gordon St; tours from $69; ☺8am-7pm; ☐12, 19, 27, 47) The ultimate embodiment of San Francisco's DIY spirit, local resident Nick Normuth custom-built a bunch of bikes, studied up on the city and started a cycling tour. The adventure begins in an adorable headquarters in SoMa, and branches out to the Mission, the Castro, Golden Gate Park and beyond, depending on which tour you've signed up for.

Cycling on Golden Gate Bridge
SPOONPHOL/SHUTTERSTOCK ©

restless souls through three spiritual stages: releasing, receiving and returning.

Diego Rivera Gallery   Gallery
(☑415-771-7020; www.sfai.edu; 800 Chestnut St; ☺9am-7pm; ☐30, ☐Powell-Mason) **FREE**

San Francisco

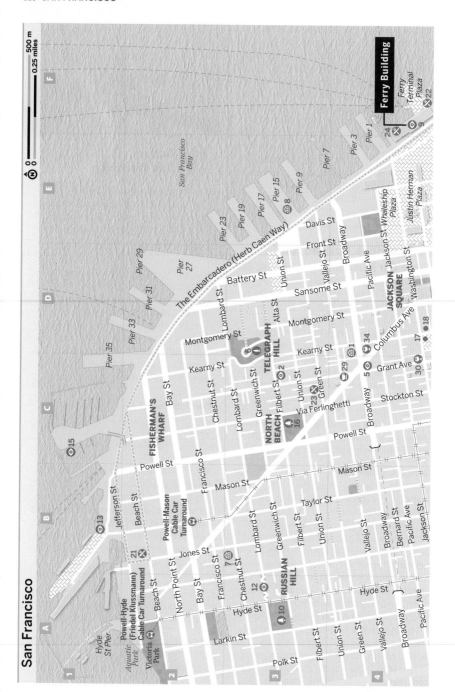

Ferry Building

0   500 m
0   0.25 miles

San Francisco Bay

Hyde St Pier

Aquatic Park

Victoria Park

Powell-Hyde (Friedel Klussmann) Cable Car Turnaround

FISHERMAN'S WHARF

Powell-Mason Cable Car Turnaround

RUSSIAN HILL

NORTH BEACH

TELEGRAPH HILL

JACKSON SQUARE

The Embarcadero (Herb Caen Way)

Pier 1
Pier 3
Pier 7
Pier 9
Pier 15
Pier 17
Pier 19
Pier 23
Pier 27
Pier 29
Pier 31
Pier 33
Pier 35

Ferry Terminal Plaza

Justin Herman Plaza

Jackson St Whaleship Plaza

Davis St
Front St
Battery St
Sansome St
Montgomery St
Kearny St
Grant Ave
Stockton St
Powell St
Mason St
Taylor St
Jones St
Leavenworth St
Hyde St
Larkin St
Polk St

Lombard St
Union St
Vallejo St
Broadway
Pacific Ave
Jackson St
Washington St
Columbus Ave

Bay St
Chestnut St
Francisco St
Filbert St
Greenwich St
Lombard St
Green St
Via Ferlinghetti
Alta St
Montgomery St
Kearny St

Jefferson St
Beach St
North Point St
Bernard St

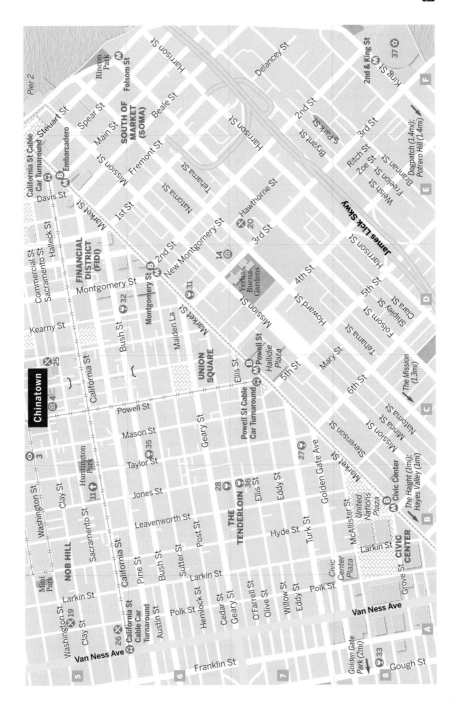

Chinatown

Pier 2

California St Cable
Car Turnaround

Rincon
Park

SOUTH OF
MARKET
(SOMA)

Folsom St

Harrison St

Delancey St

2nd & King St

37

King St

Embarcadero

Steuart St

Spear St

Main St

Beale St

Fremont St

1st St

2nd St

Bryant St

Park St

Ritch St

Zoe St

Freelon St

Bryant St

3rd St

Dogpatch (1.4mi);
Potrero Hill (1.4mi)

Davis St

Market St

Mission St

Natoma St

Tehama St

Hawthorne St

3rd St

Harrison St

Welsh St

Zoe St

James Lick Skwy

FINANCIAL
DISTRICT
(FIDI)

Commercial St

Sacramento St

Halleck St

Montgomery St

Bush St

2nd St

Montgomery St

New Montgomery St

Mission St

20

14

Yerba
Buena
Gardens

4th St

5th St

Shipley St

Clara St

32

31

Kearny St

Maiden La

Howard St

Tehama St

Folsom St

California St

25

4

Powell St

Mason St

Geary St

UNION
SQUARE

Market St

Ellis St

Powell St

Hallidie
Plaza

5th St

Mary St

6th St

The Mission
(1.3mi)

Minna St

Natoma St

3

Huntington
Park

11

Taylor St

35

Jones St

Leavenworth St

Post St

THE
TENDERLOIN

28

27

36

Ellis St

Eddy St

Golden Gate Ave

Stevenson St

Mission St

Minna St

Natoma St

Market St

Civic Center

Civic Center
Plaza

The Haight (1mi);
Hayes Valley (1mi)

Washington St

Clay St

NOB HILL

Sacramento St

California St

Pine St

Bush St

Sutter St

Hyde St

Turk St

McAllister St

United
Nations
Plaza

Mini
Park

Clay St

19

Larkin St

Washington St

California St
Cable Car
Turnaround

26

Van Ness Ave

Austin St

Polk St

Hemlock St

Cedar St

Geary St

O'Farrell St

Olive St

Willow St

Eddy St

Larkin St

Polk St

Grove St

CIVIC
CENTER

Van Ness Ave

Franklin St

Golden Gate
Park (2mi)

33

Gough St

5

6

7

8

F

E

D

C

B

A

San Francisco

Diego Rivera's 1931 *The Making of a Fresco Showing the Building of a City* is a *trompe l'oeil* fresco within a fresco, showing the artist himself pausing to admire his own work and the efforts of workers around him, as they build the modern city of San Francisco. The fresco covers an entire wall of the Diego Rivera Gallery in the **San Francisco Art Institute** (SFAI; ◷ Walter & McBean Galleries 11am-7pm Tue, to 6pm Wed-Sat, Diego Rivera Gallery 9am-7pm) FREE. For sweeping views of the city Diego admired, head to the terrace cafe for espresso and panoramic bay vistas.

Lombard Street   Street
(🚋 Powell-Hyde) You've seen the eight switchbacks of Lombard St's 900 block in a thousand photographs. The tourist board has dubbed it 'the world's crookedest street,' which is factually incorrect: Vermont St in Potrero Hill deserves that award, but Lombard is much more scenic, with its red-brick pavement and lovingly tended flowerbeds. It wasn't always so bent; before the arrival of the car it plunged straight down the hill.

◎ North Beach & Chinatown

Coit Tower   Public Art
(📞 415-249-0995; www.sfrecpark.org; Telegraph Hill Blvd; nonresident elevator fee adult/child $9/6, mural tour full/2nd fl only $9/6; ◷ 10am-6pm Apr-Oct, to 5pm Nov-Mar; 🚌 39) The exclamation mark on San Francisco's skyline is Coit Tower, with 360-degree views of downtown and wraparound 1930s Works Progress Administration (WPA) murals celebrating SF workers. Initially denounced as communist, the murals are now a national landmark. For a parrot's-eye panoramic view of San Francisco 210ft above the city, take the elevator to the tower's open-air platform. Book your docent-led, 30- to 40-minute mural tour online – tour all murals ($9), or just the seven recently restored hidden stairwell murals ($6).

City Lights Books   Cultural Center
(📞 415-362-8193; www.citylights.com; 261 Columbus Ave; ◷ 10am-midnight; 👷; 🚌 8, 10, 12, 30, 41, 45, 🚋 Powell-Mason, Powell-Hyde, Ⓜ T) Free speech and free spirits have rejoiced here since 1957, when City Lights founder

and poet Lawrence Ferlinghetti and manager Shigeyoshi Murao won a landmark ruling defending their right to publish Allen Ginsberg's magnificent epic poem *Howl*. Celebrate your freedom to read freely in the designated Poet's Chair upstairs overlooking Jack Kerouac Alley, load up on zines on the mezzanine and entertain radical ideas downstairs in the new Pedagogies of Resistance section.

Beat Museum   Museum

(☑800-537-6822; www.kerouac.com; 540 Broadway; adult/student $8/5, walking tours $30; ☺museum 10am-7pm, walking tours 2-4pm Sat; ☐8, 10, 12, 30, 41, 45, ☐Powell-Mason, MT) The closest you can get to the complete Beat experience without breaking a law. The 1000-plus artifacts in this museum's literary-ephemera collection include the sublime (the banned edition of Ginsberg's *Howl*, with the author's own annotations) and the ridiculous (those Kerouac bobblehead dolls are definite head-shakers). Downstairs, watch Beat-era films in ramshackle theater seats redolent with the odors of literary giants, pets and pot. Upstairs, pay your respects at shrines to individual Beat writers.

◎ The Haight & Hayes Valley

Haight Street   Street

(btwn Central & Stanyan Sts; ☐7, 22, 33, 43, MN) Was it the fall of 1966 or the winter of '67? As the Haight saying goes, if you can remember the Summer of Love, you probably weren't here. The fog was laced with pot, sandalwood incense and burning military draft cards, entire days were spent contemplating trippy Grateful Dead posters, and the corner of **Haight and Ashbury Streets** (☐6, 7, 33, 37, 43) became the turning point for an entire generation. The Haight's counterculture kids called themselves freaks and flower children; *San Francisco Chronicle* columnist Herb Caen dubbed them 'hippies.'

Haight Street Art Center   Arts Center

(☑415-363-6150; www.haightstreetart.org; 215 Haight St; ☺noon-6pm Wed-Sun; ☐6, 7, 22, MF)

FREE Jeremy Fish's bronze bunny-skull sculpture hints at the weird wonders inside this nonprofit dedicated to works on paper and San Francisco's signature art form: screen-printed posters. Glimpse rock-concert posters currently in progress at the on-site screen-printing studio, plus jaw-dropping gallery shows – recently featuring Ralph Steadman's original illustrations for Hunter S Thompson's *Fear and Loathing in Las Vegas*. Gracing the stairwell is a hidden SF treasure: Ruben Kaddish's 1937 WPA fresco *Dissertation on Alchemy*, surely the trippiest mural ever commissioned by the US government.

Alamo Square Park   Park

(www.sfparksalliance.org/our-parks/parks/alamo-square; cnr Hayes & Steiner Sts; ☺sunrise-sunset; ☷☷; ☐5, 21, 22, 24) Hippie communes and Victorian bordellos, jazz greats and opera stars, earthquakes and Church of Satan services: these genteel 'Painted Lady' Victorian mansions have hosted them all since 1857, and survived elegantly intact. Pastel 'Postcard Row' mansions (aka the *Full House* sitcom backdrop) along the southeastern edge of this hilltop park pale in comparison with the colorful, turreted, outrageously ornamented Queen Anne Victorians along the northwestern end.

◎ The Marina, Fisherman's Wharf & the Piers

Exploratorium   Museum

(☑415-528-4444; www.exploratorium.edu; Pier 15/17; adult/child $29.95/19.95, 6-10pm Thu $19.95; ☺10am-5pm Tue-Sun, over 18yr only 6-10pm Thu; P☷; ME, F) ✹ Is there a science to skateboarding? Do toilets really flush counterclockwise in Australia? At San Francisco's hands-on science museum, you'll find out things you wish you learned in school. Combining science with art and investigating human perception, the Exploratorium nudges you to question how you perceive the world around you. The setting is thrilling: a 9-acre, glass-walled pier jutting straight into San Francisco Bay, with large outdoor portions you can explore free of charge, 24 hours a day.

Sea Lions at Pier 39   Sea Lions

(415-623-4734; www.pier39.com; Pier 39, cnr Beach St & the Embarcadero; 24hr; ; 47, Powell-Mason, ME, F) Sea lions took over San Francisco's most coveted waterfront real estate in 1989 and have been making a public display of themselves ever since. Naturally these unkempt squatters have become San Francisco's favorite mascots, and since California law requires boats to make way for marine mammals, yacht owners have to relinquish valuable slips to accommodate as many as 1000 sea lions. These giant mammals 'haul out' onto the docks between January and July, and whenever else they feel like sunbathing.

Musée Mécanique   Amusement Park

(415-346-2000; www.museemecanique.com; Pier 45, Shed A; 10am-8pm; ; 47, Powell-Mason, Powell-Hyde, ME, F) A flashback to penny arcades, the Musée Mécanique houses a mind-blowing collection of vintage mechanical amusements. Sinister, freckle-faced Laughing Sal has freaked out kids for over a century, but don't let this manic mannequin deter you from the best arcade west of Coney Island. A quarter lets you start brawls in Wild West saloons, peep at belly dancers through a vintage Mutoscope and even learn a cautionary tale about smoking opium.

◎ The Mission, Dogpatch & Potrero Hill

Dolores Park   Park

(www.sfrecpark.org/destination/mission-dolores-park; Dolores St, btwn 18th & 20th Sts; 6am-10pm; ; 14, 33, 49, B16th St Mission, MJ) Welcome to San Francisco's sunny side, the land of street ball and Mayan-pyramid playgrounds, semiprofessional tanning and taco picnics. Although the grassy expanses are mostly populated by relaxing hipsters, political protests and other favorite local sports do happen from time to time, and there are free movie nights and mime troupe performances in summer. Climb to the upper southwestern corner for superb views of downtown, framed by palm trees.

Driving on Lombard Street (p312)

SIMON POON/SHUTTERSTOCK ©

Clarion Alley
Public Art

(www.clarionalleymuralproject.org; btwn 17th & 18th Sts; ⬚14, 22, 33, Ⓑ16th St Mission, Ⓜ16th St Mission) In this outstanding open-air street-art showcase, you'll spot artists touching up pieces and making new ones, with the full consent of neighbors and Clarion Alley Collective's curators. Only a few pieces survive for years, such as Megan Wilson's daisy-covered *Tax the Rich* or Jet Martinez' glimpse of Clarion Alley inside a forest spirit. Incontinent art critics often take over the alley's eastern end so topical murals usually go up on the western end.

TOURS

Precita Eyes Mission Mural Tours
Walking

(☎415-285-2287; www.precitaeyes.org; 2981 24th St; adult/child $20/3; ⬚12, 14, 48, 49, Ⓑ24th St Mission) Muralists lead weekend walking tours covering 60 to 70 Mission murals within a six- to 10-block radius of mural-bedecked **Balmy Alley** (btwn 24th & 25th Sts; ⬚10, 12, 14, 27, 48, Ⓑ24th St Mission). Tours last from one hour to two hours and 15 minutes (for the more in-depth, private Classic Mural Walk). Proceeds fund mural upkeep and overheads.

Sea Foraging Adventures
Tours

(www.seaforager.com; per person from $50) 🍴 For the most adventurous dining in SF, try something off the menu and on the beaches with US Fish & Game alum and James Beard Award nominee Kirk Lombard. Discover secret foraging spots around San Francisco's waterfront, from monkeyface eels under the Golden Gate Bridge to slime crabs along Fisherman's Wharf, or take fishing and foraging trips south of SF.

EATING

🍴 Downtown, Civic Center & SoMa

In Situ
Californian, International **$$**

(http://insitu.sfmoma.org; 151 3rd St, SFMOMA; mains $20-50; ⊙11am-3:30pm Thu-Mon, 5-9pm

 Best Cheap Eats in the Mission

La Palma Mexicatessen (☎415-647-1500; www.lapalmasf.com; 2884 24th St; tamales, tacos & huaraches $3-10; ⊙8am-6pm Mon-Sat, to 5pm Sun; 🖉; ⬚12, 14, 27, 48, Ⓑ24th St Mission) Follow the applause: that's the sound of organic tortilla-making in progress. You've found the Mission mother lode of handmade tamales, and *pupusas* (tortilla pockets) with potato and *chicharones* (pork crackling), *carnitas* (slow-roasted pork), *cotija* (Oaxacan cheese) and La Palma's own tangy tomatillo sauce. Get takeout or bring a small army to finish the meal at sunny sidewalk tables.

Tacolicious (☎415-649-6077; www.tacolicious.com; 741 Valencia St; tacos $5.50; ⊙11:30am-midnight; 🖉; ⬚14, 22, 33, 49, Ⓑ16th St Mission, ⓂJ) Never mind the name: once you've sampled the *carnitas* tacos and passion-fruit-habañero margaritas, you'll be in no position to debate authenticity or grammar – or say anything besides '*uno mas, por favor*' ('another, please'). Choose four tacos for $20, including seasonal vegetarian options. No reservations, but while you wait you can work through the 100-tequila menu at the bar.

Tacos
ELLARY ROSE/SHUTTERSTOCK ©

Thu-Sat, 11am-3:30pm & 5-8pm Sun; ⬚5, 6, 7, 14, 19, 21, 31, 38, Ⓑ Montgomery, Ⓜ Montgomery) The landmark gallery of modern cuisine attached to SFMOMA also showcases avant-garde masterpieces – but these

From left: Artisan bread at The Mill (p318); Sea lions at Pier 39 (p314); Haight-Ashbury neighborhood (p313)

ones you'll lick clean. Chef Corey Lee collaborates with more than 100 star chefs worldwide, scrupulously re-creating their signature dishes with California-grown ingredients so that you can enjoy Nathan Myhrvold's caramelized carrot soup, Tim Raue's wasabi lobster and Albert Adrià's Jasper Hill Farm cheesecake in one unforgettable sitting.

Benu Californian, Fusion $$$

(☑415-685-4860; www.benusf.com; 22 Hawthorne St; tasting menu $310; ☺5:30-8:30pm Tue-Thu, to 9pm Fri & Sat; ☐10, 12, 14, 30, 45) SF has pioneered Asian fusion cuisine for 150 years, but what the pan-Pacific innovation chef-owner Corey Lee brings to the plate is gasp-inducing: foie-gras soup dumplings – what?! Dungeness crab and truffle custard pack such outsize flavor into Lee's faux-shark's-fin soup, you'll swear Jaws is in there. A Benu dinner is an investment, but don't miss star sommelier Yoon Ha's ingenious pairings.

🌐 Golden Gate Park & the Avenues

Arsicault Bakery Bakery $

(☑415-750-9460; 397 Arguello Blvd; pastries $3-7; ☺7am-2:30pm Mon-Fri, to 3:30pm Sat & Sun; ☐1, 2, 33, 38, 44) Armando Lacayo left his job in finance because he, like his Parisian grandparents before him, was obsessed with making croissants. After perfecting his technique, Lacayo opened a modest bakery in the Inner Richmond in 2015. Within a year, *Bon Appétit* magazine had declared it the best new bakery in America and the golden, flaky, buttery croissants regularly sell out.

🌐 Nob Hill & Russian Hill

1760 Californian $$

(☑415-359-1212; www.1760sf.com; 1760 Polk St; dishes $15-22; ☺5:30-9:30pm Mon-Thu, to 11pm Fri & Sat; ☑; ☐45, 49) ✈ Every night is a culinary throw-down at 1760: chef Carl Foronda must find the right techniques and culinary inspirations to highlight today's star ingredients. No single cuisine

dominates and unexpected strengths shine – shiitake add depth to Korean-style short rib, while tomato confit makes papardelle with ragu sing. This is what democracy in the kitchen looks like – all equally inspired and exquisitely presented.

Swan Oyster Depot   Seafood $$

(☎415-673-1101; 1517 Polk St; dishes $10-28; ⏰10:30am-5:30pm Mon-Sat; 🚌1, 19, 47, 49, 🚋California) Superior flavor without the superior attitude of typical seafood restaurants. Justifiably famous since 1912 for signature oysters and crab salads, there's almost always a wait for the few stools at its vintage lunch counter – but the upside of high turnover is incredibly fresh seafood. Arrive before noon to avoid hour-long waits, or order takeout to enjoy in **George Sterling Park** (www.sfparksalliance. org; cnr Greenwich & Hyde Sts; 🚼; 🚌19, 41, 45, 🚋Powell-Hyde).

🍴 North Beach & Chinatown

Golden Boy   Pizza $

(☎415-982-9738; www.goldenboypizza.com; 542 Green St; slices $3.25-4.25; ⏰11:30am-midnight Sun-Thu, to 2am Fri & Sat; 🚌8, 30, 39, 41, 45, 🚋Powell-Mason) 'If you don't see it don't ask 4 it' reads the menu – Golden Boy has kept punks in line since 1978, serving Genovese focaccia-crust pizza that's chewy, crunchy and hot from the oven. You'll have whatever second-generation Sodini family *pizzaioli* (pizza-makers) are making and like it – especially pesto and clam-and-garlic. Grab square slices and draft beer at the bomb-shelter counter and boom: you're golden.

Mister Jiu's   Chinese, Californian $$

(☎415-857-9688; www.misterjius.com; 28 Waverly Pl; mains $14-45; ⏰5:30-10:30pm Tue-Sat; 🚌30, 🚋California, Ⓜ️T) Success has been celebrated in this historic Chinatown banquet hall since the 1880s – but today, scoring a table at Mister Jiu's is reason enough for celebration. Build memorable banquets from chef Brandon Jew's ingenious Chinese/Californian signatures: quail and Mission-fig sticky rice, hot and sour Dungeness crab soup, Wagyu sirloin and tuna heart fried rice. Don't skip dessert – pastry chef Melissa Chou's salted plum sesame balls are flavor bombs.

❌ The Haight & Hayes Valley

The Mill   Bakery **$**

(☎415-345-1953; www.themillsf.com; 736
Divisadero St; toast $4-7; ⏱7am-9pm; 🖋🚻; 🚌5,
21, 24, 38) Baked with organic wholegrain
stone-ground on-site, hearty Josey
Baker Bread sustains Haight skaters and
start-uppers alike. You might think SF
hipsters are gullible for queuing for pricey
toast, until you taste the truth: slathered in
housemade hazelnut spread or California-grown almond butter, it's a proper meal.
Housemade granola with Sonoma yogurt
starts SF days right, and hearty seasonal
sandwiches fuel Alamo Sq hikes.

Rich Table   Californian **$$**

(☎415-355-9085; www.richtablesf.com; 199
Gough St; mains $17-37; ⏱5:30-10pm Sun-Thu,
to 10:30pm Fri & Sat; 🚌5, 6, 7, 21, 47, 49, Ⓜ Van
Ness) 🖋 Impossible cravings begin at Rich
Table, where mind-bending dishes like por-
cini doughnuts, sardine chips, and *burrata*
(mozzarella and cream) funnel cake blow
up Instagram feeds nightly. Married co-
chefs and owners Sarah and Evan Rich riff
on seasonal San Francisco cuisine with the
soul of SFJAZZ stars and the ingenuity of
Silicon Valley regulars.

❌ The Marina, Fisherman's Wharf & the Piers

Kaiyo   Fusion **$$**

(☎415-525-4804; www.kaiyosf.com; 1838
Union St; small plates $12-28, share plates
$19-28; ⏱5-10pm Tue, Wed & Sun, to 11pm Thu
& Sat, 10:30am-3pm Sat & Sun; 🚌41, 45) For a
deliciously deep dive into the cuisine of the
Japanese-Peruvian diaspora, head to Cow
Hollow's most playful and inventive new
restaurant, where the Pisco and whiskey
cocktails are named for anime characters
and a neon-green moss wall runs the length
of the *izakaya*-style dining room.

Atelier Crenn   French **$$$**

(☎415-440-0460; www.ateliercrenn.com;
3127 Fillmore St; tasting menu $335; ⏱5-9pm
Tue-Sat; 🚌22, 28, 30, 43) The menu arrives
in the form of a poem and then come the
signature white chocolate spheres filled
with a burst of apple cider. If this seems
an unlikely start to a meal, just wait for the
geoduck rice tart in a glass dome frosted
by liquid nitrogen, and about a dozen more
plates inspired by the childhood of chef
Dominique Crenn in Brittany, France.

❌ The Mission, Dogpatch & Potrero Hill

Al's Place   Californian **$$**

(☎415-416-6136; www.alsplacesf.com; 1499
Valencia St; share plates $15-21; ⏱5:30-10pm
Wed-Sun; 🖋; 🚌12, 14, 49, Ⓜ J, Ⓑ24th St Mission)
🖋 The Golden State dazzles on Al's plates,
featuring homegrown heirloom ingredients,
pristine Pacific seafood and grass-fed
meat. Painstaking preparation yields sun-
drenched flavors and exquisite textures:
crispy-skin cod with frothy preserved-lime
dip, and grilled peach melting into velvety
foie gras. Dishes are half the size but thrice
the flavor of mains elsewhere – get two or
three and you'll be California dreaming.

Californios   Latin American **$$$**

(☎415-757-0994; www.californiossf.com; 3115
22nd St; 16-course tasting menu $197; ⏱5:30-
8:30pm Tue-Thu, to 9pm Fri & Sat; 🚌12, 14, 49,
Ⓑ24th St Mission) Parades – from Carnaval
to Día de los Muertos – are a Mission
specialty, and the parade of Latin-inspired
flavors nightly at Californios does justice
to the neighborhood's roots and unbridled
creativity. Chef Val Cantu collaborates
with local farms and artisan producers to
reinvent staples with the seasons: imagine
sourdough tortillas, foie-gras tamales, Dun-
geness crab ceviche and wild-strawberry
flan. Reserve ahead.

🍸 DRINKING & NIGHTLIFE

🍷 Downtown, Civic Center & Soma

Bourbon & Branch   Bar

(☎415-346-1735; www.bourbonandbranch.com;
501 Jones St; ⏱6pm-2am; 🚌27, 38) 'Don't
even think of asking for a cosmo' reads
the House Rules at this Prohibition-era

speakeasy, recognizable by its deliciously misleading Anti-Saloon League sign. For award-winning cocktails in the liquored-up library, whisper the password ('books') at the O'Farrell entrance. Reservations required for front-room booths and Wilson & Wilson Detective Agency, the noir-themed speakeasy-within-a-speakeasy (password supplied with reservations).

Zombie Village — Cocktail Bar

(☑415-474-2284; www.thezombievillage.com; 441 Jones St; ⊙5pm-2am Mon-Fri, from 6pm Sat; ☐27, 38) San Francisco probably didn't need anymore tiki bars, but we're certainly not going to complain about Zombie Village, the latest from Future Bars Group, also behind Bourbon & Branch, **Rickhouse** (☑415-398-2827; www.rickhousebar.com; 246 Kearny St; ⊙5pm-2am Mon, 3pm-2am Tue-Fri, 6pm-2am Sat; ☐8, 30, 45, Ⓜ Montgomery, Ⓑ Montgomery) and **Local Edition** (☑415-795-1375; www.localeditionsf.com; 691 Market St; ⊙5pm-2am Mon-Thu, from 4:30pm Fri, from 7pm Sat; Ⓜ Montgomery, Ⓑ Montgomery). Guests step off the gritty Tenderloin streets and into a dark and mystical tiki wonderland, where the rum flows like wine and skulls are everywhere.

🏠 Nob Hill & Russian Hill

Stookey's Club Moderne — Lounge

(www.stookeysclubmoderne.com; 895 Bush St; ⊙4:30pm-2am Mon-Sat, to midnight Sun; ☐1, ☐Powell-Hyde, Powell-Mason, California) Dangerous dames lure unsuspecting sailors into late-night schemes over potent hooch at this art-deco bar straight out of a Dashiell Hammett thriller. Chrome-lined 1930s Streamline Moderne decor sets the scene for intrigue, and wisecracking white-jacketed bartenders shake the stiffest Corpse Reviver cocktails in town. Arrive early to find room on the hat rack for your fedora, especially on live jazz nights.

🏠 North Beach & Chinatown

Specs — Bar

(Specs Twelve Adler Museum Cafe; ☑415-421-4112; 12 William Saroyan Pl; ⊙5pm-2am Mon-Fri;

LGBT
San Francisco

In San Francisco, you don't need to trawl the urban underworld for a gay scene. The intersection of 18th and Castro is the historic center of the gay world, but dancing queens head to SoMa for thump-thump clubs. The Mission remains the preferred 'hood for many women and a diverse transgender community. Top picks for good times:

Aunt Charlie's Lounge (☑415-441-2922; www.auntcharlieslounge.com; 133 Turk St; cover free-$5; ⊙noon-midnight Mon & Wed, to 2am Tue & Thu, to 12:30am Fri, 10am-12:30am Sat, to midnight Sun; ☐27, 31, Ⓜ Powell, Ⓑ Powell) Vintage pulp-fiction covers come to life when the Hot Boxxx Girls storm the battered stage at Aunt Charlie's on Friday and Saturday nights at 10:15pm ($5; call for reservations). Thursday is Tubesteak Connection ($5, free before 10pm), when bathhouse anthems and '80s disco draw throngs of art-school gays.

Twin Peaks Tavern (☑415-864-9470; www.twinpeakstavern.com; 401 Castro St; ⊙noon-2am Mon-Fri, from 8am Sat & Sun; Ⓜ Castro St) The vintage rainbow neon sign points the way to a local landmark – Twin Peaks was the world's first gay bar with windows open to the street. If you're not here for the Castro's best people-watching, cozy up to the Victorian carved-wood bar for cocktails and conviviality, or grab a back booth to discuss movies at the Castro over wine by the glass.

Castro district

Smuggler's Cove

8, 10, 12, 30, 41, 45, ▣Powell-Mason, ⓂT)
The walls here are plastered with mer-
chant-marine memorabilia, and you'll be
plastered too if you try to keep up with
the salty characters holding court in back.
Surrounded by seafaring mementos –
including a massive walrus organ over the
bar – your order seems obvious: pitcher of
Anchor Steam, coming right up. Cash only.

Li Po   Bar

(☎415-982-0072; www.lipolounge.com; 916
Grant Ave; ⓢ2pm-2am; ▣8, 30, 45, ▣Powell-
Mason, Powell-Hyde, ⓂT) Beat a hasty retreat
to red-vinyl booths where Allen Ginsberg
and Jack Kerouac debated the meaning
of life under a golden Buddha. Enter the
1937 faux-grotto doorway and dodge red
lanterns to place your order: Tsingtao beer
or a sweet, sneaky-strong Chinese mai
tai made with *baijiu* (rice liquor). Brusque
bartenders, basement bathrooms, cash
only – a world-class dive bar.

Caffe Trieste   Cafe

(☎415-392-6739; www.caffetrieste.com; 601
Vallejo St; ⓢ6:30am-10pm Sun-Thu, to 11pm Fri

& Sat; ☎; ▣8, 10, 12, 30, 41, 45, ⓂT) Poetry on
bathroom walls, opera on the jukebox, live
accordion jams and Beat poetry on bathroom walls: Caffe Trieste remains North
Beach at its best, since the 1950s. Linger
over legendary espresso and scribble your
screenplay under the Sardinian fishing
mural just as young Francis Ford Coppola
did. Perhaps you've heard of the movie: *The
Godfather.* Cash only.

🚌 The Haight & Hayes Valley

Smuggler's Cove   Bar

(☎415-869-1900; www.smugglerscovesf.com;
650 Gough St; ⓢ5pm-1:15am; ▣5, 21, 47, 49,
ⓂCivic Center, ⒷCivic Center) Yo-ho-ho and
a bottle of rum...wait, make that a Dead
Reckoning (Nicaraguan rum, port, pineap-
ple, bitters), unless you'll split the flaming
Scorpion Bowl? Pirates are bedeviled by
choice at this Barbary Coast–shipwreck tiki
bar, hidden behind tinted-glass doors. With
550 rums and 70-plus cocktails gleaned
from rum-running around the world – and
$2 off 5pm to 6pm daily – you won't be
dry-docked long.

🍸 The Mission, Dogpatch & Potrero Hill

Trick Dog   Bar

(📞415-471-2999; www.trickdogbar.com; 3010 20th St; ⏰3pm-2am; 🚌12, 14, 49) Drink adventurously with ingenious cocktails inspired by local obsessions: San Francisco muralists, Chinese diners or conspiracy theories. Every six months, Trick Dog adopts a new theme and the menu changes – proof you can teach an old dog new tricks and improve on classics like the Manhattan. Arrive early for bar stools or hit the mood-lit loft for high-concept bar bites.

Zeitgeist   Bar

(📞415-255-7505; www.zeitgeistsf.com; 199 Valencia St; ⏰9am-2am; 🚌14, 22, 49, 🅱16th St Mission) You've got two seconds flat to order from tough-gal barkeeps used to putting macho bikers in their place – but with 48 beers on draft, you're spoiled for choice. Epic afternoons unfold in the beer garden, with folks hanging out and smoking at long tables. SF's longest happy hour lasts 9am to 6pm weekdays. Cash only; no photos (read: no evidence).

⭐ ENTERTAINMENT

SFJAZZ Center   Jazz

(📞866-920-5299; www.sfjazz.org; 201 Franklin St; tickets $25-120; 🚹; 🚌5, 6, 7, 21, 47, 49, Ⓜ Van Ness) 🎵 Jazz legends and singular talents from Argentina to Yemen are showcased at North America's newest, largest jazz center. Hear fresh takes on classic jazz albums and poets riffing with jazz combos in the downstairs Joe Henderson Lab, and witness extraordinary main-stage collaborations by legendary Afro-Cuban All Stars, raucous all-women mariachis Flor de Toluache, and Balkan barnstormers Goran Bregović and his Wedding and Funeral Orchestra.

Booksmith   Live Performance

(📞415-863-8688; www.booksmith.com; 1644 Haight St; events free-$25; ⏰10am-10pm Mon-Sat, to 8pm Sun; 🚹; 🚌6, 7, 43, Ⓜ N) Throw a stone in SF and you'll probably hit a writer (ouch) or reader (ouch again) heading to/from Booksmith. Literary figures organize Booksmith book signings, raucous poetry readings, extra-short fiction improv, and politician-postcard-writing marathons. Head to sister shop-salon-bar the Bindery (1727 Haight St) for boozy book swaps, comedy nights, and silent reading parties hosted by Daniel Handler (aka Lemony Snicket).

Fillmore Auditorium   Live Music

(📞415-346-6000; www.thefillmore.com; 1805 Geary Blvd; tickets from $20; ⏰box office 10am-3pm Sun, plus 30min before doors open to 10pm show nights; 🚌22, 38) Jimi Hendrix, Janis Joplin, the Grateful Dead – they all played the Fillmore and the upstairs bar is lined with vintage psychedelic posters to prove it. Bands that sell out stadiums keep rocking this historic, 1250-capacity dance hall, and for major shows, free posters are still handed out. To squeeze up to the stage, be polite and lead with the hip.

Giants Stadium   Baseball

(AT&T Park; 📞415-972-2000, tours 415-972-2400; www.mlb.com/giants; 24 Willie Mays Plaza; tickets $14-349, stadium tour adult/senior/child $22/17/12; ⏰tour times vary; 🚹; Ⓜ N, T) Baseball fans roar April to October at the Giants' 81 home games. As any orange-blooded San Franciscan will remind you, the Giants have won three World Series since 2010 – and you'll know the Giants are on another winning streak when superstitious locals wear team colors (orange and black) and bushy beards (the Giants' rallying cry is 'Fear the Beard!').

ℹ️ INFORMATION

SF Visitor Information Center (www.sanfrancisco.travel/visitor-information-center) Muni Passports, activities deals, culture and event calendars.

GETTING THERE & AWAY

AIR

San Francisco International Airport (SFO; www.flysfo.com; S McDonnell Rd) is 14 miles south of downtown. BART provides a direct 30-minute ride to/from downtown. The SFO BART station is connected to the International Terminal; buy tickets ($9.65) from machines inside stations. Airport shuttles (one way $19 to $25 plus tip) take 45 minutes to most SF locations. Taxis cost $45 to $60, plus tip. Ride-share $30 to $50, plus tip.

Oakland International Airport (OAK; 510-563-3300; www.oaklandairport.com; 1 Airport Dr; ; Oakland International Airport) is 15 miles east of downtown San Francisco. BART people-mover shuttles run every 10 to 20 minutes from Terminal 1 to the Coliseum station, where you connect with BART trains to downtown SF ($10.95, 25 minutes). Taxis cost $70 to $90 to SF. Ride-share $40 to $60 off-peak for a direct-to-destination ride to SF.

TRAIN

Located outside Oakland, the **Emeryville Amtrak station (EMY)** serves West Coast and nationwide train routes; Amtrak runs free shuttles to/from San Francisco's Ferry Building, Caltrain, Civic Center and Fisherman's Wharf.

GETTING AROUND

San Franciscans mostly walk, bike, ride **Muni** (Municipal Transit Agency; 511; www.sfmta.com) or ride-share instead of taking a car or cab. Traffic is notoriously bad and parking is next to impossible.

Cable cars Frequent, slow and scenic, from 6am to 12:30am daily. Single rides cost $7; for frequent use, get a Muni Passport ($23 per day). Buy tickets at cable-car turnaround kiosks or on board from the conductor.

Muni streetcar & bus Reasonably fast, but schedules vary by line; infrequent after 9pm. Fares are $2.75 cash, or $2.50 with a reloadable Clipper card. Buy tickets from drivers (exact change required) or at underground Muni stations (where machines give change).

BART High-speed transit to East Bay, Mission St, SF airport and Millbrae, where it connects with Caltrain. Buy tickets at BART stations: you need a ticket to enter – and exit – the system.

Taxi Fares are about $3 per mile; meters start at $3.50.

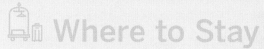
Where to Stay

San Francisco has a broad range of accommodations. In neighborhoods outside the downtown tourist fray like the Mission, Castro, Haight and Avenues, apartment rentals are often your only option besides B&Bs. Check Airbnb and VRBO. Book well in advance.

Neighborhood	Atmosphere
The Marina, Fisherman's Wharf & the Piers	Near the northern waterfront; good for kids; lots of restaurants and nightlife at the Marina.
Downtown, Civic Center & SoMa	Biggest selection of hotels; near public transportation and walkable to many sights.
North Beach & Chinatown	Culturally colorful; great strolling; lots of cafes and restaurants; terrific sense of place.
Nob Hill & Russian Hill	Stately, classic hotels atop Nob Hill; great restaurants and shopping in Russian Hill.
The Mission, Dogpatch & Potrero Hill	The Mission's flat terrain makes walking easier; good for biking; easy access to BART; gritty street scene.
The Castro	Great nightlife, especially for LGBT travelers; lots of cafes and restaurant choices.
The Haight & Hayes Valley	Lots of bars and restaurants, near cultural sights and Golden Gate Park. Gritty street scene at night.
Golden Gate Park & the Avenues	Quiet nights; good for outdoor recreation.

YOSEMITE NATIONAL PARK

Yosemite National Park at a Glance...

The jaw-dropping head-turner of America's national parks, Yosemite (yo-sem-it-ee) garners the devotion of all who enter. From the waterfall-striped granite walls buttressing Yosemite Valley to the sky-high, wildflower-splashed meadows of Tuolumne, the place inspires a sense of awe. But lift your eyes above the crowds and you'll feel your heart instantly moved by unrivaled splendors: the haughty profile of Half Dome, the hulking presence of El Capitan, the drenching mists of Yosemite Falls and the gemstone lakes of the high country's subalpine wilderness.

Two Days in Yosemite National Park

With two days in Yosemite, you'll want to head straight to the valley, where you can stand agape at the twin marvels of **Half Dome** (p330) and El Capitan. Make the most of day two with a hike to see some of the valley's **waterfalls** (p332).

Four Days in Yosemite National Park

Get deeper into this incredible park by cruising the twisting two-lane blacktop of Hwy 120 to Yosemite's high country and **Tuolumne Meadows** (p337). Make the trip up to **Glacier Point** (p328) for a bird's-eye view of the valley's monuments, or try a night or two in the backcountry.

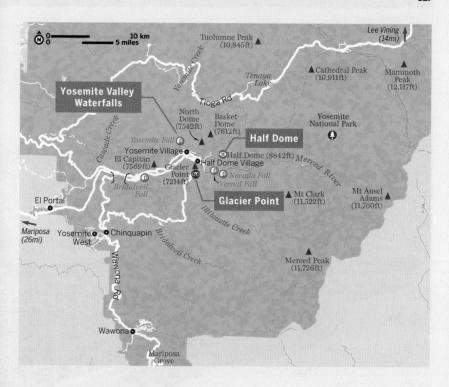

Yosemite Valley Waterfalls

Half Dome

Glacier Point

Lee Vining (14mi)

10 km
5 miles

Tuolumne Peak (10,845ft) ▲

Cathedral Peak (10,911ft) ▲

Mammoth Peak (12,117ft) ▲

Tenaya Lake

Tioga Rd

Yosemite Creek

North Dome (7542ft) ▲

Basket Dome (7612ft) ▲

Yosemite National Park

Yosemite Fall

Yosemite Village
El Capitan (7569ft) ▲
Glacier Point (7214ft)

Half Dome Village

Half Dome (8842ft)

Merced River

Nevada Fall
Vernal Fall

Cascade Creek

Bridalveil Fall

El Portal

Mt Clark (11,522ft) ▲

Mt Ansel Adams (11,760ft) ▲

Mariposa (26mi)

Yosemite West
Chinquapin

Illilouette Creek

Merced Peak (11,726ft) ▲

Wawona Rd

Bridalveil Creek

Wawona

Mariposa Grove

Arriving in Yosemite National Park

There are four main entrances to the park: South Entrance (Hwy 41), Arch Rock (Hwy 140), Big Oak Flat (Hwy 120 W) and Tioga Pass (Hwy 120 E). Visitor activity is concentrated in Yosemite Valley, which has the main visitor center and other services. Tuolumne Meadows, toward the eastern end of Tioga Rd, primarily draws hikers, backpackers and climbers. San Francisco is the nearest major gateway, some 195 miles east.

Where to Stay

All noncamping reservations within the park are handled by **Aramark/Yosemite Hospitality** (☏888-413-8869 ; www. travelyosemite.com) and can be made up to 366 days in advance; reservations are critical from May to early September. There are a few quality hotels in Groveland proper, and accommodations east along Hwy 120 in the Stanislaus National Forest. For chain hotels, check out Mariposa. Competition for campsites is fierce; reserve at www.recreation.gov.

Glacier Point

A lofty 3200ft above the valley floor, Glacier Point presents one of the park's most eye-popping vistas and practically puts you at eye level with Half Dome. It's perhaps the finest viewpoint in all of Yosemite.

Great For...

☑ **Don't Miss**

Seeing the skies on summer nights with **Glacier Point Stargazing Tours** (☏20 9-372-4386, 209-372-1240; www.travel yosemite.com; adult/child 5-12yr $45/30; ☉departure 7pm Jul-Sep; 🚐).

History

Almost from the park's inception, Glacier Point has been a popular destination. It used to be that getting up here was a major undertaking. That changed once the Four Mile Trail opened in 1872. A wagon road to the point was completed in 1882, and the current Glacier Point Rd was built in 1936.

Views

If you drove, the views from 7214ft Glacier Point might make you feel like you cheated – superstar sights present themselves without you having made any physical effort. A quick mosey up from the parking lot and you'll find the entire eastern Yo- semite Valley spread out before you, from Yosemite Falls to Half Dome, as well as the distant peaks that ring Tuolumne Meadows.

View from Glacier Point

HARRY BEUGELINK/SHUTTERSTOCK ©

ⓘ Need to Know

Parking areas fill by 10am, especially on weekends and in the summer.

✕ Take a Break

Amble over to the Glacier Point amphitheater, an ideal picnic setting with incredible panoramas.

★ Top Tip

To escape the crowds, consider a short hike down the first half-mile of the Four Mile Trail. After 15 minutes, you'll round a corner to terrific valley views.

Half Dome looms practically at eye level, and if you look closely you can spot hikers on its summit.

To the left of Half Dome lies the glacially carved Tenaya Canyon, and to its right are the wavy white ribbons of Nevada and Vernal Falls. On the valley floor, the Merced River snakes through green meadows and groves of trees. Sidle up to the railing, hold on tight and peer 3200ft straight down at Half Dome Village. Basket Dome and North Dome rise to the north of the valley, and Liberty Cap and the Clark Range can be seen to the right of Half Dome.

At the tip of the point is Overhanging Rock, a huge granite slab protruding from the cliff edge like an outstretched tongue, defying gravity and once providing a scenic stage for daredevil extroverts. Through the years, many famous photos have been taken of folks performing handstands, high kicks and other wacky stunts on the rock. The precipice is now off-limits.

Hiking Sentinel Dome

Nearby, if you're still craving views, you can hike to Sentinel's summit (8122ft), the shortest and easiest trail up one of Yosemite's granite domes. For those unable to visit Half Dome's summit, Sentinel offers an equally outstanding 360-degree perspective of Yosemite's wonders, and the 2.2-mile round-trip hike only takes about an hour. A visit at sunrise or sunset or during a full moon is spectacular.

You can combine a trip up Sentinel Dome with a walk to Taft Point and the Fissures, an equidistant hike from the same trailhead.

Half Dome

It's difficult not to feel a sense of wonder when your eyes first encounter this iconic, beautifully broken slab of granite, the most iconic physical feature of Yosemite.

Yosemite's most distinctive natural monument, Half Dome is 87 million years old and has a 93% vertical grade – the sheerest cliff in North America. Climbers come from around the world to grapple with its legendary north face, but good hikers can reach its summit via a 17-mile round-trip trail from Yosemite Valley. The trail gains 4900ft in elevation and has cable handrails for the last 200yd.

The hike can be done in a day but is more enjoyable if you break it up by camping along the way (Little Yosemite Valley is the most popular spot).

The Legend of Half Dome

According to Native American legend, one of Yosemite's early inhabitants came down from the mountains to Mono Lake, where he married a Paiute named Tesaiyac. The

Great For...

☑ **Don't Miss**

The reflection of Mt Watkins and Half Dome on Mirror Lake in spring and early summer.

R PATRICK JENNINGS/ALAMY ©

Half Dome

Half Dome Trail

Half Dome Village

ⓘ Need to Know

Rangers check for valid permits at the base of the Half Dome cables.

✕ Take a Break

Settle in for a drink at the cozy Majestic Bar (p336), inside the Majestic Yosemite Hotel.

★ Top Tip

If you want to climb it, check www.nps. gov/yose/planyourvisit/hdpermits.htm for the latest information.

journey back to the valley was difficult, and by the time they reached what was to become Mirror Lake, Tesaiyac decided she wanted to return to her people at Mono Lake. Her husband refused to live on such barren, arid land with no oak trees where he could get acorns.

With a heart full of despair, Tesaiyac fled toward Mono Lake, her husband in pursuit. When the spirits heard the couple quarreling, they grew angry and turned the two into stone: he became North Dome and she became Half Dome. The tears she cried made marks as they ran down her face, forming Mirror Lake.

Half Dome Permits

To stem lengthy lines (and increasingly dangerous conditions) on the vertiginous cables of Half Dome, the park now requires that all hikers obtain an advance permit to climb the cables.

Preseason permit lottery Lottery applications ($10) for 225 daily spots must be completed in March, with confirmation notification sent in mid-April. Applications can include up to six people, as well as specific dates. Upon acceptance, you'll pay another fee ($10 per person).

Daily lottery Approximately 50 additional day hiking permits are distributed by lottery two days before each hiking date. Apply online or by phone between midnight and 1pm Pacific Time; notification is available late that same evening. It's easier to score weekday permits. Same fees as the preseason lottery.

Backpackers Those with Yosemite-issued wilderness permits that *reasonably include* Half Dome can request Half Dome permits ($10 per person) without going through the lottery process.

Yosemite Valley Waterfalls

Yosemite's waterfalls mesmerize even the most jaded traveler, especially when the spring runoff turns them into roaring cascades and they put on a spectacular demonstration of nature's power.

Great For...

ⓘ Need to Know

By September most falls are limited by low water.

★ **Top Tip**

Be cautious around wet footpaths and railings. People have beewn swept away in Yosemite's falls.

Yosemite Falls

West of Yosemite Village, Yosemite Falls is considered the tallest waterfall in North America, dropping 2425ft (740m) in three tiers. A slick trail leads to the bottom or, if you prefer solitude, you can clamber up the Yosemite Falls Trail, which puts you atop the falls after a grueling 3.4 miles. The falls are usually breathtaking, especially when the spring runoff turns them into thunderous cataracts, but are reduced to a trickle by late summer.

Bridalveil Fall

At the southwestern end of the valley, Bridalveil Fall tumbles 620ft. The Ahwah-neechee people call it Pohono (Spirit of the Puffing Wind), as gusts often blow the fall from side to side, even lifting water back

up into the air. Peregrine falcons glide overhead. The waterfall usually runs year-round, though it's often reduced to a whisper by midsummer. Bring rain gear or expect to get soaked when the fall is heavy.

Park at the large lot where Wawona Rd (Hwy 41) meets Southside Dr. From the lot, it's a little more than a quarter-mile walk to the base of the fall.

Vernal & Nevada Falls

Vernal is one of Yosemite's iconic falls, where the thundering waters of the Merced River tumble 317ft down on the way to meet Yosemite Valley below. Mist Trail, the paved path to the falls, is one of the park's most popular. It gets extremely misty (hence the trail name) and wet along the 700 granite steps leading up to the falls.

Chilnualna Falls

Spectacular views await from Nevada Fall, ricocheting 594ft as part of the 'Giant Staircase' leading the Merced River down into Yosemite Valley. Most people take the Mist Trail (you pass Vernal Fall on the way); the John Muir Trail also gets you to the top.

Chilnualna Falls

Chilnualna Creek tumbles around 2200ft over the north shoulder of forested Wawona Dome in an almost continuous series of cascades. The largest and most impressive of these, Chilnualna Falls thunders into a deep, narrow chasm. Unlike its valley counterparts, this fall is not free leaping, but its soothing, white-water rush makes it an attractive day hike without lots of company. Carry plenty of water or a filter, as the route can be hot. The top is a nice picnic spot.

The Chilnualna Falls Trailhead is at the eastern end of Chilnualna Falls Rd. Follow Hwy 41 (Wawona Rd) a quarter-mile north of the Big Trees Lodge and Pioneer Gift & Grocery, and take a right just over the bridge on Chilnualna Falls Rd; follow it for 1.7 miles. The parking area with pit toilets is on the right, and the trailhead is marked.

The hike is 8.6 miles round trip and takes four to five hours (not counting relaxation time at the top). July and August are often too hot for an afternoon hike.

Rafting in Yosemite

From around late May to July, floating along the Merced River from Stoneman Meadow, near Half Dome Village, to Sentinel Bridge is a leisurely way to soak up Yosemite Valley views. Four-person **raft rentals** (209-372-8319; per person $28.50; 10am-4pm late May-late Jul) for the 3-mile trip are available from the concessionaire in Half Dome Village and include equipment and a shuttle ride back to the rental kiosk. Children must be over 50lb. Or bring your own raft and pay $5 to shuttle back. This activity is suitable for the mobility impaired.

River rats are also attracted to the fierce Tuolumne River, a classic class-IV run that plunges and thunders through boulder gardens and cascades. Groveland-based outfitter Sierra Mac (p337) offers guided trips.

> **✕ Take a Break**
> The Village Store (p336) in Yosemite Village has health-food items and organic produce for a picnic.

ALISHA BUBE/SHUTTERSTOCK ©

> **☑ Don't Miss**
> When the peak summer sun is hot, cool off in the refreshing mist of Vernal Fall.

Yosemite National Park

EATING & DRINKING

Village Store
Supermarket $

(Yosemite Village; ⊘8am-8pm, to 10pm summer) The biggest and best grocery store in the park is located smack in the center of Yosemite Village. Whether you're after last-minute items or full-fledged dinners, there's no denying the place comes in handy. The store carries decent produce, fresh meat and fish, and even some surprising items like tofu hot dogs, hummus, udon noodles and polenta.

You'll also find a small section of camping supplies, along with plenty of souvenirs.

Big Trees Lodge
Dining Room
American $$$

(www.travelyosemite.com; Big Trees Lodge, 8308 Wawona Rd; breakfast & lunch mains $10-21, dinner mains $23-33; ⊘7-10am, 11am-3pm & 5-9pm Easter-Dec; 🅟) 🍃 Beautiful sequoia-painted lamps light this old-fashioned dining room, and the Victorian detail makes it an enchanting place to have an upscale – though somewhat overpriced – meal. ('Tasteful, casual attire' is the rule for dinner dress.) There's a barbecue on the lawn from 5pm to 7pm every Saturday during summer.

Majestic Hotel Bar
Bar

(☏209-372-1489; www.travelyosemite.com; 1 Ahwahnee Dr, Majestic Yosemite Hotel, Yosemite Valley; ⊘11:30am-11pm) The perfect way to experience the Majestic Yosemite Hotel without dipping too deep into your pockets; settle in for a drink at this cozy bar completely remodeled in 2016. Appetizers and light meals ($11 to $23) available.

INFORMATION

Yosemite Valley Visitor Center (☏209-372-0200; www.nps.gov/yose; 9035 Village Dr, Yosemite Village; ⊘9am-5pm) The main tourist information center. Give yourself plenty of time, as lines are long in summer. Helps with self-issued wilderness permits from November to April when the **Wilderness Center** (☏209-372-0308; Yosemite Village; ⊘8am-5pm May-Oct) is closed.

ℹ GETTING THERE & AWAY

CAR & MOTORCYCLE

Yosemite is accessible year-round from the west (via Hwys 120 W and 140) and south (Hwy 41), and in summer also from the east (via Hwy 120 E). Roads are plowed in winter, but snow chains may be required at any time. Visit the National Park Service road conditions page (www.nps.gov/yose/planyourvisit/roadwork.htm) for updates before heading out.

Gas is available at Wawona, Crane Flat and El Portal 24 hours per day with a credit card. Gas is not available in Yosemite Valley.

PUBLIC TRANSPORTATION

Yosemite is one of the few national parks that can easily be reached by public transportation. **Greyhound** (☏800-231-2222; www.greyhound.com) buses and **Amtrak** (☏800-872-7245; www.amtrak.com) trains serve Merced, west of the park, where they are met by buses operated by the **Yosemite Area Regional Transportation System** (YARTS; ☏877-989-2787; www.yarts.com), and you can buy Amtrak tickets that include the YARTS segment all the way into the park. Buses travel to Yosemite Valley along Hwy 140 several times daily year-round, stopping along the way.

In summer (roughly June through September), another YARTS route runs from Mammoth Lakes along Hwy 395 to Yosemite Valley via Hwy 120. One-way tickets to Yosemite Valley are $16 ($9 child and senior, three hours) from Merced and $22 ($15 child and senior, 3½ hours) from Mammoth Lakes, less if boarding in between.

YARTS fares include the park-entrance fee, making them a bargain, and drivers accept credit cards.

ℹ GETTING AROUND

BICYCLE

Bicycling is an ideal way to take in Yosemite Valley. You can rent a wide-handled cruiser at the bike stands at **Yosemite Valley Lodge** (per hour/day $12/34; ⊘8am-6pm summer only, weather dependent) or **Half Dome Village** (per hour/day $12/34; ⊘10am-4pm Mar-Oct). Trailers for kids, strollers and wheelchairs are also for rent.

CAR & MOTORCYCLE

Traffic in the valley can feel like rush hour in LA. Glacier Point and Tioga Rds are closed in winter.

Village Garage (209-372-8320; Village Dr; 9am-5pm, towing 24hr) is available 24/7 for towing. Certainly pricey. In an emergency, might, only might, provide gas.

PUBLIC TRANSPORTATION

The free, air-conditioned **Yosemite Valley Shuttle Bus** (www.nps.gov/yose/planyourvisit/ publictransportation.htm; 7am-10pm) is a great way to get around the park. Buses operate year-round at frequent intervals and stop at 21 numbered locations, including parking lots, campgrounds, trailheads, lodges and vistas.

Groveland

From the Big Oak Flat entrance to Yosemite, it's 24 miles to Groveland, an adorable town with restored gold rush–era buildings and lots of visitor services.

⊚ SIGHTS & ACTIVITIES

Rainbow Pool   Natural Pool
(www.fs.usda.gov/stanislaus; P) FREE About 15 miles east of Groveland, in the Stanislaus National Forest, Rainbow Pool is a popular swimming hole with a small cascade; it's signed on the south side of Hwy 120. It has vault toilets and limited parking. The road to the pools may be closed in winter; in this case, park and walk to the waterfall.

ARTA River Trips   Rafting
(800-323-2782, 209-962-7873; www.arta. org; 24000 Casa Loma Rd; 1-/2-/3-day rafting $279/519/689; office hours vary) Contact ARTA for one-day and multiday Tuolumne River trips or for day trips on Merced River. Nonprofit ARTA provides all equipment (rafting gear and camping kit), plus food for the trip. The guides will take you into untouched scenery and find rapids to swim in and rocks to jump off. Tip: the overnight trips are not to be missed.

Sierra Mac   Rafting
(209-591-8027; www.sierramac.com; 27890 Hwy 120; 1-/2-/3-day rafting $279/519/694;

Tuolomne Meadows

About 55 miles from Yosemite Valley via Tioga Rd (or Hwy 120 E), 8600ft Tuolomne Meadows is the largest sub-alpine meadow in the Sierra. It provides a dazzling contrast to the valley, with its lush open fields, clear blue lakes, ragged granite peaks and domes, and cooler temperatures. If you come during July or August, you'll find a painter's palette of wildflowers decorating the shaggy meadows.

The main meadow is about 2.5 miles long and lies on the northern side of Tioga Rd between Lembert Dome and Pothole Dome. The 200ft scramble to the top of the latter – preferably at sunset – gives you great views of the meadow. An interpretive trail leads from the stables to muddy Soda Springs, where carbonated water bubbles up in red-tinted pools. The nearby Parsons Memorial Lodge has a few displays.

Hikers and climbers will find a paradise of options around Tuolomne Meadows, which is also the gateway to the High Sierra camps.

MIKE7/SHUTTERSTOCK ©

hours vary Apr-Oct) One of two outfitters running the experts-only Cherry Creek trips also offers other Tuolomne and Merced River trips. Marty McDonnell, Sierra Mac's owner, has been river guiding since the 1960s. The office is perched on a hill 13 miles east of town – look for the yellow paddle on the signpost, but best to call ahead before you show up.

Guided Tours of Yosemite

Sierra Club (☑415-977-5500; www.sierraclub.org) The national environmental nonprofit has both paid trips and free activity outings sponsored by local chapters.

Yosemite Conservancy (☑209-379-2317; www.yosemiteconservancy.org) Park-affiliated nonprofit offers multiday courses, custom trips and seminars that are great alternatives to tours.

Valley Floor Tour (☑888-413-8869; www.travelyosemite.com; adult/child $36.75/26.75; ⊙10am & 2pm year-round) Two-hour bus tour that covers the valley's highlights. Leaves from Yosemite Valley Lodge. During summer, there are additional tours at 8am and 11am, along with a special moonlight tour.

Yosemite Valley shuttle bus (p337)
MICHAEL VI/SHUTTERSTOCK ©

🍴 EATING & DRINKING

Burgers, sandwiches and pizza aren't in short supply. Groveland also has a good meat market deli and a Mexican place – both are recommended.

Mar-Val Supermarket $
(☑209-962-7452; www.marvalfoodstores.org; 19000 Main St; ⊙7am-9pm; P) This large grocery store at the eastern end of town is a good place to stock up on food and supplies before heading into Yosemite.

Iron Door Grill & Saloon Bar
(☑209-962-8904; www.irondoorsaloon.com; 18761 Main St; ⊙restaurant 7am-10pm, bar 11am-1am, shorter hours winter) Claiming to be the oldest bar in the state (established in 1852 when it served liquor to thirsty miners), the Iron Door is a dusty, atmospheric place, with swinging doors, a giant bar, high ceilings, mounted animal heads and hundreds of dollar bills tacked to the ceiling. It has live music on some weekends and also hosts open-mic and karaoke nights.

ℹ INFORMATION

There are two banks with ATMs and a gas station 1.5 miles west of town.

USFS Groveland Ranger Station (☑209-962-7825; www.fs.usda.gov/stanislaus; 24545 Hwy 120; ⊙8:30am-4pm Mon-Sat Jun-Aug, 8:30am-4pm Mon-Fri winter), about 8 miles east of Groveland, offers information for the surrounding Stanislaus National Forest and nearby Tuolumne Wild and Scenic River Area.

ℹ GETTING THERE & AWAY

There are two approaches to Groveland from the west; both involve steep mountain climbs with switchbacks.

To get to Yosemite, it's a pretty 24 miles along Hwy 120 east to the Big Oak Flat entrance. For the entrance to Hetch-Hetchy, take the turnoff from Hwy 120 near the Rainbow Pool (p337) – it's around 27 miles from town.

Mariposa

About halfway between Merced and Yosemite Valley, Mariposa (Spanish for 'butterfly') is the largest and most interesting town near Yosemite National Park. Established as a mining and railroad town during the gold rush, it has the oldest courthouse in continuous use (since 1854) west of the

Mississippi, loads of Old West pioneer character and a couple of good museums dedicated to the area's heritage.

 EATING & DRINKING

Happy Burger
Diner $

(☑209-966-2719; www.happyburgerdiner.com; cnr 5120 Hwy 140 & 12th St; mains $8-14; ☺6am-9pm; 🛜🖊🛞🐾) Burgers, fries and shakes served with a heavy dose of nostalgic Americana. Happy Burger, decorated with old album covers, boasts the largest menu in the Sierra. It's also one of the cheaper meals in town. Besides burgers, there's sandwiches, Mexican food, salads and a ton of sinful ice-cream desserts. Patio games and a 'doggy dining area' can be found outdoors.

You can call and order in advance and pick up your food at the restaurant's to-go window.

Savoury's
American $$

(☑209-966-7677; 5034 Hwy 140; mains $18-43; ☺5-9:30pm; 🖊) Upscale yet casual Savoury's is the best restaurant in town. Black-lacquered tables and contemporary art create tranquil window dressing for dishes like caramelized pork chop prepared with Sierra cider, pan-seared scallops with ginger and orange zest, Cajun-spiced New York steak with pan-seared onions, and crab cakes with cilantro-lime aioli.

Charles Street Dinner House
Steak $$$

(☑209-966-2366; www.charlesstreetdinner-house.net; cnr Hwy 140 & 7th St; mains $20-39; ☺5-10pm, plus 11am-2pm Mon-Fri) As old

school as it gets: expect wooden booths, wagon wheels for decor and hearty steaks on the menu. It's classic fare done well. Order hand-cut steaks, lobster tail or barbecue ribs. The portions are large enough to satisfy the heartiest appetite.

Alley
Bar

(☑209-742-4848; www.thealleylounge.com; 5027 Hwy 140; ☺4-10pm Mon-Thu, to midnight Fri, 2pm-midnight Sat, plus 2-8pm Sun summer only) Small batch, Californian boutique wines and 16 craft beers are served in a sophisticated, contemporary space. But it's the lovely backyard beer garden that puts the Alley at the top. Nibble on artisan appetizer plates while enjoying the laid-back atmosphere. There's live music some nights.

ℹ️ INFORMATION

Mariposa County Visitor Center (☑209-966-2456; www.mariposachamber.org/visitor-center; cnr 5158 Hwy 140 & Hwy 49; ☺8am-5pm; 🛜) Helpful staff and racks of brochures; plus public restrooms and an escape room experience.

ℹ️ GETTING THERE & AWAY

YARTS (YARTS; ☑877-989-2787, 209-388-9589; www.yarts.com; one way $5-16) Buses run year-round from Merced along Hwy 140 into Yosemite Valley (one way $16, 1¾ hours), stopping at the Mariposa County Visitor Center. Tickets include admission to Yosemite. There are several services per day, usually running between 6am to 8pm.

Hudson River Park (p53), New York City

In Focus

History   p342
The American story, from struggling colony to world superpower.

Food & Drink   p352
Chow on the nation's diverse dishes, from gumbo to barbecue, oysters to pork tacos, along with locally made wine and beer.

Sports   p356
Beers, hot dogs and baseball, football and basketball: what could be more American?

Arts & Culture   p359
The USA's music, film, literature and visual arts have had a huge impact on the world's cultural scene.

History

From the arrival of its first people up to 40,000 years ago, to its rise to number one on the world stage in the 20th century, American life has been anything but dull. War against the British, slavery and its abolishment, Civil War and Reconstruction, the post-war boom, and more recent conflicts in the 21st century – they've all played a part in shaping the nation's complicated identity.

8000 BC
Widespread extinction of Ice Age mammals. Indigenous peoples begin hunting smaller game and gathering native plants.

7000 BC–AD 100
During the 'Archaic period,' corn, beans and squash (the agricultural 'three sisters') and permanent settlements are well established.

1492
Italian explorer Christopher Columbus travels to America, making three voyages throughout the Caribbean.

Lincoln Memorial (p94), Washington, DC

LEON BIJELIC/SHUTTERSTOCK ©

Enter the Europeans

In 1492 Italian explorer Christopher Columbus, backed by Spain, voyaged west – looking for the East Indies. He found the Bahamas. With visions of gold, Spanish explorers quickly followed: Cortés conquered much of today's Mexico; Pizarro conquered Peru; Ponce de León wandered through Florida looking for the fountain of youth. Not to be left out, the French explored Canada and the Midwest, while the Dutch and English cruised North America's eastern seaboard.

Of course, they weren't the first ones on the continent. When Europeans arrived, approximately two to 18 million Native American people occupied the lands north of present-day Mexico and spoke more than 300 languages. European explorers left in their wake diseases to which indigenous peoples had no immunity. More than any other factor – war, slavery or famine – disease epidemics devastated Native American populations by anywhere from 50% to 90%. By the 17th century, indigenous North Americans numbered only about a million, and many of the continent's once-thriving societies were in turmoil and transition.

1607	**1620**	**1773**
The English found the Jamestown settlement. The first few years are hard, with many dying from sickness and starvation.	The *Mayflower* lands at Plymouth with 102 English Pilgrims. The Wampanoag tribe saves them from starvation.	Bostonians protest British taxes by dumping tea into the harbor during what would be named the Boston Tea Party.

In 1607 English noblemen established North America's first permanent European settlement in Jamestown. By 1619 the colony had set up the House of Burgesses, a representative assembly of citizens to decide local laws, and it received its first boatload of 20 African slaves.

In 1620, a group of radically religious Puritans pulled ashore at what would become Plymouth, MA. The Pilgrims were escaping religious persecution under the 'corrupt' Church of England, and in the New World they saw a divine opportunity to create a new society that would be a religious and moral beacon. The Pilgrims signed a 'Mayflower Compact,' one of the seminal texts of American democracy, to govern themselves by consensus.

Capitalism & Colonialism

For the next two centuries, European powers competed for position and territory in the New World, extending European politics into the Americas. As Britain's Royal Navy came to rule Atlantic seas, England increasingly profited from its colonies and eagerly consumed the fruits of their labors – sweet tobacco from Virginia, sugar and coffee from the Caribbean.

Over the 17th and 18th centuries, slavery in America was slowly legalized into a formal institution to support this plantation economy. By 1800, one out of every five persons was a slave.

Meanwhile, Britain mostly left the American colonists to govern themselves. Town meetings and representative assemblies, in which local citizens (that is, white men with property) debated community problems and voted on laws and taxes, became common.

However, by the end of the Seven Years' War in 1763, Britain was feeling the strains of running an empire: it had been fighting France for a century and had colonies scattered all over the world. It was time to clean up bureaucracies and share financial burdens.

The colonies, however, resented English taxes and policies. Public outrage soon culminated in the 1776 Declaration of Independence. With this document, the American colonists took many of the Enlightenment ideas then circulating worldwide – of individualism, equality and freedom; of John Locke's 'natural rights' of life, liberty and property – and fashioned a new type of government to put them into practice.

Revolution & the Republic

In April 1775 British troops skirmished with armed colonists in Massachusetts, and the Revolutionary War began. George Washington, a wealthy Virginia farmer, was chosen to lead the American army. Trouble was, Washington lacked gunpowder and money (the colonists resisted taxes even for their own military), and his troops were a motley collection of poorly armed farmers, hunters and merchants, who regularly quit and returned to their

1775	1776	1787
Paul Revere warns colonial 'Minutemen' that the British are coming. The next day the Revolutionary War begins.	On July 4, the colonies sign the Declaration of Independence.	The US Constitution is drawn up, balancing power between the presidency, Congress and judiciary.

farms due to lack of pay. On the other side, the British 'Redcoats' represented the world's most powerful military. The inexperienced General Washington had to improvise constant-ly, sometimes wisely retreating, sometimes engaging in 'ungentlemanly' sneak attacks.

In 1778 Benjamin Franklin persuaded France (always eager to trouble England) to ally with the revolutionaries, and they provided the troops, material and sea power that helped win the war. The British surrendered at Yorktown, VA, in 1781, and two years later the Treaty of Paris formally recognized the 'United States of America.'

At first, the nation's loose confederation of fractious, squabbling states was hardly 'united.' So the founders gathered again in Philadelphia, and in 1787 drafted a new-and-improved Constitution: the US government was given a stronger federal center, with checks and balances between its three major branches; and to guard against the abuse of centralized power, a citizen's Bill of Rights was approved in 1791.

With the Constitution, the scope of the American Revolution solidified to a radical change in government, and the preservation of the economic and social status quos. Rich landholders kept their property, which included their slaves; Native Americans were excluded from the nation; and women were excluded from politics. These blatant discrepancies and injustices, which were widely noted, were the results of both pragmatic compromise (eg to get slave-dependent Southern states to agree) and also widespread beliefs in the essential rightness of things as they were.

Westward, Ho!

As the 19th century dawned on the young nation, optimism was the mood of the day. The 1803 Louisiana Purchase doubled US territory, and expansion west of the Appalachian Mountains began in earnest.

In the 1830s and 1840s, with growing nationalist fervor and dreams of continental ex-pansion, many Americans came to believe it was 'Manifest Destiny' that all the land should be theirs. The 1830 Indian Removal Act aimed to clear one obstacle, while the building of the railroads cleared another hurdle, linking Midwestern farmers with East Coast markets.

In 1836 a group of Texans fomented a revolution against Mexico. (Remember the Alamo?) Ten years later, the US annexed the Texas Republic, and when Mexico resisted, the US waged war for it – and while it was at it, took California, too. In 1848 Mexico was soundly defeated and ceded this territory to the US. This completed the USA's continental expansion.

By a remarkable coincidence, only days after the 1848 treaty with Mexico was signed, gold was discovered in California. By 1849 surging rivers of wagon trains were creaking west filled with miners, pioneers, entrepreneurs, immigrants, outlaws and prostitutes, all seeking their fortunes. This made for exciting, legendary times, but throughout loomed a troubling question: as new states joined the USA, would they be slave states or free states? The nation's future depended on the answer.

1803	**1804–06**	**1849**
France's Napoleon sells the Louisiana Territory to the US, extending the nation's boundaries westward.	President Jefferson sends Lewis and Clark west. They trailblaze from St Louis, MO, to the Pacific Ocean and back.	An epic cross-country gold rush sees 60,000 'forty-niners' flock to California's mother lode.

★ **Best History Sights**

Statue of Liberty & Ellis Island (p44), New York City

National Archives (p103), Washington, DC

Ford's Theatre (p103), Washington, DC

Alcatraz (p298), San Francisco

National Archives, Washington, DC

The Civil War

The US Constitution hadn't ended slavery, but it had given Congress the power to approve (or not) slavery in new states. Public debates raged constantly over the expansion of slavery, particularly since this shaped the balance of power between the industrial North and the agrarian South.

Since the founding, Southern politicians had dominated government and defended slavery as 'natural and normal,' which an 1856 *New York Times* editorial called 'insanity.' The Southern proslavery lobby enraged Northern abolitionists. But even many Northern politicians feared that ending slavery would be ruinous. Limit slavery, they reasoned, and in the competition with industry and free labor, slavery would wither without inciting a violent slave revolt – a constantly feared possibility. Indeed, in 1859 radical abolitionist John Brown tried unsuccessfully to spark just that at Harpers Ferry.

The economics of slavery were undeniable. In 1860 there were more than four million slaves in the US, most held by Southern planters – who grew 75% of the world's cotton, accounting for more than half of US exports. Thus, the Southern economy supported the nation's economy, and it required slaves. The 1860 presidential election became a referendum on this issue, and the election was won by a young politician who favored limiting slavery: Abraham Lincoln.

In the South, even the threat of federal limits was too onerous to abide, and as President Lincoln took office, 11 states eventually seceded from the union and formed the Confederate States of America. Lincoln faced the nation's greatest moment of crisis. He had two choices: let the Southern states secede and dissolve the union or wage war to keep the union intact. He chose the latter, and war soon erupted.

It began in April 1861, when the Confederacy attacked Fort Sumter in Charleston, SC, and raged on for the next four years – in the most gruesome combat the world had ever known until that time. By the end, as many as 750,000 soldiers, nearly an entire generation of young men, were dead; Southern plantations and cities (most notably Atlanta) lay sacked and burned. The North's industrial might provided an advantage, but its victory

1861–65	1870	1880–1920
American Civil War erupts between North and South. The war's end is marred by President Lincoln's assassination five days later.	Freed black men are given the right to vote, but the South's segregationist 'Jim Crow' laws effectively disenfranchise blacks.	Millions of immigrants flood in from Europe and Asia, fueling the age of cities. New York, Chicago and Philadelphia swell in size.

was not preordained; it unfolded battle by bloody battle.

As fighting progressed, Lincoln recognized that if the war didn't end slavery outright, victory would be pointless. In 1863 his Emancipation Proclamation expanded the war's aims and freed all slaves. In April 1865, Confederate General Robert E Lee surrendered to Union General Ulysses S Grant in Appomattox, VA. The Union had been preserved, but at a staggering cost.

Great Depression, the New Deal & WWII

In October 1929 investors, worried about a gloomy global economy, started selling stocks, and seeing the selling, everyone panicked until they had sold everything. The stock market crashed, and the US economy collapsed like a house of cards.

Thus began the Great Depression. Frightened banks called in their dodgy loans, people couldn't pay, and the banks folded. Millions lost their homes, farms, businesses and savings, and as much as 25% of the American workforce became unemployed.

In 1932 Democrat Franklin D Roosevelt was elected president on the promise of a 'New Deal' to rescue the US from its crisis, which he did with resounding success. When war once again broke out in Europe in 1939, the isolationist mood in America was as strong as ever. However, the extremely popular President Roosevelt, elected to an unprecedented third term in 1940, understood that the US couldn't sit by and allow victory for fascist, totalitarian regimes. Roosevelt sent aid to Britain and persuaded a skittish Congress to go along with it.

Then, on December 7, 1941, Japan launched a surprise attack on Hawaii's Pearl Harbor, killing more than 2000 Americans and sinking several battleships. As US isolationism transformed overnight into outrage, Roosevelt suddenly had the support he needed. Germany also declared war on the US, and America joined the Allied fight against Hitler and the Axis powers. From that moment, the US put almost its entire will and industrial prowess into the war effort.

Initially, neither the Pacific nor European theaters went well for the US. In the Pacific, fighting didn't turn around until the US unexpectedly routed the Japanese navy at Midway Island in June 1942. Afterward, the US drove Japan back with a series of brutal battles recapturing Pacific islands.

Slavery

From the early 17th century until the 19th century, an estimated 600,000 slaves were brought from Africa to America. Those who survived the horrific transport on crowded ships (which sometimes had 50% mortality rates) were sold in slave markets (African males cost $27 in 1638). The majority of slaves ended up in Southern plantations where conditions were usually brutal – whipping and branding were commonplace.

1908
The first Model T car is built in Detroit, MI. Assembly-line innovator Henry Ford is soon selling one million automobiles annually.

1917
President Woodrow Wilson enters the US into WWI. The US mobilizes 4.7 million troops, and suffers 116,000 military deaths.

1920s
The Harlem Renaissance inspires a burst of African American literature, art, music and cultural pride.

The Haight, San Francisco

In Europe, the US dealt the fatal blow to Germany with its massive D-Day invasion of France on June 6, 1944: unable to sustain a two-front war (the Soviet Union was savagely fighting on the eastern front), Germany surrendered in May 1945.

Nevertheless, Japan continued fighting. Newly elected President Harry Truman – ostensibly worried that a US invasion of Japan would lead to unprecedented carnage – chose to drop experimental atomic bombs on Hiroshima and Nagasaki in August 1945. Created by the government's top-secret Manhattan Project, the bombs devastated both cities, killing more than 200,000 people. Japan surrendered days later. The nuclear age was born.

The Red Scare, Civil Rights & the Wars in Asia

The US enjoyed unprecedented prosperity in the decades after WWII, but little peace.

Formerly wartime allies, the communist Soviet Union and the capitalist USA soon engaged in a running competition to dominate the globe. The superpowers engaged in proxy wars – notably the Korean War (1950–53) and Vietnam War (1954–75) – with only the mutual threat of nuclear annihilation preventing direct war. Founded in 1945, the UN couldn't overcome this worldwide ideological split and was largely ineffectual in preventing Cold War conflicts.

Meanwhile, with its continent unscarred and its industry bulked up by WWII, the American homeland entered an era of growing affluence. In the 1950s, a mass migration left the inner cities for the suburbs, where affordable single-family homes sprang up. Americans drove cheap cars using cheap gas over brand-new interstate highways. They relaxed with the comforts of modern technology, swooned over TV, and got busy, giving birth to a 'baby boom.'

Middle-class whites did, anyway. African Americans remained segregated, poor and generally unwelcome at the party. Echoing 19th-century abolitionist Frederick Douglass, the Southern Christian Leadership Conference (SCLC), led by African American preacher Martin Luther King Jr, aimed to end segregation and 'save America's soul': to realize color-blind justice, racial equality and fairness of economic opportunity for all.

1941–45	1963	1964
WWII: America deploys 16 million troops and suffers 400,000 deaths.	President John F Kennedy is assassinated by Lee Harvey Oswald while riding in a motorcade in Dallas, TX.	Congress passes the Civil Rights Act, outlawing discrimination on basis of race, color, religion, sex or national origin.

Beginning in the 1950s, King preached and organized nonviolent resistance in the form of bus boycotts, marches and sit-ins, mainly in the South. White authorities often met these protests with water hoses and batons, and demonstrations sometimes dissolved into riots, but with the 1964 Civil Rights Act, African Americans spurred a wave of legislation that swept away racist laws and laid the groundwork for a more just and equal society.

Meanwhile, the 1960s saw further social upheavals: rock and roll spawned a youth rebellion, and the 1967 Summer of Love in San Francisco's Haight-Ashbury neighborhood catapulted hippie culture into mainstream America.

President John F Kennedy was assassinated in Dallas in 1963, followed by the assassinations in 1968 of his brother, Senator Robert Kennedy, and of Martin Luther King Jr. Americans' faith in their leaders and government was further shocked by the bombings and brutalities of the Vietnam War, as seen on TV, which led to widespread student protests.

Yet President Richard Nixon, elected in 1968 partly for promising an 'honorable end to the war,' instead escalated US involvement and secretly bombed Laos and Cambodia. Then, in 1972, the Watergate scandal broke: a burglary at Democratic Party offices was, through dogged journalism, tied to 'Tricky Dick,' who, in 1974, became the first US president to resign from office.

The tumultuous 1960s and '70s also witnessed the sexual revolution, women's liberation, struggles for gay rights, energy crises over the supply of crude oil from the Middle East and, with the 1962 publication of Rachel Carson's *Silent Spring,* the realization that the USA's industries had created a polluted, diseased environmental mess.

Civil Rights Movement

Beginning in the 1950s, a movement was under way in African American communities to fight for equality. Rosa Parks, who refused to give up her seat to a white passenger, inspired the Montgomery bus boycott. There were sit-ins at segregated lunch counters; massive demonstrations led by Martin Luther King Jr in Washington, DC; and harrowing journeys by 'freedom riders' that aimed to end bus segregation. The work of millions paid off: in 1964 President Johnson signed the Civil Rights Act, which banned discrimination and racial segregation, followed by the 1965 Voting Rights Act.

Reagan, Clinton & Bush eras

In 1980 Republican California governor and former actor Ronald Reagan campaigned for president by promising to make Americans feel good about America again. The affable Reagan won easily, and his election marked a pronounced shift to the right in US politics.

1965–75	1989	1990s
The Vietnam War tears the nation apart; 58,000 Americans die, along with 5.5 million Vietnamese, Laotians and Cambodians.	The 1960s-era Berlin Wall is torn down, marking the end of the Cold War between the US and the USSR (now Russia).	The World Wide Web debuts in 1991. Silicon Valley, CA, leads a high-tech internet revolution, remaking communications and media.

Ellis Island Immigration Museum, New York City

STEVE CUKROV/SHUTTERSTOCK ©

★ Best History Museums

National Museum of African American History & Culture (p96), Washington, DC

Ellis Island Immigration Museum (p45), New York City

Bob Bullock Texas State History Museum (p222), Austin

National Museum of American History (p97), Washington, DC

Reagan wanted to defeat communism, restore the economy, deregulate business and cut taxes. To tackle the first two, he launched the biggest peacetime military build-up in history, and dared the Soviets to keep up. They went broke trying, and the USSR collapsed.

Military spending and tax cuts created enormous federal deficits, which hampered the presidency of Reagan's successor, George HW Bush. Despite winning the Gulf War – liberating Kuwait in 1991 after an Iraqi invasion – Bush was soundly defeated in the 1992 presidential election by Southern Democrat Bill Clinton. Clinton had the good fortune to catch the Silicon Valley–led high-tech internet boom of the 1990s, which seemed to augur a 'new economy' based on white-collar telecommunications. The US economy erased its deficits and ran a surplus, and Clinton presided over one of America's longest economic booms.

In 2000 and 2004, George W Bush, the eldest son of George HW Bush, won the presidential elections so narrowly that the divided results seemed to epitomize an increasingly divided nation. On September 11, 2001, Islamic terrorists flew hijacked planes into New York's World Trade Center and the Pentagon in Washington, DC. This catastrophic attack united Americans behind their president as he vowed revenge and declared a 'war on terror.' Bush soon attacked Afghanistan in an unsuccessful hunt for Al-Qaeda terrorist cells, then he attacked Iraq in 2003 and toppled its anti-US dictator, Saddam Hussein. Meanwhile, Iraq descended into civil war.

Obama Presidency

In 2008, hungry for change, Americans elected political newcomer Barack Obama, America's first African American president. He certainly had his work cut out for him. These were, after all, unprecedented times economically, with the US in the largest financial crisis since the Great Depression. What started as a collapse of the US housing bubble in 2007, spread to the banking sector, with the meltdown of major financial institutions. The shock wave quickly spread across the globe, and by 2008 many industrialized nations were experiencing a recession.

2001	**2003**	**2005**
The September 11 terrorist attacks destroy NYC's World Trade Center and kill nearly 3000 people.	After citing evidence that Iraq possesses weapons of mass destruction, President George W Bush launches a preemptive war.	Hurricane Katrina ruptures levees, flooding New Orleans. More than 1800 people die, and cost estimates exceed $110 billion.

As Americans tried to look toward the future, many found it difficult to leave the past behind. This was not surprising since wars in Afghanistan and Iraq, launched a decade prior, continued to simmer on the back burner of the ever-changing news cycle. And the economy remained in bad shape.

With lost jobs, overvalued mortgages and little relief in sight, millions of Americans found themselves adrift, gathering in large numbers to voice their anger. On the left, this expressed itself as the Occupy Wall Street movement, which called out banks and corporations as having too much influence. On the right, it manifested as the Tea Party, a wing of politically conservative Republicans who believed that government handouts would destroy the economy. Republicans also doubted Obama's landmark 2010 health-care reform (derisively named 'Obamacare').

When Obama returned to the White House in 2013 for his second term, he did so without the same hope and optimism that once surrounded him. Obama did manage to get unemployment rates back under 5% by 2016, but he had mixed success spurring the sluggish economy. As his presidency came to a close, he turned his focus to liberal and globally minded causes that stoked resentment on the populist right, including climate change, environmental protections, LGBT+ rights and the negotiation of rapprochements with Iran and Cuba. By the time Obama left office, America was a starkly divided nation of those who believed strongly in his progressive ideals, and others who felt increasingly left behind by the global economy.

Trump Presidency

When Donald J Trump, real-estate magnate and former host of TV's reality game-show *The Apprentice,* announced he was running for President in June 2015, many around the world thought it was a publicity stunt. What ensued could only be described as a media circus.

Scandal and controversy have surrounded the Trump administration in its first term, during which the nation's democratic integrity has been challenged by conflicts of interest between public office and private enterprise. Public protest has become a key feature of the sociopolitical landscape, starting with the Women's March the day after the inauguration, the largest single-day demonstration in recorded US history with an estimated four million participants in some 653 cities around the country. The release of the Mueller Report in 2019, which summarized the findings of a two-year investigation of Trump's connections to Russia, only muddied the waters; lacking a firm conclusion and heavily redacted, the ambiguity of the report allowed both the left and the right to argue that it supports their case.

Despite Trump's controversies and continued low approval ratings, the outcome of the 2020 election is far from certain; as of this writing, a crowded field of Democratic hopefuls, including former vice president Joe Biden and senators Kamala Harris, Bernie Sanders and Elizabeth Warren, are vying for the party's nomination.

2008–09	**2015**	**2019**
Barack Obama becomes the first African American president. The stock market crashes, and the global financial crisis hits.	In a historic decision, the US Supreme Court legalizes same-sex marriage. Gay couples can now wed in all 50 states.	Several states pass abortion laws challenging *Roe v Wade* in the hope the conservative-led Supreme Court will overturn it.

Chelsea Market pizzeria (p80), New York City

BORIS-B/SHUTTERSTOCK ©

Food & Drink

The great variety found in American cuisine can be traced to the local larder of each region, from the seafood of the Atlantic to the fertile Midwestern farmlands and the vast Western ranchlands. Texas barbecue, Louisiana crawfish and California wines are but a few of the regional specialties.

Staples & Specialties

These days you can get almost every type of food nearly everywhere in the US, but regional specialties are always best in the places they originated.

New York City: Foodie Capital

They say that you could eat at a different restaurant every night of your life in New York City, and not exhaust the possibilities. Considering that there are an estimated 24,000 restaurants in Manhattan alone, with scores of new ones opening each year, it's true. Owing to its huge immigrant population and an influx of more than 50 million tourists annually, New York captures the title of America's greatest restaurant city, hands down. Its diverse

Sazerac cocktail (p355), New Orleans

neighborhoods serve up authentic Italian food and thin-crust pizza, all manner of Asian food, French haute cuisine and classic Jewish deli food, from bagels to piled-high pastrami on rye. More uncommon cuisines are found here as well, from Ethiopian to Scandinavian.

Mid-Atlantic: Global Cooking & Blue Crabs

Washington, DC, has a wide array of global fare – not surprising, given its ethnically diverse population. In particular, you'll find some of the country's best Ethiopian food.

DC also makes fine use of its unique geography, which puts it between two of the best food-production areas in America: Chesapeake Bay and the Virginia Piedmont. From the former come blue crabs, oysters and rockfish; the latter provides game, pork, wine and peanuts. Chefs take advantage of this delicious abundance.

The South: Barbecue, Biscuits & Gumbo

No region is prouder of its food culture than the South, which has a long history of mingling Anglo, French, African, Spanish and Native American foods in dishes such as slow-cooked barbecue, which has as many meaty and saucy variations as there are towns in the South. Southern fried chicken is crisp outside and moist inside. In Florida, dishes made with alligator, shrimp and conch incorporate hot chili peppers and tropical spices. Breakfasts are big, and treasured dessert recipes tend to produce big layer cakes or pies made with pecans, bananas and citrus. Light, fluffy hot biscuits are served well buttered, and grits (ground corn cooked to a porridge-like consistency) are a passion.

Louisiana's legendary cuisine is influenced by colonial French and Spanish cultures, Afro-Caribbean cooking and Choctaw traditions. Bayou-born Cajun food marries native

Vegetarians & Vegans

Most major cities have a wealth of restaurants that cater to vegetarians and vegans. Once you head out into rural areas, the options are slimmer. We note eateries that offer a good selection of vegetarian or vegan options by using the 🌱 symbol. To find more vegetarian and vegan restaurants, browse the online directory at www.happycow.net.

spices such as sassafras and chili peppers with provincial French cooking. Famous dishes include gumbo, a roux-based stew of chicken and shellfish, or sausage and often okra; jambalaya, a rice-based dish with tomatoes, sausage and shrimp; and blackened catfish. Creole food is more urban, and centered in New Orleans, where dishes such as shrimp rémoulade, crabmeat ravigote, crawfish étouffée, and beignets are ubiquitous.

Midwest: Burgers, Bacon & Beer

Residents of the Midwest eat big and with plenty of gusto. Portions are huge – this is farm country, where people need sustenance to get their day's work done. So you might start off the day with eggs, bacon and toast; have a double cheeseburger and potato salad for lunch; and fork into steak and baked potatoes for dinner – all washed down with a cold brew, often one of the growing numbers of microbrews. Chicago stands tall as the region's best place to pile a plate, with hole-in-the-wall ethnic eateries cooking alongside many of the country's most acclaimed restaurants.

The Southwest: Chili, Steak & Salsa

Two ethnic groups define Southwestern food culture: the Spanish and the Mexicans, who controlled territories from Texas to California until well into the 19th century. While there is little actual Spanish food today, the Spanish brought cattle to Mexico, which the Mexicans adapted to their own corn-and-chili-based gastronomy to make tacos, enchiladas, burritos, chimichangas and other dishes made of corn or flour pancakes filled with everything from chopped meat and poultry to beans. Steaks and barbecue are always favorites on Southwestern menus, and beer is the drink of choice for dinner and a night out.

California: Farm-to-Table Restaurants & Taquerias

Owing to its vastness and variety of microclimates, California is truly America's cornucopia for fruits and vegetables. The state's natural resources are overwhelming, with wild salmon,

★ Best Local Breweries

Angel City Brewery, Los Angeles

DAVID TONELSON/SHUTTERSTOCK ©

Dungeness crab and oysters from the ocean; robust produce year-round; and artisanal products such as cheese, bread, olive oil, wine and chocolate. Starting in the 1970s and '80s, star chefs such as Alice Waters and Wolfgang Puck pioneered 'California cuisine' by incorporating the best local ingredients into simple, yet delectable, preparations. The influx of Asian immigrants, especially after the Vietnam War, enriched the state's urban food cultures with Chinatowns, Koreatowns and Japantowns, along with huge enclaves of Mexican Americans who maintain their own culinary traditions across the state. Don't miss the forearm-sized burritos in San Francisco's Mission District. Global fusion restaurants are another hallmark of California's cuisine.

Beer, Wine & Beyond

American beer is more popular than ever, and locals are uncorking plenty of wine, as well.

Craft & Local Beer

Microbrewery and craft-beer production is rising meteorically, generating roughly $28 billion in retail sales in 2018. With around 7300 craft breweries across the USA, it's possible to 'drink local' all over the country – microbreweries are found everywhere from urban centers to small towns. According to the Brewers Association, Chicago, IL, is the current capital of the industry, with 167 craft breweries.

Thanks to this trend, beer aficionados sip and savor beer as they would wine, and some restaurants even have beer 'programs,' 'sommeliers' and cellars. Many brewpubs and restaurants host beer dinners, a chance to experience just how beers pair with different foods.

Wine

The US makes nearly 14% of the world's wine and is the third-largest wine producer in the world (behind Italy and France). About 80% of US wine comes from California, though other regions are producing wines that have achieved international status. In particular, the wines of New York's Finger Lakes, Hudson Valley and Long Island are well worth sampling, as are the wines from both Washington and Oregon, especially pinot noirs and Rieslings.

So, what are the best American wines? The most popular white varietals made in the US are chardonnay and sauvignon blanc; best-selling reds include cabernet sauvignon, merlot, pinot noir and zinfandel.

Due to higher production costs and taxes, as well as its status as a luxury item, wine isn't especially cheap in the US. But it's possible to procure a perfectly drinkable bottle of American wine at a liquor or wine shop for under $12.

Distilled Spirits

While whiskey and bourbon are the most popular American exports, rye, gin and vodka are also crafted in the USA. Bourbon, made from corn, is the only native spirit and traditionally made in Kentucky.

In the 2010s, America's long history of distilling launched a modern renaissance, much as wine and craft brewing did in preceding decades. By 2018 there were more than 2800 craft distillers in the USA – an increase of 107% since 2013. California and New York lead the charge, with 148 and 123 distilleries, respectively. Many of these distillers use local ingredients, from grains to botanicals, to inspire their spirit.

It's a fitting legacy for the country that invented the cocktail. Born in New Orleans, the first cocktail was the Sazerac – a mix of rye whiskey or brandy, simple syrup, bitters and a dash of absinthe (before it was banned in 1912, that is). American cocktails created at bars in the late 19th and early 20th centuries include such long-standing classics as the martini, the Manhattan and the old-fashioned.

Lambeau Field, home of the Green Bay Packers

JEFF BUKOWSKI/SHUTTERSTOCK ©

Sports

What really draws Americans together, sometimes slathered in blue body paint or with foam-rubber cheese wedges on their heads, is sports. It provides a social glue, so whether a person is conservative or liberal, married or single, Mormon or pagan, chances are come Monday at the office they'll be chatting about the weekend performance of their favorite team.

Seasons

The fun and games go on all year long. In spring and summer there's baseball nearly every day. In fall and winter a weekend or Monday night doesn't feel right without a football game on, and through the long days and nights of winter there's plenty of basketball to keep the adrenaline going.

Baseball

Baseball may not command the same TV viewership (and subsequent advertising dollars) as football, but with 162 games over a season versus 16 for football, its ubiquity allows it to maintain its status as America's pastime.

Chicago Clubs batter

KEETON GALE/SHUTTERSTOCK ©

Besides, baseball isn't about seeing it on TV, it's all about the live version: being at the ballpark on a sunny day, sitting in the bleachers with a beer and a hot dog, and indulging in the seventh-inning stretch, when the entire park erupts in a communal singalong of 'Take Me Out to the Ballgame.' The playoffs, held every October, still deliver excitement and unexpected champions. The New York Yankees, Boston Red Sox and Chicago Cubs continue to be America's favorite teams, even when they're abysmal.

Tickets are relatively inexpensive – the cheap seats average about $25 at most stadiums – and are easy to get for most games. Minor-league baseball games cost half as much, and can be even more fun, with lots of audience participation, stray chickens and dogs running across the field, and wild throws from the pitcher's mound. For info, click to www.milb.com.

Football

Football is big, physical and rolling in dough. With the shortest season and least number of games of any major sport, every match takes on the emotion of an epic battle, where the results matter and an unfortunate injury can deal a lethal blow to a team's play-off chances.

Football is also the toughest because it's played in fall and winter in all manner of rain, sleet and snow. Some of history's most memorable matches have occurred at below-freezing temperatures. Green Bay Packers fans are in a class by themselves when it comes to severe weather. Their stadium in Wisconsin, known as Lambeau Field, was the site of the infamous Ice Bowl, a 1967 championship game against the Dallas Cowboys where the temperature plummeted to –13°F – mind you, that was with a wind-chill factor of –48°F.

Dodger Stadium, Los Angeles

Even college and high-school football games enjoy an intense amount of pomp and circumstance, with cheerleaders, marching bands, mascots, songs and mandatory pre- and post-game rituals, especially the tailgate – a full-blown beer-and-barbecue feast that takes place over portable grills in stadium parking lots.

The rabidly popular Super Bowl is pro football's championship match, held in late January or early February. The bowl games (such as Rose Bowl and Orange Bowl) are college football's title matches, held on and around New Year's Day.

In recent years the National Football League has come under fire for failing to adjust the rules of the sport in reaction to overwhelming proof that repeated concussions (a byproduct of tackles) have a permanent effect on players. A 2017 study by Boston University of the brains of 111 NFL players showed that 110 had a degenerative brain disease, chronic traumatic encephalopathy (CTE). Though TV ratings for NFL games have taken a slight hit, the sport remains popular: 1.06 million children and teens played tackle football in 2017, according to a study by JAMA Pediatrics.

Basketball

The men's teams bringing in the most fans these days include the Chicago Bulls, the Los Angeles Lakers, the Cleveland Cavaliers, the San Antonio Spurs and, last but not least, the Golden State Warriors, which won three championships (and made it to every NBA final) between 2015 and 2019. Small-market teams such as Oklahoma City and Milwaukee have true-blue fans, and such cities can be great places to take in a game. Though not as celebrated, the women's professional basketball teams (known as the WNBA) put on thrilling performances as well.

College-level basketball also draws millions of fans, especially every spring when March Madness rolls around. This series of men's college play-off games culminates in the Final Four, when the four remaining teams compete for a spot in the championship game. The Cinderella stories and unexpected outcomes rival the pro league for excitement.

Other Sports

Auto racing has revved up interest in recent years. Major League Soccer (MLS) and the National Women's Soccer League (NWSL) are attracting an ever-increasing following. And ice hockey, once favored only in northern climes, is popular nationwide – the LA Kings are two-time Stanley Cup winners, while teams from sun-soaked Nashville, Tampa Bay and Vegas have made it to the finals.

Street jazz, New Orleans (p197)

RAINER.SU/SHUTTERSTOCK ©

Arts & Culture

The US has always been a chaotic, democratic jumble of high and low cultures: Frank Lloyd Wright and Frank Sinatra, Richard Wright and Lady Gaga, The Great Gatsby and Star Wars. America's arts are a pastiche, a crazy mix-and-match quilt of cultures and themes, of ideas borrowed and taken to create something new, often leaving dramatic new paradigms along the way.

Music

The South is the birthplace of American music. The blues developed there after the Civil War, out of the work songs, or 'shouts,' of enslaved people and out of the 'call and response' pattern of black spiritual songs, both of which were adaptations of African music. Improvisational and intensely personal, the blues remain at heart an immediate expression of individual pain, suffering, hope, desire and pride. Nearly all subsequent American music has tapped this deep well. Famous musicians include Robert Johnson, Bessie Smith, Muddy Waters, BB King, John Lee Hooker and Buddy Guy.

Jazz was born in New Orleans. There, ex-slaves adapted the reed, horn and string instruments used by the city's often French-speaking, multiracial Creoles – who themselves preferred formal European music – to play their own African-influenced music. This fertile

Art Institute of Chicago

★ **Best Art Museums**

Museum of Modern Art (p48), NYC

Metropolitan Museum of Art (p73), NYC

Art Institute of Chicago (p122)

National Gallery of Art (p97), Washington, DC

Getty Center (p280), Los Angeles

cross-pollination produced a steady stream of innovative sounds. Soon there was ragtime, Dixieland jazz, big-band swing, bebop and numerous fusions. Major players included Duke Ellington, Louis Armstrong, Billie Holiday, John Coltrane, Miles Davis and Charles Mingus.

Early Scottish, Irish and English immigrants brought their own instruments and folk music to America, and what emerged over time in the secluded Appalachian Mountains was fiddle-and-banjo hillbilly, or 'country,' music. In the Southwest, steel guitars and larger bands distinguished 'western' music. In the 1920s, these styles merged into 'country-and-western' music and became centered on Nashville, TN. For the originals, listen to Hank Williams, Johnny Cash, Patsy Cline and Dolly Parton.

Rock and roll, meanwhile, combined guitar-driven blues, black rhythm and blues (R&B), and white country-and-western music. Most say rock and roll was born when Elvis started singing. From the 1950s, it evolved into the anthem for nationwide social upheaval.

Finally, hip-hop emerged from 1970s New York, as young DJs from the Bronx began to spin and mix records together to drive dance floors wild. Synonymous with urban street culture, hip-hop soon became the defining rebel sound of American pop culture.

Film & TV

Hollywood and American film are virtually inseparable. No less an American icon than the White House itself, Hollywood is increasingly the product of an internationalized cinema and film culture. This evolution is partly pure business: Hollywood studios are the showpieces of multinational corporations, and funding flows to talent that brings the biggest grosses, regardless of nationality.

For many decades, critics sneered that TV was lowbrow, and movie stars wouldn't be caught dead on it. But times have changed. As cable TV has emerged as the frontier for daring and innovative programming, some of the TV shows of the past decade have proved as riveting and memorable as anything viewers have ever seen. Streaming services such as Netflix, Amazon and Hulu, and niche networks such as AMC and HBO, have created numerous lauded series. Recent favorites include *The Marvelous Mrs Maisel* (about a Jewish female comic trying to make it in 1950s NYC), *Atlanta* (a comedy-drama starring Donald Glover), *Stranger Things* (a supernatural saga set in the 1980s that recalls *The Goonies*) and *The Handmaid's Tale* (a near-future dystopia based on Margaret Atwood's 1985 novel).

Literature

With the dramas of world wars and a newly industrialized society for artistic fodder, American literature came into its own in the 20th century.

Dubbed the 'Lost Generation,' many US writers, most famously Ernest Hemingway, became expats in Europe. Hemingway's novels exemplified the era, and his spare, stylized realism has often been imitated, yet never bettered. F Scott Fitzgerald eviscerated East Coast society life with his fiction, while John Steinbeck became the voice of rural working poor in the West, especially during the Great Depression.

Between the world wars, the Harlem Renaissance also flourished, as African American intellectuals and artists took pride in their culture and undermined racist stereotypes. Among the most well-known writers were poet Langston Hughes and novelist Zora Neale Hurston.

After WWII, American writers delineated ever-sharper regional and ethnic divides, pursued stylistic experimentation and often caustically repudiated conservative middle-class American values. The South, always ripe with paradox, inspired masterful short-story writers and novelists Flannery O'Connor and Eudora Welty. The mythical romance and modern tragedies of the West have found their champions in Chicano writer Rudolfo Anaya, Larry McMurtry and Cormac McCarthy, whose characters poignantly tackle the rugged realities of Western life.

In recent years, ethnic identity (especially that of immigrant cultures), regionalism and narratives of self-discovery remain at the forefront of American literature.

The Great American Novel

- *The Sound and the Fury* (William Faulkner)
- *The Great Gatsby* (F Scott Fitzgerald)
- *The Sun Also Rises* (Ernest Hemingway)
- *To Kill a Mockingbird* (Harper Lee)
- *Beloved* (Toni Morrison)
- *The Grapes of Wrath* (John Steinbeck)
- *The Goldfinch* (Donna Tartt)
- *The Underground Railroad* (Colson Whitehead)
- *Native Son* (Richard Wright)
- *The Book of Unknown Americans* (Cristina Henríquez)

Visual Arts

Abstract expressionism is widely considered to be the first truly original school of American art. In the wake of WWII, painters such as Franz Kline, Jackson Pollock and Mark Rothko began exploring abstraction and its psychological potency through imposing scale and the gestural handling of paint. The movement's 'action painter' camp went extreme; Pollock, for example, made his drip paintings by pouring and splattering pigments over large canvases.

Once established in America, abstract expressionism reigned supreme. But it also inspired stylistic revolts, most notably pop art, for which artists drew inspiration from consumer images such as billboards, product packaging and media icons. Employing mundane mass-production techniques to silkscreen paintings of movie stars and Coke bottles, Andy Warhol helped topple the myth of the solitary artist laboring heroically in the studio. Roy Lichtenstein combined newsprint's humble Benday dots with the representational conventions of comics. Suddenly, so-called 'serious' art could be political, bizarre, ironic and fun – and all at once.

By the 1980s, civil rights, feminism and AIDS activism had made inroads in visual culture; artists not only voiced political dissent through their work, but embraced a range of once-marginalized media, from textiles and graffiti to video, sound and performance. Break-out artists Futura 2000, Keith Haring and Jean-Michel Basquiat moved from the subways and the streets to the galleries, and soon to the worlds of fashion and advertising.

To get the pulse of contemporary art in the US, check out works by artists such as Cindy Sherman, Kara Walker, Chuck Close, Kerry James Marshall, Eddie Martinez and Josh Smith.

South Beach (p152), Miami

ROTORHEAD 30A PRODUCTIONS/SHUTTERSTOCK ©

Survival Guide

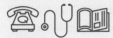

Directory A–Z

Accessible Travel

If you have a physical disability, the USA can be an accommodating place. The Americans with Disabilities Act (ADA) requires that all public buildings, private buildings built after 1993 (including hotels, restaurants, theaters and museums) and public transit be wheelchair accessible. However, call ahead to confirm what is available. Some local tourist offices publish detailed accessibility guides. For tips on travel and thoughtful insight on traveling with a disability, check out online posts by Martin Heng, Lonely Planet's Accessible Travel Manager: twitter.com/martin_heng, or download Lonely Planet's free Accessible Travel guide from http://lptravel.to/AccessibleTravel.

Telephone companies offer relay operators, available via teletypewriter (TTY) numbers, for the hearing impaired. Most banks provide ATM instructions in Braille and via earphone jacks for hearing-impaired customers. All major airlines, Greyhound buses and Amtrak trains will assist travelers with disabilities; just describe your needs when making reservations at least 48 hours in advance. Service animals (guide dogs) are allowed to accompany passengers, but bring documentation.

Some car-rental agencies, such as Budget and Hertz, offer hand-controlled vehicles and vans with wheelchair lifts at no extra charge, but you must reserve them well in advance. Wheelchair Getaways (www.wheelchairgetaways.com) rents accessible vans throughout the USA. In many cities and towns, public buses are accessible to wheelchair riders and will 'kneel' if you are unable to use the steps; just let the driver know that you need the lift or ramp.

Most cities have taxi companies with at least one accessible van, though you'll have to call ahead. Cities with underground transport have varying levels of facilities such as elevators for passengers needing assistance – DC has the best network (every station has an elevator), while NYC has elevators in about a quarter of its stations.

Many national and some state parks and recreation areas have wheelchair-accessible paved, graded-dirt or boardwalk trails. US citizens and permanent residents with permanent disabilities are entitled to a free 'America the Beautiful' Access Pass. Go online (www.nps.gov/findapark/passes.htm) for details.

Some helpful resources for travelers with disabilities:

Disabled Sports USA (www.disabledsportsusa.org) Offers sport, adventure and recreation programs for those with disabilities. Also publishes *Challenge* magazine.

Flying Wheels Travel (www.flyingwheelstravel.com) A full-service travel agency, highly recommended for those with mobility issues or chronic illness.

Mobility International USA (www.miusa.org) Advises USA-bound disabled travelers on mobility issues, and promotes the global participation of people with disabilities in international exchange and travel programs.

Accommodations

Hotels

Hotels in all categories typically include cable TV, in-room wi-fi, private baths and a simple continental

---

Book Your Stay Online

For more accommodation reviews by Lonely Planet authors, check out http://hotels.lonelyplanet.com/USA. You'll find independent reviews, as well as recommendations on the best places to stay. Best of all, you can book online.

breakfast. Many midrange properties provide minibars, microwaves, hairdryers and swimming pools, while top-end hotels add concierge services, fitness and business centers, spas, restaurants and bars.

Motels

Distinguishable from hotels by having rooms that open onto a parking lot, motels tend to cluster around interstate exits and along main routes into town. Although most motel rooms won't win any style awards, they can

be clean and comfortable and offer good value. Ask to see a room first if you're unsure.

B&Bs & Inns

These vary from small, comfy houses with shared baths (least expensive) to romantic, antique-filled historic homes with private baths (most expensive). Reservations are essential. Call ahead to confirm policies (ie minimum stay, kids, pets, smoking) and bathroom arrangements.

Resorts

Found in states like Florida and Arizona, resort facilities can include all manner of fitness and sports, pools, spas, restaurants and bars, and so on. Many also have on-site babysitting services. However, some also tack an extra 'resort fee' onto rates, so always ask.

Customs Regulations

For a complete list of US customs regulations, visit the official portal for US Customs and Border Protection (www.cbp.gov).

Duty-free allowance per person is as follows:

○ 1L of liquor (provided you are at least 21 years old).

○ 100 cigars and 200 cigarettes (if you are at least 18 years old).

○ $200 worth of gifts and purchases ($800 if you're a returning US citizen).

○ If you arrive with $10,000 or more in US or foreign currency, it must be declared.

○ There are heavy penalties for attempting to import illegal drugs. Forbidden items include drug paraphernalia, lottery tickets, items with fake brand names, and most goods made in North Korea, Cuba, Iran, Syria and Sudan. Fruit, vegetables and other food or plant material must be declared or left in the arrival-area bins.

Climate

New York City

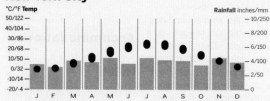

New Orleans

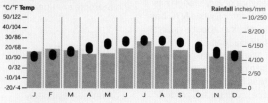

Los Angeles

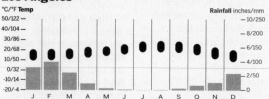

Electricity

Type A
120V/60Hz

Type B
120V/60Hz

AC 120V is standard; buy adapters to run most non-US electronics.

Health

The USA offers excellent health care. The problem is that, unless you have good insurance, it can be prohibitively expensive. It's essential to purchase travel health insurance if your regular policy doesn't cover you when you're abroad.

Bring any medications you may need in their original containers, clearly labeled. A signed, dated letter from your physician that describes all medical conditions and medications, including generic names, is also a good idea.

Availability & Cost of Health Care

In general, if you have a medical emergency your best bet is to find the nearest hospital and go to its emergency room. If the problem isn't urgent, you can call a nearby hospital and ask for a referral to a local physician, which is usually much cheaper than a trip to the emergency room. Stand-alone, for-profit, urgent-care centers can be convenient, but may perform large numbers of expensive tests, even for minor illnesses.

Pharmacies are abundantly supplied, but you may find that some medications that are available over the counter in your home country (such as Ventolin, for asthma) require a

Sleeping Price Ranges

In this book, the following price ranges refer to a double room in high season, excluding taxes (which can add 10% to 15%).

$ less than $150
$$ $150–250
$$$ more than $250

For New York City, San Francisco and Washington, DC, the following price ranges are used:

$ less than $200
$$ $200–350
$$$ more than $350

prescription in the USA and, as always, if you don't have insurance to cover the cost of prescriptions, they can be shockingly expensive.

Insurance

No matter how long or short your trip, make sure you have adequate travel insurance, purchased before departure. At a minimum, you need coverage for medical emergencies and treatment, including hospital stays and an emergency flight home if necessary. Medical treatment in the USA is of the highest caliber, but the expense could bankrupt you.

You should also consider getting coverage for luggage theft or loss and trip cancellation. If you already have

Eating Price Ranges

The following price ranges refer to a main course. Tax (5% to 10%) and tips (generally 15% to 20%) are not included in price listings unless otherwise indicated.

$ less than $15

$$ $15–25

$$$ more than $25

a homeowner's or renter's policy, see what it will cover and consider getting supplemental insurance to cover the rest. If you have prepaid a large portion of your trip, cancellation insurance is a worthwhile expense. A comprehensive travel-insurance policy that covers all these things can cost up to 10% of the total outlay of your trip.

If you will be driving, it's essential that you have liability insurance. Car-rental agencies offer insurance that covers damage to the rental vehicle and separate liability insurance, which covers damage to people and other vehicles.

Worldwide travel insurance is available at www.lonelyplanet.com/travel-insurance. You can buy, extend and claim online anytime – even if you're already on the road.

Internet Access

Travelers will have few problems staying connected in the tech-savvy USA. Most hotels, guesthouses, hostels and motels have wi-fi (usually free, though luxury hotels are more likely to charge for access); ask when reserving.

Across the US, most cafes offer free wi-fi. Some cities have wi-fi-connected parks and plazas. If you're not packing a laptop or other web-accessible device, try the public library – most have public terminals (though they have time limits) in addition to wi-fi. Occasionally out-of-state residents are charged a small fee.

If you're not from the US, remember that you will need an AC adapter for your laptop, plus a plug adapter for US sockets; both are available at larger electronics shops, such as Best Buy.

Legal Matters

If you are stopped by the police, bear in mind that there is no system of paying traffic or other fines on the spot. Attempting to pay a fine to an officer is frowned upon at best and may result in a charge of bribery. For traffic offenses, the police officer or highway patrol will explain the options to you. There is usually a 30-day period to pay a fine. Most matters can be handled by mail.

If you are arrested, you have a legal right to an attorney, and you are allowed to remain silent. There is no legal reason to speak to a police officer if you don't wish to, but never walk away from an officer until given permission to do so. Anyone who is arrested is legally allowed to make one phone call. If you can't afford a lawyer, a public defender will be appointed to you free of charge. Foreign visitors who don't have a lawyer, friend or family member to help them should call their embassy; the police will provide the number upon request.

As a matter of principle, the US legal system presumes a person innocent until proven guilty. Each state has its own civil and criminal laws, and what is legal in one state may be illegal in others.

Drinking

Bars and stores often ask for photo ID to prove you're of legal drinking age (21 years or over). Being 'carded' is standard practice; don't take it personally. The sale of liquor is subject to local government regulations – some counties prohibit liquor sales on Sunday, after midnight or before breakfast. In 'dry' counties, alcohol sales are banned altogether.

Driving

In all states, driving under the influence of alcohol or drugs is a serious offense, subject to stiff fines and even imprisonment. A blood alcohol level of 0.08% or higher is illegal in all jurisdictions.

Marijuana & Other Substances

The states have quite different laws regarding the use of marijuana, and what's legal in one state may be illegal in others. As of mid-2019, recreational use of small amounts of marijuana (generally up to 1oz/28g) was legal in Alaska, California, Colorado, Maine, Massachusetts, Michigan, Nevada, Oregon, Vermont, Washington and the District of Columbia. Another 15 states have decriminalized marijuana (treating recreational use as a civil violation similar to a minor traffic infraction), while others continue to criminalize nonmedical use, punishing possession of small amounts as a misdemeanor and larger amounts as a felony. Thus, it's essential to know the local laws before lighting up – see http://norml.org/laws for a state-by-state breakdown.

Aside from marijuana, recreational drugs are prohibited by federal and state laws. Possession of any illicit drug, including cocaine, ecstasy, LSD, heroin and hashish, is a felony potentially punishable by a lengthy jail sentence. For foreigners, conviction of any drug offense is grounds for deportation.

LGBT+ Travelers

There has never been a better time to be gay in the USA. LGBT+ travelers will find lots of places where they can be themselves without thinking twice. Beaches and big cities typically are the most gay-friendly destinations.

Hot Spots

Manhattan has loads of great gay bars and clubs, especially in Hells Kitchen, Chelsea and the West Village. A few hours away (by train and ferry) is Fire Island, the sandy gay mecca on Long Island. Other East Coast cities that flaunt it are Boston, Philadelphia, Washington, DC, Massachusetts' Provincetown on Cape Cod and Delaware's Rehoboth Beach.

In the South, Texas gets darn-right gay-friendly in Austin. Florida, Miami and the 'Conch Republic' of Key West support thriving gay communities, though Fort Lauderdale attracts bronzed boys and girls, too. New Orleans has a lively gay scene.

In the Great Lakes region, seek out Chicago. Further west, you'll find San Francisco, probably the happiest gay city in America. There's also Los Angeles and Las Vegas, where pretty much anything goes.

Attitudes

Most major US cities have a visible and open LGBT+ community that is easy to connect with. Same-sex marriage was legalized nationwide by the US Supreme Court in 2015, and a 2019 Pew Research survey showed a majority of Americans (61%) support same-sex marriage.

The level of acceptance varies nationwide. In some places, there is absolutely no tolerance whatsoever, and in others acceptance is predicated on LGBT+ people not 'flaunting' their sexual preference or identity. Bigotry still exists. In rural areas and conservative enclaves, it's unwise to be openly out, as violence and verbal abuse can sometimes occur. When in doubt, assume locals follow a 'don't ask, don't tell' policy.

Resources

The Queerest Places: A Guide to Gay and Lesbian Historic Sites by Paula Martinac is full of juicy details and history, and covers the country. Visit her blog at www.queerestplaces.com.

Advocate (www.advocate.com) Gay-oriented news website reports on business, politics, arts, entertainment and travel.

Damron (www.damron.com) Publishes the classic gay travel guides, but they're driven by advertisers and sometimes outdated.

Gay & Lesbian National Help Center (www.glnh.org) Counseling, information and referrals.

Gay Travel (www.gaytravel.com) Online guides to dozens of US destinations.

National LGBTQ Task Force (www.thetaskforce.org) National activist group's website covers news, politics and current issues.

Out Traveler (www.outtraveler.com) Gay-oriented travel articles.

Purple Roofs (www.purple-roofs.com) Lists gay-owned and gay-friendly B&Bs and hotels.

Money

ATMs widely available. Credit cards accepted at most hotels, restaurants and shops.

ATMs

ATMs are available 24/7 at most banks, and in shopping centers, airports, grocery stores and convenience shops. Most ATMs charge a service fee of $2.50 or more per transaction and your home bank may impose additional charges. Withdrawing cash from an ATM using a credit card usually incurs a hefty fee.

For foreign visitors, ask your bank or credit-card company for exact information about using its cards in stateside ATMs. If you will be relying on ATMs (not a bad strategy), bring more than one card and carry them

separately. The exchange rate on ATM transactions is usually as good as you'll get anywhere. Before leaving home, notify your bank and credit-card providers of your travel plans, to avoid triggering fraud alerts.

Credit Cards

Major credit cards are almost universally accepted. In fact, it's almost impossible to rent a car or make hotel reservations without one. It's highly recommended that you carry at least one credit card, if only for emergencies. Visa and MasterCard are the most widely accepted.

Foreign visitors may have to go inside to pre-pay at gas stations, since most pay-at-the-pump options require a card with a US zip code. Some airlines also require a US billing address – a hassle if you're booking domestic flights once in the country. It's normal for restaurant servers to take your card to a pay station to process instead of allowing you to pay at the table. Mobile pay options (Apple Pay, Google Pay) are becoming increasingly common and are a good way to bridge the technology gap.

Exchange Rates

Australia	A$1	US$0.68
Canada	C$1	US$0.76
Europe	€1	US$1.10
Japan	¥100	US$0.92
New Zealand	NZ$1	US$0.63
UK	UK£1	US$1.27

For current exchange rates, see www.xe.com

Money Changers

Banks are usually the best places to exchange foreign currencies. Most large city banks offer currency exchange, but banks in rural areas may not. Currency-exchange counters at the airport and in tourist centers typically have the worst rates; ask about fees and surcharges first. Travelex (www.travelex.com) is a major currency-exchange company, but American Express (www.american-express.com) travel offices may offer better rates.

Taxes

Sales tax varies by state and county, and ranges from 5% to 10%. Most prices you see advertised will exclude tax, which is calculated upon purchase.

Hotel taxes are charged in addition to sales tax and vary by city and state from around 10% to 18.75% (New York City).

Tipping

Tipping is *not* optional; only withhold tips in cases of outrageously bad service.

Airport & hotel porters $2 per bag, minimum per cart $5

Bartenders 15% to 20% per round, minimum per drink $1

Hotel housekeepers $2 to $5 per night, left under the card provided

Restaurant servers 15% to 20%, unless a gratuity is already charged on the bill

Practicalities

○ **Newspapers & Magazines** Leading national newspapers include the *New York Times*, *Wall Street Journal* and *USA Today*. *Time* and *Newsweek* are the mainstream news magazines.

○ **Radio & TV** National Public Radio (NPR) can be found at the lower end of the FM dial. The main TV broadcasting channels are ABC, CBS, NBC, FOX and PBS (public broadcasting); the major cable channels are CNN (news), ESPN (sports), HBO (movies) and the Weather Channel.

○ **Smoking** As of 2019, 30 states, the District of Columbia and many municipalities across the US were entirely smoke-free in restaurants, bars and workplaces; an additional six states had enacted 100% public smoking bans in at least one of these venues. For more detailed state-by-state info on smoking laws, see www.cdc.gov and www.no-smoke.org.

○ **Weights & Measures** Weights are measured in ounces (oz), pounds (lb) and tons; liquids in fluid ounces (fl oz), pints (pt), quarts (qt) and gallons (gal); and distance in feet (ft), yards (yd) and miles (mi).

Taxi drivers 10% to 15%, rounded up to the next dollar

Valet parking attendants At least $2 on return of the keys

Opening Hours

Typical opening times are as follows:

Banks 8:30am–4:30pm Monday to Thursday, to 5:30pm Friday (and possibly 9am–noon Saturday)

Bars 5pm–midnight Sunday to Thursday, to 2am Friday and Saturday

Nightclubs 10pm–4am Thursday to Saturday

Post offices 9am–5pm Monday to Friday

Shopping malls 9am–9pm

Stores 9am–6pm Monday to Saturday, noon–5pm Sunday

Supermarkets 8am–8pm, some open 24 hours

Public Holidays

On the following national public holidays, banks, schools and government offices (including post offices) are closed, and transportation, museums and other services operate on a Sunday schedule. Holidays falling on a weekend are usually observed the following Monday.

New Year's Day January 1

Martin Luther King Jr Day Third Monday in January

Presidents' Day Third Monday in February

Memorial Day Last Monday in May

Independence Day July 4

Labor Day First Monday in September

Columbus Day Second Monday in October

Veterans' Day November 11

Thanksgiving Fourth Thursday in November

Christmas Day December 25

During spring break, high school and college students get a week off from school so they can overrun beach towns and resorts. This occurs throughout March and April. For students of all ages, summer vacation runs from June to August.

Safe Travel

Despite its seemingly apocalyptic list of dangers – violent crime, riots, earthquakes, tornadoes – the USA is actually a pretty safe country to visit. The greatest danger for travelers is posed by car accidents (buckle up – it's the law).

Important Phone Numbers

Emergency	911
USA country code	1
Directory assistance	411
International directory assistance	00
International access code from the USA	011

Crime

For the traveler it's not violent crime but petty theft that is the biggest concern. When possible, withdraw money from ATMs during the day, or in well-lit, busy areas at night. When driving, don't pick up hitchhikers, and lock valuables in the trunk of your car. In hotels, you can secure valuables in your room or hotel safes.

Natural Disasters

Most areas with predictable natural disturbances – tornadoes on the Great Plains and the South, tsunamis in Hawaii, hurricanes in the Gulf and Atlantic Coasts, earthquakes in California – have an emergency-siren system to alert communities to imminent danger. These sirens are tested periodically at noon, but if you hear one and suspect trouble, turn on a local TV or radio station, which will be broadcasting safety warnings and advice. Incidentally, hurricane season runs from June to November.

The US Department of Health and Human Services (www.phe.gov) has preparedness advice, news and information on all the ways your vacation could go horribly, horribly wrong. But relax: it probably won't.

Government Travel Advice

Australia (www.smartraveller.gov.au)

Canada (www.travel.gc.ca)

New Zealand (www.safetravel.govt.nz)

UK (www.gov.uk/foreign-travel-advice)

Telephone

Cell Phones

Tri- or quad-band phones brought from overseas will generally work in the USA. However, you should check with your service provider to see if roaming charges apply, as these will turn even local US calls into pricey international calls.

It's often cheaper to buy a compatible prepaid SIM card for the USA, such as those sold by AT&T, which you can insert into your international cell phone to get a local phone number and voicemail. Telestial (www.telestial.com) offers these services.

If you don't have a compatible phone, you can buy inexpensive, no-contract (prepaid) phones with a local number and a set number of minutes, which can be topped up at will. Virgin Mobile, T-Mobile, AT&T and other providers offer phones starting around $20, with a package of minutes starting around $20 for 400 minutes, or $30 monthly for unlimited minutes. Electronics stores such as Radio Shack and Best Buy sell these phones.

Huge swaths of rural America, including many national parks and recreation areas, don't pick up a signal. Check your provider's coverage map.

Phone Cards

If you're traveling without a cell phone or in a region with limited cell service, a prepaid phonecard is an alternative solution. Phonecards typically come precharged with a fixed number of minutes that can be used on any phone, including landlines. You'll generally need to dial an 800 number and enter a PIN (personal identification number) before placing each call. Phonecards are available from online retailers such as amazon.com and at some convenience stores. Be sure to read the fine print, as many cards contain hidden charges such as 'activation fees' or per-call 'connection fees' in addition to the per-minute rates.

Phonecodes

All phone numbers within the USA consist of a three-digit area code followed by a seven-digit local number.

Typically, if you are calling a number within the same area code, you only have to dial the seven-digit number (though if it doesn't work, try adding 1 + the area code at the beginning). If you're calling long distance, dial 1 plus the area code plus the phone number. More information on dialing:

US country code 1

Making international calls Dial 011 + country code + area code + local number

Calling other US area codes or Canada Dial 1 + area code + seven-digit local number

Directory assistance nationwide 411

Toll-free prefix 1-800 (or 888, 877, 866). Some toll-free numbers only work within the US

Pay-per-call prefix 1-900. These calls are charged at a premium per-minute rate – phone sex, horoscopes...

Time

The USA uses daylight saving time (DST). At 2am on the second Sunday in March, clocks are set one hour ahead ('spring forward'). Then on the first Sunday of November, clocks are turned back one hour ('fall back'). Just to keep you on your toes, Arizona (except the Navajo Nation) and Hawaii don't follow DST.

The US date system is written as month/day/year. Thus, 8 June 2020 becomes 6/8/20.

Time Zones

The continental USA has four time zones:

- EST Eastern (GMT/UTC minus five hours): NYC, Boston, Washington, DC, Atlanta

- CST Central (GMT/UTC minus six hours): Chicago, New Orleans, Houston

- MST Mountain (GMT/UTC minus seven hours): Denver, Santa Fe, Phoenix

- PST Pacific (GMT/UTC minus eight hours): Seattle, San Francisco, Las Vegas

- Most of Alaska is one hour behind Pacific time (GMT/UTC minus nine hours), while Hawaii is two hours behind Pacific time (GMT/UTC minus 10 hours).

So if it's 9pm in New York, it's 8pm in Chicago, 7pm in Denver, 6pm in Los Angeles, 5pm in Anchorage and 4pm (November to early March) or 3pm (rest of year) in Honolulu.

Toilets

Toilets in the USA are universally of the sit-down variety and generally of high standard. Most states have rest areas with free toilets along major highways; alternatively, you can seek out toilets at gas stations, coffee shops and chain restaurants – technically these are for the use of paying customers, but you may be able to use them free of charge by asking or discreetly entering. Public buildings such as airports, train and bus stations, libraries and museums usually have free toilet facilities for public use. Some towns and cities also provide public toilets, though these are not widespread.

Tourist Information

For links to the official tourism websites of every US state and most major cities, see www.visit-usa.com. The similarly named www.visit-theusa.com is jam-packed with itinerary planning ideas and other useful info.

Visa Waiver Program

Currently under the Visa Waiver Program (VWP), citizens of 38 countries (including most EU countries, Japan, the UK, Australia and New Zealand) may enter the USA without a visa for stays of 90 days or less.

If you are a citizen of a VWP country, you do not need a visa *only if* you have a passport that meets current US standards *and* you have received approval from the Electronic System for Travel Authorization (ESTA) in advance. Register online with the Department of Homeland Security at https://esta.cbp.dhs.gov/esta at least 72 hours before arrival; once travel authorization is approved, your registration is valid for two years. The fee, payable online, is $14.

Visitors from VWP countries must still produce at the port of entry all the same evidence as for a nonimmigrant visa application. They must demonstrate that their trip is for 90 days or less, and that they have a round-trip or onward ticket, adequate funds to cover the trip and binding obligations abroad.

Visas

Be warned that all visa information is highly subject to change. US entry requirements keep evolving as national security regulations change. All travelers should double-check current visa and passport regulations *before* coming to the USA.

The US State Department (www.travel.state.gov) maintains the most comprehensive visa information, providing downloadable forms, lists of US consulates abroad and even visa wait times calculated by country.

Visa Applications

Apart from most Canadian citizens and those entering under the Visa Waiver Program, all foreign visitors will need to obtain a visa from a US consulate or embassy abroad. Most applicants must schedule a personal interview, to which you must bring all your documentation and proof of fee payment. Wait times for interviews vary, but afterwards, barring problems, visa issuance takes from a few days to a few weeks.

○ Your passport must be valid for the entirety of your intended stay in the USA, and sometimes six months longer, depending on your country of citizenship. You'll need a recent photo (2in by 2in) and you must pay a nonrefundable $160 processing fee, plus in a few cases an additional visa-issuance reciprocity fee. You'll also need to fill out the online DS-160 nonimmigrant visa electronic application.

○ Visa applicants are required to show documents of financial stability (or evidence that a US resident will provide financial support), a round-trip or onward ticket and 'binding obligations' that will ensure their return home, such as family ties, a home or a job. Because of these requirements, those planning to travel through other countries before arriving in the USA are generally better off applying for a US visa while they're still in their home country, rather than while on the road.

○ The most common visa is a nonimmigrant visitor's visa: type B-1 for business purposes, B-2 for tourism or visiting friends and relatives. A visitor's visa is good for multiple entries over one or five years, and specifically prohibits the visitor from taking paid employment in the USA. The validity period depends on what country you are from. The actual length of time you'll be allowed to stay in the USA is determined by US immigration at the port of entry.

● If you're coming to the USA to work or study, you will need a different type of visa, and the company or institution to which you are going should make the arrangements.

Women Travelers

Women traveling alone or in groups should not expect to encounter any particular problems in the USA. The community website www.journeywoman.com facilitates women exchanging travel tips, and has links to other helpful resources.

If you're assaulted, consider calling a rape crisis hotline before calling the police, unless you are in immediate danger, in which case you should call ☎911. But be aware that not all police have much sensitivity training or experience assisting sexual-assault survivors, whereas staff at rape crisis centers will tirelessly advocate on your behalf and act as a link to other community services, including hospitals and the police. Telephone books have listings of local rape-crisis centers, or contact the 24-hour National Sexual Assault Hotline on ☎800-656-4673. Alternatively, go straight to a hospital emergency room.

Transportation

Getting There & Away

Flights, cars and tours can be booked online at lonelyplanet.com/bookings.

Entering the USA

● Everyone arriving in the US needs to fill out the US customs declaration. US and Canadian citizens, along with eligible foreign nationals participating in the Visa Waiver Program, can complete this procedure electronically at an APC (Automated Passport Control) kiosk upon disembarking. All others must fill out a paper customs declaration, which is usually handed out on the plane. Have it completed before you approach the immigration desk. For the question, 'US Street Address,' give the address where you will spend the first night (a hotel address is fine).

● No matter what your visa says, US immigration officers have absolute authority to refuse admission to the country, or to impose conditions on admission. They may ask about your plans and whether you have sufficient funds; it's a good idea to list an itinerary, produce an onward or round-trip ticket and have at least one major credit card.

● The Department of Homeland Security's registration program, called Office of Biometric Identity Management, includes every port of entry and nearly every foreign visitor to the USA. For most visitors (excluding, for now, most Canadian and some Mexican citizens), registration consists of having a digital photo and electronic (inkless) fingerprints taken; the process takes less than a minute.

Passport

Every visitor entering the USA from abroad needs a passport. Visitors from most countries only require a passport valid for their intended period of stay in the USA. However, nationals of certain countries require a passport valid for at least six months longer than their intended stay. For a country-by-country list, see the latest 'Six-Month Club Update' from US Customs and Border Protection (www.cbp.gov). If your passport does not meet current US standards, you'll be turned back at the border. All visitors wishing to enter the USA under the Visa Waiver Program must have an e-Passport with a digital photo and an integrated RFID chip containing biometric data.

Air

The USA has more airports than any other country, but only a baker's dozen form the main international gateways. Even travel to an international gateway sometimes requires a connection in another gateway city (eg London–Los Angeles flights may involve transferring in Houston). That said, in recent years many mid-size airports in cities like Austin, Charleston, Indianapolis and Nashville have begun offering at least one nonstop flight to hub cities in Europe.

The USA does not have a national air carrier. The largest USA-based airlines are American, Delta, United and Southwest.

International gateway airports in the USA:

Atlanta Hartsfield-Jackson International Airport (ATL; ☏800-897-1910; www.atl.com)

Boston Logan International Airport (BOS; ☏800-235-6426; www.massport.com/logan-airport)

Chicago O'Hare International Airport (ORD; ☏800-832-6352; www.flychicago.com/ohare; 10000 W O'Hare Ave)

Dallas DFW International Airport (DFW; ☏972-973-3112; www.dfwairport.com; 2400 Aviation Dr)

Fort Lauderdale-Hollywood International Airport (FLL; ☏866-435-9355; www.broward.org/airport; 100 Terminal Dr)

Honolulu International Airport (HNL; ☏808-836-6411; www.airports.hawaii.gov/hnl; 300 Rodgers Blvd)

Houston George Bush Intercontinental Airport (IAH; ☏281-230-3100; www.fly2houston.com/iah; 2800 N Terminal Rd, off I-59, Beltway 8 or I-45)

Los Angeles International Airport (LAX; www.lawa.org/welcomeLAX.aspx; 1 World Way)

Miami International Airport (MIA; ☏305-876-7000; www.miami-airport.com; 2100 NW 42nd Ave)

New York JFK International Airport (JFK; ☏718-244-4444; www.jfkairport.com)

Newark Liberty International Airport (EWR; ☏973-961-6000; www.newarkairport.com)

San Francisco International Airport (SFO; www.flysfo.com; S McDonnell Rd)

Seattle Sea-Tac International Airport (SEA; ☏206-787-5388; www.portseattle.org/Sea-Tac; 17801 International Blvd)

Washington Dulles International Airport (IAD; ☏703-572-2700, 703-572-8296; www.flydulles.com)

Getting Around

Air

When time is tight, book a flight. The domestic air system is extensive and reliable, with dozens of competing airlines, hundreds of airports and thousands of flights daily. Flying is usually more expensive than traveling by bus, train or car, but it's the way to go when you're in a hurry.

Main 'hub' airports in the USA include all international gateways plus many other large cities. Most cities and towns have a local or county airport, but you usually have to travel via a hub airport to reach them.

Airlines in the USA

Overall, air travel in the USA is very safe (much safer than driving out on the nation's highways); for comprehensive details by carrier, check out airsafe.com.

Climate Change & Travel

Every form of transport that relies on carbon-based fuel generates CO_2, the main cause of human-induced climate change. Modern travel is dependent on airplanes, which might use less fuel per mile per person than most cars but travel much greater distances. The altitude at which aircraft emit gases (including CO_2) and particles also contributes to their climate change impact. Many websites offer 'carbon calculators' that allow people to estimate the carbon emissions generated by their journey and, for those who wish to do so, to offset the impact of the greenhouse gases emitted with contributions to portfolios of climate-friendly initiatives throughout the world. Lonely Planet offsets the carbon footprint of all staff and author travel.

The main domestic carriers:

Alaska Airlines (www.alaskaair. com) Has direct flights to Anchorage from Seattle, Chicago, Los Angeles and Denver. It also flies between many towns within Alaska.

American Airlines (www. aa.com) Nationwide service.

Delta Air Lines (www.delta. com) Nationwide service.

Frontier Airlines (www. flyfrontier.com) Denver-based airline with service across the continental USA.

Hawaiian Airlines (www. hawaiianairlines.com) Nonstop flights between the Hawaiian islands and various spots on the mainland.

JetBlue Airways (www.jetblue. com) New York City–based airline serving many East Coast cities, plus other destinations across the USA.

Southwest Airlines (www. southwest.com) Dallas-based budget airline with service across the continental USA and Hawaii.

Spirit Airlines (www.spirit. com) Florida-based budget airline; serves many US gateway cities.

United Airlines (www.united. com) Nationwide service.

Virgin America (www.virgin-america.com) California-based airline serving over two dozen cities, from Honolulu to Boston.

Bicycle

Cyclists must follow the same rules of the road as automobiles, but don't expect drivers to respect your right of way. Better World Club (www.betterworldclub. com) offers a bicycle roadside-assistance program.

For advice, route maps, guided tours and lists of local bike clubs and repair shops, browse the websites of Adventure Cycling (www. adventurecycling.org) and the League of American Bicyclists (www.bikeleague. org).

Bus

To save money, travel by bus, particularly between major towns and cities. Middle-class Americans prefer to fly or drive, but buses let you see the countryside and meet folks along the way. As a rule, buses are reliable, cleanish and comfortable, with air-conditioning, barely reclining seats, lavatories and no smoking.

Greyhound (www.grey-hound.com) is the major long-distance bus company, with routes throughout the USA and Canada. Other long-distance bus lines that offer decent fares and free wi-fi (though it doesn't always work) include Megabus (www.megabus.com) and BoltBus (www.boltbus.com).

Sample Greyhound standard one-way adult fares and trip times: Chicago –New Orleans ($130; 20 to 30 hours), Los Angeles–San Francisco ($25; 7½ to 13 hours), New York–Chicago ($65; 18 to 23 hours), New York–San Francisco ($75; 72 hours), Washington, DC–Miami ($150; 25 to 30 hours).

Reservations

Tickets for most trips on Greyhound, Trailways, Megabus and BoltBus can be bought online. You can print all tickets at home or, in the case of Megabus or BoltBus, simply show ticket receipts through an email on a smartphone. Greyhound also allows customers to pick up tickets at the terminal using 'Will Call' service.

Car & Motorcycle

Automobile Associations

The American Automobile Association (AAA; www. aaa.com) has reciprocal membership agreements with several international auto clubs (check with AAA and bring your membership card from home). For its members, AAA offers travel insurance, tour books, diagnostic centers for used-car buyers and a wide-ranging network of regional offices. AAA advocates politically for the auto industry.

A more ecofriendly alternative, the Better World Club (www.betterworldclub. com), donates 1% of revenue to assist environmental cleanup, offers ecologically sensitive choices for every service it provides and advocates politically for environmental causes.

With these organizations, the primary member benefit is 24-hour emergency roadside assistance anywhere in the USA. Both also offer trip planning, free travel maps, travel-agency services, car insurance and a range of travel discounts (eg on hotels, car rentals, attractions).

Driver's License

Foreign visitors can legally drive a car in the USA for up to 12 months using their home driver's license. However, an International Driving Permit (IDP) will have more credibility with US traffic police, especially if your home license doesn't have a photo or isn't in English. Your automobile association at home can issue an IDP, valid for one year, for a small fee. Always carry your home license together with the IDP.

To ride a motorcycle in the USA, you will need either a valid US state motorcycle license or an IDP specially endorsed for motorcycles.

Insurance

Don't put the key into the ignition if you don't have insurance, which is legally required. You risk financial ruin and legal consequences if there's an accident. If you already have auto insurance, or if you buy travel insurance that covers car rentals, make sure your policy has adequate liability coverage for where you will be driving, as different states specify different minimum levels of coverage.

Car-rental companies will provide liability insurance, but most charge extra. Rental companies almost never include collision-damage insurance for the vehicle. Instead, they offer an optional Collision Damage Waiver

(CDW) or Loss Damage Waiver (LDW), usually with an initial deductible cost of between $100 and $500. For an extra premium, you can usually get this deductible covered as well. Paying for some or all of this insurance increases the cost of a rental car by as much as $30 a day.

Many credit cards offer free collision damage coverage for rental cars if you rent for 15 days or less and charge the total rental to your card. This is a good way to avoid paying extra fees to the rental company, but note that if there's an accident, sometimes you must pay the car-rental company first and then seek reimbursement from the credit-card company. There may be exceptions that are not covered, too, such as 'exotic' rentals (eg 4WD or convertibles). Check your credit-card policy.

Car Rental

Car rental is a competitive business in the USA. Most rental companies require that you have a major credit card, be at least 25 years old and have a valid driver's license. Some major national companies may rent to drivers between the ages of 21 and 24 for an additional charge of around $25 per day. Except in Michigan and New York, those under age 21 are not permitted to rent at all.

Car-rental prices vary wildly, so shop around. The average daily rate for a small

car ranges from around $25 to $75, or $125 to $500 per week. If you belong to an auto club or frequent-flier program, you may get a discount (or earn rewards points or miles).

Road Conditions & Hazards

Road hazards include potholes, city commuter traffic, wandering wildlife and cellphone-wielding, kid-distracted or enraged drivers. Caution, foresight, courtesy and luck usually gets you past them. For nationwide traffic and road-closure information, check www.fhwa.dot.gov/trafficinfo.

○ In places where winter driving is an issue, many cars are fitted with steel-studded snow tires, while snow chains can sometimes be required in mountain areas.

○ Driving off-road, or on dirt roads, is often forbidden by car-rental companies, and it can be very dangerous in wet weather.

○ In deserts and range country, livestock sometimes graze next to unfenced roads. These areas are signed as 'Open Range' or with the silhouette of a steer.

○ Where deer and other wild animals frequently appear roadside, you'll see signs with the silhouette of a leaping deer. Take these signs seriously, particularly at dusk and dawn.

Road Rules

• In the USA, cars drive on the right-hand side of the road.

• The use of seat belts is required in every state except New Hampshire, and child safety seats or seat belts for children under 18 are required in every state. Most car-rental agencies rent child safety seats for $10 to $14 per day, but you must reserve them when booking.

• In some states, motorcyclists are required to wear helmets.

• On interstate highways, the speed limit is usually 70mph. Unless otherwise posted, the speed limit is generally 55mph or 65mph on highways, 25mph to 35mph in cities and towns, and as low as 15mph in school zones (strictly enforced during school hours). It's forbidden to pass a school bus when its lights are flashing.

• Unless signs prohibit it, you may turn right at a red light after first coming to a full stop – note that turning right on red is illegal in NYC.

• At four-way stop signs, cars should proceed in order of arrival; when two cars arrive simultaneously, the one on the right has the right of way. When in doubt, just politely wave the other driver ahead.

• When emergency vehicles (ie police, fire or ambulance) approach from either direction, pull over safely and get out of the way.

• In many states, it's illegal to talk on a handheld cell phone while driving; use a hands-free device instead.

• The maximum legal blood-alcohol concentration for drivers is 0.08%. Penalties are very severe for 'DUI' – driving under the influence of alcohol and/or drugs. Police can give roadside sobriety checks to assess if you've been drinking or using drugs. If you fail, they'll require you to take a breath test, urine test or blood test to determine the level of alcohol or drugs in your body. Refusing to be tested is treated the same as if you'd taken the test and failed.

• In some states it's illegal to carry 'open containers' of alcohol in a vehicle, even if they're empty.

• If you are pulled over by the police, do not get out of your car. Wait for the officer to approach your window – in the meantime, collect your license, proof of insurance and registration or rental agreement, and have them ready for the officer to inspect.

Local Transportation

Except in large US cities, public transportation is rarely the most convenient option for travelers, and coverage can be sparse to outlying towns and suburbs. However, it is usually cheap, safe and reliable.

More than two-thirds of the states in the nation have adopted 511 as an all-purpose local-transportation help line.

Subway

The largest subway systems are in New York City, Chicago, Boston, Washington, DC, the San Francisco Bay Area, Philadelphia, Los Angeles and Atlanta. Other cities have small, one- or two-line rail systems that mainly serve downtown areas.

Taxi & Ridesharing

Taxis are metered, with flagfall charges of around $3 to start, plus $2 to $3 per mile. They charge extra for waiting and handling baggage, and drivers expect a 10% to 15% tip. Taxis cruise the busiest areas in large cities; elsewhere, it's easiest to phone and order one.

Ridesharing companies such as Uber (www.uber.com) and Lyft (www.lyft.com) have seen a surge in popularity as an alternative to taxis.

Tours

Group travel can be an enjoyable way to get to and tour around the USA.

Reputable tour companies:

American Holidays (www.americanholidays.com) Ireland-based company specializes in tours to North America.

Contiki (www.contiki.com) Party-hardy sightseeing tour-bus vacations for 18- to 35-year-olds.

North America Travel Service (www.northamericatravel-service.co.uk) UK-based tour operator arranges luxury US trips.

Trek America (www.trekameri ca.com) Active outdoor adventures for 18- to 38-year-olds.

Train

Amtrak (www.amtrak.com) has an extensive rail system throughout the USA, with Amtrak's Thruway buses providing connections to and from the rail network to some smaller centers and national parks. Compared with other modes of travel, trains are rarely the quickest, cheapest, timeliest or most convenient option, but they turn the journey into a relaxing, social and scenic all-American experience, especially on western routes, where double-decker Superliner trains boast spacious lounge cars with panoramic windows.

Commuter trains provide faster, more frequent services on shorter routes, especially the northeast corridor from Boston, MA, to Washington, DC.

Amtrak's high-speed Acela Express trains are the most expensive, and rail passes are not valid on these trains. Other commuter rail lines include those serving the Lake Michigan shoreline near Chicago, IL, major cities on the West Coast and the Miami, FL, area.

Classes & Costs

Amtrak fares vary according to the type of train and seating. On long-distance lines, you can travel in coach seats (reserved or unreserved), business class, or 1st class, which includes all sleeping compartments. Sleeping cars include simple bunks (called 'roomettes'), bedrooms with en-suite facilities and suites sleeping four with two bathrooms. Sleeping-car rates include meals in the dining car, which offers everyone sit-down meal service (pricey if not included). Food service on commuter lines, when it exists, consists of sandwich and snack bars. Bringing your own food and drink is recommended on all trains.

Generally the earlier you book, the lower the price. To get many of the standard discounts, you need to reserve at least three days in advance. If you want to take an Acela Express or Metroliner train, avoid peak commute times and aim for weekends.

Sample Amtrak standard, one-way, adult coach-class fares and trip times: Chicago–New Orleans ($130; 20 hours), Los Angeles–San Antonio ($125; 29 hours), New York–Chicago ($130; 19 hours), New York–Los Angeles ($250; 72 hours), Washington, DC–Miami ($140; 23 hours).

Reservations

Reservations can be made any time from 11 months in advance up to the day of departure. Space on most trains is limited, and certain routes can be crowded, especially during summer and holiday periods, so it's a good idea to book as far in advance as you can. This also gives you the best chance of fare discounts.

Behind the Scenes

Acknowledgements

Climate map data adapted from Peel MC, Finlayson BL & McMahon TA (2007) 'Updated World Map of the Köppen-Geiger Climate Classification', *Hydrology and Earth System Sciences*, 11, 1633–44.

Cover photograph: Colorado River from South Rim, Grand Canyon National Park. Francesco Carovillano/ 4Corners Images©

Illustrations pp42-3, pp98-9 by Javier Zarracina; pp300-1 by Michael Weldon.

This Book

This third edition of Lonely Planet's *Best of USA* guidebook was curated by Karla Zimmerman and researched and written by Karla, Ray Bartlett, Andrew Bender, Alison Bing, Stephanie d'Arc Taylor, Ashley Harrell, Adam Karlin, Ali Lemer, Vesna Maric, MaSovaida Morgan, Christopher Pitts, Kevin Raub and Greg Ward. This guidebook was produced by the following:

Destination Editors Ben Buckner, Trisha Ping, Sarah Stocking

Senior Product Editors Grace Dobell, Vicky Smith, Martine Power

Regional Senior Cartographer Alison Lyall

Product Editor Paul Harding

Book Designer Clara Monitto

Assisting Editors Lou McGregor, Gabrielle Stefanos

Cover Researcher Meri Blazevski

Thanks to Jess Boland, Karen Henderson, Wibowo Rusli, Amanda Williamson

Send Us Your Feedback

We love to hear from travelers – your comments keep us on our toes and help make our books better. Our well-traveled team reads every word on what you loved or loathed about this book. Although we cannot reply individually to postal submissions, we always guarantee that your feedback goes straight to the appropriate authors, in time for the next edition. Each person who sends us information is thanked in the next edition, the most useful submissions are rewarded with a selection of digital PDF chapters.

Visit lonelyplanet.com/contact to submit your updates and suggestions or to ask for help. Our award-winning website also features inspirational travel stories, news and discussions.

Note: We may edit, reproduce and incorporate your comments in Lonely Planet products such as guidebooks, websites and digital products, so let us know if you don't want your comments reproduced or your name acknowledged. For a copy of our privacy policy visit lonelyplanet.com/privacy.

Index

N

Symbols & Map Key

Look for these symbols to quickly identify listings:

- ◉ Sights
- ✪ Activities
- ◐ Courses
- ◑ Tours
- ✪ Festivals & Events
- ✪ Eating
- ◐ Drinking
- ✪ Entertainment
- ◐ Shopping
- ❶ Information & Transport

These symbols and abbreviations give vital information for each listing:

- ✤ Sustainable or green recommendation
- **FREE** No payment required

- ☎ Telephone number
- ◷ Opening hours
- P Parking
- ◐ Nonsmoking
- ✳ Air-conditioning
- @ Internet access
- ⌘ Wi-fi access
- ⛱ Swimming pool

- 🚌 Bus
- ⛴ Ferry
- 🚋 Tram
- 🚆 Train
- 📖 English-language menu
- ✒ Vegetarian selection
- ♿ Family-friendly

Find your best experiences with these Great For... icons.

- Art & Culture
- Beaches
- Budget
- Cafe/Coffee
- Cycling
- Detour
- Drinking
- Entertainment
- Events
- Family Travel
- Food & Drink
- History
- Local Life
- Nature & Wildlife
- Photo Op
- Scenery
- Shopping
- Short Trip
- Sport
- Walking
- Winter Travel

Sights

- Beach
- Bird Sanctuary
- Buddhist
- Castle/Palace
- Christian
- Confucian
- Hindu
- Islamic
- Jain
- Jewish
- Monument
- Museum/Gallery/ Historic Building
- Ruin
- Shinto
- Sikh
- Taoist
- Winery/Vineyard
- Zoo/Wildlife Sanctuary
- Other Sight

Points of Interest

- Bodysurfing
- Camping
- Cafe
- Canoeing/Kayaking
- Course/Tour
- Diving
- Drinking & Nightlife
- Eating
- Entertainment
- Sento Hot Baths/ Onsen
- Shopping
- Skiing
- Sleeping
- Snorkelling
- Surfing
- Swimming/Pool
- Walking
- Windsurfing
- Other Activity

Information

- Bank
- Embassy/Consulate
- Hospital/Medical
- Internet
- Police
- Post Office
- Telephone
- Toilet
- Tourist Information
- Other Information

Geographic

- Beach
- Gate
- Hut/Shelter
- Lighthouse
- Lookout
- Mountain/Volcano
- Oasis
- Park
- Pass
- Picnic Area
- Waterfall

Transport

- Airport
- BART station
- Border crossing
- Boston T station
- Bus
- Cable car/Funicular
- Cycling
- Ferry
- Metro/MRT station
- Monorail
- Parking
- Petrol station
- Subway/S-Bahn/ Skytrain station
- Taxi
- Train station/Railway
- Tram
- Underground/ U-Bahn station
- Other Transport

Alison Bing

Over many guidebooks and 20 years in San Francisco, author Alison has spent more time on Alcatraz than some inmates, become an aficionado of drag and burritos, and willfully ignored Muni signs warning that safety requires avoiding unnecessary conversation.

Stephanie d'Arc Taylor

A native Angeleno, Stephanie grew up with the west LA weekend ritual of going for Iranian sweets after ten zaru soba in Little Osaka. She quit her PhD to move to Beirut and become a writer and has since published work with the New York Times, the Guardian, Roads & Kingdoms and Kinfolk Magazine (among others), and co-founded Jaleesa, a venture-capital funded social impact business in Beirut.

Ashley Harrell

After a brief stint selling day-spa coupons door-to-door in South Florida, Ashley decided she'd rather be a writer. She went to journalism grad school, convinced a newspaper to hire her, and started covering wildlife, crime and tourism, sometimes all in the same story. Fueling her zest for storytelling and the unknown, she traveled widely and moved often, from a tiny NYC apartment to a vast California ranch to a jungle cabin in Costa Rica, where she started writing for Lonely Planet. From there her travels became more exotic and farther flung, and she still laughs when paychecks arrive.

Adam Karlin

Adam has contributed to dozens of Lonely Planet guidebooks, covering an alphabetical spread that ranges from the Andaman Islands to the Zimbabwe border. As a journalist, he has written on travel, crime, politics, archeology and the Sri Lankan civil war, among other topics. He has sent dispatches from every continent barring Antarctica (one day!) and his essays and articles have featured in the BBC, NPR, and multiple nonfiction anthologies. Adam is based out of New Orleans, which helps explain his love of wetlands, food and good music. Learn more at http://walkonfine.com.

Ali Lemer

Ali has been a Lonely Planet writer and editor since 2007, and has authored guidebooks and articles on Russia, Germany, NYC, Chicago, Los Angeles, Melbourne, Bali, Hawaii, Japan and Scotland, among others. A native New Yorker, Ali has also lived in Melbourne, Chicago, Prague and the UK, and has traveled extensively around Europe, North America, Oceania and Asia.

Vesna Maric

Vesna has been a Lonely Planet writer for nearly two decades, covering places as far and wide as Bolivia, Algeria, Sicily, Cyprus, Barcelona, London and Croatia, among others. Her latest work has been updating Florida, Greece and North Macedonia.

MaSovaida Morgan

MaSovaida is a Lonely Planet writer and multi-media storyteller whose wanderlust has taken her to more than 35 countries across six continents. Prior to freelancing, she was Lonely Planet's Destination Editor for South America for four years and worked as an editor for newspapers and NGOs in the Middle East and United Kingdom. Follow her on Instagram @MaSovaida.

Christopher Pitts

Chris' first expedition in life ended in failure when he tried to dig from Pennsylvania to China at the age of six. He went on to study Chinese in university, living for several years in China. After more than a decade in Paris, the lure of Colorado's sunny skies and outdoor adventure proved too great to resist.

Kevin Raub

Atlanta native Kevin started his career as a music journalist in New York, working for Men's Journal and Rolling Stone magazines. He ditched the rock 'n' roll lifestyle for travel writing and has written nearly 50 Lonely Planet guides, focused mainly on Brazil, Chile, Colombia, USA, India, the Caribbean and Portugal. Along the way, the confessed hophead is in constant search of wildly high IBUs in local beers. Follow him on Twitter and Instagram (@RaubOnTheRoad).

Greg Ward

Since youthful adventures on the hippy trail to India, and living in Spain, Greg Ward has written guides to destinations all over the world. As well as covering the USA from the Southwest to Hawaii, he has ranged on recent assignments from Corsica to the Cotswolds, and Dallas to Delphi. Visit his website at www.gregward.info to see his favorite photos and memories.

Other Contributors

Barbara Noe Kennedy contributed to the Washington, DC section.

Our Story

A beat-up old car, a few dollars in the pocket and a sense of adventure. In 1972 that's all Tony and Maureen Wheeler needed for the trip of a lifetime – across Europe and Asia overland to Australia. It took several months, and at the end – broke but inspired – they sat at their kitchen table writing and stapling together their first travel guide, *Across Asia on the Cheap*. Within a week they'd sold 1500 copies. Lonely Planet was born.

Today, Lonely Planet has offices in Franklin, London, Melbourne, Oakland, Dublin, Beijing, and Delhi, with more than 600 staff and writers. We share Tony's belief that 'a great guidebook should do three things: inform, educate and amuse'.

Our Writers

Karla Zimmerman

Karla lives in Chicago, where she eats donuts, yells at the Cubs, and writes stuff for books, magazines and websites when she's not doing the first two things. She has contributed to 70-plus Lonely Planet guidebooks and travel anthologies covering destinations in Europe, Asia, Africa, North America and the Caribbean. To learn more, follow her on Instagram and Twitter (@karlazimmerman).

Ray Bartlett

Ray Bartlett has been travel writing for nearly two decades, bringing Japan, Korea, Mexico, Tanzania, Guatemala, Indonesia and many parts of the United States to life in rich detail for top-industry publishers, newspapers and magazines. His acclaimed debut novel, *Sunsets of Tulum*, set in Yucatán, was a Midwest Book Review 2016 Fiction pick. Among other pursuits he surfs regularly and is an accomplished Argentine tango dancer. Follow him on Facebook, Instagram, Twitter or www.kaisora.com, his website.

Andrew Bender

Award-winning travel and food writer Andrew Bender has written three dozen Lonely Planet guidebooks (from Amsterdam to Los Angeles, Germany to Taiwan and over a dozen titles about Japan), plus numerous articles for lonely planet.com. His coverage of Palm Springs and California's deserts for Lonely Planet received the prestigious Eureka! Travel Writing Award from Visit California in 2017. Outside of Lonely Planet he writes the Seat 1A travel site for Forbes.com and is a frequent contributor to the *Los Angeles Times*, inflight magazines and more.

More Writers

STAY IN TOUCH LONELYPLANET.COM/CONTACT

AUSTRALIA The Malt Store, Level 3, 551 Swanston St, Carlton, Victoria 3053
☏ 03 8379 8000,
fax 03 8379 8111

IRELAND Digital Depot, Roe Lane (off Thomas St), Digital Hub, Dublin 8, D08 TCV4, Ireland

USA 155 Filbert St, Suite 208, Oakland, CA 94607
☏ 510 250 6400,
toll free 800 275 8555,
fax 510 893 8572

UK 240 Blackfriars Road, London SE1 8NW
☏ 020 3771 5100,
fax 020 3771 5101

 twitter.com/ lonelyplanet

 facebook.com/ lonelyplanet

 instagram.com/ lonelyplanet

 youtube.com/ lonelyplanet

 lonelyplanet.com/ newsletter